# CROSSROADS

# THE GREAT AMERICAN EXPERIMENT

## THE RISE, DECLINE, AND RESTORATION OF FREEDOM
## AND
## THE MARKET ECONOMY

E. BARRY ASMUS
DONALD B. BILLINGS

91159

UNIVERSITY
PRESS OF
AMERICA

LANHAM • NEW YORK • LONDON

University Press of America,™ Inc.

4720 Boston Way
Lanham, MD 20706

3 Henrietta Street
London WC2E 8LU England

**Library of Congress Cataloging in Publication Data**

Asmus, E. Barry.
  Crossroads: the great American experiment.
  Bibliography: p.
  Includes index.
   1. United States—Economic conditions. 2. United
States—Economic policy. 3. Comparative economics.
I. Billings, Donald B. II. Title.
HC103.A86   1984     338.973     84-20962
ISBN 0-8191-4362-6 (alk. paper)
ISBN 0-8191-4363-4 (pbk. : alk. paper)

For

Andrew and Angela

and

Peter and Cathy

# ACKNOWLEDGEMENTS

The debts to be acknowledged in the writing of this book are represented by the long list of scholars and their works which are contained in the "Selected Sources and Recommended Readings" after the final chapter. They are so numerous that it is not possible to list but a few of those who have been most influential on our views of the issues raised. A great debt of appreciation to the Nobel Laureate in economics Freidrich A. Hayek must be expressed. His writings in economics, law, and social philosophy have had a profound impact on our thinking. Likewise, it is difficult to imagine us writing this book without having studied the scholarship of Bernard Bailyn, James M. Buchanan, Milton Friedman, Ludwig von Mises, Robert Nisbet, Robert Nozick, Murray N. Rothbard, Thomas Sowell, and from an earlier time, John Locke and Adam Smith. While others remain nameless in this acknowledgement, the following pages clearly demonstrate our gratitude in bringing to a wider audience their profound insights on the social, political, and economic relationships that exist in a community of individuals.

In the arduous task of getting it down on paper, we benefited from the willingness of P. J. Hill of Montana State University to read part of the manuscript at an early stage of the effort and provide important insights and encouragement. Hopefully, the book is better because of his wise counsel. Thomas and Marti Janstrom read most of the manuscript and assisted us in the problem of indentifying the audience with which we hoped to communicate. Our colleague D. Allen Dalton at Boise State University read the entire manuscript and brought to the project important  professional skills with respect to the economic analysis and suggested sources, as well as significant improvements in the narrative. Finally, C. Gaye Bennett not only read the manuscript at a late stage in the project and made substantive improvements in its style, but she also facilitated the project by innumerable hours of support assistance which eased the difficult task of finishing the book. Needless to say, the limitations of the book which remain are solely the responsibility of the authors.

# TABLE OF CONTENTS

*THE RESTORATION OF FREEDOM
AND THE MARKET ECONOMY*

# PART
# I

## THE RISE OF INDIVIDUAL FREEDOM AND THE MARKET ECONOMY

# CHAPTER 1

## THE GREAT AMERICAN EXPERIMENT

> Fortunately...we are as a people, still free to choose which way we
> should go--whether to continue along the road we have been following
> to ever bigger government, or to call a halt and change direction.
> --Milton and Rose Friedman

Most people of the world remain today, as they have for centuries,
under the yoke of barbaric dictatorships or, at the very least, continue to glorify the state and the politicization of human affairs. The
first experiment in human liberty, the United States of America, remains its last bastion; yet, even here, government continues to slip
towards the abyss of tyranny. For too many Americans, government
is still viewed as a solution rather than the problem. However, as
Milton and Rose Friedman remind us, Americans are still "free to
choose" a change in direction and to restore the American dream of
human liberty. We are at a profound crossroads, and a decision must
be made between the collectivist vision which worships the state and
political solutions *and* the Great American Experiment in liberty and
individual dignity.

The issue is human freedom. History, in varying degrees, indicates
that human creativity under freedom is a low cost, self-sustaining,
and synergistic process. But like oxygen in a space craft, liberty remains in very short supply. Government, almost by definition, inevitably reduces liberty or even eliminates it. Not by design, of
course, but pathologically and operationally liberty is eradicated.
State power has always worked that way. The nature of the conflict
between power and liberty, and therefore the nature of the
crossroads at which human civilization stands, has been summarized
by Clarence B. Carson in his series of articles entitled "World in the
Grip of an Idea:"

> If the twentieth century were a play, it would have long since driven the
> audience mad. The incongruity between the words spoken by the actors
> and the action on stage would be too great to be borne. The actors speak
> of peace, prosperity, progress, freedom, brotherly love, and a forthcom-
> ing end to the age-old ills of mankind. The action on stage has been
> world wars, dictatorships, slave labor camps, police states,
> totalitarianism, class and racial animosities, terrorism, and a more general
> coarsening of human behavior. The promises bespeak a beatific vision;
> the reality is a descending barbarism. We are continually led to believe
> that the barbarism is a temporary phenomenon, and that just beyond it

lies the realization of the bright promise. Meanwhile, the terror and disorder continue to spread. It is my contention that it is possible to grasp what has been happening in the twentieth century on a worldwide scale. To do so, it is necessary to ignore the promises, to keep our eyes firmly fixed on the action, and to attend to the ideas that are producing it...

This book is about the action, not the promises. Dictatorships of the left and right talk of freedom and progress, but if, following Clarence Carson, we "keep our eyes firmly fixed on the action," it is abundantly clear that these objectives were most nearly realized in the Great American Experiment of 1776. Most of the world's people failed to participate in and adopt the crucial ingredients of this revolution and, as a result, remain poverty stricken and tyrannized by government.

## WORLD POVERTY

From the beginning of time, few individuals have had the privilege of living in freedom and material well-being. Even today, the vast majority of people live under totalitarian regimes, political dictatorships and an almost inevitable poverty. Though Rome experienced some freedom for a time, and centuries ago China breathed faintly the air of freedom, for the most part, freedom has been the exception not the rule. Poverty seems the natural condition, wealth an aberration. Yet, a thousand years ago it appeared that China would be an exception. Blessed with abundant natural resources, a strong work ethic, and personal incentives, the country produced wealth and culture. Impressively inventive, their achievements included papermaking, moveable type, the compass, gun powder, the production of fine silk and porcelain, and significant advances in medicine, mechanics, and astronomy. Although block printing was used in the seventh century in Europe, Guttenberg's invention of moveable type, which was developed in the eleventh century, didn't have an impact on European progress until late into the fifteenth century. In fact, papermaking in China goes back at least two thousand years while European papermaking did not become widespread until the twelfth century.

The Chinese also possessed a singular advantage in that they could record and store knowledge. Information was made accessible and this proved beneficial to all disciplines and lines of progress. For example, by discovering the magnetic properties of the lodestone, the Chinese were the first to use the compass and, subsequently, ocean navigation developed. Advancement and higher living standards were the direct result of such activity. China indeed led the world in attempting to better the human condition. A "classical age" took hold in which its most memorable prose was written, domestic and international markets were opened, and a money economy appeared.

4

The fact that laws were actually written down and that property rights were partially protected from the whims of government were stunning in their impact. Fertilizers, the traction plow, and the displacement of bronze by iron represent but a few more examples of the creative genius of the Chinese.

Although rooted in the most impressive advances in human culture, somehow their economic progress broke down. Advocates arose who believed in subservience to the state. Individual freedom was thought to be subordinate to government. In fact today, China is poor, backward and seemingly technologically incapable. The scientific and industrial revolution either by-passed China, or its bureaucratic brand of feudalism resisted change. And, in the twentieth century at least, China's practice of socialism and public ownership of the means of production so stultifies human incentives and degrades the human spirit, that the economy is practically inoperative. Something is dreadfully wrong.

Fox Butterfield, first head of the *New York Times* bureau in Peking, writes in his book *China: Alive in the Bitter Sea:*

> Almost every Chinese I got to know during my 20 months in Peking, had a tale of political persecution...from their stories it seemed as if a whole generation of Chinese (over 600 million since 1949) had known nothing but arbitrary accusations, violent swings in the political line, unjustified arrests, torture, and imprisonment. Few Chinese I knew felt free from the fear of physical or psychological abuse and a pervasive sense of injustice.

Could it be that Chinese leaders failed to recognize that the wealth of a nation is its people, and in order to energize individuals their property rights must be secure, personal incentives must be encouraged, and their freedoms promised and delivered?

On yet another continent, Africa, the experiment with liberty and its pronounced effects on living standards has barely begun. Not unlike a billion others on this planet, the typical East African is very poor. Their hutlike homes are made of mud, dung, and plastered stone. On the average, the one-room dirt floor contains a fire used to heat water and cook food, and without a chimney, the hut is often filled with smoke. Family members accept pinkeye as the price for hot water and cooked food because the smoke that stains the walls also strains the eyes. Diets are mostly inadequate, as sorgum is often in short supply.

Poverty is everywhere. The sacred oxen is seldom harnessed and, without animal power, sticks and hand tools are used for digging and cultivating. Agriculture without adequate equipment makes life hard, unproductive and short. Doctors estimate that three-out-of-five children never reach the age of sixteen, and nearly twenty of every thousand mothers die in childbirth. In fact, most East Africans cannot get into a hospital, but because of a lack of appropriate medicines, those that do often die anyway. Without the necessary fuels to generate refrigeration, hospitals are also often short of blood supplies.

5

Naturally, the average age remains low, as almost sixty percent of the population are under twenty years of age. It is easy to see why most East Africans are discouraged and fatalistic. Life for the masses offers little hope, persistent hunger and little chance for material improvement.

The poor of the world, in particular the agricultural peasants, have always sowed and reaped by sweat and season. It is they who should benefit from their back-breaking and laborious efforts. But the effects of government taxes, controls, regulations, graft, export taxes, import controls, and especially the threat or implementation of government ownership of the land submerges them in dire poverty. Naturally, human effort is reduced, and the linkage between reward and production is obscured. What is a person to believe when one reads that the food minister of India blames its poverty on rich Indians that eat too much? Preposterous, yet interesting to note that India also has placed price controls on food. Can the laws of supply and demand be repealed and thus negated? Hardly. But, government continues to believe so and inevitably produces disastrous effects.

How pitiful is the spectacle of Soviet and Chinese leaders reducing their farmers to mere wage earners! These are men and women who are divorced from ownership and are, therefore, unconscience of the enormous amounts of energy and stewardship it takes to grow a crop. The day-to-day decisions of preparing the soil, planting the seed, irrigating and fertilizing the plants, and harvesting the crop, requires a covetous attention to detail. All these self-motivating activities are relinquished in behalf of collectivist goals. Stewardship, production and efficiency are sacrificed on the alter of forcing the farmer to work for the state for a weekly wage. Predictably and understandably, it does not work! Malcome Muggeridge, in his biography, tells of a journey to a fertile soiled Rostovian area of the Soviet Union in 1933:

> Stalin's collectivization of agriculture was...a general idea in a narrow empty mind, pursued to the uttermost limit, without reference to any other consideration, whether an individual or collective humanity. To be oppressed by an individual tyrant is terrible enough; but an outraged deity, as the Old Testament tells us, even more terrible; but Paine is right when he contends that the worst of all fates is to be oppressed by a general idea. This was the fate of Russian peasants, as it is, increasingly the fate of all of us in the twentieth century.

And yet, as always, the fault was not with the dogma. Indeed, it was the "...peasant who had to be re-educated." Ideology is never wrong. Patience with today's difficulties and hopes for a glorious future are restated, widely declared, and reinforced with the state's every move. Somehow the world must be alerted to the fact that the peasants of this modern world face a new enemy. It is no longer the parasitical monarch or feudal master who extracts his due. It is rather the all-powerful state. It extracts. It exploits. It inhibits.

6

The scenario repeats itself: hungry children, families in dire poverty and individuals with few opportunities. Much of Mexico, most of Central America, a large part of South America, nearly all of Africa and major portions of Asia reflect living standards incomprehensible to most Americans.

## THE MAINSPRING OF HUMAN PROGRESS

Why have circumstances been so different in the United States? Why such abundance in concert with so much liberty in our part of the world? What are the characteristics of this Great American Experiment which solved the critical problems of man's physical needs while providing wealth and opportunities to the masses that were once confined to kings? Could liberty be the prerequisite to and mainspring of human progress? Unfortunately, the experiment with human liberty under a regime of private ownership has not been properly appreciated by most Americans.

This book analyzes the fundamental issues which have determined the rise, decline and restoration of freedom and the market economy. It is imperative that we understand those factors which made the American dream a reality. Can it once again be harnessed? What were the primary causes of its decline? Can America experience a restoration? Indeed, how can today be made better than yesterday and tomorrow improve on them both? The next few decades will undoubtedly answer these questions. It is our hope that this effort represents a rethinking of the necessary attributes of a free society, and that future generations can experience a dream which can too easily be taken for granted.

## THE GREAT AMERICAN EXPERIMENT UNFOLDS

We will analyze the rise of the market system, its decline in the eyes of many, and the prospects of restoring market capitalism and limiting government's role in society. The central argument is the proposition that human liberty *is* the mainspring of human progress and impossible to maintain without the institution of private property. This book represents both a personal statement regarding the socially beneficial implications of a private property, free-market economic system, and an important survey of the people and ideas which produced capitalism and its particular set of economic and social institutions. As an exposition on the ideas of the proponents and opponents of a spontaneous, competitive order, important contributors to the ideas developed are cited and quoted. In order to avoid excess clutter in the narrative, but at the same time to provide the reader with the appropriate sources and citations, a detailed bibliographical appendix is placed after the concluding chapter. We believe it to be an excellent reading list on the principles and issues raised in the body of the work.

By way of orientation, the book is divided into three parts. *Part I* traces the evolution of the philosophy of individualism and the crucial role of property rights. The evolution of political ideas in the seventeenth and eighteenth centuries which contributed importantly to the rise of competitive capitalism is discussed. The revolution in economic understanding is described through analysis of the contributions of Adam Smith and other "classical liberal" economists. The development of these revolutionary political and economic principles is followed by a description of the socially beneficial characteristics of the Industrial Revolution in England and the economic transformation of the United States. This section concludes by defending the moral results of a private property, free-market order.

*Part II* analyzes the factors, singularly and in combination, which have contributed to the decline in both intellectual and practical support for competitive capitalism and its fundamental institutions. This part of the book deals with changes in the legal and judicial interpretations of the American constitutional order, the contructivist or planning mentality, socialism in its various manifestations, and its appeal to most intellectuals. The expansion in government intervention for economic stabilization purposes is also analyzed. Because of the present-day emphasis placed on the notion of equality, the relationship between freedom and equality is discussed at some length. Finally, the general question of the desirability and meaning of progress concludes this section.

*Part III* sets an agenda and a bill of particulars for the restoration of the market economy and voluntary social arrangements. The character of the counter revolution in economic thinking of the past twenty-five years, which supports the potential for restoration, is identified while simultaneously demonstrating the anatomy of government's many failures. Drawing on the Austrian School of Economics in particular, the essential nature of the competitive process is developed and a more realistic and appropriate meaning of monopoly is offered. A strong case against government regulation, in most circumstances, is documented, and the possibilities for privatization and a turn from government controlled production are discussed in depth. The renewed interest in a national industrial policy is shown to be old medicine in a new bottle. And finally, the absolute size of government is analyzed and alternative means to reduce the scope of government budgets and get politics out of the money creation business are explored.

This section makes a strong, affirmative case in support of the market system and private property when dealing with the many dimensions of the human predicament. It provides an agenda for the rest of the twentieth century and into the twenty-first. Privatization, deregulation, free and open markets, entrepreneurship and limited government will not, unfortunately, quickly replace the seemingly irresistable march of politicization. An increased understanding of voluntary and peaceful arrangements, alongside the historical failure of government solutions for human problems, warrants a mild optimism for liberty. Government as a delivery system, a social organizer, an allocator of resources, or even a corrector of market failures, increasingly reveals "the emperor has no clothes."

The book argues, as powerfully as we know how, that the human community is involved in a great struggle between two fundamentally irreconcilable social systems. One is a system which emphasizes individual responsibility, private property, and voluntary social arrangements. It requires that government's role in economic and personal matters be strictly limited if individual freedom is to be sustained in coming decades. The system of competitive capitalism is shown to produce standards of living and opportunities for individuals unparalleled in human history. The alternative system, which relies on government control and the use of force and coercion, would increasingly politicize economic exchange and suppress the individual's sphere of autonomy. Only the future will reveal whether the supposedly omniscient and benevolent force of government employs the velvet glove or the steel fist. History indicates that government intervention eventually uses the steel fist.

The Great American Experiment was an effort to control the power of government while at the same time freeing individuals to pursue economic gain and personal happiness by serving the interests of consumers. A crossroad has been reached: whether a system relying on private ownership, market exchange and carefully defined limits to government intervention in economic life can be sustained beyond our immediate time. The people of this country are making these momentous decisions whether conscious of the on-going debate or not. This book hopefully makes a contribution by assisting the American people in understanding the fundamental issues and the historical development of the relevant principles. Human liberty is at stake.

# CHAPTER 2

# HUMAN NATURE AND HUMAN ACTION

The man of system...seems to imagine that he can arrange the different members of a great society with as much ease as the hand arranges the different pieces upon a chessboard. He does not consider that the pieces upon the chessboard have no other principle of motion besides that which the hand impresses upon them; but that, in the great chessboard of human society, every single piece has a principle of motion of its own, altogether different from that which the legislature might choose to impress upon it. If those two principles coincide and act in the same direction, the game of human society will go on easily and harmoniously, and is very likely to be happy and successful. If they are opposite or different, the game will go on miserably and the society must be at all times in the highest degree of disorder.

--Adam Smith

"Why should it be," asked Walter Lippman, a famous observer of the American scene, "that in a time when men are making the prodigious claim that they can plan and direct society, they are so profoundly impressed with the unmanageability of human affairs?" Especially in the twentieth century, we have seen more elaborate attempts through government to manage and control the private actions of individuals, yet, as Lippman observed, "....this more elaborate organization can be operated only if there is more intelligence, more insight, more discipline, more disinterestedness, than exists in any ordinary company of men. Unfortunately this is the sickness of an overgoverned society, and at this point the people must seek relief through greater freedom if they are not to suffer greater disasters." Even the casual observer senses that government actions to solve problems are not working, and that as government attempts to do more, the less successful it becomes. Many are asking why.

## HUMAN NATURE AND SOCIAL ORGANIZATION

A major theme of this book is the proposition that government is that institution which requires individuals to act contrary to their own interests and to be something they are not. Men are not gods, and though some modification is possible, history suggests that moral improvement is a very slow process. For example, the illusion that reward can be separated from effort and that people can be treated as things without losing their dignity, though sincere, is contemporary "wishthink." Personal self-interest, after all, differs markedly from governmental interests. As the introductory quotation from Adam Smith suggests, we continue to forget that "... in the great chessboard of human society, every single piece has a principle of motion of its own, altogether different from that which the legislature might choose to impress upon it." Government, however, attempts to do otherwise. The goals of those with the reigns of power seldom coincide with the preferences and ambitions to which people actually aspire. The great German libertarian Wilhelm von Humboldt made the fundamental point:

> The true end of man--not that which capricious inclination prescribes for him, but that which is prescribed by eternally immutable reason--is the highest and most harmonious cultivation of his faculties into one whole. For this cultivation, freedom is the first and indispensable condition.

Since individual human action is purposeful, human behavior is said to be goal-oriented. Action is a process of reducing the degree of uneasiness in one's life, and in that sense human beings are rational. Enlightened self-interest is an inherent characteristic of human kind. To act purposefully or rationally means that individuals can and do identify what they want. Everyone has preferences, and the act of choosing among alternative desires involves a ranking of wants from most to least preferred. As individuals reduce their uneasiness, they will choose among alternative wants in a manner which maximizes their net satisfaction. Net benefits are simply benefits minus costs of acquisition.

Consider a person's action in the following situations: The first, a baby drowning in a shallow swimming pool; the second, finds that same baby in the middle of the Niagra River just moments away from going over the falls. Most people would rescue the baby in the small pool. But what about the baby ready to go over Niagra Falls? In that case the rational person would likely conclude the personal costs to be too high. The same baby but different costs produce a different response. Although most choices involve decisions that are less extreme, people are constantly prioritizing and making decisions which involve both benefits and sacrifices. Not surprisingly, we all choose differently. The science of economics can usually predict the *direction* of change in response to a new package of relative benefits and costs. But there is no accurate and reliable way of predicting how a single individual will respond to a particular situation. And, therefore, we can be quite confident that government doesn't know either.

Even when explaining interpersonal human behavior in a social setting, it is necessary to recongize the essential role of *personal* wants. It is the purposeful actions of individuals which explain the nature of group behavior. The analysis of human behavior in an interpersonal environment requires that we look to the behavior of individual human beings making up the group in question. This idea is usually called the principle of "methodological individualism." In the euphoric rush to collectivism and government control in the twentieth century, we have forgotten the implications of the essentially individualistic character of human communities. Consequently, individualism is one of the dominant and recurring themes of this book.

Perhaps the most exciting aspect of Western civilization has been the recognition of individual personality and the potential for human achievement and growth. Although life is an arduous and sometimes discouraging journey, a better tomorrow is possible through self-evaluation, determination, and hard work. In short, we each seek to discover our reason for living and the position we might occupy in the scheme of things. As we attempt to overcome our personal weaknesses and insecurities, profound truths emerge: each individual is a unique and responsible creature; no individual can think for another; and government imposed preferences are in reality the shibboleths of our time.

When any person or group of persons, through the institution of government, attempts to impose their preferences on other members of the community, inevitably the use or threat of force is required. Those who would have us act contrary to our own individual interests "...seem to imagine that (they)...can arrange the different members of a great society with as much ease as the hand arranges the different pieces upon a chessboard." Since government seeks to have individuals act contrary to their own interests, of necessity it must use coercion.

Therein lies an important reason for the unworkability of government solutions. The first principle of morality simply states that each man has a right to live his life in accordance with his own preferences so long as he does not forcibly interfere with the same right of other persons. Moral philosophy assumes the proposition that individuals are responsible for their actions. Human beings are morally autonomous, and this autonomy means that individuals are both free and accountable. There exists a fundamental contradiction between this principle of autonomy and the essential nature of government. The philosopher Robert Paul Wolff advises us: "The defining mark of the state is authority, the right to rule. The primary obligation of man is autonomy, the refusal to be ruled. It would seem, then, that there can be no resolution of the conflict between the autonomy of the individual and the punitive authority of the state." Inevitably, the most important characteristic of a moral order is therefore violated with the passage of most if not all laws. Regulations, controls, rules, procedures, entitlements, edicts, and laws of all kinds attempt to force individuals into actions that would not otherwise occur. In economics in particular, the voluntary exchanges between human beings are often prohibited outright, or they are so distorted that they create outcomes which are unintended and in conflict with their original purpose.

In contrast to government, which acts in opposition to the peaceful and goal-oriented individual action so characteristic of human beings, an alternative set of institutions has evolved. Adam Smith labels it the "system of natural liberty" and Nobel Laureate Friedrich Hayek writes of the "spontaneous order." Both ideas express the complementary interaction between the institution of private property and the social convention of mutually beneficial and voluntary exchange. Private property is the recognition that justly acquired "rights" to physical and intellectual "property" accrue to individuals. Examples of such rights would include the freedom to use, profit from, dispose of, and control property, including one's own body, without interference from others. Limits to an individual's control of property could only be justified if one's actions were to interfere with or prevent the exercise of similar rights by other individuals in the use of their property.

By voluntary exchange we mean a situation in which individuals agree to trade or exchange values (property) without the threat of force. Both parties to the exchange necessarily believe they are going to personally benefit from the transaction. It is a mutually beneficial arrangement (some would say "positive-sum game") which encourages individuals to specialize in production and carry out market trades which, from their necessarily different viewpoints, will bring personal gain.

## HUMAN ACTION AND ALTERNATIVE ECONOMIC SYSTEMS

The rise, decline, and restoration of the market economy is in large part about the relative advantages and disadvantages of two overarching principles of social organization. Following the work of the German sociologist Franz Oppenheimer, Albert Jay Nock distinguishes between the "political means" and the "market means" as social organizers or delivery systems. Which of these institutions works best when organizing interpersonal social and economic behavior; and, which most closely conforms to the basic nature of man?

The political means necessarily requires the use of the coercive apparatus of government. It forces individuals to take actions which are contrary and in opposition to their own desires and goals. After all, the essential characteristic of government is its claim to a monopoly right on the use of force in society. As individuals, you and I would be arrested if we attempted to do those things which governments do as standard fare.

The market means refers to social arrangements in which only voluntary transactions between persons are permitted. In a market economy involuntary or forced exchanges would be criminal acts legitimately subject to appropriate penalties and government action. The fundamental distinction is between mine and thine. Individuals would pursue their own goals through the voluntary exchange of justly acquired rights in property.

The market means is consistent with both human nature and the purposeful action of individuals. In contrast, the political means operates at cross-purposes to human nature and individual choice. Minimum wage laws, rent controls, usury laws, price controls, tariffs, subsidized rents, interest rate ceilings, agricultural price supports, federal loan guarantees, passenger rail service subsidies, and fixing public utility rates are just a few of the ways that government tries to alter human behavior. In every case it limits the number of exchanges that would have normally taken place and necessarily involves government force to ensure compliance. Constraining the purposeful behavior of individuals reflected in the laws of supply and demand, government tries to supersede the market in the name of the "public good."

But, the use of government force to restrict private actions presents important difficulties. Before government can create a miracle for one group, for example farm price supports for agriculture or rent controls for current renters, the money must first be taken away from someone else. Taxes are the anti-miracle imposed on people who would rather spend their money in a different way. This raises a fundamental question regarding the morality of allowing person A to meet with person B to determine how the money of person C will be used to help person D. The issue is a matter of justice in the acquisition of things (i.e., property) and therefore an important topic of discussion.

There is also the question of economic efficiency. Does government intervention in fact produce the intended consequences? Do minimum wage laws really help the poor? Have price supports in agriculture helped the farmer in the long run? Did price controls on energy solve the "energy crisis" or create it? Although many of government's actions are sincere and well intended, they have for the most part been disastrous in their unintended consequences. Government inherently demands that individuals act contrary to their personal objectives. This creates a situation analogous to the problem of forcing water to run uphill; although it can be done, it is very costly in terms of economic efficiency. But more importantly, the process involves a continual and growing abridgment of individual liberty.

In contrast, the market means encourages the spontaneous and mutually beneficial exchange of property which is in perfect harmony with the purposeful actions of free and sovereign human

14

beings. As Adam Smith pointed out more than two hundred years ago in his *Wealth of Nations*, if the organizing principles of society agree with and are complementary to human nature, then "...the game of human society will go on easily and harmoniously, and is very likely to be happy and successful. If they are opposite or different, the game will go on miserably and the society must be at all times in the highest degree of disorder."

The mystery, posed by Walter Lippman, regarding the simultaneous increase in the growth and power of government and our receding confidence in government's ability to deal with society's ills, disorder, decay, and malaise should be no surprise. Chaotically, we have come to rely on institutions of social organization that operate at cross purposes to the essential nature of purposeful human beings. Every individual has his very own principle of motion. There is no mystery at all; pushing square pegs into round holes simply does not produce socially beneficial results.

## MORALITY AND INALIENABLE RIGHTS

Economists generally compare private and public (i.e., government) actions in terms of their relative efficiencies. Economizing is required by the pervasive existence of resource scarcity, and economists have found the use of government and political solutions to be comparatively inefficient when compared to market solutions. Furthermore, most of what government does is not only economically inefficient but also immoral and inconsistent with the basic principles of human freedom. Adam Smith's system of natural liberty and Thomas Jefferson's Declaration of Independence, which states that "all men have certain unalienable rights, among which are life, liberty, and the pursuit of happiness," embody the fundamental premise that every human being owns and is personally responsible for his own life and consequently has the right to act however he chooses so long as no force is used to interfere with the life of any other individual. Governments only exist to guarantee and protect these rights. In other words, "human rights" or, equivalently, "natural rights" exist and a moral order requires that they be respected.

The concept of inalienable rights provides the cornerstone for the implementation and maintenance of a free society. The philosopher Tibor Machan in his book *Human Rights And Human Liberties* reminds us that "...the idea of natural rights has been the most powerful and valuable contribution made to the political life of mankind. It has provided the best intellectual support for the liberation of millions of human beings from the caprice and malice of others, including those who have carried out their assault on the innocent 'for reasons of state'."

We are asserting the proposition that, in the name of a supposedly

15

more important public purpose, the rights of one individual cannot be violated in behalf of the "needs" of another individual; or, that the end never justifies the means where individual rights and freedom are concerned. The violation of an individual's rights is immoral and should rightfully be condemned. This concept of individual freedom and inalienable rights dominates our view of the social interaction of purposeful human beings.

For individuals to have inalienable rights to control their own lives, which means to have a property right in one's own person, they must be able to acquire and hold rights in things and ideas which will enable them to sustain that life. Following John Locke, men have rights to "life, liberty, and property." Or put another way, human rights are not possible without property rights. We seek to explore the proposition that government coercion (i.e., the use of the "political means") is inconsistent with the inalienable rights of human beings. On the other hand, private property and voluntary exchange (i.e., the use of the "market means") define peaceful and, therefore, permissable human actions. As a Justice of the United States Supreme Court once said: "One's right to life, liberty, and property...and other fundamental rights may not be submitted to a vote; they depend on the outcome of no elections." To summarize, again quoting Tibor Machan, "...the right to be free...is best understood to mean: we are (morally, naturally) entitled to relate to others on a voluntary basis, not by coercion."

In the seventeenth century, and especially in the eighteenth century, there occurred a great intellectual revolution in which a set of social institutions and rules of conduct were identified and described which were consistent with mankind's nature. Man is a purposeful, goal-oriented being, and Adam Smith's "system of natural liberty" is characteristic of and consistent with a moral order. This intellectual revolution was tested in the American colonies and came to fruition with the American Declaration of Independence. The Pulitzer Prize winning historian Bernard Bailyn, in *The Ideological Origins Of The American Revolution,* has captured the essential spirit of this revolutionary change in the relationship between individuals and their government:

> The details of this new world, were not as yet clearly depicted; but faith ran high that a better world than any that had ever been known could be built where authority was distrusted and held in constant scrutiny;...and where the use of power over the lives of men was jealously guarded and severely restricted. It was only where there was this defiance, this refusal to truckle, this distrust of all authority, political or social, that institutions would express human aspirations, not crush them.

# CHAPTER 3

## POLITICAL REVOLUTION & THE INDIVIDUAL

> We hold these truths to be self-evident, that all men are created equal, that they are endowed by their Creator with certain unalienable rights, that among these are life, liberty, and the pursuit of happiness. That to secure these rights, governments are instituted among men, deriving their just powers from the consent of the governed. That whenever any form of government becomes destructive of these ends, it is the right of the people to alter or to abolish it.
>
> --The Declaration of Independence

It is more than coincidental that Adam Smith's *Wealth of Nations,* which proposed an "obvious and simple system of natural liberty" in economic affairs, was published in the same year that the Declaration of Independence was written and signed. Indeed, one "unblemished system," joining moral and political rights and economic freedom in a complementary package, dominated the thinking in the American colonies during the eighteenth century. The political transformation, culminating in the American Revolution, fundamentally changed the relationship between an individual and his government from that which had existed in the past. This political change both preceded and coincided with a radical, intellectual revision in what men believed to be the "nature and causes of the wealth of nations." In this chapter, we describe and illustrate the important characteristics of the political movement which came to fruition in the view of individual rights and the limited role of government so beautifully expressed in the Declaration of Independence.

### JOHN LOCKE AND NATURAL RIGHTS

The emergence of the "classical liberal" political tradition of natural rights, of individual freedom, and limited government, arose in opposition to the "ancient regime" in Europe and the all powerful state. Beginning in England during the English Civil Wars of the 1640's, sophisticated and convincing attacks on the omniscient state was in full bloom by the time of the Glorious Revolution of 1688. A new set of ideas was emerging on the relationship between the people and their government. While there were other important figures in the English Revolution, like the Levelers in the 1640's who proposed a *real* "social compact" which would explicitly define the appropriate relationship between a free people and their government, the philosopher John Locke became the driving force in the revolutionary political change of the period. Locke's ideas on individual liberty eventually were incorporated by Thomas Jefferson in his draft of the American Declaration of Independence.

Locke's major political work is *Two Treatises of Government*, which was written before but published following the Glorious Revolution of 1688 in England. The second treatise, *Of Civil Government*, remains the classic defense of natural rights and the limits to government power implied by the existence of these individual rights. In Chapter Two of *Of Civil Government*, Locke declares: "The state all men are naturally in...is a state of perfect freedom to order their actions, and dispose of their possessions, and persons as they think fit, within the bounds of the Law of Nature, without asking leave, or depending upon the will of any other man." Furthermore, "...reason, which is that law, teaches all mankind, who will but consult it, that being all equal and independent, no one ought to harm another in his life, health, liberty, or possession." Individuals have sovereignty over themselves and their property. In Chapter Five he states, "...every man has a property in his own person. Thus no body has any right to but himself. The labour of his body, and the work of his hands, we may say, are properly his."

But in this state of nature, where as Thomas Hobbes had said life would be "solitary, poore, nasty, brutish, and short," man is, according to Locke, "...very unsafe, very insecure. This makes him willing to quit a condition which however free, is full of fears and continual dangers...he seeks out, and is willing to join in society with others...for the mutual preservation of their lives, liberties and estates." However, Locke's government is to be limited and established by the consent of the people. The absolute state is rejected and government's responsibility is explicitly defined: "Government has no other end but the preservation of property." It is crucial to note that government's purpose is the "preservation" of rights already naturally belonging to individuals.

Here then, is the magnificent reversal of that proposition of the "Old Order" in which individuals were perceived to be the servant and property of the state. Man has a nature and that nature implies certain rights: the right to life, liberty, and property. These views of Locke were widely read in the American colonies and can, therefore, rightly be said to be the intellectual cornerstone for the American Revolution. The Great American Experiment, without question, has Lockean roots. But his abstract philosophic defense of individual rights and limited government, would not have alone moved men to revolution.

It remained for the radical and revolutionary "true Whigs" of the first half of the eighteenth century, primarily in England, to apply Locke's principles *Of Civil Government* to the actual practices of government and the preservation of individual rights. Two representatives and persuasive leaders of this impassioned group were John Trenchard and Thomas Gordon, who published a series of newspaper articles in London during the early 1720's entitled Cato's Letters. Widely reprinted and read in the American colonies throughout the period before the American Revolution, the Cato Letters represented the smoldering sparks of an inevitable explosion. The intense and fervent defense of human freedom and their integration of political and economic freedom, is suggested by the following quotation from one of Cato's Letters:

> By liberty, I understand the power which every man has over his own actions, and his right to enjoy the fruit of his labour, art, and industry, as far as by it he hurts not the society, or any members of it, by taking from any member, or by hindering him from enjoying what he himself enjoys. The fruits of a man's honest industry are just rewards of it, ascertained to him by natural and eternal equity, as is his title to use them in the manner which he thinks fit. And thus, with the above limitations, every man is sole lord and arbiter of his own private actions and property.

Years later, British constraints on free human action in the colonies, such as the Sugar Act of 1764, the Stamp Act of 1765, and the Intolerable Acts of 1774, would signal the beginning of the revolution which had its foundation in the appealing arguments of Trenchard and Gordon.

Trenchard and Gordon also recognized, so relevant to our own misplaced and exclusive allegiance to majority rule today, the implications for individual freedom which can arise from the tyranny of the majority:

> It is a mistaken notion in government, that the interest of the majority is only to be consulted, since in society every man has a right to everyman's assistance in the enjoyment and defense of his private property; otherwise the greater number may sell the lesser, and divide their estates amongst themselves; and so, instead of a society, where all peaceable men are protected, much equity may one man wantonly dispose of all, and violence may be sanctified by mere power.

## NATURAL RIGHTS IN THE AMERICAN COLONIES

Cato's Letters were very popular and influential in the American colonies. According to the scholarship of Gerald O'Driscoll, William Grampp, David L. Jacobson and especially Bernard Bailyn, the essays by Trenchard and Gordon were even more influential than the writings of Locke in describing the desirable characteristics of the good society. As their ideas prevailed, a growing unrest with government interference in private affairs occurred. Evidence of the commitment to individual liberty in the colonies appeared in the writing and correspondence of many Americans. John Adams, for instance, included Locke, Trenchard, and Gordon in his list of the great political thinkers. Josiah Quincy, Jr. bequeathed to his son, in 1774, the works of John Locke and the Cato Letters.

From this tradition, came the arguments which would ultimately justify and sustain the American Revolution. The United States of America was founded on these unyielding principles which said individuals had inalienable rights to property and peaceful exchange. Changing long held relationships between a citizen and his government is never easy, but the seeds of revolution had been planted. A sermon by the Massachusetts minister Jonathan Mayhew in early 1750 used the natural rights arguments and came to be called the "warning gun of the (American) Revolution." While Mayhew forcefully argued an individual's right to resist tyrannical government, Locke's influence was especially visible in the 1744 pamphlet by the Reverend Elisha Williams of Massachusetts entitled *The Essential Rights and Liberties:*

> As reason tells us, all are born thus naturally equal (i.e., with an equal right to their persons) so also with an equal right to their preservation...and every man having a property in his own person, the labour of his body and the work of his hands are properly his own, to which no one has right but himself...And if every man has a right to his person and property; he has also a right to defend them.

In New York, during the early 1750's, William Livingston published a periodical which was patterned after London's *Independent Whig* by Trenchard and Gordon. Bernard Bailyn's pulitzer prize winning book, *The Ideological Origins of the American Revolution,* documents the important role that these mid-eighteenth century Americans had on the founding fathers who signed the Declaration of Independence and/or drafted the United States Constitution.

So the great political tradition of natural rights, individual freedom, and closely constrained government was deeply imbedded in the American intellectual makeup on the eve of the American Revolution. The men who signed the Declaration of Independence in 1776, and therefore gave birth to one of the world's great experiments, were influenced by a movement which had its important beginnings in England a century earlier. Fortunately, neither a great ocean nor thousands of miles in distance could prevent the spreading influence of the writings of John Locke, the Cato Letters, and other writings like *Discourses Concerning Government* by Algernon Sidney. Like fertile seeds blown by the wind, their ideas on individual rights came to America and took root. Since many of the feudal institutions of the ancient regime were missing in the colonies, a fresh start could be made to form a more perfect union. For the first time in history, the state was to have well specified limits to its power and authority. These constraints were specified in the Articles of Confederation, the various State Constitutions and their bills of rights, and later in the U. S. Constitution. Bernard Bailyn, in an important summary paragraph from his *Ideological Origins,* has captured the essential libertarian character of the revolutionary period in America:

> The modernization of American politics and government during and after

the Revolution took the form of a sudden, radical realization of the program that had first been fully set forth by the opposition intelligentsia...American leaders moved swiftly and with little social disruption to implement systematically...the whole range of radically liberating ideas. In the process they...infused into American political culture...the major themes of eighteenth century radical libertarianism...The first is the belief that power is evil, a necessary perhaps but an evil necessity; that it is infinitely corrupting; and that it must be controlled, limited, restricted in every way compatible with a minimum civil order. Written constitutions; the separation of powers; bills of rights; limitations on executives, on legislatures, and courts; restrictions on the right to coerce and wage war--all express the profound distrust of power that lies at the ideological heart of the American Revolution and that has remained with us as a permanent legacy ever after.

Many Americans have forgotten (or perhaps the public schools no longer teach) that the American Revolution was so fundamentally libertarian in its origins. The Revolution was neither "liberal" or "conservative" in any modern meaning of those terms. There were no distinctions between what some people today call civil rights and property rights. Human rights were inseparable. According to the founding fathers and their teachers, rights of individuals to use and dispose of real and personal property were no different than the rights associated with personal conscience and freedom of speech.

## THOMAS JEFFERSON AND THE DECLARATION OF INDEPENDENCE

The Great American Experiment came to be summarized in the historic document given us by Thomas Jefferson. The Declaration of Independence declared that "...all men...are endowed by their Creator with certain unalienable rights," and that "...only to preserve and secure these rights, governments are insituted among men." Further, this government, with limited responsibilities, is not absolute but derives its "...just powers from the consent of the governed." As Frank Chodorov has pointed out, "...it is not at all the charter of a new nation. It is a rationalization of rebellion."

The indictment of the British crown was but a springboard from which Jefferson launched a political principle that: "Government, far from being an end in itself, is but an instrument invented by man to aid him in bettering his circumstances." Years later, Jefferson repeated in his private correspondence the essential nature of his political philosophy. In 1786 he wrote to Mrs. John (Abigail) Adams: "The spirit of resistance to government is so valuable on certain occasions that I wish it to be always kept alive." This spirit of resistance to government (the Jeffersonian/Lockean political philosophy) is indeed the taproot of liberty. And it is important to remember that this

21

proposition is based on our fundamental, but admittedly unprovable, premise: That human beings have inalienable rights and that these rights are inherent in an individual by the fact of that person's existence.

The Declaration set the tone for the revolutionary changes in the relationship between an individual and his government, but it remained for the practical implementation to be carried out in the constitutions drafted by the various states during the course of the revolution. In a history of the American scene, two prominent historians, Samuel Elliot Morrison and Henry Steele Commager, note that in these state constitutions: "Truly no governments on earth have ever been instituted with so little authority to do ill, as those of the American states. Yet, not content with that, the framers of constitutions even limited their government's power to do good, lest it be perverted to their hurt." For example, George Mason of Virginia, another important revolutionary figure, was asked to draw up a Bill of Rights at Williamsburg for the Constitution of the State of Virginia. Mason produced a set of articles which were later incorporated into other state constitutions and the first ten amendments to the federal constitution. George Mason's first two articles, with utmost clarity, define this taproot of liberty as follows:

I. That all men are created equally free and independent and have certain inalienable rights, which they cannot by any compact derpive or divest their posterity, among which are the enjoyment of life and liberty, with the means of acquiring property, and pursuing and obtaining happiness and safety.

II. That all power is by God and nature vested in and consequently derived from the people; that magistrates are their trustees and servants, and at all times amenable to them.

In addition to the contributions of Thomas Jefferson, George Mason, James Madison, John Adams, Samuel Adams, and many others, it was probably in Thomas Paine's *Common Sense* and later his *Rights of Man*, that the Great American Experiment in human freedom was developed most passionately. Shortly before the signing of the Declaration of Independence, Thomas Paine wrote the following eloquent plea for human liberty:

These are the times that try men's souls. The summer soldier and the sunshine patriot will, in this crisis, shrink from the service of their country...Tryanny, like hell, is not easily conquered...What we obtain too cheap, we esteem too lightly...it would be strange indeed if so celestial an article as freedom should not be highly rated. Society in every state is a blessing, but government, even in its best state, is but a necessary evil; in its worst state an intolerable one.

# THE UNITED STATES CONSTITUTION

The Articles of Confederation and then the Constitution of 1787, established what the framers thought to be viable constraints on government power consistent with the principles which had evolved over the previous century. But James Madison, among others, was not unaware of the problems associated with the granting of coercive power to government and the fragile character of human freedom:

> But what is government, but the greatest of all reflections on human nature? If men were angels, no government would be necessary. If angels were to govern men, neither external nor internal controls on government would be necessary. In framing a government, which is to be administered by men, the great difficulty lies in this: You must first enable the government to control the governed; and in the next place, oblige it to control itself.

Madison was concerned that "...the accumulation of all powers...in the same hands, whether of one, a few, or many, and whether hereditary, self-appointed, or elective, must just be pronounced the very definition of tyranny," and therefore the powers of government "...are guarded against by a division of the government into distinct and separate departments...the power surrendered by the people is first divided between two distinct governments, and then the portion alloted to each subdivided among distinct and separate departments. Hence a double security arises to the rights of the people. The different governments will control each other, at the same time each will be controled by itself." Still, those who opposed the ratification of the Constitution, the so-called Anti-Federalists, argued that the national government would extend its authority "...to every case that is of the least importance."

Clearly, many of the founding fathers believed that this principle of the separation of powers, in combination with the Bill of Rights as the first ten amendments to the Constitution, would be sufficient to prevent the state from becoming a leviathan. Furthermore, it would provide the ground rules for economic production and socially beneficial exchange by providing, even if not explicitly stated, for the security of private property. The Constitution would be the mechanism for securing both political *and* economic freedom. By reducing individual uncertainty regarding human rights and specifying the limits to government intervention in private spheres, the Constitution of the United States was to become the stabilizing force for a workable free market economy. Alexander Hamilton, in debating the ratification of the Constitution, argued that the system of checks and balances "...is so complex, so skillfully contrived, that it is next to impossible that an impolitic or wicked measure should pass the scrutiny with success." There were those who doubted the reliability of the safeguards, especially the Anti-Federalists, but nevertheless the Constitution represented a giant step forward relative to the ancient regime

## THE GREAT AMERICAN EXPERIMENT BEGINS

So the die was cast. The Constitution was ratified. And the Great American Experiment moved into another phase. It would take decades before the full implications of the Supreme Court's interpretation of the Constitution, and later with amendments to the document, would be fully known.

Nevertheless, the political revolution of the seventeenth and eighteenth centuries contributed significantly to the successful revolution in the economic sphere which followed. The transformation in economic thought came to fruition with the publication of Adam Smith's *An Inquiry into the Nature and Causes of the Wealth of Nations* in 1776. Stimulated by the same political commitment to individual liberty, the Industrial Revolution began in England during this same period.

# CHAPTER 4

## THE REVOLUTION IN ECONOMICS

The role of competitive capitalism (or a market based private enterprise system) in supporting and extending personal liberty ("freedom to" as well as "freedom from") is little known among the lay public compared to, say, the intended roles of public education, constitutional government, or a free press. Indeed, the workings of capitalism are usually more subtle, and its effects on the range of human choice have generally been unintended by those bringing them about. That is, they often occur as by-products of actions motivated by quite other ends in view (e.g., making a profit).

--Robert G. Perrin

During the political revolution which transpired between the seventeenth and eighteenth centuries, changes were also taking place in the economic life of England, Holland, and other parts of Europe. The proposition that individuals had natural rights contributed to a relaxation of the rigidities which existed in economic life during the middle ages. Fortunately, the more open characteristics of English society were transferred to the English speaking colonies in North America. While government's influence on both political and economic life, and indeed religious life too, was still important, it was clear that significant change was underway.

Both events and ideas in the eighteenth century brought radical revisions in the interpretation of economic phenomena and the contemporary understanding of the nature and sources of economic progress. In this chapter, we look briefly at the events and ideas which produced this economic revolution and in turn document the intellectual case for the economic system of competitive capitalism.

### FEUDALISM AND MERCANTILISM

The high point of competitive capitalism, and as close as we have ever come to a truly laissez faire economic order, occured during the nineteenth century. In England and the United States the evolution of the market system was a long and tortuous process which slowly came to fruition over many centuries. The medieval social and economic system of feudalism, which characterized the Middle Ages and continued to influence the early modern period, was governed by custom and tradition. The medieval manorial system of lord and serf reflected a "natural and eternal ordering" which was viewed as being handed down by God. Individuals were born into particular stations and this assignment was not to be questioned. The whole

25

feudal system of reciprocal responsibility, as governed by the tradition and custom of the manor, critically depended on each member of the community recognizing their place in the scheme of things.

Nevertheless, the feudal order came unraveled. A new social mobility associated with rising productivity in agriculture and an increase in trade, especially trade between the cities of Europe and beyond, was the initial catalyst. The relationships of status and reciprocal obligation in an unchanging social and economic system of tradition and custom, fell before the forces of money exchange, contracts, and the acquisitive and purposeful nature of people who perceived the opportunity to improve their material condition and station in life.

A very important technological change during the Middle Ages which contributed to the breakdown of the feudal system involved the transition from a two-field to a three-field crop rotation system. Similar to the results of contemporary experience with multi-cropping, agriculture efficiency increased dramatically. Following gains in agricultural productivity, the rapid growth in Europe's population during the twelfth and thirteenth centuries encouraged the growth of cities. This, in turn, encouraged the spread of trade and commerce throughout most of Europe.

The growth of economic exchange and the institutions and instruments of this trade (i.e. money exchange, negotiable instruments, credit facilities, new systems of commercial law, contract law, and other modern business institutions), resulted in a rapid and irreversible decline in the restrictive and traditional system of feudalism. In the relatively more relaxed political environment characteristic of England, trade-for-profit by merchant capitalists came to control the issues of production, resource allocation, and the distribution of economic goods.

Competitive capitalism, the economic system characterized by the exchange of property for profit and the accumulation of capital, really became the driving force in Europe, at least with regard to export trade, by the end of the sixteenth century. Change in the seventeenth century was even more dramatic. Large cities in England, France, Spain, and Holland were becoming thoroughly capitalisitc; an environment in which a growing middle class of merchants and shopkeepers were intimately involved in commerce, manufacturing, and even finance.

The institutional arrangements of this period of early capitalism were known as the system of mercantilism. Although private trade and commerce were becoming increasingly important, the most influential view continued to be that government should direct economic life to the benefit of the nation state. Then as now, merchants, labor guilds, and businesses formed coalitions of special interest groups to restrict competition. Wanting competition for others and monopoly for themselves, they sought government protection in order to preserve particular markets for their very own. Mercantilism meant in large part the implementation of restictive practices and the use of government granted monopoly charters for specific interests. During this period, most European contries adopted extensive export and import regulations. For example, the English Navigation Acts of 1651 and 1660 promoted a monopoly in Britain's international trade. The Statute of Artificers (1563) granted the government in England many of the functions performed by the craft guilds of that time and by the market in today's economy. Regulation of wages, quality controls over many goods, the allocation of labor among different occupations, and conditions of employment all came under government purview and control.

In France, regulation, specification, and restriction were carried to the extreme by Jean Baptiste Colbert, minister and economic advisor to Louis XIV. As an example, the width of a piece of cloth and the precise number of threads contained within it, were rigidly specified by the government. Eli Heckscher, in his classic volume *Mercantilism*, recorded the extremes to which the Crown would go in its "attacks on innovations." The following account by Heckscher concerns an attempt by the French government to prevent the production, import, or consumption of printed calicoes:

> It is estimated that the economic measures taken in this connection cost the lives of some 16,000 people, partly through executions and partly through armed affrays, without reckoning the unknown but certainly much larger number of people who were sent to the galleys, or punished in other ways. On one occasion in Valence, 77 were sentenced to be hanged, 58 were to be broken upon the wheel, 631 were sent to the galleys, one was set free, and none were pardoned.

While entrepreneurship and market arrangements were slowly gaining the ascendency, the state continued to dominate.

As is usually the case with government intervention, the restrictive practices of the mercantalist period, while beneficial to some, actually harmed many others. For example, the principal European nations tried to exclude the merchants and traders of other countries from their own colonial empires. This would prove to be a very important issue in the resolution of the American Revolution. Government was also an instrument of control for the established merchant-capitalist class: Potential competitors were prevented from competing while those with the monopoly charter benefited. As might have been expected, protests arose from important segments of the rising new middle class and industrial capitalists against government restrictions. They simply wanted more freedom and free trade. With the exception of special interest groups that benefited from the mercantilist restraints on production and trade, most of the newly emerging capitalists believed themselves constrained by state regulations aimed against their entrepreneurial efforts.

Another factor contributing to the evolution of this wealth

maximizing individualism was the development of the protestant work ethic. Stemming from protestant theology following the Reformation and explained by Max Weber *(The Protestant Ethic and the Spirit of Capitalism)* and Richard Tawney *(Religion and the Rise of Capitalism)* among others, the individual conscience was seen as the fundamental constraint on human behavior. Particular actions were judged according to their consistency with one's faith in God. The merchant, tradesman, and artisan of the sixteenth and seventeenth century in certain parts of Europe, for example London and Amsterdam, believed that the principle of private property had been ordained by God. Purposeful action on their part to achieve material gain was not only consistent with God's law, but indeed their economic efforts represented a glorification of Him. These protestant sects were admittedly rigid and doctrinaire in practice. Nevertheless, salvation was an individual matter and the behavior which was encouraged by the new faith was conducive to economic growth.

The "protestant ethic," as interpreted by the Calvinists and other groups, necessarily contributed to economic growth and rising living standards. The ethic emphasized the importance of diligence and hard work as a person's earthly calling while at the same time condemning conspicious consumption and extravagance. Through long hours of labor, efficiency promoting effort, and a savings ethic, one would not only glorify God but would secure his personal salvation in the Kingdom of Heaven. One's calling acted then as a powerful inducement to rising productivity and economic progress. Personal limits on consumption in combination with greater work effort unavoidably caused an accumulation of capital. Economists have long known that the surest and best way to produce economic growth is capital expansion and better tools through investment.

Sadly, in our own time, a large majority of God's representatives on earth are not so much concerned with individual responsibility and the work ethic, as they are with equality, socialism and collectivist solutions to the human predicament. This flavor was also present in the English colonies in North America, but it remains true, as we believe Weber and Tawney have shown, that a change of emphasis to the individual and his or her personal salvation played a significant role in the rise of the individualistic society during the colonial period.

Though briefly described, such were the forceful economic events over the many centuries which fashioned the economic revolution. The changes in human behavior, encouraged by the political revolution described in the last chapter and sometimes encouraged by the changes in religious belief, helped to bring about a revolution in the way economic events were to be interpreted. A new view emerged during the eighteenth century as to the ultimate sources of economic growth and progress.

## IDEAS ON THE MARKET BEFORE ADAM SMITH

John Locke, whose ideas had contributed so importantly to the political revolution of this period, also had important things to say about economic matters. According to Locke, the formation of government under the "social contract," was largely to protect individuals in the enjoyment of the fruits of their labor. The protection of private property rights was a device to generate incentives conducive to production and the creation of wealth. As a result, Locke believed that the role of government in economic life should be limited to the preservation of rights. He thought the market place preferable to the "bungling of men."

In England, the Whig followers of this tradition also stressed the limits which should be placed on government intervention and the importance of secure property for economic advancement. John Trenchard and Thomas Gordon, whose views, as we have noted, were very popular in the American colonies during the eighteenth century, stressed the role of personal incentives in economic life: "Man will not spontaneously toil and labour but for their own advantage, for their pleasure or their profit, and to obtain something which they want or desire, and which, for the most part, is not to be obtained but by force or consent." Trenchard and Gordon were precursors to the interest in "supply-side" economics in our own time. Where government confiscates the rewards to productive effort through high tax rates, self-interested men and women will respond by working less and producing less: "Learning, the arts, commerce, all would sicken under arbitrary governments."

A number of other important contributions during the eighteenth century helped produce ideas regarding the socially beneficial effects of private property and the free-market system. Bernard de Mandeville, in 1714 published *The Fable of the Bees or Private Vices and Public Benefits*, which anticipated much of what Adam Smith would say in the *Wealth of Nations*. Baron De Montesquieu's *The Spirit of Laws* in 1748, emphasized the role of incentives in guiding human behavior in productive ways. Montesquieu was convinced that purposeful acting human beings would respond positively to greater rewards and that high tax burdens would discourage work effort and productivity. Thomas Jefferson is known to have studied Montesquieu's ideas and thought a great deal of what he had written about spontaneous economic arrangements. Jefferson translated into English another important French work on the free market system, Count Destutt de Tracy's *A Treatise on Political Economy*, and was therefore thoroughly familiar with the newly emerging defense of competitive capitalism.

David Hume, in *Political Discourses* (1752), was also an important contributor to the ideas which were to be summarized and integrated in the later work on political economy by Adam Smith. While the mercantilists had advocated high taxes and low wages to encourage work effort, Hume was adament in his view that high tax rates discouraged production. Following the lead of John Locke, he felt that government's role in economic life was to be a limited one. Private individuals, acting in an enlightened self-interest, would respond positively to an open market system in which rewards would accrue to hard working, efficient producers. Both Benjamin Franklin and Alexander Hamilton, among others, respected Hume's ideas and assisted in bringing them to America.

During the middle of the eighteenth century, the Physiocrats, a school of political economy in France, led by the French writers Quesnay and Turgot, also wrote critically of the mercantilist doctrine that wealth was a matter of accumulating precious metals. Quesnay emphasized that wealth was a matter of increasing the level of production of goods and services. Turgot and other Physiocrats objected to the considerable intervention in the French economy by government and the extremely high tax rates which burdened the economy. In fact, they argued that government tax revenues could be increased by lowering tax rates, a proposition which sounds very much like Arthur Laffer's recommendations in the 1980's. It remained for someone who was aware and knowledgeable of all these eighteenth century economic writers to gather together the theoretical bits and pieces on private market arrangements and to identify the essential characteristics of a spontaneous economic order.

## ADAM SMITH AND THE WEALTH OF NATIONS

While Locke, Trenchard, Gordon, Mandeville, Montesquieu, Hume, Quesnay, Turgot, and the founding fathers, especially Benjamin Franklin, made important contributions to the intellectual defense of competitive capitalism, it was the Scotsman Adam Smith who fundamentally and permanently changed the way in which economic phenomena were to be explained. Beginning his revolutionary book during a two year stay in Toulouse, France in 1764-1766, *An Inquiry into the Nature and Causes of the Wealth of Nations* was finally published in 1776. The book was a tremendous success. Translated throughout Europe, including at least four French translations, it was widely read in Europe and America. Most of the important institutional changes during the transition from a feudal order to the system of competitive capitalism were examined by Smith. The centuries of change which transformed the British economy prior to the Industrial Revolution, including the nature of human motivations, the role of private property, the sources of wealth, were systematically analyzed in the *Wealth of Nations*.

The center piece of Smith's "model" was what he called the "system of natural liberty." His analysis of the spontaneous origin of economic institutions and arrangements and the proposition that this spontaneous order would generate socially beneficial results was the clarion call to a new economic order:

> This marvelous institution is not originally the effect of any human wisdom, which forsees and intends that general oppulence to which it gives occasion. It is the necessary, through very slow and gradual, consequence of a certain propensity in human nature which has in view no such extensive utility; the propensity to truck, barter, and exchange one thing for another.

It is the desire to better one's own situation which guides human behavior. Enlightened self-interest works because it describes the way man is, not the way some think he should be. Smith, in a famous and frequently quoted passage from the *Wealth of Nations*, captures the nature of the human predicament:

> Man has almost constant occasion for the help of his brethren, and it is in vain for him to expect it from their benevolence only. He will be more likely to prevail if he can interest their self-love in his favour, and show them that it is for their advantage to do for him what he requires of them. Whoever offers to another a bargain of any kind, proposes to do this: Give me that which I want, and you shall have this which you want, is the meaning of every such offer; and it is in this manner that we obtain from one another the far greater part of those good offices which we stand in need of. It is not from the benevolence of the butcher, the brewer, or the baker that we expect our dinner, but from their regard to their own interest. We address ourselves, not to their humanity, but to their self-love, and never talk to them of our own necessities, but of their advantages.

Self-interested individuals, spontaneously and voluntarily exchanging private property rights in order to better their condition, generate socially beneficial results. Again, we believe it is important to recite a famous passage from Adam Smith's book which continues to have such a profound impact on all of our lives:

> (an individual)...intends only his own security; and by directing that industry in such a manner as its produce may be of the greatest value, he intends only his own gain, and he is in this, as in many other cases, led by an invisible hand to promote an end which was not part of his intention. Nor is it always the worse for the society that it was not a part of it. By pursuing his own interest he frequently promotes that of society more effectually than when he really intends to promote it. I have never known much good done by those who affected to trade for the public good.

The beneficial results of voluntary exchange could only be realized in a society where property rights were secure and contractual arrangements between individuals were enforced. The reduced uncertainty associated with the security of individual rights broadens the range of mutually beneficial exchange and encourages individuals to work, save, and accumulate capital in order to improve their circumstances.

Smith was no apologist for the business class and was well aware of the potential for monopoly to suppress the competitive process.

When the individuals of a single industry got together for drink and meriment, he believed the conversation would sooner or later turn to rigging the market in their favor. Nevertheless, Smith was confident that open markets, without artificial barriers to the entry of new producers, would practically eliminate the likelihood of private monopoly. For Smith, the important source of monopoly involved the granting of special privilege by government.

Through the division and specialization of labor, Smith's system of natural liberty makes possible an enormous increase of wealth which is the fundamental source of economic progress and individual well-being. The combination of human freedom, enlightened self-interest and economic specialization is bound to increase productivity and therefore produce greater wealth.

In order to extend the market and broaden opportunities, Smith condemned domestic restraints to trade and commerce and presented a persuasive argument for the socially beneficial effects of free international trade. He maintained that the degree of specialization is limited by the extent of the market. Productivity and wealth are a function of how wide and far the nexus of the competitive process can be spread.

After the division of labor and the invention of money, Smith believed that there was nothing as important as the accumulation of capital to increase productivity and promote economic progress. The fundamental propositon that the quantity and quality of tools and machines available to complement the application of human effort determines the productivity of the population and therefore standards of living stems from the important passages in Adam Smith's *Wealth of Nations*.

In recent years we have had to relearn Adam Smith's dictum regarding the underlying source of the wealth of nations. Material standards of living depend crucially on the process of investment in new and more productive capital goods. Investment is made possible by personal savings and the retained earnings of business. In turn, decisions to save depend on the existing structure of incentives, including, for example, the rate of inflation, interest rates and tax burdens. Personal saving decisions depend on the appropriate structure of incentives. The underlying determinant of our behavior in this regard, Smith reminded us long ago, is the "...desire of bettering our condition." No grand designs or central plans are required:

> The uniform, constant, and uninterrupted effort of every man to better his condition, the principle from which public and national as well as private opulence is originally derived, is frequently powerful enough to maintain the natural progress of things toward improvement, in spite both of the extravagance of government, and of the greatest errors of administration.

Therefore, he argued, the sufficient condition for economic progress is the system of natural liberty in which individuals have certain inalienable rights. The right to truck, barter, and exchange property and the spontaneous and natural tendency of individuals to better their condition by hard work, through the specialization of labor and capital accumulation, were to Smith the necessary prerequisites to economic growth. "It is a game," according to Nobel Laureate Friedrich Hayek, "which serves to elicit from each player the highest worthwile contribution to the common pool from which each will win an uncertain share."

Smith was adament in his proposition that there existed an essential harmony between the private interest and the public interest with relatively few exceptions. This conclusion, according to Smith, could be demonstrated through observation: it was the universal experience of history. The socially beneficial results of the spontaneous order left relatively little that government could do and almost nothing that it could do well. Government would do well to avoid taking on tasks which are beyond its capacity to discharge. The direction of economic activity should be left to the purposeful behavior of individuals. Government's role would be to secure property rights, enforce contracts, and little else.

Since 1776, Adam Smith's arguments regarding the legitimate functions of government as well as its inefficiencies have been the primary source of most arguments by opponents of economic intervention by government. For Smith, the functions and responsibilities of market participants and the ministers of government in the social order were distinctly different. Government was to preserve order and enforce property rights so that the socially beneficial results of the market order might be achieved. An additional problem, as we have come to know so well in the twentieth century, is that governments, when involved in economic affairs, are "...always and without exception, the greatest spendthrifts in the society." His warnings on this score influentially shaped the thinking of the leaders of the American Revolution and those who would draft the United States Constitution.

Misguided belief to the contrary, it is important to remind the reader that Adam Smith was also conscious of and sensitive to those on the bottom of the economic ladder. The working class, he said, would share in the benefits of progress, and the poor would be important beneficiaries of economic growth. Or, as Smith put it:

> ...it deserves to be remarked, perhaps, that it is in the progressive state, while the society is advancing to the further acquisition rather than when it has acquired its full complement of riches, that the condition of the laboring poor, of the great body of people, seems to be the happiest and most comfortable. It is hard in the stationary, and miserable in the declining state. The progressive state is in reality the cheerful and the hearty state to all different orders of society.

In summary, and in spite of the reservations one can find by appealing to selected passages, Adam Smith's *Wealth of Nations* represents a passionate plea for the economic freedom of the individual. Smith, like few before him, recognized that the wealth of a nation is its people. With humans acting to better their own condition while simultaneously benefiting society, he saw that private ownership and freedom were inextricably tied to wealth and progress. He made eloquent appeals to the private and public benefits of a free society with private property, voluntary exchange, and the economic growth and progress which would necessarily occur in that system of natural liberty. The *Wealth of Nations* was one of the most influential books ever written. Generations of academics, political leaders, and opinion makers felt the influence of this gentle man from Scotland. The appropriate conduct of business and the legitimate scope of government were eloquently demonstrated by the moving passages in Smith's great book. Most important of all, he taught us there were practically no limits to the possibility of economic progress in which both the rich and poor would share.

## THE IDEA OF ECONOMIC FREEDOM SPREADS

Smith's ideas spread rapidly to Europe. In France the word was passed by Jean Babtiste Say, another great champion of individual freedom and the market order. After reading the *Wealth of Nations* as a young man of twenty-three, Say described it as containing "...a number of positive truths." He was much impressed with Smith's characterization of the system of natural liberty. In 1803 Say published his own book, *Le Traite' d'Economie Politique*, in which the important ideas first developed by Smith were reproduced and a number of Smith's points were improved upon. Published almost a quarter of a century after the *Wealth of Nations*, Say's treatise considered the implications of the industrial revolution in England which, by 1803, was in full fury. While Smith had given agriculture the prime spot in his scheme, Say focused on the manufacturer.

Other significant advances by Say included the emphasis he placed on the entrepreneur in the system of competitive capitalism and the distinction between the functions performed by the entrepreneur and those performed by the capitalist. According to Say, it is the entrepreneur who determines the allocation of resources among competing uses and, motivated by profits, produces wealth and progress in a free society. The fundamental role of the entrepreneurial function in the competitive market process is an important point of discussion later in this book.

Because of Mandeville, Hume, Smith, and J. B. Say, the essential ingredients of free and voluntary economic arrangements in society were recorded and passed into the nineteenth century. The banner would be carried by James Mill, Nassau Senior, and until at least his latter years, John Stuart Mill in England, by Friedrich Bastiat in France, Karl Menger in Austria, and a number of lesser known economists and philosophers in the United States. In the twentieth century the banner of personal freedom and the market order has been carried by Irving Fisher, Frank Knight, Henry Simons, Milton

Friedman, James Buchanan, Ludwig von Mises, Friederich Hayek, Armen Alchian, Murray Rothbard, Thomas Sowell, and many others. Although individual freedom and private property rights have been eloquently stated and defended by these great minds, in large part the twentieth century has unfortunately embraced other ideas in practice and policy. Socialism, public ownership, and government planning are also ideas that have been presented with great force and emotional plea. We will look at what the champions of a free society have had to say regarding the beneficial and socially desirable implications of a competitive market order throughout the rest of this book. We will also explore the ideas of those persons who would politicize society and make the case against competitive capitalism.

## THE SYSTEM OF NATURAL LIBERTY IS COLORBLIND

The marketplace has another important attribute. It is generally blind to social class, personal honor, estate, elitist prerogatives and other impediments to free and voluntary human interaction. An individual's worth under a system of private property and voluntary exchange is determined in the market place. In no small way is it the result of the interaction of the pressures of demand and supply. In particular, the market rewards all kinds of human activity with which you and I might or might not agree. Professional sportsmen make millions of dollars, and so do punk rock groups, attractive movie stars, and soap salesmen. On the other hand, millions of people are engaged in positions that, though important, are not rewarded as handsomely. The market overlooks race, color, creed, occupation, and even the value of self-worth by efficiently delivering what people want. No one is forced to see a movie or a football game, but if enough people attend, then the performers involved will be richly rewarded. The market gives people what they want and to argue otherwise is analogous to blaming the waiter for obesity.

The transition from a feudal society to a capitalistic society increased social mobility and broadened the boundaries of free choice. The effects of these changes were to be seen in the increase in political freedom and the resulting appearance of representative political institutions. For example, the Glorious Revolution of 1688 in England was largely the consequence of the development of trade, commerce, and the altered property arrangements that occurred during the previous centuries. As the end of the twentieth century approaches, almost without exception the political democracies in the world remain devoted to economic arrangements emphasizing private ownership and a market system. We have already shown in an earlier chapter that property rights are human rights. Without security in one's property, other human rights (i.e., religious, speech, and political freedom) cannot and will not long endure. As the Nobel Laureate Friederich Hayek has said: ''We must once again make economic freedom an intellectually exciting and stimulating issue if we are to maintain our freedoms.''

35

# CHAPTER 5

## THE INDUSTRIAL REVOLUTION

With the best will in the world, the transition from farms and cottages to factories and cities could never have been smooth...those who dwell on the horrors that arose from the fact that the products of the sewers often got mixed up with the drinking water, and attribute this, as all other horrors, to the Industrial Revolution, should be reminded of the obvious fact that without the iron pipe, which was one of the products of that revolution, the problem of enabling people to live a healthy life together in towns could never have been solved.

--T. S. Ashton

Since the dawn of civilization economic progress has generally been slow. Centuries have passed without perceptible changes in standards of living. Generation replicated generation, and bone wearying labor provided only bare subsistence. Whole populations were susceptible to serious diseases, disorders, and the incomplete development of minds and bodies. Drought, flood, insect plagues, failure of a staple crop, a disproportionate increase in the population relative to the food supply, crop destruction caused by wars, and political and property right instability could all be listed as reasons for famine, starvation, and poverty.

To cite examples, in 436 B.C. Rome experienced one of the earliest recorded famines during which thousands committed suicide by drowning rather than face starvation. Famines struck the entire world during the middle ages: One in 879 A.D. and another in 1162. Because of the famine of 1586, England passed the "Poor Laws" in an attempt to provide relief for the distressed. India suffered three consecutive famines in the latter half of the 18th century and eight during the 19th century. Almost ten million persons died in the famine which struck Northern China in 1877. To this day, hunger continues to plague parts of the world. Of the billions of people who are living or have lived, most have had to worry about food. It seems that the struggle to nourish and feed the family has been man's primary concern. Even the more advanced cultures have faced starvation. The ancient Asyrians, Egyptians, and Greeks, though blessed with resources and fertile lands, were often incapable of producing enough food. For the most part their lives were wretched.

Although the Industrial Revolution changed all of this for many countries, it is nevertheless a most misunderstood episode in human history. Professor Freidrich A. Hayek, the 1974 Nobel Laureate in Economics, writes in his book *Capitalism and the Historians* that the one historical myth which has probably done more to discredit the economic system from which we owe our present day civilization concerns the asserted deterioration of the working class's position due to the rise of capitalism.

## THE BIRTH OF THE INDUSTRIAL REVOLUTION

A century after the political revolution in England and beginning on the eve of the publication of *The Wealth of Nations* there occurred a great transformation of the British economy. The time period encompasses the last few decades of the eighteenth century and the first half of the nineteenth. During this great upheaval known as the Industrial Revolution, an economic system relying on private ownership of the means of production, individual initiative, and market exchange was predominant. The material standard of living rose, and a slow but persistent increase in per capita real income continued from generation to generation. While the economic gains varied among different skill groups and geographic areas in Great Britain, a belief in the inevitability of economic progress was a widespread and popular point of view. This was in stark contrast to earlier centuries in which poverty and deprivation were viewed as pre-ordained.

Yet, the dominant intellectual interpretation of this period is one of a worsening situation for the poor and unparalleled misery and degradation. Both scholars and students alike have argued that capitalism might be fine in its properly constrained place, but not at the expense of human beings and the working poor. Without government legislation, they say, we would still have child labor and sweatshop conditions. Deeply instilled into the national psyche, few ideas are more earnestly held. But then as today, the real news is really just the opposite. In point of fact, because of the Industrial Revolution, the laboring class finally began their long climb from poverty. Yes, material conditions were not as favorable as today, but they were improving considerably over what had been.

In truth, government cannot wave the wand of restrictive legislation and thereby abolish poverty and hard work. Any improvement that a law makes in working conditions, for example, comes directly out of the wages of the worker. The tough, long road from misery and poverty to rising standards of living must, of necessity, go through the stage of higher savings, investment, hard work, and even "sweatshops." To prohibit child labor in India, for example, would be to automatically condemn millions to starvation. With few exceptions, immigrant families in the United States improved their economic positions through what economists call multi-family participation of labor. For the layman, that means dad works, mom works, sister works, brother works, everyone works. The irony of the myth of deteriorating conditions for the poor is that while capitalism has brought unprecedented increases in living standards to the masses it continues to be blamed as the cause of their misery.

## THE ROMANTIC INTERPRETATION OF EARLIER TIMES

Wishful thinking and humanitarian zeal will not do. The implications and results for living standards, especially among the working poor, must be compared not to today's standards, which are incontestably the result of the evolution of capitalism, but to the miserable conditions which had existed before. Even Karl Marx agreed in his *Communist Manifesto* on the proposition that capitalism represented a great engine of economic growth:

> The bourgeoisie, during its rule of scarce one hundred years, has created more massive and more colossal productive forces than have all preceding generations together.

The results of the Industrial Revolution have largely been criticized by socialist or socialist-leaning historians who have had a very idealized view of the conditions of the poor in the pre-capitalist, feudal period. The flavor of this mythical view, which is in conflict with the actual facts of the case, can be seen in the following passage from Friedrich Engels, the collaborator of Karl Marx, in his *The Condition of the Working Classes in England in 1844*. Before the sordid conditions of the Industrial Revolution appeared, according to Engels romantic view:

> ...the workers vegetated throughout a passably comfortable existence, leading a righteous and peaceful life in all piety and probity; and their material condition was far better than that of their successors. They did not need to overwork; they did no more than they chose to do, and yet earned what they needed. They had leisure for healthful work in garden or fields, work which, in itself, was recreation for them, and they could take part besides in the recreation of games of their neighbors, and all these games--bowling, cricket, football, etc.--contributed to their physical health and vigour. They were, for the most part, strong, well-built people, in whose physique little or no difference from that of their peasant neighbours was discoverable. Their children grew up in fresh country air, and, if they could help their parents at work, it was only occasionally; while of eight or twelve hours work for them there was no question.

Unfortunately for the view reflected in this quotation, there exist any number of accounts of earlier periods suggesting far worse conditions than those existing in the first few decades of the nineteenth century in England's cities. For example, P. Boissonnade in the *Life and Work in Medieval Europe,* describes the hardship, brutality, and human suffering associated with the earlier period. Attempts like Engels' to romanticize the pre-industrial world, in which life for the great many was, in fact, "brutish, nasty, and short," have done a great injustice to the period of transition to the modern factory system and the high living standards which followed.

The statistical evidence indicating the capacity to produce greater quantities and selections of goods and services for the laboring

38

classes is there for all to see. For millions of peasants the evolution of a secure and, therefore, productive system of property arrangements meant that abject poverty was avoidable for the first time in human history. The new factory system was, in fact, a potential "road to freedom" for an overwhelming majority of the population and represented nothing less than a revolutionary change from all that had gone before.

## PROPERTY RIGHTS AND THE INDUSTRIAL REVOLUTION

The Industrial Revolution seems to have been the result of an inter-related series of events which came together in the latter half of the eighteenth century in a tiny corner of the known world: England. Of great importance, a more efficient set of property rights evolved from the seventeenth century. Also, there was an increase in the growth rate of population in the eighteenth century which was accompanied by a wave of urbanization. Simultaneously, international trade also flourished in England. Further, there was a significant increase in the pace of technological change and invention during this period. And tying it all together was the intellectual revolution associated with the rising respect for the individual person. With political stability and security in his property rights, the individual was turned loose to invent, innovate, and produce.

Douglas North and Robert Paul Thomas are but two of the economic historians who have written how the increased security in property for individuals, which evolved during the seventeenth and eighteenth centuries, contributed greatly to specialization in production and market exchange. The parliament, they argue, gained the upper hand over the King of England, and gradually the system evolved from sovereignty of the king to "consumer sovereignty." Finally, individuals mattered and personal incentives were recognized as important.

While the revolution in England's agriculture is usually assigned to the eighteenth century, the enclosure movement had been well underway by the seventeenth century. By eliminating the common property characteristics of land ownership, the economic gains associated with more efficient farming techniques now accrued to those who actually worked a particular piece of ground. The economic proverb "...give a man a permanent lease on a desert and he will turn it into a garden, but give him a one year lease on a garden and he will turn it into a desert..." seems universal in its application.

Progressive changes in industry were also a result of a more efficient assignment of property rights. For example, the Statute of Monopolies ended the king's authority to grant monopoly franchises, and according to North and Thomas in *The Rise of the Western World*:

...it was the Statute of Monopolies which not only reflected the fundamental change in organization between Crown monopoly and voluntary group organization, but institutionalized the internalization of the benefits from innovation, so that they became a part of the legal system of the society. In effect the rewards of innovating were no longer subject to royal favor, but were guaranteed by a set of property rights embedded in the common law.

The beginnings of a system of property arrangements then, in which the economic gains from innovation would be captured by the individual who undertook that innovative activity, were well underway by the eighteenth century. Secure property rights encouraged enlightened self-interest and purposeful activity which in turn became prime activators.

In England at the beginning of the eighteenth century a set of property arrangements was in place which provided a "hospitable environment" in which economic growth might take place. When property rights were finally embedded in the common law and a judiciary system was framed to protect them, the door of opportunity was opened to the many. The Industrial Revolution occurred in England largely because of the rearrangement and greater security of property rights.

Not surprisingly, in the twentieth century, the absence of sustained economic advance in many parts of the world is largely a consequence of the insecurity of individuals about the land with which they are asked to work. Adam Smith argued the necessity of an efficient system of property rights if economic growth and change were to occur. The revision of property arrangements in England that led to sustained economic growth was largely the result of fee-simple ownership of land, security in one's property, and the other institutional arrangements which allowed and encouraged people to personally benefit from their individual efforts. These new arrangements, complete with the technological innovations that followed, were brought to the American colonies and played a crucial role in the economic transformation of the United States during the nineteenth century. Thomas Jefferson and John Adams, to name but two, clearly understood that property rights were crucial to human freedom and that human freedom was the main catalyst to entrepreneurship and economic progress.

## POPULATION AND PROGRESS

One of the more striking features of the Industrial Revolution was the large increase in population. In 1700, for example, the population of England and Wales was five million, but in 1750 it had increased to more than six million. Growth accelerated, and by 1801 population had reached nine million and by 1831 it was over fourteen million. In the second half of the eighteenth century the population had increased by 40 percent, and in the first three decades of the nineteenth century it increased by more than 50 percent. The large gains in population, mostly the result of a decline in mortality rates, offer important evidence that the Industrial Revolution was producing important and positive benefits for the masses. Rising productivity on the farms, better diets, increased standards of personal cleanliness, new technology, better drainage conditions in the cities, running water, improved disposal of refuse and waste, and "the proper burial of the dead" all made important contributions. The growth in production and wealth clearly contributed to the growth in population.

But whatever the direction of causation, acreage under cultivation increased during this period, and there was also a rapid increase in investment and capital accumulation. As T. S. Ashton points out in *The Industrial Revolution:* "The central problem of the age was how to feed and clothe and employ generations of children outnumbering by far those of any earlier time." Ireland in the nineteenth century, for example, failed to solve its population problem. England, by contrast, solved the problem of more people by transforming the economy to the factory system which characterizes all industrial economies today. Ashton has captured the importance of this monumental accomplishment:

> She (England) was delivered, not by her rulers, but by those who, seeking no doubt their own narrow ends, had the wit and resource to devise new instruments of production and new methods of administering industry. There are today on the plains of India and China men and women, plague-ridden and hungry, living lives little better, to outward appearance, than those of the cattle that toil with them by day and share their places of sleep by night. Such standards, and such unmechanized horrors, are the lot of those who increase their numbers without passing through an industrial revolution.

A notoriously neglected aspect of the population growth in England during the period of the Industrial Revolution appears in the failure to recognize, as observed by the British economist P. T. Bauer, that the "...position of those who have failed to die has certainly improved, as has the situation of those whose children continue to live." Those who have been critical of the impact on the poor during the economic transformation of the British economy have failed to recognize this very important point: In the development of statistics on per capita income and real wages "...the satisfaction derived from living longer and from having children are ignored." Professor Bauer, as well as Julian Simon in a very important book *The Ultimate Resource,* has identified an issue which is crucial to the ultimate question of progress and living standards. To ignore the decline in mortality and increasing longevity in England during the Industrial Revolution represents a serious omission in the measurement of progress. We make a similar mistake in the twentieth century when we ignore the benefits associated with lower mortality and longer life in the less developed countries of the world. In *Dissent on Development*, Bauer makes his important point as follows:

> Health and life expectation, perhaps the most important components of well-being outside the field of emotions, are not included in the conventional national income compilations. Indeed, better health and longer life expectations often reduce conventionally measured per capita incomes (compared to what they would have been otherwise), with the paradoxical and indeed perverse result that what is clearly an improvement in people's conditions is represented as a deterioration. Longer life expectation of people and of their children implies a psychic benefit, an increase in well-being, in psychic income. The reality of this benefit is obvious on reflection; and it is clear also from the readiness of people to pay for doctors' services to postpone their own death and that of their children...in statistics of national income the birth of a calf represents an increase in living standards but the birth of a child represents a fall.

## THE IMPACT ON STANDARDS OF LIVING

Those who criticize the uneven economic progress during the industrialization and urbanization of England would do well to remember that in addition to the rapid increase in population growth, there occurred a steady increase in real wages and material standards of living for the great bulk of the English people. This was especially true in the century following the last of the Napoleonic Wars and the War of 1812. By the end of the nineteenth century, material standards of living in England were much higher than anyone could have imagined just a century before. Such sustained economic progress, shared by almost all segments of the population, is in marked contrast to the pessimistic view of Karl Marx in *Capital*: "It follows therefore, that in proportion as capital accumulates, the lot of the labourer, be his payment high or low, must grow worse. The law...establishes an accumulation of misery, corresponding with accumulation of capital. Accumulation of wealth at one pole is, therefore, at the same time accumulation of misery, agony of toil, slavery, ignorance, brutality (and) mental degradation at the opposite pole..." Obviously, Marx was wrong.

In a collection of essays edited by the economic historian R. M. Hartwell, *The Long Debate on Poverty*, the available evidence on English working-class living conditions during these revolutionary times is presented. Through the use of reconstructed British national income figures, Hartwell shows that the per-capita production of goods and services increased by fifty percent between 1700 and 1780, by 50 to 100 percent between 1780 and 1850, and by 80 to 100 percent between 1850 and 1914. Indicating that output per person quadrupled during the nineteenth century, the evidence shows that the average Englishman was six or seven times better off in terms of material wealth in 1950 than he had been prior to the Industrial Revolution in 1750. In fact, it is persuasively argued in *The Long Debate on Poverty* that the increased *sensitivity* to the issue of poverty and the adverse circumstances of the poor during this period, was largely the result of the comparatively higher standard of living being generated for the great majority of people because of the Industrial Revolution.

The evolution of the factory system and large scale techniques of production was accompanied by a steady increase in the degree of urbanization in England. While enclosures were reducing the agricultural population by pushing peasants toward towns and cities, the new industrial cities were also pulling people to these urban places in anticipation of bettering their lives. As Manchester, Liverpool, and London grew rapidly during this earlier transition, so today do peasants migrate to Mexico City, Sao Paulo, Bangkok, and Nairobi. Urbanization has invariably been associated with rising living standards and a reduced demand for people to work the land. For those like Charles Dickens, J. L. and Barbara Hammond, and Sidney and Beatrice Webb, who could see nothing beneficial in the teaming urban centers of the nineteenth century, we recommend those accounts of the brutish, short, and nasty lives led by the rural inhabitants of earlier periods. For example, read the work of P. Boissonnade, *Life and Work in Medieval Europe,* who, according to the economic historian Louis M. Hacker, "...so effectively stripped bare all the pretensions of those who were seeking to pretty up the medieval world."

## INTERNATIONAL TRADE AND ECONOMIC GROWTH

The pace of economic change in England also quickened during this period due to an increase in the volume of international trade. Adam Smith had recognized that the wealth of a nation is determined by the division of labor and specialization. Since the specialization of labor was limited by the extent of the market, further progress could be facilitated by broadening the market and encouraging international commerce. Standards of living for the working people of England rose during this period largely because of their widened choice of commodities. Tea, sugar, raw cotton for clothing, and timber for housing were representative of the imported commodities which considerably improved the average Englishman's life. But importantly, they gave the less developed countries the purchasing power to buy English textiles and machinery.

After about 1780, increasing numbers of English workers depended on the export industries for their livelihood. Phyllis Dean and W. A. Cole have argued that: "The existence of exploitable international markets at the end of the eighteenth and beginning of the nineteenth centuries was probably crucial in initiating the process of industrialization and the growth in real incomes which was associated with it." They estimate that during this period, about one third of British industrial output was being exported. While some argue that foreign markets were being exploited, we would emphasize that British textile exports, especially cotton goods, provided much of the world with improved and less expensive clothing. Voluntary trade and exchange are always mutually beneficial.

Efficient private property arrangements; a structure of incentives conducive to innovation; entrepreneurial activity by English merchants, industrialists, and scientists; market transactions for profit; and expanded markets for the products of English factories, literally transformed this relatively small and insignificant island nation into a society in which economic progress was taken for granted. Today the poor nations of the world wish to emulate this accomplishment. They too would like to achieve an industrial revolution.

## INVENTION, INNOVATION AND PROGRESS

Coinciding with the expansion of markets at home and abroad, and encouraged by the increased efficiency associated with the larger role of private property arrangements and the rapid increase in population, a great wave of invention and innovation in agriculture, transportation, manufacturing, trade, and finance began during the 1760's. The eminent British historian T. S. Ashton, writes: "It is difficult to find a parallel at any other time or place." The inventions and innovations began with the "gadgets" of Brindley, Roebuck, Wedgwood, Hargreaves, Arkwright, and Watt and lasted for more than a half a century. New production techniques were applied in agriculture, in mining, in the iron industry, and in the manufacture of textiles. The steam engine, made economically viable by the partnership of Matthew Boulton and James Watt, had enormous implications. The new form of power, gradually replacing the muscles of both man and beast, was the basis of the transition to the modern industrial age. The potential of the new steam power brought new technologies and production processes. The changes in the textile industry were startling. In 1813, there were still fewer than 2,400 power-looms in the whole of England; by 1820, the number had increased to about 14,000; and by 1833, about 100,000 power-looms were in operation in Britain.

While productivity increased in industry, the extent of the market was widened by improvements in internal communication and transportation. Engineering came to prominence during the eighteenth century with a very large increase in bridge construction and other engineering projects. Of special importance, the people who built the bridges, canals, roads, and railways were in the private sector and were motivated by the possibilities of increasing their incomes. They were *not* tax-supported government employees.

Great Britain became an epicenter of a veritable whirlwind of economic change during the last few decades of the eighteenth century and the early part of the nineteenth century. The people of England passed through the Industrial Revolution, and its impact was felt in most parts of the world. Those other countries which were prepared to adopt and defend the institution of human freedom and secure man's inalienable rights to property, also would share in this progress. In contrast, history is replete with examples of collectivist and statist schemes which have not produced wealth, let alone personal well-being. The Industrial Revolution was different. Individualism was recognized; purposeful activity was made personally beneficial; and increasing wealth rather than eternal poverty became the expectation of all those who participated in this new experiment. All previous human arrangements for dealing with poverty were impossibly primitive by comparison.

## THE LEGEND ABOUT THE POOR GETTING POORER

Much has been written, as we have already indicated, on the impact of the Industrial Revolution on the working class and the poor. The conventional wisdom has been that "...the struggle against the machine had brought only misery and poverty," and presumably it was not worth the cost. Illusionary history notwithstanding, living standards in England increased dramatically during the nineteenth century. Such an increase in productivity and therefore wealth was directly and immediately a function of that revolutionary economic change which took place in the period 1760-1830. In fact, according to Ashton, "it would have been strange, indeed, if the industrial revolution had simply made the rich richer and the poor poorer. For the commodities which it gave rise were not, in general, luxuries but necessaries and capital goods." Cotton textiles, pottery, utensils, furniture, sugar, grain, tea, and coffee represented the consumption goods of the masses, not the rich.

The legend that the rise of capitalism produced a broad based deterioration in the living standards of the working classes has contributed importantly to the intellectual and emotional aversion to competitive capitalism in the twentieth century. Myth to the contrary, the eminent British historian Sir John Clapham, in *An Economic History of Modern Britain,* voicing the sentiments of most modern economic historians on this matter, has summarized the more accurate and optimistic case:

> The legend that everything was getting worse for the working man, down to some unspecified date between the drafting of the People's Charter and the Great Exhibition, dies hard. The fact that, after the price fall of

1820-21, the purchasing power of wages in general--not, of course, of everyone's wages--was definitely greater than it had been just before the Revolutionary and Napoleonic Wars, fits so ill with the tradition that it is very seldom mentioned, the works of statisticians of wages and prices being constantly disregarded by social historians.

Even J. L. and Barbara Hammond, important contributors to the myth of falling standards of living, admitted toward the end of their lives that the "...general view is probably more or less correct...": real wages were rising and most Englishmen were sharing in the greater productivity.

There can be no doubt that the Industrial Revolution was, in large measure, a direct consequence of the increase in the individual's political and economic freedom. The writings of Locke, Trenchard, Gordon, Mandeville, Hume, and especially Adam Smith, were ideas that had consequences. Where these ideas were adopted, the standard of living increased to levels unheard of in previous centuries. The acceleration in economic activity and the wealth which was generated, represented, in Nobel Laureate Hayek's words, "...an almost accidental by-product of the limitations which the revolution of the seventeenth century had placed on the powers of government."

# CHAPTER 6

## THE ECONOMIC TRANSFORMATION OF THE UNITED STATES

How is it that 4 million people, located between the Atlantic coastline and the Mississippi River, starting with very little in 1789, ended up with more than enough for 76 million people by 1900?

--Unknown

The English Industrial Revolution of the late eighteenth and early nineteenth centuries created new technologies, production processes, and machines of both marvel and miracle. Many became available to the rest of the world following the War of 1812. But it was the American entrepreneur who successfully borrowed, adapted, and applied these new ideas in the United States. Complemented on the American continent by the rich endowment of land and resources and a limited but literate population, but unencumbered by vestiges of feudal restrictions, the technologies begun in Great Britain were utilized by the industrious people of this new nation.

In addition, the presence of a political and social environment which rewarded work, encouraged saving and investment, and in large part left individuals alone in the pursuit of their own interests, also contributed importantly to the transformation of the American economy. Material living standards soared in the nineteenth century. In the second half of the century alone, per capita national income tripled when measured by the relationship between money wages and wholesale or retail prices. Between 1840 and the eve of World War I, according to economic historians, the purchasing power of American wages rose by a factor of three. Today, benefiting tremendously from these earlier advances, the great majority of Americans live on a scale of affluence that compares favorably with the way even the wealthy lived during the revolutionary period. A crucial ingredient in that advance was a set of economic institutions which provided the impetus for individuals to better their own condition: private ownership of the means of production, voluntary exchange in open and free markets, and a price system which assigned resources to their highest and most valued uses.

## THE OPEN SOCIETY AND ECONOMIC PROGRESS

The benefits attributable to the "open qualities of American society" produced a willingness to consider and adapt new and better ways to get things done. In this environment, the propensity to "truck, barter, and exchange" was encouraged, and "the uniform, constant, and uninterrupted effort of every man to better his condition," in combination with the richness of the American continent's natural environment, generated the most remarkable increase in wealth and progress mankind had ever experienced. Viewed as a long term process of raising living standards, competitive capitalism in the nineteenth century was eminently successful.

In contrast to the success of private property arrangements in the nineteenth century, it is interesting that in the earlier phases of the British colonization of the eastern seaboard, attempts were made to transfer communal arrangements of land ownership to America. The Virginia Company, for example, tried to establish a structure of property rights reflecting the late feudal system of Europe. Such efforts at common ownership discouraged individual motivation, however, and gave settlers little incentive to better their own condition. The Virginia Company was eventually dissolved, and a system of private property rights in the land, a system of "freeholds," came to dominate American agriculture.

Following the successful revolutionary break with England, the new nation sought to establish the institutional arrangements necessary for economic growth. This would involve, as Adam Smith had said, securing the property rights of individuals, extending the market so that specialization might be encouraged, and insuring that gains in productivity might become part of a self-sustaining process of economic expansion. Fundamental decisions were made which increased and encouraged the role of the private sector of the economy and left relatively few functions for government.

As an example, a significant consequence of the constitutional convention in Philadelphia in 1787 involved the prohibition on tariffs between the several states. Drawing on the ideas of Adam Smith and his *Wealth of Nations,* free trade was encouraged among the United States. The relevant market was thus extended and future economic expansion was assured. The provision in the new Constitution for a patent system further strengthened private property rights, thereby encouraging inventions and entrepreneurship. The increased security of individual rights to property in combination with provision for the enforcement of private contracts laid the basis for a large and continuous increase in production and wealth. Since rights were protected and enforced, business risk was limited to that arising from the vagaries of the market, exclusive of government changing the legal environment. Thousands upon thousands were willing to take a chance at reaching the golden ring.

This constitutional period set the stage for the economic revolution which would follow in the nineteenth century. As stated in the highly acclaimed *American Economic Growth:* "In short, the whole structure of the institutions and the legal enactments of this period, was designed to encourage the growth of the private sector by reducing transaction costs, with the supplemental result of shifting the private-public mix in favor of the former." Government was largely restrained to protecting property rights and private individuals were allowed to work and produce.

The emphasis on private property and, therefore, private initiative was also stimulated by the massive shift of resources from public lands to the private sector. Land grants to railroads and the Homestead Act of 1862 are notable examples of getting resources into the hands of producers. As the economic historian Douglas North said: "...it is hard in retrospect to conceive of a land policy that would have encouraged a higher rate of economic growth."

## GOVERNMENT INVOLVEMENT IN THE AMERICAN ECONOMY

For good or evil, government did play a role in the economic transformation of the American economy. Since raising capital for large, risky "public works" was thought to be important, both federal and state governments helped in their financing. Some roads, most of the canals, and to a very limited degree railroads (excluding the land grants) were financed by government monies. Private investment built thousands of miles of roads in the period 1800 to 1830, and these private turnpikes remained the basic means of transporting people and goods into the West.

Expenditures for "public" education also came to be an important kind of government outlay as the century proceeded. The national government also provided for the national defense. Unfortunately, government's role was not limited to roads, schools, and defense. Special interest groups began lobbying Congress for money and the passage of laws beneficial to themselves. In 1828, for example, manufacturers were moderately successful in obtaining higher tariffs on foreign products (it was known as "The Tariff of Abominations"). Farmers also tried in the nineteenth century, with limited success, to increase their incomes through government price supports and other special interest legislation.

Government, after all, is the seat of considerable economic power. The federal treasury is irresistible. Individuals, associations, businesses, and states are constantly lured to obtain for their constituents the dollars earned and paid in taxes by someone else. The federal government is, in fact, a gold mine. Frederich Bastiat wrote brilliantly to the point when he said "...there is another tendency that is common among people. When (people) can, they wish to live and prosper at the expense of others. Man can live and satisfy his wants only by ceaseless labor; this process is the origin of property. But it is also true that a man may live and satisfy his wants by seizing and consuming the products of the labor of others. This process is the origin of plunder." There are two ways to make a living: The first is to work and trade, and the other is to steal. Viewed by recipients as manna from the heavens, the "hand-outs" process, or "stealing," can only be stopped with great difficulty.

It is true that government in the nineteenth century did respond to the demand for transportation, education, and the need for internal and external order. But, inappropriately and with disastrous consequences, the seedbed for income redistribution and government intervention in economic life was laid. Late in the nineteenth century, a process of relentless growth in government accelerated from what appeared to be inconsequential beginnings. Today, policies of redistributing income and wealth, and using government as an instrument to suppress competition and encourage monopoly, have reached flood proportions.

Nevertheless, during the nineteenth century, the American economy was transformed by the entrepreneurship which flowed from the private property, market system. Living standards rose significantly, and the system of competitive capitalism was undoubtedly the driving force. Concerning government's participation in and contribution to production, the book *American Economic Growth,* authored by an eminent group of American economic historians, summarizes the role of public sector investment: "Overall, government investment probably did not play a major role in nineteenth century economic growth. It was a very small share of total investment in that period. Some of it was wisely distributed and some was not. Even if the overall social rate of return on government investment was twice the market rate of return on private investment, it would still have made a relatively small contribution to the overall growth of the economy." Government's main role then, as visualized by the founding fathers, and supposedly assured by the constitution, was national defense, enforcing property rights, and, in general, providing for a peaceful domestic and international commerce.

## AMERICAN GROWTH BEFORE THE CIVIL WAR

According to one historian, the economic development of the United States which took place in the decades following the Civil War represented the "...most rapid and striking transformation of a major social order in the history of mankind." But note that this sensational growth had its roots in the pre-Civil War period. The embryonic economic change in the first half of the nineteenth century determined and literally paved the way for the change and economic growth which would take place in the second half of the century. During the decades before the War-between-the-States, significant

50

changes were taking place in agriculture, transportation, and manufacturing which were destined to quicken the pace of economic activity.

Following the improvements in internal transportation in the first decades of the nineteenth century, American agriculture experienced rapid increases in efficiency. Increased productivity was obtainable by economizing on labor which was relatively scarce in comparison to the abundance of land. Inventions and their agricultural applications were designed to be labor saving and capital intensive. John Deere, for example, developed a light polished plow in the 1830's which required significantly less man and animal power. Factory produced in large quantities by the 1850's, they became the superior plow throughout the world. Another entrepreneur, Cyrus McCormick, patented his reaper in 1834 just a few months after Obed Hussey had patented his. According to one economic historian, it was "...probably the most revolutionary innovation in agricultural machinery ever made in the United States." By the time of the Paris Exposition in 1855, in 22 minutes a horse-drawn American reaper produced the equivalent of what it took an English machine 66 minutes, and a French machine 71 minutes.

On the eve of the Civil War, many other labor saving machines, including cultivators, harrows, hay mowers, threshing machines, and corn planters were being used. In 1860 a typical farmer in Ohio required only two-thirds of the labor required in 1840 to produce the same crop. In other words, the introduction of the harvesting reaper meant that two or three men could now accomplish in a day what had previously taken 15 men. As machinery makes mankind more productive, it allows labor to leave agriculture and move to other useful activities. The net result is that we get our food, and, in the example cited, 12 workers can now be employed to produce other products. Technological change did not destroy jobs, but created new ones. It increased productivity which in turn guaranteed higher wages and incomes for workers. Labor saving innovations during the nineteenth century were, it should be remembered, accompanied by larger and larger employment figures. Dudley Dillard has summarized the implication of these revolutionary changes in American agriculture:

> Increased agricultural productivity by means of labor saving devices made possible the rapid industrialization of the United States. A smaller proportion of the population was employed in agriculture, and a larger proportion became available for industry. Put in another way, farmers using machinery produced larger surpluses above their own family needs. These farm surpluses supported men working in nonagricultural pursuits. The surpluses were large enough not only to provide food and raw materials for American industries but also to provide an export surplus to pay for the imported capital goods needed for industrial development. A principle of general applicability in economic experience is that increased agricultural productivity is a prerequisite for large scale industrialization.

It must be remembered that this great wave of invention and innovation was driven by entrepreneurs who were motivated by enlightened self-interest and the associated desire to better their own condition. Adam Smith's "invisible hand" was at work. Increases in American agricultural productivity not only produced higher standards of living in the United States, but also fed a portion of the rest of the world. It is interesting that Thomas Malthus, the great pessimist regarding man's ability to feed himself, died the year before the reaper was patented, the machine that helped make the United States the bread basket of the world.

In large part, the stimulus to agriculture was closely associated with the improvements in transporation. For example, many turnpikes, the most famous being the Cumberland Road, were built in the years following the inauguration of George Washington. This National Road, as it was also known, provided greatly improved transportation between the Ohio River Valley and the Atlantic coast. More importantly, thousands of miles of private roads opened up the West to commerce. Americans pioneered in the use of the steamboat for river transportation, and canal building also became very important. The Erie Canal, through the Appalachian barrier, was 363 miles long and connected Albany on the Hudson River with Buffalo on Lake Erie. Completed in 1825, the canal produced a significant decline in the costs of shipping between East and West. While steamboats were mainly financed and operated privately, turnpikes were financed using both private and government funds. Most canals, however, were built using government money.

As a result of the railroad construction in the decade-and-a-half before the Civil War, the American economy became an integrated whole from the Atlantic coast to the Great Lakes region and Ohio Valley. In the process, the United States was thrust into the first rank of nations. During the 1850's, the Baltimore and Ohio Railroad, the Pennsylvania Railroad, the New York Central Railroad, and the Erie Railroad completed the trans-Appalachian connection which almost immediately produced lower freight costs. Total railway mileage in the United States tripled during the decade before the Civil War. Largely because of the railroads, the western cities of Chicago, St. Louis, Cincinnati, and Cleveland all grew rapidly.

The most important implication of the rapid improvement in transportation, however, involved the expanding size of the American market, and, therefore, the division of labor and speicialization made possible among the geographic regions of the country. Even the South was tied to the West through the riverboat traffic propelled by steam. This integrated national economy, at least as far west as the Mississippi River, represented the foundation upon which the industrialization of America would take place following the Civil War.

The pace of manufacturing also accelerated in the two decades preceding the Civil War. The same structure of positive incentives which generated entrepreneurial activity in agriculture and transportation was present in the fledgling manufacturing sector. Self-interest and the potential for beneficial production and exchange in an overwhelmingly free economy produced significant technological change which would come to benefit almost all Americans. "What American manufactures lacked in artistic elegance that appealed to European artistocrats," according to economic historian Dillard, "they more than made up in utility and rough-and-ready serviceability that, in keeping with the times, appealed to mechanics, farmers, and the host of other energetic, dynamic Americans who were preoccupied with their material welfare."

As with the new machines in agriculture which were designed to economize on labor, the manufacturing sector speedily adopted new ways. Similarly propelled by monetary incentives, Americans, including the British immigrants who brought known technologies with them, enthusiastically borrowed and adapted the many new machines introduced during the English Industrial Revolution. The "American system of manufacturing" was driven by a unique, American discovery: the assembly of complex mechanical devices with interchangeable parts.

The principle of manufacturing with interchangeable parts, which was first introduced by Eli Whitney in the production of army muskets early in the nineteenth century, significantly reduced the demand for costly piece-fitting labor. Consequently, manufacturing costs fell dramatically. The technique spread to many other industries including clocks, sewing machines, agricultural implements, locomotives, ammunition, locks, typewriters, and bicycles. According to the economic historian Nathan Rosenberg, manufacturing by the production of interchangeable parts ". . . has been insufficiently appreciated. . ." in terms of the revolutionary impact it has had on productivity, and, therefore, standards of living.

The widespread application of James Watt's steam engine to industry and transportation, the substitution of machines for handicraft skills, and the development of the machine tool industry, also contributed substantially to the process of economizing on scarce and expensive labor. But at the same time, these labor saving innovations produced large increases in labor productivity and wage rates. The machine tool industry, in particular the metal shaping and metal cutting industries, became a very specialized activity. The entrepreneurial skills involved in designing, manufacturing, and marketing these machines and tools were not only rewarded but had important long term ramifications. According to Rosenberg:

Technological change in the nineteenth century, then, was generated and eventually institutionalized in a very special way. It emerged in large measure as an accumulation of solutions to a range of technical problems facing a group of specialized manufacturing firms. These firms were the producers of capital goods--machinery and equipment used as inputs in other sectors of the economy. The growing skill exhibited by these firms in solving problems of specialized machine production ought to be regarded as the basic learning process underlying nineteenth-century industrialization.

Today, as in the previous century, the machine tool and capital goods industries, which are now involved in the design of microprocesssors and robots, represent the driving force behind economic change and rising incomes. The current evolution in the development of the electronic processor of information represents an excellent example of the beneficial results of competitive capitalism at work.

Finally, the complementary relationship between the growth in the iron and steel industry, and the growth in the railroad industry, played an important role in the transition to an industrialized America during the nineteenth century. The demand for steel rails stimulated iron and coal mining, and consequently, steel production. The railroads, in turn, provided the capacity to ship heavy metals of all kinds over long distances. In summary, the rise of competitive capitalism in the United States during the nineteenth century had its important beginnings before the Civil War. And after the "Tariff of Abominations" in 1828, the quickening pace of industrial growth occurred during a period of falling tariff rates.

## THE GILDED AGE

The Civil War represented a watershed period. Some industries, mostly in the North, such as woolen textiles, shoe and boot manufacturing, sewing machines, and farm machinery were stimulated by the hostilities. Other industries were contracting. According to Dudley Dillard and other economic historians ". . . the Civil War was a major disrupting influence to American life and retarded, perhaps, as many economic activities as it stimulated." Based on available statistics on employment and the value of output by economic sector, it is apparent that the Civil War separated an agricultural America from the industrial economy that followed.

The "Gilded Age" or the "Age of Excess," as historians have characterized the period after the Civil War to the eve of World War I, produced what one author called "the most rapid and striking transformation of a major social order in the history of mankind." The United States was propelled to the rank of being the wealthiest country and having the highest standard of living in the world. While progress was uneven due to cyclical changes in the level of economic activity, the real material standard of living, as measured by the real earnings of nonfarm employees, showed an accelerating advance. Not only did real wages rise significantly, but at the same time the work day was becoming shorter. The average work day in manufacturing and mechanical establishments was 11.5 hours in 1850, 9.8 hours in 1900, and down to 8.5 hours in 1920. Dorothy Brady, in *American Economic Growth,* observed that "...the refinements that households with modest means were introducing into their homes in the 1830's and earlier, became available to the poor. By the 1870's such articles as beds, bedding, chairs, tables, dishes, knives, and forks were considered indispensable even to the poor." And these material gains, it must be remembered, occurred before labor unions were at all significant as a portion of the American labor force.

Historically, we must remind ourselves, economic progress has been very slow throughout the world. Generations and even centuries would pass without noticeable differences in the standard of living. This so-called "Age of Excess" in the United States, and the earlier Industrial Revolution in Great Britain, represented an unprecedented break with the past. Per capita income was doubling every 30 years, and Americans came to expect a constantly improving economic life. The die was cast, there was no turning back. The agricultural revolution in America was giving way to an industrial revolution. By the late 1870's, employment in non-agricultural occupations exceeded employment in agriculture. Between 1860 and 1910, the percentage of the labor force engaged in agriculture fell from about 60 percent to approximately 30 percent. Today it is less than 3 percent. The value of output in the manufacturing sector surpassed that of agriculture during the decade of the 1880's.

The massive and rapid transition to a fully industrialized economy was assisted by the building of the transcontinental railroads. While railroad building involved a curious "mixture of government paternalism," it was essentially a laissez faire philosophy that marked public policy. Government was careful not to offend the strident individualism of the post-Civil War period. In order to stimulate and accelerate the pace in the construction of a transcontinental rail connection with the West, more than 130 million acres of land adjacent to railway right-of-ways were granted to railroad companies between 1850 and 1871. For example, the Union Pacific received 20 million acres, while the Northern Pacific acquired 42 million. Nevertheless, and in spite of these landgrant subsidies, the actual construction of the railroads was with private money and was carried out through the entrepreneurial skills of the Vanderbilts, Goulds, Hills, and Morgans. Capital was more generously available in part because of the decline in the federal debt during this period. On the eve of the Civil War there were roughly 30,000 miles of track, by 1890 there were 170,000 miles, and by 1916 there were 250,000 miles. The railroad construction boom created a truly integrated national market for the products of American farms, mines, and factories. Indicative of this growth in markets was the growth in ton-miles of freight hauled. In 1859 railroads carried 2.6 billion ton-miles, by 1890 the figure had exploded to 80 billion ton-miles.

Since more geography meant expanded markets, economies of

scale could be attained by specialization in production and distribution. Mass production techniques were encouraged by the new national market, and assembly line principles of production were employed by a number of industries. Automobile companies adopted the "process experiments" conducted by the slaughterhouses and grain mills. The "disassembly" of pigs in slaughterhouses during the first decade of the 20th century provided the guidelines followed by Henry Ford's assembly lines in the second decade. The "rationalization of the work process" permitted larger volumes of production and lower costs than would have otherwise been possible. In 1916, the Ford Motor Company sold more than one-half million Model T's at a retail price of less than $400 and shipped them all across the country on the radically improved and integrated national transportation network. Ford's experiment, which relied on an industrial system that used "the principles of power, accuracy, economy, system, continuity, speed, and repetition," made available to the growing middle class the autombile: America's great "freedom machine." Henry Ford literally placed a steering wheel in the hands of every working person in America. This is a feat which most industrialized countries of the world have still not totally accomplished.

In the process of rationalizing techniques of production, the great entrepreneurs of the Gilded Age brought to the American people ever greater quantities of consumer goods at continuously lower prices. Since an essential input to most, if not all, of the new industries was steel, it was Andrew Carnegie who, through his entrepreneurial leadership and production techniques, filled the void and brought remarkable results. Writes William Greenleaf:

> Carnegie's unrelenting insistence of cost-cutting through progressive technology reduced the price of a ton of steel from $65 a ton in 1872 to $20 a ton in 1897. Between 1889 and 1900, Carnegie boosted his annual steel output from 322,000 tons to 3 million tons. During that time his profits increased eight times over, reaching $40 million in 1900.

Rising productivity also meant higher real wages for steel workers. In the process of searching for entrepreneurial profits, Carnegie's efforts generated large increases in the output of steel at drastically lower prices, but higher wages for those in the industry. Unfortunately, the clearly beneficial results of Carnegie's cost cutting efforts are still viewed by many as selfish profiteering. This is a most unfortunate twisting of the facts.

John D. Rockefeller was another "Robber Baron" who, with the assistance of entrepreneurial partners Samuel Andrews, Henry Flagler, and his brother William Rockefeller, led the race in petroleum refining and distribution. This competitive race, in which Rockefeller set the pace for a while, revolutionized the average American's life and standard of living. The Rockefeller organization began refining petroleum products in 1865. By 1870, Rockefeller's share of total refined output was 4 percent, and at that time there were approximately 250 independent refiners. By 1880 the Rockefeller share was more than 80 percent, and the number of independent refiners had fallen to less than 100. The decrease in numbers was encouraged by the generally deflationary movement in prices during the 1870's, and by the economies of large scale production associated with the introduction of destructive distillation (petroleum "cracking"). The myth of predatory pricing, as the source of Rockefeller gains, has been soundly refuted by John S. McGee. In actual fact, rival refineries were frequently purchased by the Standard Oil Company at "outrageously" high prices. One George Rice in 1882, literally tried to "bribe and blackmail" Standard Oil into paying a price for his refinery which was inflated by a factor of ten.

For economic growth and American living standards, however, we are interested in the implications of the competitive forces for costs of production and consumer prices. During the period in which the Rockefeller interests were supposed to have monopolized the petroleum industry, Dominick Armentano has captured the flavor of what was in fact going on:

> Between 1870 and 1885 the price of refined kerosene dropped from 26 cents to 8 cents per gallon. In the same period, the Standard Oil Company reduced the average costs per gallon from almost 3 cents in 1870 to 0.452 cents in 1885. Clearly, the firm was relatively efficient, and a good share of that efficiency was transmitted profitably to the consumer in the form of lower prices for a much improved product.

As costs and prices continued to fall into the twentieth century, Standard Oil experienced a progressively less important and less secure position. Fuel oil, lubricating oils, and gasoline began to replace the kerosene age; new crude supplies were discovered in Southwest and California; and additional integrated petroleum companies entered the competitive oil business. Standard's share of crude supply fell from 34 percent of total market supplies in 1898 to just 11 percent in 1906. On the eve of the government anti-trust suit against the Standard Oil Company in 1911, its share of the petroleum products market was 64 percent, down from a high of 88 percent in 1890. The per gallon barrel price of refined oil, which had been 9.33 cents in 1880, declined to 5.91 cents in 1897, and continued to decline into the twentieth century.

Yet in the face of these facts, on May 15, 1911, the United States Supreme Court ruled that the Standard Oil Company had "unreasonably" conspired to restrain trade, and, therefore, was in violation of the Sherman Antitrust Act of 1890. The socially beneficial effects of lower prices, and very large increases in the production and consumption of petroleum, was apparently not considered at all. The accepted meaning of monopoly--the restriction of output and higher prices--was to be turned on its head. Standard Oil was to be dissolved for increasing output and lowering prices. This case is just one example of where government chooses to interfere with economic activities regardless of the actual situation. In our own time, government agencies find fault with IBM for increasing production and lowering the price of processing information through innovation. If the price is too high, then government charges monopoly. If the price is too low, government charges unfair competition. What about the same price? Then, of course, the government charges price fixing. The government rule seems to be: no matter the price, it is suspect.

## COMPETITION AND GOVERNMENT IN THE GILDED AGE

In fact, the conventional wisdom that the American economy in general, was controlled by giant monopoly trusts around the turn of the century, is itself incorrect. As the railroad tycoon James J. Hill said in 1901: "...the trust...came into being as the result of an effort to obviate ruinous competition." According to the economic historian Gabriel Kolko, monopoly during this period "...was the exceptional and not routine characteristic of most industries, and the use of the term 'monopoly' or 'trust' by defenders of the status quo, was based more on wish-fulfillment than on economic reality." Kolko quotes from an issue of *The Iron Age* in 1900 which sadly summarized the difficulty encountered in short-circuiting the competitive process:

> Experience has shown that very few of the promises of the promoters of consolidation have materialized. That some of them are satisfactorily profitable is undoubtedly true...Others are less so, some are conspicuously unprofitable, some have dissolved, and more will have to dissolve within the next two or three years.

The pressures of the inherently competitive open market system required that those wishing to protect themselves from new and potential competition had to turn to government for aid and protection. But imagine the kind of world we would have if business was generally successful in hiding behind government. Instead of solving problems through individual initiative, people would be encouraged to lobby, demonstrate, coerce, threaten, and use government power to their own ends. In most cases, government action is synonymous with monopoly and the naked use of power. Seldom can a company maintain a monopoly position for long without the mantel of government protection. Profits attract entry. The life of the incumbent is quite uneasy, and they must constantly be looking over their shoulder for potential competitors. However, through licensing, controls, import restrictions, tax credits, depletion allowances, and other devices, government can successfully impede rivalry, and, hence, reduce or eliminate competition. In reality, government is controlled by powerful special-interest groups, and it is these minority interests that, without exception, work at cross-purposes to the private interests of the average citizen. It is this movement to state enforced monopoly which Gabriel Kolko has termed "The Triumph of Conservatism."

In general, then, most historians have this thing backwards. Seldom have antitrust laws ever been used against a firm that was restricting production and raising prices, but almost always the firms that get prosecuted are the ones that expand production and lower prices. The result is that they get a larger market share. The question is: Should that be construed as bad? Suits are brought against these firms because they attract and hold customers day-after-day, and conduct transaction-after-transaction in markets where new entrants are always a realistic possibility. In the final analysis, these firms are merely being responsive to the consumer because they recognize that the consumer is king. As an example, and contrary to popular assumptions, the Interstate Commerce Commission was not created to regulate a natural monopoly. It was lobbied in the Congress by influential eastern railroad interests as a means of enforcing their price fixing agreements and other cartel-type behavior; enforcement which had proven to be impossible in the free and open market place. Kolko summarizes this more realistic perspective:

> Despite the large number of mergers, and the growth in the absolute size of many corporations, the dominant tendency in the American economy at the beginning of this century was toward growing competition...As new competitors sprang up, and as economic power was diffused throughout an expanding nation, it became apparent to many important businessmen that only the national government could rationalize the economy...ironically, contrary to the consensus of historians, it was not the existence of monopoly that caused the federal government to intervene in the economy, but the lack of it.

## THE GREAT TRANSFORMATION

On the eve of World War I, after a century of remarkable progress in the United States, economic growth and its benefits for raising the standard of living were evident for all to see. It was a time during which capitalism (cynics call it "Social Darwinism"), was given a chance, the role of government in economic affairs, while substantial in some instances, was quite limited in scope. Living standards, longevity, and economic opportunity grew to levels unimaginable merely a hundred years earlier. Though progress was uneven, and some people grew fabulously rich, it was in large part the poor who experienced the greatest improvements. By the end of the nineteenth century, America's poor enjoyed material living standards significantly higher than most of the world's population.

Something indeed must have been right in America. If not in the view of many historians and their social theories, then in the actions of the "teaming millions" who immigrated to the United States by voting for competitive capitalism with their feet. The truth was out that America offered economic opportunity and political freedom. Between 1860 and 1890, more than ten million immigrants came to America to seek their fortunes. During the period between 1895 and 1915, on the average, more than one million immigrants a year came to the United States. Thomas Sowell, a contemporary economist, documents in his *Race and Economics,* the important degree to which these immigrants, mostly carrying just the clothes on their backs, were largely assimilated, within a generation or two, into the mainstream of American economic life.

The great increase in wealth and economic progress in the nineteenth century, which was shared by most if not all Americans, can largely be attributed to the revolutionary ideas of John Locke, Thomas Jefferson, and Adam Smith. They redefined the relationship of the sovereign individual to his government, and clearly demonstrated the socially beneficial results of a system of natural liberty. Political and economic freedom, after all, go hand-in-hand, and they produced living standards which even Karl Marx recognized would occur.

But "capitalism" in many quarters is, nevertheless, perceived to be morally unacceptable. While agreeing to its material advantages, academicians, pastors, parlor groups, people in the media, and other word merchants, believe capitalism is unworthy of complement or retention. Even in the face of Stalin and Mao, the gulag and bureaucracy, and repeated socialistic failures worldwide, the dream lives on that there exists a better system than capitalism. Perhaps there is. But history, and especially the United States and its economic system during the nineteenth century, shows clear and overwhelming evidence that private ownership and limited government produce a system of natural liberty that allows man more freedom, economic opportunity, and a better chance to improve himself than any other system known to man. Though falling far short of utopian dreams, it would seem far ahead of whatever is in second place.

# CHAPTER 7

## THE MORAL CASE FOR COMPETITIVE CAPITALISM

What is under attack is the capitalist system; and it is attacked mainly on ethical grounds, as being materialistic, selfish, unjust, immoral, savagely competitive, callous, cruel, and destructive. It is futile today to defend it merely on technical grounds (as being more productive, for example) unless we can show also that the socialist attacks on ethical grounds are false and baseless.

--Henry Hazlitt

In previous chapters a powerful and factual case has been made for the remarkable and unprecedented economic progress which inevitably follows the adoption of competitive capitalism and its central institutions of private property and voluntary social arrangements. Even Karl Marx, in the *Communist Manifesto*, pronounced capitalism a great "engine of growth." Undeniably, however, the market system of capitalism continues to be viewed as materialistic, ethically unjust, and consequently immoral by great numbers of people all over the world. This view is especially strong among the majority of so-called intellectuals. For these critics of private, market arrangements, it follows that some sort of socialism is the only solution.

### THE MORAL CASE FOR SOCIALISM

Economic efficiency has surely not been the great appeal of socialism, especially in its Marxist variety. Frankly, we do not believe that Karl Marx in *Das Capital*, nor the analysis of his many follwers, have had much to do with the coherency or reasonableness of "Marxian economics" or with the real world workability of socialism. While most economists will admit that Marx had a few insights about the classical theories of exchange and value, very few would agree that his arguments involved good economics. Although his many economic errors overwhelmed his insights, the revolutionary nature of his ideas have nevertheless had a great influence on social and economic thinking.

By and large, the people of this planet are not concerned with acquiring economic understanding of exchange and value, of "diminishing marginal utility," "Gresham's law," supply, demand, and comparative advantage in international trade. The esoteric, theoretical, and mathematical explanations that economists have often used to explain the way the world works are of little interest to the average man. But almost everyone has a sense of right and wrong. Socialism, in all of its varieties, is a moral vision rather than an economic one.

The concepts of justice, fairness, and equity, quite frankly, evoke a gut feeling in most of us. Even though economists have repeatedly shown that tariffs and trade barriers are disastrous, that minimum wage laws hurt the very people they are intended to help, and that government prescriptions have unintended and negative consequences, often doing more harm than good, government continues to be seen as the institution which can best foster brotherhood and friendship, while gradually eliminating alienation and isolation. Not surprisingly, the politicians and academicians of the far left have effectively used the symbolism that is easily understood by the electorate. By playing the politics of envy and attacking the ethical basis of capitalism, they conjure up the evils of profits, wealth, tycoons,and round-stomached capitalists. Playing on the theme that business doesn't care for the little guy, and that capitalism runs roughshod over the poor, their portrayal of exploitation sets well with ordinary people who are merely seeking a better life.

Nevermind the historical fact that systems other than capitalism trample freedoms, spawn totalitarian political regimes, reduce opportunity, and make a mockery of economic efficiency. Despite the evidence that central planning and economic equality lead to government intervention in private actions, and often ruthless dictatorship, the committed socialist of the left or right nevertheless believes that a small dose of socialism will one day glorify the human situation.

Interestingly, an increasing number of America's intellectual elite, known for their belief in "the mixed economy," "the middle way" or "economic democracy," are emerging from the socialist closet. They either admit to being socialists or, at the very least, are expressing preferences for an institutional mix other than free markets. Motives aside, their contention is that capitalism is inherently unfair. Without a moral basis, say the critics, the private property, free-market system could never be humanistic and compassionate.

In the past, defenders of competitive capitalism have been just as guilty as anyone for perpetuating this wrong-headed view. They have literally spent thousands of hours extolling the virtues of the efficiency of capitalism, free markets, and of the socially useful information generated by prices, wages, interest rates, profits, and losses. Pontificating on the efficiency aspects of capitalism, its supporters have failed to devote enough time and attention to the morality of the system. If the case for the morality of capitalism is not made, either through comparisons to its real world alternatives or on the basis of principle, then the probability of the great American experiment surviving is slim indeed.

## ALTRUISM VERSUS ENLIGHTENED SELF-INTEREST

Although history does provide ample evidence, year after year, in favor of the market and against socialism, making the case *for* enlightened self-interest and *against* the benevolent sounding idea of altruism requires a more sophisticated argument. The challenge is enormous. It is difficult to quarrel with public lands, public forests, public education, public television, and of course, the "public good." Compare by contrast the faint praise heard for private enterprise, private schools, private forests, commercial cable television, and the private interest in general. Sharing, cooperation, equality, and public ownership, irrespective of their actual results for human wellbeing, are, on the surface, more easily argued than competition, profits and self-interest.

Under socialism, sincerity and good intentions replace actual outcomes as the measuring rod of success. But, unfortunately for collectivized citizens, outcomes do matter. It is in the area of actual performance where socialism's failure is so readily apparent. Food, clothes, opportunity, and freedom are, in large part, the very stuff of life. If a good dose of self-interest increases productivity, raises material standards of living, and thereby widens individual human choice, then let's have more of it. Enlightened self-interest, personal choice, and individual responsibility are inseparably tied to the good of mankind. The morality of capitalism is a case well worth making.

## THE STATE AND MORALITY

People throughout the world, especially the purveyors of knowledge, continue to view the market order and its allegiance to private property with disdain. Alexander Solzhensitsyn, in a *National Review* article in 1978, acknowledged that "...it is almost universally recognized that the West shows all the world a way to successful economic development." However, and unfortunately, he goes on "...many people living in the West are dissatisfied with their own society. They despise it or accuse it of not being up to the level of maturity attained by mankind." Such being the case, we continue to witness attempts by supposedly beneficent dictators to remake mankind in terms of some utopian, although vague and unspecified, image. Unfortunately, societies designed by government planners, either to promote morality or economic efficiency, are rarely successful. The Ayatollah's Iran is an excellent example of a spiritual intolerance totally incompatible with a moral order.

Indeed, totalitarian regimes often appeal to morality as a convenient device to subjugate their peoples. Henry Hazlitt cites an incident at the Communist First International, recorded in Marx's correspondence with Engels, in which Marx admits that "I was obliged to insert in the preamble two phrases about 'duty and right,' ditto 'truth, morality, and justice.' But these lamentable phrases are placed in such a way that they can do no harm." Marx, the revolutionist, smartly included rhetoric and high sounding phrases of morality and the brotherhood of man. But the consequences of his system have been uniformly the opposite. Seldom has socialism's results accorded with expectations. In fact, as Max Eastman records: "The notion of an earthly paradise in which men shall dwell together in millennial brotherhood is used to justify crimes and depravities surpassing anything the modern world has seen."

## MORALITY AND THE RISE OF CAPITALISM

The morality and justice of the system of competitive capitalism, therefore, cannot be fully appreciated until its alternatives are observed and evalutated. As Arthur Shenfield reminds us: "It is a plain historical fact that the treatment of man by man became conspicuously more humane side by side with the rise of capitalism." Attitudes and policies toward the punishment of crime, treatment of women, care for the insane and feeble minded, slavery and serfdom, and the treatment of workers changed significantly for the better during the rise of industrial capitalism. Henry Thoreau was once asked if he thought the railroad a great improvement over the stagecoach, and he answered: "Only if it carries better people." Capitalism seems to allow that. There was an explosion of charitable endeavor in those countries where capitalism was leading the way. Charity for the poor, educational endowments, medical research, and other kinds of private giving experienced significant growth during the most explosive period of the market economy. The economic system of private property, voluntary exchange, and free markets brought with it an improvement on what had gone before, and very definitely an improvement over the right-wing and left-wing socialist dictatorships of the twentieth century.

## THE MORAL CASE FOR CAPITALISM

The most important part of the case for economic freedom is not its vaunted economic efficiency nor its dramatic success in promoting economic wealth and well-being, but rather that capitalism is consistent with certain fundamental moral principles of life itself. Principles that respect the dignity and individuality of each person, that don't try to manipulate people as objects but recognize a person's rights and values, and that seek to use persuasion and voluntary exchange rather than coercion and force. Competitive capitalism thrives on the non-aggression principle of human freedom. The requirement that transactions in the private property market order must be voluntary guarantees that the moral and physical autonomy of persons is protected from violent attack by others. Force is inadmissable in human relationships under a regime of capitalism. Personal freedom, and therefore economic and political freedom, is not "ethically indifferent," but a necessary condition of morality. Violence or the use of force against other individuals, which necessarily denies the most fundamental character of human freedom, the safety of person and his property, is inconsistent with a moral order. The moral life requires that individuals act and make choices free of external intimidation and coercion. Friedrich Hayek reminds us of certain fundamental conditions of the moral life: "It is only where the individual has choice, and its inherent responsibility, that he has occasion to affirm existing values, to contribute to their further growth, and to earn moral merit."

Consider, for example, what Aristotle would call man's habits or choices in the context of a moral theory. He argued that man's virtues, moral or intellectual, were habits, as were his vices, Virtues are good. Vices are bad. They are both so constituted as to have a moral quality connoted by these words. Since virtue is praiseworthy and vice is not, it is only when a person is responsible for his own actions that the choices made can be viewed as freely chosen. Furthermore, such choices employ man's mental faculties in a fashion which belong peculiarly to an individual as a human being. Therefore, man's actions are uniquely moral. Examples would include purposeful actions of all kinds, especially self actualization. Man, unlike any other creature on the face of the earth, has a faculty for thinking and knowing that continually develops and expands with decision making. Moral choice presumes the necessary freedom to exercise our responsibilitie.

The free market system, in which only voluntary and mutually beneficial exchange is permitted, is consistent with freedom-of-choice, and, therefore, offers the greatest potentiality for a moral order in which the integrity of the individual conscience is respected. Hayek, in a warning to us about the undesirable consequences of a planned, socialist order, wrote in his book *The Road to Serfdom* that only:

> ...where we ourselves are responsible for our own interest...has our decision moral value. Freedom to order our own conduct in the sphere where material circumstances force a choice upon us, and responsiblity for the arrangement of our own life according to our own conscience, is the air in which alone moral sense grows and in which moral values are daily recreated in the free decision of the individual. Responsibility to bear the consequences of one's own decisions are the very essence of any morals which deserve the name.

It is frequently asserted that the materialistic character of capitalism is at the very least amoral. However, it is surely an error to blame a social system for being too concerned with material things simply because the individuals in that system remain free to decide for themselves those goals which are to be pursued.

The practice of blaming capitalism for being materialistic is to miss the point. Most would agree that capitalism does have a record of organizing resources efficiently. It is also important to note that very few people go hungry under this system. In comparison, socialism fails on both counts. Yet, material abundance is admittedly but one of the positive attributes of living. In most societies of which we are familiar, it is only a minority who are not concerned with economic growth and material gain. As much or even more than market economies, socialist nations of both the left and right, place most of their emphasis on economic growth, industrial production, and personal sacrifice in the pursuit of material ends.

Unfortunately, the people in planned societies who are not materially oriented, those, for example, who might want to pursue the life of a recluse, take a vow of poverty, or seek some spiritual end, are persecuted. Freedom, it seems, is more important to the minority of those who do not have material objectives than it is to those who do. Only in a decentralized, pluralistic, private property order can inalienable rights of these persons who are different be secure. But whatever the goals of individuals, whether virtuous, materialistic, or whatever, the market still seems to be the most humane way mankind has found for dealing with the economic problems of scarcity and the efficient allocation of resources.

One of the great advantages of a social system characterized by social cooperation through mutually beneficial exchange is the opportunity and scope for sympathy, beneficience, and human friendships. Indeed, the libertarian scholar Murray Rothbard, reminds us that "...it is far more likely that feelings of friendship and communion are the effects of a regime of contractual social cooperation rather than the cause." Each individual has a uniqueness. In that sense, it is difficult for anyone else to say what will or will not lead to another's fulfillment. Naturally, when we disagree with a person's actions, there exists the tendency to save that person from himself. Fortunately, capitalism tends to favor those who respect the sanctity of the other person's autonomy because of the respect for and enforcement of private property rights. The deterioration in many socially useful conventions, and the decay of morality which many people have felt in recent years, are partially the result of our shift in thinking from personal to social responsibility. As persons are told their behavior and circumstances are not their fault, behavior is modified, society is indicted, and government is viewed as the only institution capable of solving the problem.

The work ethic, encouraged by the institution of private property, represents an important source of moral responsibility as well as a continuous reminder that our actions always entail costs. The essential ingredients of a free market order define a set of social institutions which encourage mutual respect for each and every individual. In contrast with all other economic systems, competitive capitalism operates on a set of rules which encourages mutual respect for persons with whom we interact.

The processes by which we satisfy material wants through social cooperation do not exhaust the goals which individuals might hope to achieve. The serach for personal happiness and inter peace, for example, must be found within the individual alone. Nevertheless, mankind's social relationships are generally far more peaceful under a system of private property and free trade. The period between the Napoleonic Wars and World War I, the heyday of competitive capitalism, represented a century relatively free of the brutality of war. Furthermore, Shenfield, Hayek, and others remind us that competitive capitalism was the first social system in human history to direct man's desire to become rich by peacefully supplying greater quantities of goods and services for his fellow human beings. The market process has been especially productive in providing greater abundance for the working class and the poor. Unfortunately, the alternative to serving other men's wants through voluntary exchange is to try to control their lives through the use of force. Wherever socialism has prevailed, it has invariably meant lower living standards for most people, and the subjugation of the many by the privileged few. A socialist country of the left or right, with few if any exceptions, means a totalitarian political regime in which other civil and human freedoms disappear and a form of slavery ensues.

## CAPITALISM AND RELIGION

The case for morality and justice of the system of capitalism rests on the intimate and complementary connection between private property and voluntary arrangements, and the sovereignty of the individual over his own life. We tend to take the concept of individuality for granted, but in reality, this concern and interest for the individual came into its own only with the rise of capitalism. In fact, the market system, far from dehumanizing man, finally allowed him to assume his full individuality. The individual conscience and its potential for discerning right and wrong, which was recognized during the early Christian period, came to full fruition under the system of competitive capitalism.

The "dawn of conscience," that point in history in which individuals were first argued to be morally free, and, therefore, responsible for their actions first appeared in Egypt, and was later borrowed and developed by the Jews. Later Jesus and the Apostle Paul outlined a view which recognized the unique personality of each human being. Essentially, this account represented an individualistic view of mankind which maintained that the individual's soul is the most important thing about him. Christianity provided an environment in which individuals, in order to gain salvation, made choices from a position of free will.

Not only did the church discover that individual souls were worth saving, but Christianity also implanted the concept of the "rule of law." This attention to the notion of legality also proved to be important in the development of the idea of freehold property and the land deed in the Western world. Admittedly, these contributions were largely to protect the church and its institutions and property from the power of the secular State. But over time, the principles of the "rule of law", and the private ownership of property were progressively expanded to the relationships between individuals. There is a distinct and important connection between the Judeo-Christian morality and a free-market economy. This relationship rests on the established view of the central importance of the individual in the analysis of social relationships.

The system of free and open markets is most conducive to the perfection, or at least improvement, of man's free will, which tends to generate and make moral behavior possible. One can learn correct behavior only if one is allowed to make mistakes, and hopefully, to learn from them. After all, one possible consequence of making a mistake is wisdom. Unfortunately, the larger the influence of government in peoples lives, the less opportunity there exists for an unhindered and free exercise of a person's moral faculties. Society itself cannot be moral or immoral; only individuals are moral agents. Following the argument developed by Arthur Shenfield, it would appear that in an economic system, "...if its essential characterisitics on balance positively nurture or reinforce moral or immoral individual behavior, (then)...it is a moral or immoral system in its effects." Competitive capitalism, under the rule of law, positively nurtures moral behavior, and therefore, can be moral in its effects. Where justly acquired property rights are defended, and where contracts are enforced, and where the rule of law applies, then "the voluntary nature of capitalist transactions propels us into respect for others."

## MORALITY AND PERSONAL TASTE

It is, of course, impossible to argue that a system of competitive capitalism will always produce values and behavior of which we would individually approve. However, it is important that we tolerate the "undefendable," undesirable or annoying behavior of others as long as it is peaceful. An individual should not violate what the nineteenth century sociologist Herbert Spencer called his "law of equal freedom," which states that "...every man has freedom to do all that he wills, provided he infringes not the equal freedom of any other man." Consequently, peaceful, non-violent human action is not a crime. Those who really believe in freedom must oppose coercive acts which would deny the possibility of a moral life by preventing that freedom of choice which morality requires. Given the uniqueness of individuals and the varied goals they pursue, we must allow actions which, while permissable in a free society, are offensive to personal tastes.

Lysander Spooner, a great and passionate defender of individual liberty during the nineteenth century, recognized an important distinction: the criminal and/or violent invasion of one's person or property is different in kind from behavior, "...whilst perhaps immoral in some broader sense, must be allowed to flourish, and even be given the full protection of the law." Morality is impossible unless one has the freedom to choose between alternative courses of action without external coercion. It was the great humanitarian, Albert Schweitzer, who said that civilization can only revive when there shall come into being in a number of individuals who would develop a new tone of mind, independent of and in opposition to, the prevalent one among the crowd; a point of view which gradually wins influence over the collective mind and in that manner determines its character. Only a movement grounded in a revised ethical perspective can rescue us from this relentless slide into collectivism. Necessarily, the revised moral point of view will come into existence *only by individual choice*. Once again, we encounter the proposition that it is the free market economic system of private property and voluntary exchange which maximizes the *potential* for leading a moral life.

The effects and results of the competitive process under capitalism are generally consistent with a moral order, but even when they are not it is still terribly important to oppose coercive restrictions of human behavior unless they violate the law of equal freedom. Diverse lifestyles and unique opinions represent one of the main arguments for human liberty. It is under a system of private property and free markets where this sometimes annoying or even obnoxious activity is protected by the laws of a free society.

## MORALITY AND AVAILABLE ALTERNATIVES

In summary, the system of institutional arrangements called "capitalism," a disparaging reference for many people, is unquestionably more consistent with morality and justice in our social arrangements than any alternative set of social institutions presently conceivable to us. The obviously immoral character of the socialist dictatorships in Poland, Cuba, East Germany, the Peoples Republic of China, the Soviet Union, the Ayatollah's Iran, and the right-wing facist dictatorships in countries like Argentina and Chile, where the most elementary human freedoms are suppressed, and where millions of human beings have been murdered in the name of a new social order, documents the case for the free, open, and decentralized market system.

Poverty and brutality are repulsive. From any point of view, starving children must be viewed as detestable. We ask then, under what economic systems are the greatest number of people leading lives with sufficient food, self-chosen occupations, and the greatest degree of inward and outward independence? In which countries do individuals have the opportunity to be free, really *free*? Have the socialist countries delivered this choice, mobility, and independence? Or, in fact, is it best nurtured in an open market, private property, and limited government social order? These questions have already been answered. The Soviet Union talks about "freedom" and "democracy," but they don't seem to have much of an immigration problem. Communist East Germany, on the other hand, must build massive steel and concrete walls and guard them continuously to prevent an exodus of their people. Even in the so-called "social democracies," the construction of peaceful and egalitarian systems is failing. In recent years, the declining French economy, under a more intense Mitterand brand of socialism has been on international display. The myth of the Swedish utopia has been fully revealed for what it really is in *The New Totalitarians* by Roland Huntford.

The great French economist and social critic, Frederic Bastiat, writing in the nineteenth century, captured what would be the desirable characteristics of a truly just and moral order. He asked an important question:

> ...which countries contain the most peaceful, the most moral, and the happiest people? Those people are found in the countries where the law least interferes with private affairs; where the government is least felt; where the individual has the greatest scope, and free opinion the greatest influence; where the administrative powers are fewest and simplest; where taxes are lightest and most nearly equal;...where individuals and groups most actively assume their responsibilities, and, consequently, where morals of...human beings are constantly improving; where trade, assemblies, and associations are the least restricted;...where mankind most nearly follows its own natural inclinations;...in short, the happiest, most moral, and most peaceful people are those who most nearly follow this principle: although mankind is not perfect, still, all hope rests upon the free and voluntary actions of persons whithin the limits of right; law or force is to be used for nothing except the administration of universal justice.

Understanding that the case we have made for the moral basis of capitalism requires further refinement, we defer to the wisdom of St. Augustine. He argued that material well-being does not necessarily bring better choices, a finer morality, or even more happiness. Referring to earth and the human predicament, he writes: "The things which the earthly city desires cannot justly be said to be evil, for it is itself, in its own kind, better than all other human goods. For it desires earthly peace for the sake of enjoying earthly goods. It is all right for men to seek these things, for they are good things, and without doubt, the gifts of God. But there is something better and that is the heavenly city which is secured by eternal victory and peace never ending." That kind of morality is between each person and his God. Salvation is quite another matter.

Despite the arguments of Bastiat, Hayek, Shenfield, and others, a very interesting and important question remains to be asked. Why has a system of social organization which has produced historically unprecedented increases in living standards in those countries where the principles were practiced, and which simultaneously did so much to reduce man's inhumanity to man during its ascendancy, come to have such a low standing in the minds of so many millions of people? Hayek is surely right when he insists that we must once again make the study of freedom an exciting intellectual issue. Not just for economic, philosophical, or historical reasons, but for the billions of people who, whether they know it or not, must faintly perceive that ideas do have consequences, and that their lives are bound to be affected dramatically by the scribblings of philosophers. "Liberty," said Alexis de Tocqueville, "cannot be established without morality, nor morality without faith." If America is to survive, its indisputably modern elements must be conjoined with what Russell Kirk calls the "permanent things," and George Nash calls "...the spiritual things and the institutions that sustain them."

# PART II

## THE DECLINE AND FALL OF PERSONAL AND ECONOMIC FREEDOM

# CHAPTER 8

## POLITICAL, LEGAL AND JUDICIAL REVERSALS

> The American Revolution . . . marked the turning point in American development; the checking of the long movement of decentralization and the beginning of a counter movement of centralization--the most revolutionary change in three hundred years of American experience. The history of the rise of the coercive state in America, with the ultimate arrest of all centrifugal tendencies, was implicit in that momentous counter movement.
>
> --Vernon L. Parrington

It is a frequently but erroneously repeated view that the decline and fall of the experiment of freedom in America, and economic freedom in particular, began with Roosevelt's "New Deal" response to the Great Depression. Admittedly, the steepness of the slide into a parternalistic state was accelerated by Roosevelt's legislative program enacted by Congress in the 1930's. Nevertheless, we must look for the beginning of the decline in personal liberty, and the enlarged role of the state, in the very first years of the Republic. Although our previous argument demonstrated the benefits an essentially free people derived from the institutions of capitalism throughout the nineteenth and into the twentieth century, the nationalism and centralization of federal power, following almost immediately upon ratification of the Constitution, was a first, but very important step, in a process which now, two hundred years later, threatens to terminate the great American experiment. The Declaration of Independence summarized and brought to fruition on the North American continent a movement which had begun with the Magna Carta. Firmly rooted in the ideas of Locke from the seventeeenth century, the Declaration of Independence captured the attention and confidence of almost all educated Americans. By the time of the ratification of the Constitution, however, tendencies to centralization in government resumed.

While freedom remains the hallmark of America, the limits to individual freedom in the last decades of the twentieth century are a result of events which took place in the very first American administrations. Acts of Congress and judicial interpretations of the Constitution during the nineteenth century progressively diminished and constrained human liberty, especially those rights we characterized as economic freedoms. The "classical liberalism" of John Locke, Adam Smith, Thomas Jefferson, and Thomas Paine came to be progressively more restricted in its application in the two centuries following the Declaration. In our own time the pace of restraint and restiction has of course accelerated. Freedom's vitality has continually been diffused with the passing of each new law. In the following pages the important factors which have slowly, but methodically, reduced the scope and degree of personal freedom in America, far below that which is attainable, are identified and described.

## ALEXANDER HAMILTON'S NATIONALISM

Hardly had the ink dried on the Declaration of Independence that the advocates of larger and more powerful government came out of the woodwork. The American Revolution brought to an end more than a century in which the ideas supporting a free society had been slowly evolving, first in the United Kingdom and then in the colonies. According to the historian Vernon L. Parrington, the revolution represented a turning point in America. Although human freedom remained a characterizing feature of American society, this period marked the beginning of a fundamental change in direction.

Decentralization had reached its zenith, and the "counter movement of centralization" was to strongly infuence American politics in the Federalist administrations of Washington and Adams and even, ironically, the administration of Jefferson. This momentous reversal was observed in the threatened coup d'etat by American army officers in 1783 which had as its purpose the restoration of a monarchy in America. But in practical terms the efforts at centralization of power were identified with the nationalistic program of Alexander Hamilton, largely implemented during George Washington's administrations.

The conservative reaction in American political thought between the Declaration of Independence and the drafting of the Constitution in 1787 represented an important watershed in our history. The delegates to the constitutional convention wished to achieve a compromise between the radical individualism and states rights of the Jeffersonian Republicans, and the reactionary Hamiltonian Federalist who wished to create a constitutional monarchy.

The process of ratifying the Constitution involved a whole series of heated debates throughout the thirteen states on whether the proposed Constitution gave the national government too much power. The Anti-Federalist, those who opposed ratification of the document drafted in Philedelphia in 1787, believed that " . . . there is no way more likely to lose ones liberty in the end than being too niggardly of it in the beginning." The Anti-Federalist believed that the federal government didn't need to be as powerful as that proposed in the Constitution. They believed, as Herbert J. Storing tells us in *What the Anti-Federalists Were For,* that the "supremacy" and "necessary and proper" clauses in combination with the explicit and broad grants of power amounted to "...an unlimited grant of power to the general government to do whatever it might choose to do." A number of the

Anti-Federalists were concerned with the emphasis that some proponents of the Constitution placed on the issues of national defense
and a vigorous commercial policy. They were concerned that
government's proper concern with individual liberty was being
sacrificed to the pursuit of "noble purposes" which would make us
"...respectable as a nation abroad, and rich as individuals at home."
When observing the Federalists promoting "...the grandeur and importance of America," Anti-Federalists like Patrick Henry worried
about the preservation of liberty: "You are not to inquire how your
trade may be increased, nor how you are to become a great and
powerful people, but how your liberties can be secured, for liberty
ought to be the direct end of your government." Unfortunately, the
problems which the Anti-Federalists anticipated have generally come
to pass.

The ratified Constitution, which came out of that convention in
Philadelphia, would only have explicit meaning in light of how it was
interpreted. Its vagueness and silence on so many issues meant of
necessity that future legal and judicial decisions would ultimately
determine whether the power of government could be controlled. As
reflected in the Bill of Rights, the Constitution did provide for the
basic protection of political or civil rights. On the other hand, the
Constitution gave the national government broad and far-reaching
powers over the nation's economic affairs. The Federal government
was given the authority over international and interstate commerce,
to coin money, and to provide for the general welfare. These and
other provisions of the Constitution meant, according to the historian
Arthur Ekirch, "...the stage was set for the abandonment of laissez-
faire liberalism and the substitution of a policy of economic nationalism or government paternalism."

In 1791 for example, an enlarged role for the national government
in economic life was illustrated in the debate over Hamilton's proposal to charter the first United States Bank. Thomas Jefferson objected to this proposal as being an unwarranted and unnecessary role
of the national government. Hamilton responded with the
"doctrine" of implied or resulting powers. "The Constitution,"
Hamilton argued, "contains certain implied powers which result
from other powers specifically enumerated." This broad interpretation of the Consitution, even to this day, dominates judicial decisions, especially those concerned with economic issues.

Another illustration of the degree to which the Hamiltonian
Federalists were willing to extend government power is represented
by the Alien and Sedition Acts which were passed in 1798 during
John Adams' administration. Laws approved by Congress to supposedly deal with our confused and uncertain involvement in the
Napoleonic Wars between France and Britain, they frightfully
demonstrated the power of our growing government. The Alien Act
provided for the deportation and imprisonment of "dangerous

aliens" during time of war. However, it was the Sedition Act which startled and angered the Republicans and radical individualists. This act made it a crime to oppose the operations of the government, and "...if any person shall write, print, utter, or publish...any false scandalous and malicious writing..." against the government "...with intent to defame," then that person could be fined and imprisoned. The Sedition Act was enforced against the opposition party through the arrest of Republican newspaper editors and politicians. Both John Adams and Alexander Hamilton later tried to disclaim responsibility for this legislation which was in direct contradiction to the principles of the revolution. James Madison responded in a manner which seems applicable today: "Perhaps it is a universal truth that the loss of liberty at home is to be charged to provisions against danger, real or pretended, from abroad." Furthermore, if it is not a foreign threat that makes governments grow, it is perhaps the power-seeking politician who, though honest as a man, truly believes in the necessity of force to govern men.

## THOMAS JEFFERSON AS NATIONALIST

It is interesting that when Thomas Jefferson became President, he too joined in the spirit of economic nationalism. As one economist was later to write, "...Jefferson, anti-Hamiltonian out of supreme office, became in good part Hamiltonian as President." Concerned with the European struggles during his presidency, Jefferson took positions which were in direct opposition to his "classical liberalism." Aware of his dilemma, he tried in vain to reconcile his actions with his underlying belief in human liberty. It is indeed one of the great ironies of history that the period of Jefferson's presidency witnessed such important refutations of his principles.

For example, Jefferson's purchase of Louisiana, which doubled the national debt, could not be reconciled with his earlier pronouncements on government's role; but it was the renewal of hostilities in Europe in 1803 which led the Jefferson Administration "...into domestic policies more autocratic and sweeping than Hamilton's boldest enterprise." Various Enforcement Acts and the Embargo Act of 1807, which restricted the freedom of American merchant ships, significantly reduced individual liberties. The growth in the Navy and Army, a policy followed by Jefferson, also contributed importantly to the increase in the power of the national government. The tariff legislation, federal participation in internal improvements, and the Second Bank of the United States sponsored by the Republican administrations of Jefferson and Madison all represented greater government involvement in the national economy.

Though Jefferson came to regret the growth of federal power during his retirement years at Monticello, the damage was done. The path of federal supremacy had been established and would characterize America's future development. While economic activity would continue to be mostly a private matter during the nineteenth century, conducted in an overwhelmingly free market environment, federal encroachment would nevertheless continue. Even Jefferson later admitted in correspondence, that from a strict constructionist interpretation of the Constitution, "...I have corrected some erring opinion into which I had slidden without sufficient examination." John Randolph of Virginia, a severe critic during this period of the broadened interpretation of constitutional authority, commented upon reading of Jefferson's regrets, that "...the old gentleman seems from this correspondence, to be more alarmed at the rapid and increasing encroachments of the federal government than I could have imagined." Unfortunately out of this period came a truly "nationalistic philosophy" which eventually produced the proposition that it was government's responsibility to guarantee the economic well being of all its citizens. This, of course, was a reversal from the older position of individual responsibility and individual freedom.

Resulting in hostilities with Great Britain in the War of 1812, American involvement in Europe's Napoleonic conflicts provided the foundation for perpetual taxation and a permanent military establishment. This, according to Albert Gallatin, Secretary of the Treasury, was most "...unfavorable to the happiness and free institutions of the country." During the administrations that followed Jefferson, both James Madison and James Monroe made relatively feeble attempts at a return to the principles of limited national government power. The tokenism, however, of acts such as Monroe's veto of a bill to repair the Cumberland Road with federal funds was too little too late to stop the trend toward economic nationalism.


## THE SUPREME COURT AND FEDERAL POWER

The supremacy of federal power over individual and states' rights was consolidated by the judicial decisions of John Marshall's Supreme Court. With respect to the balance between states' rights and federal supremacy, Chief Justice Marshall in his famous decision on *McCulloch vs. Maryland* (1819) forcefully depicted the broad interpretation of federal power under the Constitution: "Let the end be legitimate, let it be within the scope of the Constitution, and all means which are appropriate, which are plainly adapted to that end, which are not prohibited, but consist with the letter and spirit of the Constitution are constitutional." The Court's efforts at making the U. S. Constitution supreme was successful, but the consequences of this centralization have evolved in a manner which has reduced individual freedom far below that which is both sustainable and desirable.

Supported by the judicial decisions of the Marshall court, and the precedents established by the Hamiltonian nationalism of George Washington, John Adams, and even Thomas Jefferson, President John Quincy Adams' goals for government were even more far reaching. Taking office in 1825, his policies for internal economic improvements and even federal aid to cultural projects were numerous. Following the lead of Henry Clay's *American System,* which called for a massive increase in the role of the federal government in the economic life of the nation, Adams' plans for consolidation and centralization represented but the next step in what would become a very much enlarged role for government in private economic affairs.

Morton J. Horwitz, in *The Transformation of American Law, 1780-1860,* documents the extent to which this intervention would frequently be to the benefit of commercial interests in the name of economic progress. The judicial branch of government, with economic growth its intention, relentlessly pursued policies of "helping" business. These changes not only affected the distribution of income and wealth in society and the degree to which business interests sought government favors, but they also represented the principle means by which tort, nuisance, and trespass liability under the law were weakened. In the name of economic growth, strict liability concepts of the common law were progressively relaxed by judicial decision. That is, property rights were allowed to be violated. Today, the burden of this "transformation in American law" is crucial to our understanding of the problems of pollution and the environment and the associated issue of property rights assignment which continue to plague us.

To make this point, assume that a large 18 wheel truck drove across a person's property and did considerable damage. However, when the damaged party took the case to court they were surprised to learn that no damages would be awarded because in the name of economic growth, efficiency, and progress, the truck was found by the courts to be saving time by driving across private property. The courts of this era were continually making decisions that allowed property rights to be violated in this fashion. For example, in recent years an Ohio court permitted the construction of a new airport runway in spite of the noise and, therefore, falling property values in the surrounding residential neighborhood. The court's decision was rationalized, of course, in the name of growth and progress. Is it any wonder that we have polluted rivers and dirty air when these kinds of compromises are made on property rights? The courts reinforced the incentive that "it pays to pollute."

The early nineteenth century requests for economic advantage and subsidy through legislation and judicial decision, always in the name of the "public interest" and economic progress, can be viewed as analogous to calling on the fox to guard the chickens. It was only a matter of time before the federal government called the tune. These seemingly harmless changes in the law and/or its interpretation for some slight immediate benefit to business or commercial interests have in our own time come to be a reflection of the leviathan state. That same government which offered those economic advantages would now control, or at least intervene to some degree, in almost every important business decision.

## WAR AND THE DECLINE OF FREEDOM

Fortunately, the interventionist policies of the nationalists were only partially accepted prior to the Civil War. There were still many radical Jeffersonians who remained concerned about the expanding scope of government power. Most of John Quincy Adams' internal improvements, for example, were rejected by the Congress. The idea that government should be distrusted and its intrusions into economic and social life be kept to a minimum was still very popular. Unfortunately, war or even the threat of war, both then and now, has inevitably been associated with an increase in government power and a corresponding decrease in individual freedom. From Lincoln's prosecution of the Civil War we received the first federal income tax, the chartering of national banks, and the inflationary printing of paper money ("green backs").

Interestingly, the intervention was not limited merely to the economic sphere. Lincoln, again supposedly in the "public interest" and in order to save the union, suspended constitutionally guaranteed rights of American citizens, including the suspension of the Writ of Habeus Corpus, and the arbitrary arrest and imprisonment of Americans not convicted of any crime. By the end of the Civil War, the federal government had become the dominant institution in American society. This was a role from which it would not withdraw. In fact, the heroic view of the Civil War which continues to appear in our history books is at odds with another view much more critical of the illiberal results of the "demands of the war." Although slavery was at long last ended in America, the loss of civil liberties during the war and the conservative reaction associated with Reconstruction in the postwar period represented a darker side.

## GOVERNMENT AND BUSINESS IN THE GILDED AGE

While the dominant force for economic progress from the Civil War to the end of the century continued to be competitive capitalism, Republican administrations, as well as the federal courts, continued to increase the involvement of the national government in the economic life of the nation. Land grant subsidies to the railroads and the creation of the land grant college system permanently enlarged government's role in the economy. According to the economic historian Gabriel Kolko, the Interstate Commerce Commission was in large part created in 1887 to enforce a cartel for eastern American railroads which had proven to be unenforceable without the aid of government coercion. The economist Dominick Armentano even argues that the Sherman (Antitrust) Act of 1890 was not, in fact, legislation to prevent monopoly, but represented an attempt to solidify the market dominance of the "trusts" which were losing their positions through fierce market competition. The expanded transportation network, led by the great railroad building boom, created competition among regional producers and created a truly national market. Analogous to the role of international trade today, drastically lower transportation costs intensified competition during the very period the trusts reached their zenith.

Unfortunately, the turn toward legislation to deal with what were, in reality, mostly imaginary problems, reinforced the political centralization. The precedents established very early on by the Hamiltonian program, fostered by Jefferson and then accelerated by Henry Clay, John Quincy Adams and Abraham Lincoln, provided on the eve of World War I the intellectual support for the dominant and decisive role the federal government would play in the twentieth century.


## FREEDOM AND THE WAR TO END ALL WARS

In light of his visits to and study of America in the nineteenth century, Alexis de Tocqueville warned that our fears should not be concerned with decentralization or an excess of individual freedom, but instead should be concerned with "...inadequate securities which exist against tyranny." And especially, "...a long war almost always reduces nations to the wretched alternative of being abandoned to ruin by defeat or to despotism by success...no protracted war can fail to endanger the freedom of a democratic country." The American involvement in World War I on the European continent provided just such an opportunity. Government economic intervention occured everywhere. And as Tocqueville had warned, the growing democratic tendency facilitated a move toward greater uniformity as well as the centralization of power in Washington D.C.

On the eve of World War I there were two monumental legal changes in the American environment, both of which were to have profound implications for the course of American history and the relative role of government and the market in the lives of individual Americans. First, the Sixteenth Amendment to the Constitution, ratified in 1913, provided that "...The Congress shall have power to lay and collect taxes on incomes, from whatever source derived, without apportionment among the several States, and without regard to any census or enumeration." The path was laid open. From a maximum rate of seven percent in 1913, the rate on income taxes increased to seventy-seven percent by 1918! Admittedly, the personal income tax did not become a tax on the "masses" until World War II. Nevertheless, the income tax amendment to the Constitution provided the ultimate foundation upon which the enormous increase in the federal tax bill of the American people would be derived. Later, with the adoption of "withholding" at the source of wages and salary income, the enforcement of collections was made easier and also softened the end-of-year burden that represented such a convenient reminder of just how costly government was becoming.

In 1913, Congress also enacted the Federal Reserve Act, which created a national central bank in the United States. The Federal Reserve System, composed of twelve regional banks located throughout the United States and a Board of Governors located in Washington, D.C., was a compromise solution and was largely in response to the severe financial panic of 1907-08, which we might add was quickly over without a central bank's assistance. While a strong national central bank was desired by some, there were still those who feared the concentration of financial power in New York City or Washington, D.C. The Federal Reserve System was opposed for the same reasons that the radical Jeffersonians had opposed the First and Second Bank of the United States (1791 and 1816). However, those who believed an active central bank would effectively deal with financial distress carried the day. As a result, the Federal Reserve System would play an important role in the marketing of massive U.S. Treasury borrowing requirements during World War I and during World War II. Large federal deficits continue to plague us, and unfortunately, the FED's role in all this is to "monetize" U.S. government bonds. Economists use this phrase "debt monetization" to describe what the public calls "running the printing press." The end result, in any case, is more inflation.

## THE "NEW DEAL" OF FRANKLIN ROOSEVELT

The legal and judicial environment was drastically affected by the momentous change brought on by the Great Depression. Although a thorough analysis of modifications in the law and changes in its interpretation would require volumes, we must briefly look at the legislation of the "New Deal" of Franklin Roosevelt: its role in reducing our liberties and increasing the police power of the state. Originally, the "New Deal" was presumably required because of the failure of capitalism. However, it is now widely accepted that the blame for the depth and duration of the decline rests squarely with the federal

82

government and its agencies. Though Roosevelt was jesting when he said Hoover possessed the intellectual and economic power to create the worldwide depression, it was not far from wrong, given the events which in fact transpired during the Roosevelt years.

The combined effects of the infamous Smoot-Hawley Tariff of 1930 and the inappropriate monetary policy of the Federal Reserve System in the early 1930's were unquestionably sufficient to generate a depression which would otherwise have been a relatively mild recession. Economic historian Peter Temin and other economists have documented the devastating impact of the Smoot-Hawley tariff which increased the average rate on dutiable imports into the United States to over fifty percent. Naturally, foreign countries retaliated and world trade collapsed as a result of the war of protection. Nobel Laureate economist Milton Friedman and Anna Schwartz place appropriate blame on the failure of the Federal Reserve System to prevent a precipitous thirty percent decline in the money supply during the great contraction of the early 1930's.

A good many of the legislative proposals by the leftist intellectuals who joined the Roosevelt Administration came directly from Hoover's policy of aiding business. Before becoming President, and while serving as Secretary of Commerce in the 1920's, Herbert Hoover decided that it was his responsibility to support business interests both at home and abroad. He advocated that codes of ''fair'' competition be established by business groups and that trade associations be formed in which common interest might be discussed. He was convinced that the U.S. was ''...passing from a period of extremely individualistic action into a period of associational activities.'' Trade associations proliferated and by the time Hoover left the presidency in 1933 more than two thousand groups were active, compared to the dozen or so in 1920.

The cozy relationship between big business and government continues to this day. The Lockhead, Chrysler, and Continental Illinois loans, the subsidies to the dairy industry and the protection offered to automobiles, steel and textiles by tariffs and ''voluntary'' quotas are among the many government intrusions into the private sector. Wanting short term benefits while neglecting the deleterious long term effects of increased government intervention, business, then as today, prepares its own grave. Henry Ford serves as an example: ''Mr. Ford was for Mr. Wilson when Mr. Wilson was President. Mr. Ford was for Mr. Harding when Mr. Harding was President. Mr. Ford is for Mr. Coolidge while Mr. Coolidge is President. Mr. Ford is a marvelous businessman!''

Lobbying for government handouts one day, the business community continues to be amazed at government's insistence on intervening tomorrow. But one can't have it both ways. Nevertheless, business and other interest groups in the economy, agriculture and labor especially, perceived a friendly marriage with government to be in their best interest. Temporarily, that might have been true, but it has never been beneficial to the consumer. Although not that concerned about economic freedom, Supreme Court Justices Brandeis and Oliver Wendell Holmes were both concerned with the growth in centralized power. Brandeis, writing on the decline in state rights, said that "...the extremes of concentration are proving its failure to the common man."

Writing to a friend a few months before the onset of the Great Depression, a period which would drastically increase the role and power of the state in economic affairs, the historian Vernon L. Parrington expressed his concern over the ultimate implications of the growth in government's sphere of power:

> Wherever power is lodged a great struggle for control and use of that power follows. When one controls the political state, whatever one wants can be done under the cover of the law and with the sanction of the courts. Have you been able to convince yourself that the corporative wealth of America will permit the centralized political state to pass out of its control? We must have a political state powerful enough to deal with corporative wealth, but how are we going to keep that state with its augmenting power from being captured by the force we want it to control?

This power would increase almost without limit during the administrations of Franklin Roosevelt. He accomplished what Jefferson would have deplored. And, because of him, the United States would never be the same. William Allen White wrote that "...Roosevelt was the most enemy-baffling president that the U.S. has ever seen, displaying a capacity for statesmanship in the large and simple billboard language that the common people can understand, that the people admire even when it is their deadly poison." There is no question that Roosevelt was a politician par excellence. But more than any other politician, Franklin Delano Roosevelt released government from the restraint of the law to the murky, ever changing whims of men.

On the occasion of Franklin Roosevelt's inauguration in 1933 the American economy had reached an unprecedented low. Unemployment was nearly twenty-five percent of the labor force and industrial production and the Gross National Product were down by more than a third. Social and economic despair was widespread. In accepting the nomination of his party, Roosevelt had promised "...a new deal for the American people...," and the contemplated changes might very well include national economic planning of the collectivist sort practiced in the Soviet Union. The "brain trust" which gathered in Washington, D.C., was convinced, in spite of the important role government had played in producing the depression, that a tremendously enlarged responsibility for the national government was necessary. The Committee of Social Studies of the American Historical Association reported: "The age of individualism and laissez faire in economy and government is closing and a new age of collectivism is emerging." Out of this philosophy of paternalistic government intervention and planning, the decade of the 1930's witnessed federal legislation that radically transformed and modified the relationship between citizens and their government.

Unquestionably the most far-reaching legislation was the National Recovery Act, a Rooseveltian version of national economic planning. "Codes of fair competition" were mandated for each industry, and, as might be expected, the members of the respective industries prepared the regulations for prices and production. Within a year there were over four hundred codes covering about ninety per cent of American businesses and more than twenty million workers. President Roosevelt boasted that the Act was "...the most important and far-reaching legislation ever enacted by the American Congress." But, in fact, its real impact was to legalize the formation of cartels in most every sector of the U. S. economy. Entrepreneurship and market competition were either suppressed or eliminated.

Adam Smith, in the *Wealth of Nations,* had warned that whenever "...people of the same trade...meet together, even for merriment and diversion...the conversation ends in a conspiracy against the public, or in some contrivance to raise prices." Roosevelt's "brain trust" in effect ignored Smith's warning. Fortunately for the American people, the Supreme Court of the United States unanimously declared the National Recovery Act to be unconstitutional. But the disease was now widespread, and the national government would be intimately involved in the economic affairs of the nation. Although government creates no wealth, provides jobs in one area only by taxing which reduces jobs elsewhere, blocks trade between willing individuals, destroys psychological capital by regulating the entrepreneur, creates inflation, and reduces economic freedom; the myth that government intervention was necessary would now rule the industrial nations of the world.

In the farm sector, legislation passed by the "New Deal" Congress created the Agricultural Adjustment Administration and later the Commodity Credit Corporation. These new agencies significantly increased the role of the federal government in agriculture. The massive farm programs in our own time, wasteful and inefficient as they are, represent a direct legacy of the massive federal intervention into agriculture during the 1930's.

Organized labor obtained its magna carta with the passage of the National Labor Relations Act which created the National Labor Relations Board. This legislation, in effect, exempted labor from the antitrust laws and gave organized labor monopoly powers generally unavailable to business or other sectors of the economy. The coerced requirement that an employer "negotiate in good faith" with a particular labor organization is an obvious and clear violation of the liberties of employers. In a free society the requirements of the National Labor Relations Act impose a fundamental contradiction.

Government's coercive powers can either be used to force an employer to negotiate with and hire an employee not of his choosing, or, alternatively, the force of government can be used to protect the employer from the employee who threatens violence in the name of demanding a job. But what is clear is that we cannot have it both ways. The state is either used to prevent violence or to force exchanges even if one of the parties does not wish to participate. What a far cry from our country's beginnings!

Ironically, however, the most collectivist New Deal programs have traditionally been those receiving the least amount of criticism. The Tennessee Valley Authority Act of 1933, a massive socialist experiment in regional economic planning, is a prime example. Initially expanding an existing facility on the Muscle Shoals section of the Tennessee River, the TVA came to involve not only hydroelectric power generation, but it established cooperatives, subsidized homesteads, encouraged rural zoning, and basically provided for general regional planning. According to one of the original commissioners of the Authority, "...the TVA showed the possibilities of collectivism without the sacrifice of democracy." Unfortunately, the TVA produced many undesirable and costly consequences, including the generation of differential federal benefits for the southeastern part of the country as a result of subsidized government produced electricity.

An equivalent boondoggle in the 1980's is represented by the Northwest Power Act which has generated the Northwest Regional Power Plan, another collectivist effort to nationalize part of the energy industry in the United States. While its supporters claim the Act "...finally offers an intelligent, common-sense approach to satisfying the region's needs," the planning to be done by the Northwest Power Planning Council presumes a degree of knowledge by government officials and political appointees which the Nobel Laureate Friedrich Hayek reminds us is simply unavailable to ordinary men. And yet, as David Shapiro, an economist at the Hoover Institute, has stated in the *Wall Street Journal*: "The Bonneville Power Administration and its erstwhile (past) administrator, Mr. Hodel (the key player in the multi-billion dollar WPPSS failure), have prospered rather than suffered in the aftermath of the regional power problems. The entire Washington Public Power Supply System (WPPSS) imbroglio illustrates the failure of a government agency in economic planning. The appointment to cabinet office of the head of that agency by a president (Reagan) devoted to free-market principles is so fraught with irony as to defy all description."

Viewed through rose colored glasses in 1935, the Social Security Act, which created a system of nationally determined and mandatory tax payments and old-age pensions, represented a revolutionary movement away from a system of individual responsibility and private retirement programs. Beginning with tax rates that were very low, the Social Security System has become a great Ponzi scheme, a chain-letter arrangement in which current recipients receive in retirement benefits their life-time tax contributions in the first two or three years of their retirement. This collectivist experiment in a government mandated and compulsory retirement program faces bankruptcy and ultimate collapse. The elderly of the early part of the twenty-first century and those still employed and working will bear the brunt of such a sham.

There were, of course, many other legislative "victories" for the New Deal administration during these times. Major banking legislation was passed in 1933 and 1935 which simultaneously created monopoly protection for commercial banks and other financial intermediary institutions and drastically strengthened and centralized the power of the Federal Reserve System in Washington, D.C. The Civil Aeronautics Board was created in 1938 and, until the deregulation legislation of 1978, had for all practical purposes created an airline cartel in the United States. The Interstate Commerce Commission's authority over railroads was expanded to trucking, which further increased the inefficiency in America's surface transportation industries. Communications and broadcasting were also brought under tighter federal control during this period through the Federal Communications Commission (FCC).


## JUDICIAL DECISIONS AND INDIVIDUAL FREEDOM

By the second Roosevelt term, the "new Roosevelt court" began to change the rules of the game. The Supreme Court, while defending so-called civil rights of free speech and the like, modified or eliminated a number of the constitutional barriers to federal government regulation of the economy. The court believed the government's intevention into economic affairs could be justifiably much broader in those situations in which businesses affected that nebulous thing called the "public interest." As early as 1934 the Supreme Court (Nebbie vs. New York) upheld the conviction of a small merchant for selling milk below the price established by a state legislated minimum price law. A majority of the court ruled that it was not unreasonable for New York to enact legislation that deprived Nebbie of the liberty to sell milk at a price of his own choosing. A dissenting opinion by Justice McReynolds that "...the legislature cannot lawfully destroy guaranteed rights of one man with the prime purpose of enriching another, even if for the moment, this may seem advantageous to the public..." was to no avail. In the late 1930's these kind of court decisions, which presumed in the public interest to benefit one group of individuals at the expense of other groups, came to be a common theme. In large part, the Federal judiciary moved with and complemented the legislative legacy of the "New Deal."

The incredible growth in government and its intervention in the lives of individual citizens during the period of the Great Depression has never been rolled back. Constitutional lawyer Henry Mark Holzer in *Sweet Land of Liberty?: The Supreme Court and Individual Rights,* documents the extent to which government continues, today, to intervene in *private* affairs, often in direct and explicit contradiction to the U.S. Constitution. Government's political power to determine the uses to which property might be put was changed fundamentally in 1926 when the U.S. Supreme Court in *Euclid vs. Ambler Realty Company* placed the stamp of approval on local zoning ordinances in which, according to the court, ''...a majority of Euclid (Ohio's) inhabitants...'' were merely ''...voicing their will.'' Since that time, Holzer tells us that ''...to the extent that there has been disagreement between the justices, it has not been over the fundamental principle of whether government *should* control people's lives, but merely over the details of how, when, and to what extent their lives *will* be controlled.''

Ruling on a case in which a local zoning ordinance was changed after a man purchased five acres for development, the Supreme Court recently reinforced its earlier decision. In *Agins vs. City of Tiburon* (1980) the court rejected the argument by Mr. Agins that the Fifth Amendment to the U.S. Constitution precluded a ''taking'' of property without just compensation--the so-called eminent domain clause of the Constitution. ''The term 'police power','' said the majority of the Supreme Court, ''connotes the time-tested conceptual limit of public encroachment upon private interests.'' But the limit seemed to offer no constraint to the power of the state. ''The interests of the public...require such interference,'' the U.S. Supreme Court had said way back in 1894, and the only limit is that the intervention ''...not *unduly* (be) oppressive upon individuals...'' (emphasis added). In other words, the property rights of *some* individuals can be constrained by government power if undertaken on the behalf of the public--that is to say, on behalf of *other* individuals.

Probably the most important factor in the transformation of the law in the United States has been the interstate commerce clause of the U.S. Constitution. Article I, Section 8 provides that the federal government is ''...to regulate Commerce...among the several States...'' and ''...to make all laws which shall be necessary and proper for carrying into execution the foregoing powers...'' Especially since the 1930's, although of course it really got rolling back in 1887 with the passage of the Interstate Commerce Act, Congress has used the interstate commerce clause to protect certain business interests from potential competitors. It has used the ''law'' on behalf of businesses that were deemed in need of protection from the rigors of competition. Congress has thus justified government control of transportation, banking, investments, labor relations, communications, energy retail trade, food and drugs, and almost anything else one would care to imagine.

The courts have decreed that government has the right to interfere in the establishment of wage rates, in maximum hours of work, in the control over production levels, and in the contracts between the owners and customers of businesses, including private schools. In *Robins vs. Prune Yard Shopping Center* (1980) the U.S. Supreme Court, in summing up the outcome of decisions made over the previous decades, affirmed its disregard for the inalienable rights to private property: "Neither property rights nor contract rights are absolute...Equally fundamental with the private right is that of the public to regulate it in the common interest." However, the "public interest" is invariably and unavoidably the interests of particular individuals who gain at the expense of those whose rights are compromised. In *Prune Yard Shopping Center* the court ruled that it did not "...*markedly* dilute (the owner's) property rights..." (emphasis added) to allow high school students to seek signatures on petitions in this privately owned shopping center. But it surely created "rights" in the shopping center for strangers.

There are innumerable examples that show the extent to which the federal courts have compromised the protection of property rights. The Constitution provides in Article I, Section 10 that state governments could enact no "...law impairing the obligation of contracts." The state governments and, by implication, the federal government could not rewrite contracts for the state's own purposes or for the benefit of third parties. But these constitutional safeguards have failed to constrain government's ever larger encroachment on private action. Legal tender laws were passed in 1862 so that the federal government could print paper money ("greenbacks") in order to finance the Civil War. The Congress of the United States in a Joint Resolution on June 5, 1933, suspended "gold clauses" in private contracts between consenting adults, thereby taking property from creditors. In the 1930's, mortgage contracts were, in effect, rewritten by state governments. Contracts containing restrictive land covenants between private citizens, admittedly for racist and bigoted motives, were declared null and void in spite of the protection of the U.S. Constitution. "The Supreme Court of the United States," according to Holzer, "nakedly yet unashamedly admitted that some individuals can be oppressed (though not 'unduly') by government power exercised on behalf of the public (i.e., other people)."

Bernard Siegen, in his book *Economic Liberties and The Constitution*, documents the way in which the United States Supreme Court has almost eliminated the "economic due process" to "life, liberty, and property" which had been guaranteed by the Fourteenth Amendment to the Constitution. Following the important Supreme Court decision in 1897, *Allgeyer vs. Lousiana*, limits were placed on the powers of the federal and state governments to interfere with the rights of individuals to contract, which is to say exercise their economic liberties. For these so-called substantive due process

Justices, there were important limits to the coercive power of government to prevent peaceful and voluntary exchange. Justice Peckham, writing the unanimous opinion of the Supreme Court in *Allgeyer,* identified what he believed to be the limits to the state's authority to restrict the liberty of contract:

> The liberty mentioned in that (fourteenth) amendment means not only the right of the citizen to be free from the mere physical restraint of his person, as by incarceration, but the term is deemed to embrace the right of the citizen to be free in the enjoyment of all his faculties; to be free to use them in all lawful ways; to live and work where he will; to earn his livelihood by any lawful calling; to pursue any livelihood or avocation, and for that purpose to enter into all contracts which may be proper, necessary and essential to his carrying out to a successful conclusion the purposes above mentioned.

Justice Peckman relied in part on an earlier opinion by Supreme Court Justice Harlan who also defended the proposition that "...acquiring, holding and selling property, is an essential part of his right of liberty and property" under the Constitution. The substantive due process protection of economic freedoms continued to be supported by the Court, although by bare majorities, until 1937. Finally, economic rights were sacrificed by a court which came to passionately defend intellectual freedoms of speech and the like, but no longer recognized the intimate and fundamental connection between the two. As Justice Holmes suggested: "When this seemingly absolute protection is found to be qualified by the police power, the natural tendency of human nature is to extend the qualification more and more until at last private property disappears."

With the *Nebbie vs. New York* U.S. Supreme Court decision of 1934 mentioned earlier, the beginning of the end for economic due process occurred with the conviction of that small New York store owner for selling milk below a legislatively enacted minimum price. The end of economic due process came in 1937 when, in *West Coast Hotel vs. Parrish,* legislated minimum wages for women and minors were supported by the Court. Nevermind that the legislation discriminated against women and minors who were willing to take these jobs and thereby favored male workers, the liberty to freely contract was no longer to be defended by the Court. What has unfortunately developed is an almost unlimited use of the police power of government to regulate and constrain what would otherwise be mutually beneficial and otherwise legal contracts. The regulation of wages, air fares, shipping rates, selling "below cost," discriminatory pricing, and all the rest are justified in the name of a very vague notion of the "public interest."

Government's intrusions into the private affairs between "consenting capitalist adults" continue to take place in religious issues, speech and sex, as well as specifically economic exchanges. This tragic record of the denial of inalienable rights, even when specifically provided for in the U. S. Constitution, has already been documented in other volumes. The following quotation, which is an excellent summary of this mentality that denies individual rights in the name of some greater good, is from a majority opinion by Charles Evans Hughes, Chief Justice of the United States. It succinctly summarizes the unfortunate transformation of the law in the United States since the Declaration and the increased police power over private arrangements:

> It is manifest from this review of our decisions, that there has been a growing appreciation of public needs and of the necessity of finding ground for a rational *compromise between individual rights and public welfare.* The settlement and consequent contraction of the public domain, the pressure of a constantly increasing density of population, the interrelation of the activities of our people and the complexity of our economic interests, have inevitably led to an increased use of the organization of society in order to protect the very bases of individual opportunity. Where, in earlier days, it was thought that only the concerns of individuals or of classes were involved, and that those of the state itself were touched remotely, it has later been found that the fundamental interests of the state are directly affected; and that the question is no longer merely that of one party to a contract as against another, but the use of reasonable means to safeguard the economic structure upon which the good of all depends.

Government intervention for most any "worthwhile" purpose is carved into stone by this interpretation of the Constitution. The reader must evaluate the merits of Chief Justice Hughes position; whether we have gone too far or not far enough. Back in 1944, John Flynn in his *As We Go Marching* believed we had already gone far too far. He compared at great length the similarities between the kinds of arguments presented by Justice Hughes and Roosevelt's "brain trust" and the kinds of arguments which, during the 1930's, were being made by the facist movements of Adolph Hitler in Germany and Benito Mussolini in Italy.

However desirable it may be to restore economic freedom in the United States, the problems associated with cutting back the state, piece by piece, program by program, are going to be more difficult as a result of the Supreme Court's failure to protect economic freedoms which presumably had been guaranteed by the Constitution. Even prestigious supporters of the New Deal in its early stages came to regret much of what transpired. Therefore, we must conclude that there is hope for a restoration of the great American experiment. Walter Lippman, the great American pundit and insightful observer of the American scene, and an avowed socialist in his younger days, recognized the terrible cost which had been born through the growth in government power over individual lives. Writing in his *Inquiry Into the Principles of the Good Society,* published in 1937, Lippman summarized the results of the legal and judicial changes of that momentous period:

> The premises of authoritarian collectivism have become the working beliefs, the self-evident assumptions, the unquestioned axioms, not only of all the revolutionary regimes, but of nearly every effort which lays claim to being enlightened, humane, and progressive...Throughout the world, in the name of progress, men calling themselves communists, socialists, fascists, nationalists, progressives, and even liberals, are unanimous in holding that government with its instruments of coercion must, by commanding the people how they shall live, direct the course of civilization and fix the shape of things to come.

Though the principles involved may have been sincere and the judicial pronouncements well intended, the outcome was the erosion and dilution of the rule of law. Legal relativism gave certain individuals enormous powers to mold society according to the prevailing ideologies and predilections of a small cadre of judges and legislators whose operational powers were nearly unbounded. The growth in government's potential for inappropriate and even abusive behavior cannot be denied. The essential limits to unbounded state power were to have been the Constitution, state's rights, representative government, the rule of law, and the committment to individual and personal responsibility. "Where law ends, tyranny begins," stated John Locke. "And whoever in authority exceeds the power given him by the law and makes use of the force he has under his command, ceases to be a good magistrate."

In spite of the warnings by Lippman and many other thoughtful and concerned Americans, the growth and centralization of government has continued in America to this day. Important insights into the intellectual, ideological, and other factors which have contributed to and fostered the move to centralized planning of economic affairs, collectivist solutions to individual problems, and the welfare-state mentality in general will be provided in the following pages.

# CHAPTER 9

## RATIONAL CONSTRUCTIVISM AND THE PLANNED ECONOMY

When I remember how many of my private schemes have miscarried, how speculations have failed...how the things I desperately strove against as a misfortune did me immense good--how while the objects I ardently pursued brought me little happiness when gained...I am struck with the incompetence of my intellect to prescribe for society.

There is a great want of this practical humility in our political conduct...Though we have ceased to assume the infallibility of our theological beliefs and so ceased to enact them, we have not ceased to enact hosts of other beliefs of an equally doubtful kind. Though we no longer coerce men for their spiritual good, we still think ourselves called upon to coerce them for their material good: not seeing that the one is as useless and as unwarrantable as the other.

--Herbert Spencer

The sincere desire of intellectuals and bureaucrats to plan, protect and control the lives of others for the "public good" has been a most influential factor in the decline and fall of the spontaneous, free market economic system in the United States. It happened in academic circles where "rational constructivism" became the popular methodology for explaining social processes. In contrast to the emphasis attached to the socially beneficial implications of Adam Smith's system of natural liberty, this preference for social engineering (often described as "positivism," or "utilitarianism") has come to dominate the political, legal and economic thinking in our time. It suggests a view of human arrangements which maintains that the good society can be deliberately designed to specification. According to this argument, combining government of, by and for the people, with thoughtful plans and sincere implementation, represents the most rational and therefore appropriate way of obtaining the society we desire. Well, almost! Interestingly enough, people can sometimes be stubborn and have personal plans of their own (e.g., Ukranian peasants, Polish workers, Afghanistan rebels, Cuban emigrants, etc.). The modern socialist movement is but a reflection of this "constructivist" mentality; applied in an attempt to collectivize and centrally plan society's parts in order to produce the rationally designed whole.

93

## CONSTRUCTIVISM, THE AGE OF REASON AND UTILITARIANISM

Today's experiments with social engineering have evolved directly from the constructivist ideas promoted during the so-called "Age of Reason." Society appeared to these thinkers as a deliberate construction in which plans could be generated for the attainment of specific and intended purposes. Infinite possibilities exist when rational thought is used to design and create the perfect order. Following philosophers like Descartes, caution was thrown to the winds. Thomas Hobbes expressed this positivist proposition when he said "...every rule of law must be derivable from a conscious act of legislation." To obtain a moral order, Auguste Comte asserted the unquestionable superiority of morals demonstrated by man's reason as opposed to morals revealed by the test of time. And Voltaire went so far as to argue that "...if you want good laws, burn those you have and make yourselves new ones." With supporting arguments from such respected thinkers as Rousseau, Francis Bacon and Hegel, these proponents of such an extreme form of rationalism provided the foundation for the development during the nineteenth century of the doctrines of "utilitarianism" and "legal positivism." The ideas of Thomas Jefferson as written into the Declaration and Bill of Rights contradicted such beliefs in social engineering, arguing instead the rule of law not the rule of men.

It was during the nineteenth century that Jeremy Bentham's utilitarianism, at least for most intellectuals, replaced the earlier belief in natural law and natural rights. Instead of inalienable rights and individualism, the utilitarian philosophers proposed that the aggregate happiness of society be maximized. They called it the greatest good for the greatest number of people. If, for example, you had to make two people sick to make three people well, then the numbers have it. Or, stated differently, the marginal units of income held by the rich were less valued than those held by the poor, and therefore, it made quite good sense to "transfer" (i.e., take!) that income from the rich, supposedly increasing the level of societal happiness in the process. Since the morality of "taking" said money from its rightful owner was apparently neglected, a momentum began to build for the redistributive society. And continue to build it did.

## SOCIAL ENGINEERING AND THE EDUCATORS

In the United States this utilitarian pragmatism or social engineering came to have its impact on social arrangements largely through the work of the philosopher and educator John Dewey. Following the pragmatic urgings of William James, in the 1890's Dewey justified his theories by way of his "progressive school" experiment at the University of Chicago. Dewey's influence was staggering. Through the explosion of public (or government) education in this century, largely the result of Dewey's efforts, three or four generations of American leaders have had their minds distinctively shaped by the appeal of planning the good society and government enforced social arrangements. The following quotation from one of John Dewey's books explicitly reveals how far government should go in molding society: "Whether [the use of force] is justifiable or not...it is in substance a question of efficiency of means in the accomplishing of ends. The criterion of values lies in the relative efficiency and economy of the expenditure of force as a means to an end." Stalin, Hitler, and even less controversial liberal and conservative leaders in the West, working for their own particular pet projects, have always believed the ends justify the means, especially when it is intended for the "public good."

Other followers of Dewey, many of whom believed in the possibility of building a utopia, also recommended abandoning the inalienable rights tradition of the founding fathers. In practice the sacrifice of Locke's natural rights, unfortunately meant an "...open ended coercion in the hands of policy makers." For example, Harold Lasswell, a political scientist at the University of Chicago, insisted that centralized political control of society was the only "rational" way to order society. Thorsten Veblen imagined the task of social organization as a simple engineering problem; and the very respected sociologist Lester Frank Ward wrote near the end of the nineteenth century that "...the individual has reigned long enough. The day has come for society to take its affairs into its own hands and shape its own destinies." In fact, according to Ward, society was suffering from "under government." This judicious mixture of "utilitarianism" and "rational constructivism" provided the intellectual foundation for the planners and social engineers who would plan the individual's every move.


## SOCIAL COMPLEXITY DEMANDS SOCIAL ENGINEERING


One of the most frequently heard claims of these technocrats is the proposition that the market system may have been adequate for an earlier and less complex age but is no longer applicable to modern circumstances. They argue that with the urbanization and industrialization of the American economy following the Civil War the spontaneous forces of the market cannot be synchronized with the wants and needs of the people; centralized planning is necessary because of the rising complexity of social arrangements. Speaking in San Francisco on the eve of the 1932 presidential election, Franklin

Roosevelt recommended the use of government as an elightened administrator and argued that we should formulate "...an economic constitutional order." Happily," he asserted, "the times indicate that to create such an order not only is the proper policy of government, but is the only line of safety for our economic structure as well."

But indeed, this greater complexity provides the most persuasive argument *against* constructing and planning from the center. Communities face what Nobel Laureate Friedrich A. Hayek has called the "knowledge problem." It is unimaginable that any single person or group of people could have had the necessary knowledge earlier in this century, let alone today, to institute an efficient centralized plan. In a modern society information is always and everywhere widely dispersed among millions and millions of separate individuals. Hayek has wisely noted "...that we have been able to achieve a reasonably high degree of order in our economic lives despite modern complexities only because our affairs have been guided, not by central direction, but by the operations of the market and by competition." Such a spontaneous order is the only way we may assume mutual adjustment and the smooth functioning of a very diverse and complex economy.

It is a great puzzle that so many educated and informed individuals have seriously believed that a centralized bureaucracy would be able to correctly anticipate the ongoing changes of an industrial society. Who indeed can respond more efficiently to consumer tastes, invention, product innovation, and new ways of doing things? Is it government? Or, could it be those individuals actually on the spot pursuing enlightened self-interest? The rational constructivist who would plan even the last detail of a modern industrial economy obviously has forgotten the reminder that Adam Smith gave us in *The Theory of Moral Sentiments:* "The man of systems...seems to imagine that he can arrange the different members of a great society with as much ease as the hand arranges the different pieces upon a chessboard. But in the great chessboard of human society, every single piece has a principle of motion of its own, altogether different from that which the legislature might choose to impress upon it."

## INTENTIONS AND OUTCOMES

We find, not surprisingly, that government plans continue to produce results other than those desired. Instead of producing the greater mastery over our environment that John Dewey and the others promised, it seems that situations become even more confused. Far from goal attainment, or approximations thereof, the route is wayward and often opposite of the direction intended. Indirect effects of government intervention are not recognized or are slighted. Many examples could be cited to contrast a law's original intention with its eventual outcome. Housing subsidies, regulation of business, anti-trust, poverty programs, and price controls are but a few of the conspicuous failures. Government price regulation provides a case in point. Wherever government places an effective maximum price on a product, whether medical care, credit, rental housing, or, as in the following example, petroleum products, two things are inevitable: the amount demanded increases above what would have otherwise been the case and supplies shrink due to the reduced incentive to discover and produce additional amounts. Or, in a word: shortages! Government placed price controls on natural gas in the late 1950's and effective price controls on petroleum in 1971; the inevitable result was an energy shortage felt by almost all Americans. Artificially low prices stimulated consumption while at the same time discouraged the search and discovery of new supplies. That the "crisis" was legislated in Washington, D.C. is seldom discussed. Predictably, government responded by readying another barrage of laws and even created a new Department of Energy to solve the problem that government price controls caused in the first place. Taking more than $10 billion more from U.S. taxpayers, and employing nearly 20,000 bureaucrats to regulate energy markets, to plead conservation, and to subsidize alternative energy forms, the federal government proceeded to "solve" a problem that should never have occurred.

Failures notwithstanding, those at the helm of government zealously intensify their efforts to "rationally plan our future." And it almost always produces additional intervention in private spheres to correct and modify unintended consequences of previous government actions which inevitably occur. The profound question submitted by Walter Lippman, as his disillusionment with socialism intensified, bears repeating: "Why should it be that in a time when men are making the prodigious claim that they can plan and direct society, they are so profoundly impressed with the unmanageability of human affairs?"

**PLANNING FOR EQUALITY**

There are also the social engineers who would plan society in the name of achieving "social justice." Defending *their* perception of an equitable and "just" distribution of income and wealth, they would gladly accept a reduction in real material standards of living in order to accomplish their goal. But let there be no misunderstanding on this point: Schemes of distribution and redistribution can only be realized under a totalitarian regime which denies individuals the opportunities to live their personal lives in accordance with their own preferences. Welfare voted by majorities necessarily violates rights of minorities who are forced to give up resources they rightfully believe are theirs.

## MARKETS VERSUS PLANNING

The underlying dilemma in the attempt to deliberately design social arrangements was captured by Hayek forty years ago in his book *The Road to Serfdom:*

> The dispute between the modern planners and their opponents is, therefore, not a dispute on whether we ought to choose intelligently between the various possible organizations of society. It is a dispute about what is the best way of doing so...The question is whether for this purpose it is better that the holder of coercive power should confine himself in general to creating conditions under which the knowledge and initiative of individuals are given the best scope so that they can plan most successfully, or whether a rational utilization of our resources requires central direction...according to some consciously constructed blueprint.

The relevant issue then is to examine the alternatives--competitive capitalism and elightened self-interest versus socialism and central planning--in terms of actual outcomes rather than utopian intentions.

Following the persuasive arguments of the Scottish philosophers David Hume, Adam Smith, and Adam Ferguson, social arrangements are, according to Hayek, ''...the result of human action but not of human design.'' In fact, even before Charles Darwin's work on the theory of evolution and natural selection, these men were arguing that a ''natural'' order exists where modes of conduct conducive to an efficient social order survive a process of cultural selection. The viability of society rests in great measure on the ''wisdom of our ancestors'' as reflected in inherited institutions. This favorable view of a socially beneficial, spontaneous order was preserved in England largely as a result of the important traditions embodied in the common law: a legal system of justice which was not the result of the arbitrary pronouncements of the ruler, but of a long evolutionary process. This was the tradition which the great English jurist Edward Coke defended in the name of human liberty against King James I and the divine right of kings.

It is profoundly important to recognize the extent to which the centrally planned economies of the world have, without exception, recognized the need to decentralize their economies, reintroduce competitive markets, and begin to use the price system. Kruschev, upon returning to the Soviet Union from the United States in 1957, suggested reforms which would entail a greater reliance on the market. Shortly thereafter he was deposed. In the People's Republic of China, Deng Xiaoping, in a significant denuciation of Mao Tse Tung's policies, restructured a middle Chinese province that permitted more economic freedom. Based on observations, this experiment is succeeding. The Soviet Union today recognizes the need for personal incentives and has been introducing them in its agricultural programs. Selected countries in Africa, South America and Asia are beginning to realize the economic efficiency of private ownership, or at the very least, the workability of markets and enterprise. Incentives *do* matter, and centralized direction from above, without regard to the pattern of personal reward, has led to economic inefficiency, chaos and even starvation. These outcomes should really not surprise us. The great Austrian economist, Ludwig von Mises, demonstrated conclusively the impossibility of rational economic calculation under socialism more than a half-century ago. As history unfolds, we necessarily see a sort of capitalism, with prices and profits, surfacing in the centrally planned economies. Unfortunately, the totalitarian regimes would collapse if this liberalization were allowed to go too far. They seem to know what we seem to have forgotten: the market system and private property produce and protect individual freedom. Only the armed might of the Soviet army has prevented Hungary, Romania, Czechoslovakia, and Poland from leaving the socialist camp.

## LEGAL POSITIVISM

As already suggested, there are two strains to the rational constructivist dogma of the nineteenth and twentieth centuries. The implications of a pragmatic and government enforced utilitarianism have been briefly analyzed. "Legal positivism" is the other influence. It, too, has had a profound effect on the decline of the free market order of private property and voluntary exchange. Positivism comes from the Latin *positus* which means "to set down" or "to impose." It suggests a preference for things deliberately created and designed.

The intellectual support for legal positivism arises from the importance attached to the power of abstract reasoning. According to the argument, there are no limits to man's ability to invent and design justice. Natural law and natural rights are metaphysical clap-trap according to the famous German legal scholar Hans Kelsen. Rules of justice in society stem from reason and deliberate design. In fact, as already observed, Voltaire, following the teachings in the rationalism of the philosopher Rene Descartes, suggested that "...if you want good laws, burn those you have and make yourselves new ones."

## THE RULE OF LAW AND LEGAL POSITIVISM

There have been many great minds, such as the great English legal scholar Edward Coke, the philosopher David Hume, the Whig Edmund Burke, Henry Maine, Adam Ferguson, Bernard Mandeville and especially Friedrich Hayek, who have insisted in their writings that "the law" and, therefore, justice are much older than legislated law. Adam Ferguson noted in 1767 that "...nations stumble upon establishments, which are indeed the result of human action, but not the execution of any human design." In large part, according to this tradition, we do not "create the law," but we "discover" it. The great common law tradition in England involved "law-finding" among the studied opinions of legal scholars. This is a radical departure from the legal positivism which maintains that we "set law by the deliberate will of men." Neither the law of gravity or the "law" of consumer demand in economics are valid because Congress so decreed. And good intentions notwithstanding, nor can they be repealed by government decree. This fundamental contradiction between the constructivist point of view and the perspective emphasizing the value of experience and time-tested principles requires another notable quotation from the work of Friedrich Hayek:

> To modern man...the belief that all law governing human action is the product of legislation appears so obvious that the contention that law is older than law-making has almost the character of a paradox. Yet there can be no doubt that law existed for ages before it occurred to man that he could make or alter it...In the form in which it is now widely held, however, namely that all law is, can be, and ought to be, the product of the free invention of a legislator, it is factually false, an erroneous product of that constructivist rationalism...We shall...see that the whole conception of legal positivism which derives all law from the will of a legislator is a product of the intentionalist fallacy characteristic of constructivism, a relapse into those design theories of human institutions which stand in irreconcilable conflict with all we know about the evolution of law and most other human institutions.

This statement, from Hayek's *Law, Legislation and Liberty,* serves to remind us that proposals to legislate occur in the context of a pre-existing "...framework of generally recognized but often unarticulated rules of justice." And, this framework is largely the result of a long and arduous evolutionary process which has stood the test of time and therefore has been socially beneficial. The law in this sense represents "abstract rules" which are revealed or found; not the result of deliberate design or creation.

In our time, legal positivism has come to mean that majorities can, and do, legislate for particular outcomes in which individuals are treated differently by design. We find it an interesting paradox that the same people who argue equal pay for equal work inconsistently also believe in the progressive income tax. Yet, this is discriminatory by definition. If a person chooses to work harder (two shifts perhaps), or smarter, or whatever, is a heavier tax burden on this person justifiable? Certainly the progressive tax runs counter to the notion of "equal pay for equal work." Roscoe Pound, for example, interested in the pursuit of equality in the distribution of material things, believed "social justice" to be an appropriate pursuit of the law, where government should legislate equal shares. But, the attempt to coerce distributive outcomes would necessarily be "law" that was arbitrary, capricious, and unpredictable. Law, in fact, in a free society embodies a set of abstract rules of conduct which define permissable social relations and protect individual rights. Such "negative" law would not concern itself with particular ends, but would entail "...rules applicable to an unknown and indeterminable number of persons and instances," in Hayek's words. We are describing a community of free individuals with perfect "equality before the law;" not equality in the holdings of things.

John Dewey's pragmatic and utilitarian use of government and the constructivist's utilization of legal positivism to correct the perceived ills of society have converged to create the unmanageable leviathan state which we experience in the final decades of the twentieth century. These forces of deliberate design are now combined in the great and arbitrary power of "legislation" that is wielded by governments.

## NATIONAL ECONOMIC PLANNING

The implications of this "blank check for coercion" in the United States of America are illustrated by the forceful pleas during the last decade for national economic planning and in the 1980's for an "industrial policy." In the early 1970's a group of new-deal liberals and socialists, including United Auto Workers president Leonard Woodcock, Myron Sharpe, John Kenneth Galbraith, Nobel Laureate Gunnar Myrdal, Arthur Schlesinger, Jr., Leon Keyserling, and Nobel Laureate Wassily Leontief, formed the Initiative Committee for National Economic Planning. They published *The Case for Planning* and, at least in part because of their efforts, the Balanced Growth and Economic Planning Act of 1975 was sponsored in the United States Senate by Senators Hubert Humphrey, Jacob Javits, and George McGovern, among others. At the time, the *New York Times* hailed the event, declaring "...why is planning considered a good thing for individuals and business but a bad thing for the national economy?"

The committee for National Economic Planning rejected, of course, the use of totalitarian methods for the achievement of their goals: "It should be clear that the Planning Office would not set specific goals for General Motors, General Electric, General Foods, or any other individual firm. But, it would indicate the number of cars, the number of generators, and the quantity of frozen foods we are likely to require in, say, five years, and it would try to induce the relevant industries to act accordingly." Yes, "the means of influencing" the decisions of industry would include "selective credit controls; guidance of basic capital flows; limits to the use of air, water, and land; and, mandatory resource allocation." However, "selective," "guidance," "limits," and "mandatory" all simply the same outcome: *FORCE!* Government *is* force. It makes people and institutions do things they would not otherwise do.

The morality of it all is obvious, but the intriguing part is the innocent naivety of such ideas of grandeur. What a presumption of knowledge of an unknown future! Imagine, if you will, in 1978 trying to forecast the demand (or supply for that matter) for desktop personal computers in 1984. Why would the U.S. government's estimates be better than IBM's or Apple's? Is it not ironic that the institution of government, which is so notorious in its inability to plan its own affairs, should be asked to centrally plan the most complex economy on the face of the earth. The draft of the Balanced Growth and Economic Planning Act of 1975 itself indicts government for its current practices which fail to deal with the longer term consequences of its own actions. In recent years there have been demands for a "Consumer Protection Agency" in the federal government, and an important part of its responsibility would be to protect Americans from other federal agencies!

Leontief and the others tell us that their planning effort would be perfectly consistent with democratic institutions, that the planning bureaucracy and the "law" would only "induce" actions. There would be no "mandatory resource allocation." What would be the implications, however, when the plans of a business were inconsistent with the great master plan? A warning? A slap? A fine? Or, perhaps jail? Surely individual plans must be subservient to the "national plan."

The Balanced Growth and Economic Planning Act of 1975 proposed a very drastic increase in federal intervention in the American economy. Yet, the larger government bureaucracy to do all this planning has always been unsuccessful in improving on the demonstrated results of the free market system. Witness the terrible consequences of the Mitterand socialist government in France that has sought to nationalize and centrally plan the French economy. In the meanwhile, the Sino-Soviet bloc countries continue to decentralize in recognition of the difficulties associated with the implementation of their central plans.

It is characteristic that the chief sponsor in the United States Senate of the Planning Act, Hubert Humphrey, who boasted that it was his "...single most important piece of legislation...," was quoted as follows: "This is advisory and consultative, and hopefully out of this dialogue and discussion...we will come down to a much more clear and precise understanding of exactly what we are taking about and what we mean." Remember, as Adam Smith observed in the *Wealth of Nations:* "The statesman who should attempt to direct private people in what manner they ought to employ their capitals, would not only load himself with a most unnecessary attention, but assume an authority which would safely be trusted, not only to no single person, but to no council or senate whatever, and which would nowhere be so dangerous as in the hands of a man who had folly and presumption enough to fancy himself fit to exercise it." The same warning is in order for the latest version of centralized planning now appears in the 1980's as the debate on the "new industrial policy" or the question of "reindustrialization."

## FREEDOM AND THE SPONTANEOUS ORDER

The growth of government intervention in the American economy and the associated decline in the vitality of the market economy has proceeded hand-in-hand with the rise of rational constructivism. If a free market economy is to be restored in the United States, we must learn to recognize the severe limitations that exist with respect to creating and designing the ideal social order. Much of the loss of respect for American economic institutions and the recent reduction in productivity gains can be attributed to the uninformed and misguided intervention in the economy by government. Such intervention, of course, is always supported by the unwarranted proposition that government knows best.

We must come to recognize once again the important propositions established by David Hume, Adam Smith, Friedrich Hayek, and others regarding the socially beneficial effects of institutions which have evolved and stood the test of time. There are severe limits to social engineering by government because of the difficulty of collecting useful and important knowledge in a timely and usable form at a central location. But further, the whole process, by definition, must violate the property rights and distort incentives of individuals seeking mutually beneficial, voluntary exchanges through enlightened self-interest. It is important to recognize the socially beneficial implications of a system of spontaneous order, guided far more successfully by the "invisible hand" than most intellectuals would care to admit. Smith's system of natural liberty offers opportunities for individuals to use their knowledge for their own purposes to a far greater extent than any known centrally planned alternative. It is worth remembering that those countries which have opted for centralized plannning are devoid of the most rudimentary civil and human freedoms, like speech, petition, emigration, assembly, and press, let alone contract and property freedoms.

Legislating the particular outcomes ends up treating people unequally before the law. The preservation of individual freedom requires that we reject measures which assist one group at the expense of another. "A successful defense of freedom must," Hayek reminds us, "...be dogmatic and make no concessions to expediency." What is required are general rules of acceptable behavior, and a determination that these rules are not to be violated for temporary advantage or to achieve particular positions for particular individuals.

# CHAPTER 10

## EQUALITY VERSUS FREEDOM

From the fact that people are very different it follows that, if we treat them
equally, the result must be inequality in their actual position, and that the
only way to place them in an equal position would be to treat them differently. Equality before the law and material equality are therefore not
only different but are in conflict with each other; and we can achieve
either the one or the other, but not both at the same time.
                                                    --Friedrich A. Hayek

Those who would construct and plan the good society almost invariably propose to do so in the name of equality. An underlying
theme in the previous chapter on constructivism and utilitarianism
entailed a complementary concern with equality and social engineering. In the following chapters on the modern socialist movement and
the politicization of society the notion of equality of material conditions plays a fundamental role. Therefore, we must deal with the profound conflict which exists between equality of outcome and individual freedom under the rule of law.

In the whole history of mankind probably no idea has been so
carelessly defined, so passionately championed, and so
misrepresented among believers than the idea of equality. Western
civilization must choose between two systems: The system of individual freedom, private property and limited government, and the
system of collectivism which would restrain the individual and
socialize property in the name of "justice" and "equality." An important illustration of the transition from the former to the latter is the
egalitarian movement which began in England in the last decades of
the nineteenth century. The Fabian Society of England was formally
constituted in England in 1884 with the agreed aims of affecting a
gradual transition from capitalism to socialism by parlimentary enactments. The Fabian's name, in fact, came from the ancient Roman
consul Fabian, whose policy during the Second Punic War was one
of wearing down the strength of the enemy by continual
harassments. Ten years after its founding, the Fabian Society became
influential in shaping the programs and policies of the newly founded
Independent Labor Party of England. By 1919 it had become, in effect, an educational arm of the Labor Party, and soon it was on its
way to making and shaping British socialist policy.

Much of the agenda was in the name of inequality, and with the
passage of time ideas, even bad ones, do have consequences. Unfortunately, the ideas of the socialist movement in Great Britain failed to
incorporate a fundamental fact: That the great inventors and industrialists of the previous century, such as Watt, Bolton, and

Archwright, acting through the competitive market process, had done more to rid England of poverty than all previous men of history had accomplished under the paternalistic and totalitarian regimes of the past. The antidote for poverty is increased productivity and production, not welfare and redistribution.

The twentieth century welfare state, in the name of "social justice," labors to reduce inequalities wherever found and with whatever force necessary. Society faces a profound crossroads at which the idea of individual liberty first instilled in the Magna Carta, then the Glorious Revolution of 1688, and finally in the Declaration of Independence is in conflict with the pursuit of equality. Let there be no doubt: there is an irreconcilable conflict between individual autonomy, the freedom to be different *and* the depressing emphasis on equality of condition. This is true not only in material things, but in the intellectual, physical, and psychological differences which exist among individuals.


## THE REDISTRIBUTIVE SOCIETY AND THE APPEAL TO JUSTICE

The notion that material living conditions should be basically the same, that everyone should finish the race at the same time, has, according to many observers, pushed American society beyond the welfare state to the "redistributive society." At one time individuals "gave to government a part of *their* income. Today in the redistributive society individual incomes are supposedly part of a common pool which belongs to society as a whole. As one alert observer has noted: when assigning tax liabilities to individuals, government appears to be deciding *not* how much of the citizen's own income it will take, but how much of society's income the state will allow the individual to keep. Those who display the bumper sticker *Vote Liberal: Ban Take-Home Pay* are sarcastically making this very point.

Equality of outcome, however, is good business for some. Irving Kristol reminds us that there is a "new class" of government bureaucrats, academics, journalists, and other intellectuals carrying the argument for this equality of outcome and condition who stand to benefit directly from their cries for equality. While belonging to income groups with higher than average incomes, these proponents of material equality also stand to gain from increased power and prestige. "Fair shares for all" has replaced Karl Marx's "To each according to his needs, from each according to his ability." Milton and Rose Friedman in *Free to Choose* capture the essential dilemma in this conflict when they recite the words of Dodo in Alice in Wonderland: "Everybody has won, and ALL must have prizes." But Dodo is bombarded from the crowd with a fundamental question: "But who is to give the prizes?"

The "who" will inevitably be government. But where does government get it? Does government create wealth? Can the federal government really create jobs through the CETA "jobs" program when it must tax others to pay for the training? Do we really increase material standards of living over the long run by taxing producers and entrepreneurs and in turn use these funds to, in effect, pay other individuals *not* to work? The Russians and the Chinese swallow this bitter pill daily by attempting the impossible task of prescribing the exact amount of freedom necessary to be creative and to produce. The creativity of the intellectual, the artist, the scientist and the entrepreneur in "equal" societies becomes so thwarted, leaving so few personal incentives, that the normally dignified, industrious and self-reliant human being learns to be a dependent, unproductive and, therefore, parasitical creature.

## ALL MEN ARE CREATED EQUAL

When Thomas Jefferson wrote that "all men are created equal," he obviously meant something quite different than the allegiance to equality of material condition which has come to be so much a part of the twentieth century mindset. Jefferson argued for an equality of liberty, that all men are "...endowed by their Creator with certain unalienable rights." That men were "equal in the eyes of God," that the principle of "equality of rights" and "equality before the law" was "self-evident." But the idea of "economic equality" was inconceivable to Jefferson and to the other founding fathers. As George Mason clearly pointed out in the Virginia Bill of Rights: "...men are created equally free and independent." The founding fathers recognized the manifest and obvious differences in individuals and their capacities for material, intellectual, and artistic success. In fact, equal treatment before the law and the protection of "unalienable rights" was required precisely because of the obvious differences in talent, ability, and drive which existed in any ordinary company of men.

In contrast to the system of political equality through which individual differences are respected and inalienable rights are protected, the "passion for equality" of outcome, in the words of Oliver Wendell Holmes, is "...merely idealizing envy." The current intellectual cry for "social justice," which largely means equality in the distribution of income and wealth, has become a very serious threat to individual liberty. President Franklin Delano Roosevelt, on the subject of social security, said: "We are determined to make every American citizen the subject of his country's interest and concern...The test of our progress is not whether we add more to the abundance of those who have much; it is whether we provide enough for those who have too little." Tocqueville saw clearly the weakness of this argument when he said: "The foremost or indeed sole condition required in order to succeed in centralizing the supreme power in a democratic community, is to love equality or to get men to believe that you love it."

## THE EMPTINESS OF THE PHRASE "SOCIAL JUSTICE"

The question of social or "distributive justice" has been a crucial ingredient in the rapid growth in government and its larger role in our day to day lives. Without doubt the appeal to social justice has now become the most widely used argument in political discussion. Almost every claim for government action is advanced in its name.

Envy or jealousy aside, it is a colossal presumption that we can somehow know what one "deserves." When using "merit" as a measure of one's contribution, as opposed to the values placed on the benefits provided to others through exchange, it requires that one set of individuals can determine what in fact another individual is "worth" and therefore what that person will be allowed to achieve. There is a presumption in all this that some of us (which ones?) can know others better than we even know ourselves. Either we allow the market to decide the economic value of janitors, football players, factory workers, professors, artists, and other professions, or we choose to put this awesome and impossible responsibility in the hands of those presently running the government. This kind of government power, history tells us, has inevitably meant the loss of economic freedoms first and then the gradual erosion of our other cherished political, religious, and personal freedoms.

Equality, therefore, perceived as a distributively just pattern of income shares, cannot be objectively discovered nor can anything claiming to be "social justice" be pursued without bringing to bear the coercive and potentially violent force of government. Equality of outcome is, in fact, an empty phrase, as Friedrich Hayek has noted:

> The complete emptiness of the phrase 'social justice' shows itself in the fact that no agreement exists about what social justice requires in particular instances; also that there is no known test by which to decide who is right if people differ; and that no preconceived scheme of distribution could be effectively devised in a society whose members are free, in the sense of being allowed to use their own knowledge for their own purposes. Indeed, individual moral responsibility for one's actions is incompatible with the realization of any such desired overall pattern of distribution.

Without universally accepted methods of discovering the appropriate degree of equality in things--criteria that we would *all* agree to, "economic equality" is objectively incapable of being discovered. It is a problem very much analogous to obtaining agreement on the relative merits of pianists, flutists or rock groups. It is simply impossible.

## EQUALITY OF OUTCOME AND GOVERNMENT FORCE

It is inevitable that the force of government will be required to implement what some, those in power, deem to be "socially just" changes in income shares. The effort to legislate equality, to mandate relative material conditions upon a large heterogeneous population, inevitably means greater and greater infusions of government power. It starts with the utopian vision of Plato and eventually ends up with the secret police.

The fundamental dilemma is that there is no way in which Harvard philospher Robert Nozick's description of an "end-state principle" of distributive justice, where particular shares are assigned in an attempt to achieve equality of income and/or wealth, can be maintained unless government continuously rearranges shares. In order to maintain a particular *pattern,* the voluntary exchange of income for goods and services will of necessity have to be constrained. For example, if individuals continue to pay to see Moses Malone, Fernando Valenzuela, Barbra Striesand, Luciano Pavarotti, and the Beach Boys, government will be required to continuously intervene, taking from some people and giving to others. The police power of the state would necessarily have to be brought to bear "...to forbid capitalist acts between consenting adults."

The problem is an ethical one. Is it consistent with a moral order that men be subjected to the police powers of the state to achieve social equality? And, what if the people don't want it? "Isn't it interesting," says Robert Nisbet, the internationally recognized sociologist and professor in the humanities at Columbia University, that even with the teachers in our "free" public schools constantly bombarding America's youth with the egalitarian views of left intellectuals "...the people still cannot be counted on to adore equality as the first of the social virtues."

Christopher Jencks, one of the high priests of equality, is concerned that "...the crucial problem today is that relatively few people view income inequality as a serious problem." Therefore, in the chapter entitled "What Is To Be Done?" from his book *Inequality,* he suggests "...we will not only have to politicize the question of income inequality, but alter people's basic assumptions about the extent to which they are responsible for their neighbors and their neighbors for them." Rousseau, history's greatest defender of equality according to Robert Nisbet, states that the family must be sacrificed, if necessary, in order for the very young to be separated from "...the intelligence and prejudices of fathers (so that they might be)...early accustomed to regard their own individuality only in its relation to the body of the state, to be aware, so to speak, of their own existence merely as part of that of the state." There are apparently no limits to the force and violence which may be applied in the name of equality, irrespective of the underlying differences which obviously exist among people. In fact, the left-intellectual philosopher Ronald Dworkin is prepared to argue that "...a more equal society is a better society even if its citizens prefer inequality."

In addition, the complaints regarding existing inequalities of income, which have so often been followed by inequalities in political power, have in turn contributed importantly to the large increase in government's role in economic affairs. Government is called upon to distribute "differential benefits," and the state, therefore, becomes an important prize worth capturing. Groups of individuals who control the apparatus of the state tend obviously to make use of that power for their own ends. Power attracts, and what could be more attractive and exciting than using the coercive arm of government to force the world into the mold you most desire. Compounding this problem is the additional proposition that policies designed to equalize economic conditions, or patterned principles of distributive justice, involve appropriating the actions of other persons. The propositions of self-ownership and private property proposed by Locke, Sydney, Gordon, and the founding fathers are suddenly reinterpreted to mean that individuals have property rights in *other people*. We agree with philosopher Robert Nozick, therefore, that redistributive efforts by government force "...are not achievable by any morally permissible available means."

All attempts at making "social" or "distributive justice" the primary goal of social organization, wherever found, have resulted in a reign of terror and bloodshed. There is an irreconcilable conflict between individual liberty and the goal of equal shares. The Soviet Union, the People's Republic of China, and Cambodia are all witness to the violence which necessarily accompanies government imposed actions to achieve equality of outcome. Hayek in his *Law, Legislation and Liberty* poses the ultimate question: "Whether it is possible to preserve a market order while imposing upon it (in the name of 'social justice' or any other pretext) some pattern of remuneration based on the assessment of the performance or the needs of different individuals or groups by an authority possessing the power to enforce it." Hayek's analysis of this fundamental issue is crucial:

> The great problem is whether this new demand for equality does not conflict with the equality of the rules of conduct which government must enforce on all in a free society...Since people will differ in many attributes which government cannot alter, to secure for them the same material position would require that government treat them differently...Strict equality of those benefits which government could provide for all on the other hand, would clearly lead to inequality of the material positions...While an equality of rights under a limited government is possible and an essential condition of individual freedom, a claim for

equality of material position can be met only by a government with totalitarian powers.

## INDIVIDUAL RIGHTS, VOLUNTARY EXCHANGE, AND JUSTICE

Not only does the striving for distributive justice generate totalitarian solutions, but there are other implications of equality of condition which lead to negative consequences. The claim that individuals have *rights* to particular things (to a job, to "free" medical care, to a "decent" standard of living) necessarily requires that other individuals be prepared (i.e., forced) to relinquish "entitlements" to such things and to other property rights. Or, in other words, individuals claim to have rights over other individuals. What are the conditions under which the rights of some individuals to particular things are to be sacrificed in order to satisfy the claims of those with "needs" and "rights" to particular outcomes? In a truly *free* society of private and protected property rights, the only "rights" one can morally enforce are those inalienable rights to an equal protection of the laws that apply uniformly to all individuals. The "rights" to adequate housing, a job, a minimum income, and all the rest must be acquired by enlisting the voluntary cooperation of our fellow man. Force and theft, even when justified by majorities, are inconsistent with a moral order. What kind of society is it, we ask, that would force people to do good? Is it really humanitarian, let alone just, to rob one neighbor to feed another known to be hungry?

We would all like a world of wine and roses; where individuals were uniformly good to each other. But economic charity, to be truly charitable, must possess at least the following characteristics: to give something to another it must first be mine to give; without clear title of ownership the gift becomes merely the transfer of stolen property. Further, the transfer must be voluntary. Acts that require obligations are not charitable, but rather enslaving. Beneficience through enslavement inevitably produces dependence and permanent obligation. It is only sham charity which allows the giver to breastbeat and the receiver to become indebted. Yet inevitably, the mass programs of social dependency and socialized "charity" produce this very result. Again, we emphasize that the whole process necessitates government force by continuously applied.

## INEQUALITY, INCENTIVES, AND STANDARDS OF LIVING

While Smith, Hayek, Nozick, and many others recognize the immorality of violating legitimate claims to property justifiably acquired, the drive to equality of outcome in the twentieth century has an even more practical adverse implication. Those who place equality of condition as their highest value apparently are unaware, or possibly do not care, that the distribution of income and wealth under a private property, market economy creates a structure of economic incentives which encourage greater productivity and stimulate economic growth and progress. As a result of such growth, history suggests that everyone benefits, though not necessarily to the same extent. Those who march to the tune of equality, however, ignore this important fact. The incentives of the market system work so well because they do indeed produce differential returns for different efforts. And, the benefits of a voluntary exchange economy accrue to us all. Wealth of any kind to be enjoyed must first be produced. Entrepreneurship and risk taking, savings, and investment are the only real ways of producing wealth.

In fact, our high income levels in the United States depend on the inequalities in shares. All humans dream. We would wish that everyone had everything. Not only is it a distinguishing mark of our individuality but it evidences the compassionate and humanitarian side of our beings. But dreamwishes should be recognized for what they are: fanciful thought divorced from reasonable expectations. There is a world of difference, afterall, between probability and outright impossibility. If such distinctions are not made, a utopian's dream becomes madness, a world of phantasmagoria. A society suffused with unreasonable expectations, that confuses words with deeds, making sincerity more important than actual outcomes, is terribly imperilled. The rhetoric of equality, of equal distributions, makes wonderful slogans: "Nothing is impossible for a government that wants the good of its citizens," noted FDR at a fireside chat. But chats don't produce wealth, nor do good intentions, and certainly neither does government. The philosopher Erick Mack summarrizes the nature of the incentives issue:

> A false assumption underlies all these equality theories of justice. The theorists assume that the economic goods are just there, that wealth is like manna from heaven. And now these theories claim that the state has the right to decide who gets what and whose favorite pattern will be carved out of these miraculously appearing goods. Manipulative theories of this sort assume that how or why the goods exist makes no difference as to who is entitled to them.

The creation of wealth and therefore economic progress is not random in its occurence. The physical, physchological and mental acumen of individuals are so diversely endowed, their health, strength, and abilities so unalike, that to argue otherwise is absurd. Further, the specialized skills needed in an advancing industrial nation further insures that some will be more valued than others. Entrepreneurs, individuals prepared to take risks in the use of their time, ideas and capital, and in anticipation of differential economic gain, produce goods and services in accordance with the wishes of the consumer in a market economy. Some are successful, many are not.

111

But with economic growth all of us benefit, although admittedly to different degrees. Those who demand a reduction in the inequality of outcomes not only threaten the survival of the goose which lays such golden eggs, but in addition make the highly questionable claim that they are entitled to await the outcome of the entrepreneurial game before claiming their "fair share."

Human nature's weakness has and always will be the belief that something can be had for nothing. Governmental propagandists and economically illiterate commentators, by condemning the rich, are really laying the foundation for economic decline, even tragedy. Is there any doubt that the consequences of equality of outcome would be reduced personal freedoms, warped incentives, the decline of production and entrepreneurship, and fewer goods and jobs? Robert Nozick sees the inconsistency quite clearly:

> Often people who do not wish to bear risks feel entitled to rewards from those who do and win; yet these same people do not feel obligated to help out by sharing the losses of those who bear risks and lose...The case for such asymmetrical sharing is even weaker for businesses where success is not a random matter. Why do some feel they may stand back to see whose ventures turn out well (by hindsight determine who has survived the risks and run profitably) and then claim a share of the success; though they do not feel they must bear the losses if things turn out poorly, or feel that if they wish to share in the profits or the control of the enterprise, they should invest and run risks also?

Where are the altruists, public do gooders and people willing to use their *own* money to soothe the misfortunes of Braniff Airlines, International Harvester, Osborne Computer, and the thousands of other businesses which either fail or are on the verge of failing? "Why," the philosopher Tibor Machan asks simply and to the point, "is it that the intellectual left is so hell-bent on believing that it is more important to make it difficult for the rich than to actually make it better for the poor?"

There is the story of a man being exposed for the first time to the Niagra Falls and when asked as to whether he was impressed, his answer was "I'd be more impressed if the water ran the other way." It would be impressive indeed if we could all live finely and contented without the entrepreneurial risk taker who sometimes becomes rich. But history indicates that it cannot be done. Without these special individuals, capital expansion would lag, savings would fall, and the economic pie would fail to grow. Yet we continue the relentless drive to extinguish differential economic rewards in the name of equality! Envy undoubtedly plays an important role in this dogmatic push for equality in material things. Nevertheless, the way to help those with less is not to waste time, energy, and capital in wresting the fruits of labor from the rich, but rather it is to create an environment of freedom and opportunity from which the poor can most benefit. What doctor would make the well sick in order to make the sick well? It is truly a mystery why the concern with distributive justice is so recipient oriented and, therefore, unconcerned with the property rights of producers who make it all possible.

## GOVERNMENT WELFARE AND THE POOR

The great irony in all this, however, is that in spite of an incredible increase in government spending on behalf, supposedly, of the poor (hundreds and hundreds of billions of dollars in the post-World War II period in the United States) almost all studies suggest that the net benefits to the poor *as a whole,* after taxes, are relatively meager. Both proponents of competitive capitalism and the radical advocates of socialism have been in basic agreement that after throwing all this money at poverty, the poor have probably not benefited significantly. These perverse results of spending for the poor were observed long ago by Sir G. Nicholl in his *History of the English Poor Law* in which he observed: "We find, on the one hand, that there is scarcely one statute connected with the administration of public relief which has produced the effect designed by the legislature, and that the majority of them have created new evils and aggravated those which they were intended to prevent."

The figures are always startling. Between 1934 and 1976, for example, total social welfare spending in the U.S. increased from $13.7 billion to $284.2 billion per year, yet during that same time period the number of Americans on welfare increased from less than one million to 11.2 million people. During the period 1960 through 1971, while the population of New York City was actually stable or declining, the number on welfare in the City, with massive amounts of money being devoted to poverty, actually increased from 330,000 to 1.2 million.

In recent years, federal, state, and local government budgets indicate that to "fight poverty" nearly $400 billion is being spent annually. Many economists and other interested observers have noted that if we just divide that level of expenditure among those officially declared to be below the poverty line, each poor family of four would receive an annual income in excess of $34,00. Unfortunately, the greater part of these welfare expenditures never reach the poor, but rather are eaten up by the welfare bureaucracy and the middle and upper income classes which build the subsidized housing and produce the goods supposedly destined for the poor.

The massive amounts of money which are transferred by the political means turn out to be mostly transfers within the middle class and not from rich to poor. The "welfare" payments drift towards those in the community who know how to use the political process and are taken from those who are not politically powerful. Thomas Sowell, the brilliant author/economist, has commented: "My theory of how to get rid of poverty is to hold a meeting of all the leading experts on poverty somewhere in the middle of the Pacific Ocean and not let them go home for ten years. When they come back, they would discover there was no more poverty."

As a whole, the tax system in the United States assigns tax burdens roughly in proportion to incomes, except at the higher income levels where higher average tax burdens are borne. This result is observed in spite of the highly progressive rate structure in the federal personal income tax. On the other hand, in large part because of the ineffectiveness of the truly poor in championing their cause, government expenditures go mostly to subsidize the middle class and above. While the empirical studies which attempt to sort this thorny issue out are both difficult reading and subject to alternative interpretations (See for example the study by Henry Aaron and Martin McGuire in *Econometrica*), it is quite likely that the overall impact of government spending and taxing involves a net transfer of wealth to higher income groups and away from the *least* well off.

It all started so simply with noble intentions: take from those that have and give to those that don't. Progressive tax laws were formulated to do just that. But special interest groups, seeing Washington, D.C., as the seat of economic power, sought special legislation to modify outcomes. Farmers got their price supports. The oil industry needed its double depreciation. Realtors needed subsidized interest rates. Cities got their tax-free bonds. Or more specifically, legislators and governments responded to special interest group politics. The merchant marine, the tobacco growers, the military-industrial complex, the dairy lobby, the physicians, Chrysler Corporation--these are the groups with the time, money, and expertise required to obtain government favors. Legislators are themselves political entrepreneurs: "Their palms are soft, their grip lacks clout, yet they win votes with each hand out." The system is skewed in favor of the wealthy, the organized, the influential. But the poor have none of these prerequisites. So, in the name of equality, we provide through the political means massive subsidies, tax breaks, and other largess to those already successful. With friends like these, the poor don't need enemies.

## THE MAINSPRING OF HUMAN PROGRESS ONCE AGAIN

A system of equality of rights in liberty based on the private ownership of the means of production, differential economic rewards to generate wealth producing incentives, and the system of competitive capitalism have always served the poor. The important and relevant question can be stated as follows: historically, has the market means dealt more effectively with poverty than government's coercive transfer of wealth? The answer is unequivocally *YES*. It was upward economic mobility, after all, and not government handouts that represented the driving force behind the efforts of individuals to better themselves. And, stable and secure property rights in combination with entrepreneurial activity--core attributes of capitalism--fundamentally changed the prospects for mankind to eliminate poverty. But unfortunately, the politicization of an economy lends legal credibility to violating property rights, thereby cutting off upward mobility and even throttling any remaining private concern for the poor.

We know that rapid economic growth increases labor productivity and that even the most menial occupation tends to share in this newly produced wealth. Isabel Patterson urges us to remember that ''...if the full role of sincere philanthropists were called, from the beginning of time, it would be found that all of them together by their strictly philanthropic activities have never conferred upon humanity one-tenth of the benefit derived from the normally self-interested efforts of Thomas Alva Edison, to say nothing of the greater minds who worked out the scientific principles which Edison applied.''

An increase in the rate of growth in real output of one percent per year would raise living standards for the poorest by much more than any amount that government redistribution might provide. The answer to the poverty problem is faster growth and rising productivity in general. For example, a barber "produces" a haircut in the same manner his predecessors used two hundred years ago, yet the barber is far better off today. Their wages are higher because wages are determined by the overall productivity of labor. We pay the barber a price which keeps this person from taking employment in a factory, a brewery, a bakery, or a construction company. We must pay the barber to not accept his or her next best alternative employment opportunity. Productivity is in turn a function of education, experience, work effort, saving, investment in modern plant and equipment, and innovation and entrepreneurial alertness to new opportunities of serving consumers.

The benefits of rising productivity do not accrue to just those already at the top. In spite of the degree of government intervention in the economy and the existing tax burdens, there continues to be a significant vertical movement of individuals into higher income groups. The movements are in fact in both directions. Bradley R. Schiller has summarized the results of his study of this matter:

> The American economy is characterized by a very high degree of individual income mobility. Specifically, individuals move significant distances up and down the earnings distribution, implying tremendous mobility of relative economic status. The rigid shape of the aggregate income distribution is a misleading index of opportunity stratification because it camouflages a great deal of individual mobility between the separate points of that distribution. The inequalities observed at any particular time are reduced over time as individuals exchange relative economic position.

One very simple reform to further encourage upward economic mobility would be to repeal legislation which prevents or discourages mutually beneficial exchange. These include minimum wage laws, occupational licensing, anti-peddler statutes, tariffs, interest rate ceilings, price floors, and many other laws which have had the effect of cutting the bottom rungs from the economic ladder. Economists Walter Williams in *The State Against The Blacks* and Thomas Sowell in *Markets And Minorities* have carefully documented the adverse consequences of minimum wage and licensing statutes to entry level employment, especially for blacks and minorities.

But what of the truly needy, the incapacitated, the lame? A restored system of competitive capitalism would undoubtedly generate more rapid productivity gains, but would this rising "surplus" go to the poor and involuntarily unemployed? In recent years, Americans, in spite of the existing tax burdens, have donated more than $30 billion per year to charity. Even before high tax rates, earlier in this century, voluntary charity in the United States was very large. Assuming that with a robust and healthy economy there still would be 6 million poor in need of assistance, even this level of giving would represent a potential payment of about $5,000 for every poor individual in the nation. With federal and state tax burdens substantially lower  as a result of a significant decline in the politically coerced "charity" and the privatization services currently performed by government, we believe private charity, through some of the older "intermediate institutions," such as churches and other private organizations, would be restored to their place of honor in a civilized society. A significant indirect benefit would be that the middleman in the existing network of "poverty programs," namely the massive government bureaucracy, would be largely eliminated. The charitable aid would then mostly go directly to the truly needy. Moral choices would once again be made from a position of freedom of choice.

## ENVY, EQUALITY, AND LIBERTY

Why is it that in the politicized society, in spite of the massive increase in poverty programs, there appears to have been little progress in the achievement of human happiness? Irving Kristol has commented on the irony of all this:

> Somehow, the fact that more poor people are on welfare, receiving more generous payments, does not seem to have made this country a nice place to live--not even for the poor on welfare, whose condition seems not noticeably better than when they were poor and off welfare. Something appears to have gone wrong; a liberal and compassionate social policy has bred all sorts of unanticipated and perverse consequences.

It seems, the sociologist Robert Nisbet points out, that "...on the evidence, it is not monetary differentiation--much as equalitarians like to dwell upon it--that galls and occasionally humiliates; it is rather the type of differentiation that comes from unequal intellectual and moral strengths, unequal applications of resolve and aspiration, and unequal benefactions of luck." If we do away with differentials in economic conditions, something else will replace the material differences in the minds of the envious and those who would somehow equalize personal self-esteem. In fact, it is quite clear that with each additional attempt to pursue equality of outcome the level of dissatisfaction in society has risen. It has become obvious that "fair share" is incapable of being operationally defined, and, as Hayek insists, the concept of "...social justice is entirely empty and meaningless."

There is, however, a profound and meaningful sense of equality which is essential to a free society. There is, Robert Nisbet tells us, "...a large and historically indispensable sphere of liberty--that relating to the pragmatic capacity of individuals and groups to express their essence, to fulfill chosen objectives, to initiate, to create, and to do--in which the thought of equal shares is plainly absurd." It is the liberty of the founding fathers, which was to share equally in the protection of the laws, but incapable of being divided into specific shares of material or spiritual well-being. We believe, along with Hayek, that "...if the differences," in initiative, creativity, and motivation among individuals, "are not very important, then freedom is not very important and the idea of individual worth is not very important."

The level of dissatisfaction in society has risen. Furthermore, we have seen how the envious desire for equality leads to attitudes of hating those who have achieved a preferred material outcome. The mentality is: never admit that another's success has anything to do with hard work, risk taking, and personal abilities. Rather it should be attributed to luck, exploitation, or some other coincidence. Personal weaknesses, moral failings, laziness, or a mistaken decision, unfortunately, are influences rarely examined. To ignore the characteristics of personal responsibility means we risk the failure of both individual and cultural resolve. Freedom is a delicate flower which requires constant attention for its survival.

When examined for actual outcomes, equality of result looms as synonymous with the worst of all possible worlds. The idea could be a measure of our senility, indeed a barometer registering our decline. Nothing is quite so alien to creativity, genius, and production as is a mathematical envy that measures distances from one person to the other. Equality in fact is an emphereal dream. Although utopians will continue their hallucinations, we believe that freedom and equality are eternal enemies. One cannot prevail without the destruction of the other. Whenever inequality is checked, freedom dies. When freedom lives, inequality of material condition prevails. The funda-

117

mental contradiction between equality of liberty and economic equality is poignantly summarized by Friedrich Hayek in his magnificent book *Constitution of Liberty*:

> (The)...problem is whether it is desirable that people should enjoy advantages in proportion to the benefits which their fellows derive from their activities OR whether the distribution of these advantages should be based on other men's views of their merits.

## EQUALITY BEFORE THE LAW AND INALIENABLE RIGHTS

Justice in a free society requires generally applicable "rules of conduct" which necessarily generate inequalities in income and wealth. But in the system of natural liberty there should not be rules which try to define anyone's material position. Inalienable rights and equality before the law--yes. "Rights" to equal incomes--*no!* If individuals, more fortunately situated, wish on moral grounds to assume additional charitable responsibilities for the disadvantaged, that is their right. But charity should not be determined by the *force* of law. Adam Smith, justifiably famous for his monumental work, *The Wealth of Nations*, in which he emphasized enlightened self-interest, also wrote another book in which the notion of "sympathy" and fellow-feeling towards other individuals was highlighted. The issues of freedom and equality, and our views about where we must stand, are summarized in this important passage from Smith's *The Theory of Moral Sentiments:*

> And upon this is founded that remarkable distinction between justice and all the other social virtues...that we feel ourselves to be under a stricter obligation to act according to justice, than agreeably to friendship, charity, or generosity; that the practice of these last-mentioned virtues seems to be left in some measure to our own choice. We feel, that is to say, that force may, with the utmost propriety, and with the approbation of all mankind be made use of to constrain us to observe the rules of the one, but not to follow the precepts of the other.

In other words, government may use force to preserve inalienable rights to equal protection of the law--governments are, according to the Declaration of Independence, instituted to preserve these rights; but the force of government may not be used for the purpose of making men generous or fellow-feeling.

# CHAPTER 11

## SOCIALISM AND THE STATE

What history will think of our times is something that only history will reveal. But, it is a good guess that it will select collectivism as the identifying characteristic of the twentieth century...that society is a transcendent entity, something apart and greater than the sum of its parts, possessing a superhuman character and endowed with like capacities...It follows, therefore, that society, which may concern itself paternalistically with individuals, is in no way dependent on them.

--Frank Chodorov

Near the end of the nineteenth century the eminent British statesman Sir William Harcourt professed that "...we are all socialists now." At that time there was already a degree of truth to this viewpoint in England, Germany, and other parts of Europe, but in the United States of America it was surely not the case. Today, as the twentieth century comes to a close, most countries in the world can indeed be characterized as socialist in orientation, and the United States continues to move in that direction. Michael Novak has reminded us that: "Socialism is no longer a dream or a vision to be found only in books; some fourscore or more nations have built themselves firmly upon its deals. One can now, as one could not thirty years ago, study socialism as it actually functions in actual experience and practice. The results do not accord with expectations."

Whether defined to be the public ownership of the means of production, or alternatively, and probably more realistically, control over the *results* of production, a large majority of the world's people live in societies devoted to the principles of socialism. The predominant world paradigm is authoritarian control over people's lives and their economic affairs. In America the transformation of the law since the time of the Constitution, the call for rationalist revisions in institutions predicated on the desire to create and construct the good society, and the emotional appeal to the need for equality of material condition, have all been heavily influenced by the writings of those intellectuals who have championed socialism as the solution to human problems.

The system of competitive capitalism, say the collectivists, is an immoral system of exploitation and guarantees undesirable consequences for the bulk of the population (the "proletariat"). Greater misery and falling living standards are inevitable. Socialism, on the other hand, would produce an unlimited bounty of material things and everlasting happiness for everybody. Unfortunately for these contentions, even a hurried and fairly casual look at the real world-- countries like Cambodia, East Germany, Poland, Cuba, and the Soviet Union--suggests a totally different picture. One of the great champions of personal liberty and economic freedom, Ludwig von Mises, captured the full measure of the contradictions which have always been part and parcel of the socialist faith:

> The champions of socialism call themselves progressives, but they recommend a system which is characterized by rigid observance of routine and by a resistance to every kind of improvement. They call themselves liberals, but they are intent upon abolishing liberty. They call themselves democrats, but they yearn for dictatorship. They call themselves revolutionaries, but they want to make the government omnipotent. They promise the blessings of the Garden of Eden, but they plan to transform the world into a gigantic post office.

Following the analysis of scholars like Mises and Joseph Schumpeter, we strive to capture the flavor of both the intellectual defense and factual character of socialism. A movement which, through collectivist solutions to human problems, threatens to terminate the great American experiment of 1776. The evolutionary change in the intellectual climate is investigated, from a time when the founding fathers believed government should be given a minimum number of responsibilities, but then must be watched very closely that it not expand beyond those limits. However intentioned, government evolved from its limited role to where it is now supposedly endowed with omniscient and omnipotent powers to provide unlimited benefits, subsidies, protection, and other favors. In spite of the obvious fact that government can provide benefits only when it taxes or constrains others, socialism in its many variations currently commands the active or implicit support of the great majority of the world's intellectual community. How and why should this be, when, in our view, it is manifestly impossible for the institution of government to simultaneously improve the living standards of everybody. In order to explain the decline and fall of the free market, private property system, we must first attempt an explanation of the socialist dream.

## THE SOCIALIST ARGUMENT

A measure of the harsh brief against capitalism by the advocates of socialism can be found in the rather strong conclusion reached by Samuel Bowles and Herbert Gintis in their book *Schooling In Capitalist America:* "We venture to suggest that *all* of the glaring inadequacies of political democracy in the United States are attributable to the private ownership of the means of production and the lack of a real economic democracy" (emphasis added). The popularity of this collectivist case against capitalism by the intellectual comunity has produced great numbers of "secondhand dealers in ideas" who market the socialist product with great passion. Supported by the religious importance of their mission, a crossroads has

120

been reached where it is uncertain whether the institution of private property and, therefore, human freedom will survive into the twenty-first century.

The appeal of socialism has been rationalized by a combination of factors which we have already discussed. First, a "moral absolute" is assumed which provides that the fundamental role of government policy should be equality of material condition as opposed to the administration of justice under the rule of law. Yet, the meaning of equality is at its root metaphysical, utopian, and, as discussed earlier, in mortal conflict with freedom.

Second, and also previously noted, a "false analogy" presumes that we can engineer a social order according to a predetermined plan like those in the physical sciences where professionals engineer a bridge or high-rise office building. Third, following the preoccupation with equality, the proponents of collectivist solutions to individual problems perpetuate the myth that the successes of capitalism have come at the expense of the working class and the poor. However, this is an essentially incorrect description of changes in living standards during the Industrial Revolution, a point already made.

And finally, there is the influential contribution to the socialist movement by Karl Marx: The notion of a historical inevitability of a socialist order which can be discovered from the study of history. In combination, these are the assumptions and misconceptions which have resulted in the massive politicization of society in this century. As one famous British historian noted: "Until August, 1914, a sensible law-abiding Englishman could pass through life and hardly notice the existence of the state, beyond the post office and the policeman." That is obviously no longer an accurate description of the American scene, let alone the state of affairs in Great Britain. The State has, in fact, not withered away as Marx told us it would. Indeed, those nations committed to communism find that the most elementary personal rights of free speech, freedom of the press, and the right of assembly are non-existent.

## SOCIALISM BEFORE KARL MARX

Advocates of socialism, such as Plato and Sir Thomas More, have always existed. However, the "father of the modern socialist movement, according to many observers, was the French nobleman Comte Henri de Saint-Simon, who made his mark in the early nineteenth century. His immediate followers forged the underlying intellectual defense of public ownership of property and asserted the exploitation of labor arising from the institution of private property. Both Karl Marx and Friedrich Engels, the founders of communism, held the name of Saint-Simon in high esteem. There is some irony in this, for Saint-Simon's complex system of views were in many ways

121

consistent with the open-market, limited government ("classical liberal") order described by Adam Smith in Great Britain and J. B. Say in France. Both of these defenders of human liberty were quoted by Saint-Simon with explicit approval. There is a subtle distinction between the "...other principle of respect for property and proprietors," according to Saint-Simon. While we believe this to be an inappropriate distinction, there is still a recognition and important utilitarian respect by Saint-Simon for the socially beneficial results of the increase in material well-being which would surely follow from secure property and the efforts of entrepreneurial producers. This had of course been an important lesson learned by the Soviet bloc countries in recent years.

Unfortunately, Saint-Simon argued that government was required to administer things, even govern men directly: "Under the new system the aim must be to combine all the forces of society in such a fashion as to secure the successful execution of all those works which tend to improve the lot of its members either morally or physically." The followers of Saint-Simon, the Saint-Simonians, including August Comte and B. A. Enfantin, attached an even more radical view to the role of government. According to one follower: "Far from admitting that the direct control of government in social matters ought to be restricted, we believe that it ought to be extended until it includes every kind of social activity." Engels wrote that this was the most important doctrine, as interpreted by his followers, which Saint-Simon ever proposed.

In 1829 the Saint-Simonians published *Expostion de la Doctrine de Saint-Simon* (largely the work of St. A. Bazard) which, according to the French economic historians Charles Gide and Charles Rist, represented a very important exposition of modern socialism. Following the so-called labor theory of value--the proposition that all value (or cost) stems from labor, the Saint-Simonians insisted that the institution of private property guarantees that the worker is forced to share the fruits of his labor. The capitalist owns the machinery of production, resulting in the payment of interest and rent (although Saint-Simon himself had justified these payments), and therefore the necessary "exploitation of one man by another" takes place. What should belong to the worker is stolen by the capitalist property owner. Interestingly enough, the entrepreneur who directs production is also exploited through the interest which he pays to the capitalist who supplies the funds. Profit for the Saint-Simonians is not the result of exploitation but represents the justified reward to entrepreneurship.

This view of exploitation represents both an early and important example of a misguided view regarding the value of time and ignores the payment (interest) necessary if capital is to be allocated to its most productive uses. David Ricardo's labor theory of value is almost universally rejected by economists today. Even the Soviets have recognized, Marx to the contrary notwithstanding, the importance of attaching an interest rate to the time value of money for the efficient allocation of capital. Nevertheless, bad ideas often die slowly.

It is difficult to overstate the importance to the collectivist movement of the Saint-Simonian statement of exploitation by the capitalist of the working class. Karl Marx adopted a variation on the same theme, and concluded that both interest and profit were in the nature of theft. In his *Das Capital,* labor is the source of all value. This proposition is demonstrably false and without intellectual merit as a general theory of value. Value is in fact a subjective matter which is registered by individuals when they make choices regarding production and consumption, and not something to be measured by man-hours of labor. An artist, for example, might paint a number of pictures that sell for less than $100 each. But time and changing tastes could one day find the paintings selling for $2,000 each. Same artist. Same paint. Same number of hours of labor. But the value has changed because people's subjective valuations have changed. The whole process has little if anything to do with the "man hours of labor."

There are other problems with private property according to the Saint-Simonians. They argue that the roles of exploiter and exploited rarely are reversed because of the right of inheritance under capitalism. Inheritance of property is not only ethically wrong, from their point of view, but also means that capital will not be placed in the most capable hands. Hence, they argue that the means of production should be in the hands of government, a questionable conclusion at best. From this view comes the utilitarian argument (as opposed to the equity argument) against all private property and inheritance.

According to the Saint-Simonians: "The law of progress as we have outlined it would tend to establish an order of things in which the state, and not the family, would inherit all accumulated wealth and every other form of what economists call the funds of production." One problem with this view is that it presumes that capital acquired by the accident of birth will long remain in the hands of the lazy or dull. The complaint by the Saint-Simonians is that "...each individual devotes all his attention to his own immediate dependents. No general view of production is ever taken." Here we have a precursor to the arguments in the twentieth century for central economic planning. But as we have already noted, this kind of planning requires a degree of centralized knowledge of particular circumstances which is unattainable by ordinary men and has shown little if any success in the real world experiments in centrally planned socialist or fascist nations.

In summary, the Saint-Simonians, in the *Doctrine de Saint-Simon,* provide a clear statement of their commitment to the state ownership of property, a point of view which is shared by all modern socialist movements. The Saint-Simonian St. A. Bazard summarized their position on the question of private property rights:

> The general opinion seems to be that whatever revolutions may take place in society, this institution of private property must forever remain sacred and involable; it alone is from eternity unto eternity. In reality nothing could be less correct. Property is a social fact which, along with other social facts, must submit to the laws of progress. Accordingly, it may be extended, curtailed, or regulated in various ways at different times.

This statement surely offers no security in the protection and enforcement of property rights. There are important questions which we are entitled to ask regarding this view. By whom and how are we to extend or curtail property rights? Is it indeed true that property rights exist only through the courtesy of society? John Locke thought that there are in fact natural rights to property which supercede societal courtesies. Governments were to be insituted among men to protect those rights.

Whatever the answers to these questions, the followers of Saint-Simon can indeed be identified as the founding fathers of the modern socialist movement. Views quite similar to those briefly repeated here continue to hold the attention and admiration of most intellectuals.

## THE UTOPIAN CHARACTER OF SOCIALISM

Socialist doctrine invariably contains a good deal of utopianism. Unfortunately, this utopian bent fails to correspond with what we know about human nature and the factors which motivate individuals to pursue their own enlightened self-interest. We find it interesting that Karl Marx appealed (and appeals) to the educated and refined classes in society, but seldom to the masses. In any case, this utopian view fails to consider the undeniable propositon that the state does not have the intelligence or the ability to discharge the responsibilities which government would be asked to perform.

Before turning to the influence of Karl Marx and his followers on the socialist movement, we will briefly examine a group known as the "utopian socialists," sometimes called the "associated socialists." Convinced that a tendency to monopoly was the inevitable result of the forces of competition and possessing an accompanying distaste for profits, they proposed a system of voluntary, communal arrangements that would lead to equality. Equal rewards for labor hours would be the essential characteristic of their collectivist economic system. These nineteenth century proponents of socialism included the famous, like Robert Owen, and those who, though less famous, would be persuasive defenders of the new order, like Charles Fourier and William Thompson.

Robert Owen, a rich and successful English manufacturer, argued and published his defense of an "associative socialism" during the period 1813-1858. Owen, who was the first person to use the word socialism in the title of a book, in his *What is Socialism?* in 1841, was very fearful of the phenomenon of competition and its presumed outcome: business combinations and monopoly. His answer to this "problem" was voluntary associations in cooperative ventures which would eliminate the undesirable consequences of competition. Ultimately, a new social milieu would be created if the environment could be changed. He believed that it might be necessary that a "good despot" be selected to bring this new socialist order into existence. Force might be necessary to rid the world of evil profit--the driving force of this assumed system of monopoly power. Remember that one of the central tendencies of human beings is to "buy low and sell high." Seeking their own personal satisfaction and well-being, individuals want to strike the best deal they can. Interestingly, the result of such action is beneficial to everyone. Wealth is not fixed, but rather created. All parties benefit from a voluntary exchange and the creation of new wealth. This important proposition is repeated in order to contrast it with the utopian fear of profit and the zero-sum game mentality of if you win, I lose. It's just not so.

Like the Saint-Simonians, Owen believed that the source of all value was labor. He advocated a system of payment according to work hours rather than ability, capacity, or consumer preference, and furthermore favored absolute equality in the distribution of income. Owen's preference for equality of material condition followed from his belief in the labor theory of value and a deterministic belief in the supreme role of environment in determining outcomes. He dismissed entirely the notion of individual responsibility. Unfortunately Owen, and the Saint-Simonians before him, accepted the idea that an objective and absolute measure of value could be found. There are still those who cling to this false notion. It would be interesting to see how many people would show up at the stadium to watch the peanut vendor throw bags of peanuts to the outreached hands of customers rather than to see famous quarterbacks tossing footballs to the stretched arms of split ends. Since vendor's arms are about the same as arms of quarterbacks, shouldn't they be paid the same? Or could it be the labor theory of value is both false and unadulterated nonsense?

Fortunately, today the generally accepted point of view is that value is a subjective phenomenon and can be discovered only in the act of individual choice. For some reason people pay more to see good quarterbacks than they do to see good peanut vendors. At the very least, it is totally inappropriate to ascribe all value to labor hours, for as we have already suggested, waiting or time requires a payment, a reward in the form of interest, to induce individuals to postpone immediate consumption.

In the end Robert Owen realized his attempt to mold and recreate society has failed, and he renounced any ambitions to build a new social order. He is mostly remembered with regard to the cooperative movement, although the cooperative association movement was considered by Owen to be an unimportant and unrepresentative part of his system. His actual experiments in socialism failed miserably. His New Harmony, Indiana commune failed after just six months. The attempts to replace money with "labor notes," which Owens said were "...more valuable than all the mines of Mexico and Peru," were generally unsuccessful and in fact came to be in direct conflict with his doctrine of equality of payment for work. The volume of labor notes one might acquire depended on one's intelligence, greater effort, and even the capacity for surviving reversals of fortune. A necessary consequence was inequality of income in accordance with differential abilities and circumstances. In his experiment with labor notes at the National Equitable Labour Exchange in London, "associates" would deposit the product of his labor and receive the "price" for it in labor notes. Unfortunately, his assumptions regarding human nature were quite inappropriate. Members announced the value of their own production and invariably inflated the value. The society began to attract members who were not as honest as earlier members, and the exchange tended to be inundated in products which were of inferior quality and generally unsaleable. But the labor notes exchanged for these goods could then be used to acquire more realistically valued and superior goods from the exchange. The exchange found itself acquiring goods which cost more than they were worth in exchange value and having to sell products below their exchange value. The exchange was soon emptied of quality merchandise, and the whole thing came to a sudden and inglorious end. So much for a system based on an unrealistic, utopian view of mankind and the idea that value can be established in terms of manhours of labor!

A number of associative colonies were founded in the United States, especially during the 1840's, and were linked with famous American names like Nathaniel Hawthrone. Though dozens were started, the misspecification of man's basic nature in combination with an intellectual love affair with the discredited labor theory of value insured that *none* of these settlements would last very long. Nevertheless, these were generally voluntary arrangements, and a belief in liberty requires that those who would band together in an egalitarian system, if that is their wish, be supported; as long as it does not require the coercive use of government or infringe on the equal rights of others to pursue their own goals. We say three cheers for voluntary socialism!

## KARL MARX AND COMMUNISM

Rather than recite the related and complementary views of the

126

other utopian socialists of this period, like Charles Fourier or Louis Blanc, we will look at the intellectual defense of socialism by the great intellectual giant of the socialist movement, Karl Marx, his collaborator Friedrich Engels and their student Vladimir Illyitch Lenin. Though their ideas have universally resulted in totalitarian systems of government, the Marxist dogma continues to capture the imagination of great numbers of people thoughout the world.

The socialist movement of Karl Marx was inaugurated by the publication of a small pamphlet entitled *The Communist Manifesto*. Friedrich Engels summarized the "fundamental proposition" of the Marxian fremework:

> That in every historical epoch the prevailing mode of economic production and exchange, and the social organization necessarily following from it, form the basis upon which is build up, and from which alone can be explained, the political and intellectual history of the epoch; that consequently the whole history of mankind...has been a history of class struggles, contests between exploiting and exploited, ruling and oppressed classes; that the history of these class struggles forms a series of evolution in which, now-a-days, a stage has been reached where the exploited and oppressed class (the proletariat) cannot attain its emancipation from the sway of the exploiting and ruling class (the burgeoise) without, at the same time, and once and for all, emancipating society at large from all exploitation, oppression, class-distinction and class-struggles.

From these words in the preface of the *Manifesto*, then, comes the proposition which explains the call for a new socialist order and defines the nature of the human predicament. As Michael Novak so brilliantly described in his book *The Spirit of Democratic Capitalism*, socialism from its beginning was a mythical force. The all red flag adopted by the socialists represented a dramatic simplifying device as contrasted to the tri-color flags of the other republics. It was really a simple and understandable idea uniting and/or transcending every nation. Victor Hugo described its red glow as ominous by torchlight, representing fire, danger, struggle, and the universal symbol of bloodshed for a cause. Socialism was a kind of secular fundamentalism, eschewing an oppression every workingman could potentially understand.

Unfortunately for their argument, capitalism has been in fact the most important vehicle known to man for the breakdown and erosion of "class," "status," and "caste." Of the many illustrations of class conflict in the *Manifesto*, there were *none* drawn from the important capitalist countries of the nineteenth century. Invariably, Marx looked to the status and caste conditions of precapitalist society. Before the full-blown appearance of the capitalist system of markets and private property, it was always easy to identify the aristocracy, the petty bourgeoisie, and the peasantry by their dress and manners. However, today it would be impossible to label by class the people walking down Fifth Avenue in New York City or touring Fisherman's Wharf in San Francisco.

Contrary to the fundamental tenet of the Marxian system, competitive capitalism has been an important instrument in *reducing* the importance of class distinction. In a market economy poor people are continuously becoming rich, and some of the rich are losing their wealth and returning to the ranks of the poor. We have already quoted from the study by Schiller which documented the very high degree of individual income mobility in the United States, both up and down the rankings. Under the system of natural liberty everyone has the opportunity of changing his or her economic status. Competitive capitalism, far from being a system of class distinction and caste, represents in fact a great social engine of mobility and therefore social and economic freedom. To doubt or deny this proposition and its importance for economic opportunity is to fail to recognize the thousands, even millions, of success stories of people producing material wealth and attaining living standards once thought possible only for kings. One striking source of this kind of evidence appears in the obituary notices in America's newspapers. Documenting the move from rags to riches, they represent striking examples of the economic opportunity characteristic of competitive capitalism.

In contrast, Karl Marx, the father figure of the world socialist movement in the twentieth century, was a pitiful figure. His whole life was one of extreme poverty and general obscurity. He was unable to make a living as a writer or journalist, and, without the aid of his disciple and collaborator, Friedrich Engels, who had a wealthy capitalist father, would have been a ward of the state. Max Eastman in his book *Reflections on the Failure of Socialism* captures some of the man:

> If he ever performed a generous act, it is not to be found in the record. He was totally undisciplined, vain, slovenly, and an egotistical spoiled child. He was ready at the drop of a hat with spiteful hate. He could be devious, disloyal, snobbish, anti-Semitic, anti-Negro. He was by habit a sponge, an intriguer, a tyrannical bigot who would rather wreck his party than see it succeed under another leader.

This man of few friends and little political impact at the time of his death, came to have a tremendous impact on the human community. Marx and Engels collaborated on the three volume work *Das Capital* which set out the Marxian system of value, exploitation, class struggle, and the historical inevitability of revolution and the socialist order. Socialist parties, founded all over Europe before World War I, revered Marx as the founding father. But the world was not permanently transformed until the Russion revolutionary Vladimir Lenin adopted the Marxian program in its entirety. Marxism became the political creed of the new revolutionary government in Russia after 1917.

While few have ever read *Das Capital,* and only a few more have even read the short phamplet *The Communist Manifesto,* the appeal of Marxism has had world-wide repercussions. As one author pointed out, "...there comes an intoxicating sense of being in step with history, of professing a creed that is based on infallible science." Unfortunately, or rather we should say happily for the survival of a free society and private property, Marx made many fundamental mistakes with respect to his economic and historical analysis. The errors in his "model" have become increasingly evident. History simply has not conformed to what Marx predicted as being "historically inevitable." And, interestingly, Marx or Engels never did indicate how we get to the new millennium in which the conditions of human existence will be nothing but milk and honey and the state will just "whither away."

This is not a book on the Marxian system, and therefore we will limit our discussion to identifying the more important problems and failures of this version of socialism. First and foremost, the historical inevitability of an even larger proletariat in which, according to *Das Capital,* "...there occurs a corresponding increase in the mass of poverty, oppression, enslavement, degeneration, and exploitation..." has not occurred in market economies. It just has not come to pass that "...the knell of capitalist private property sounds. The expropriators are expropriated." In point of fact, it has been precisely the opposite. In countries whose leaders remain sympathetic to the Marxian rhetoric, for example India, Ghana, Cuba, East Germany, and China, poverty remains the way of life for the masses. Capitalism, on the other hand, has brought to overwhelming majorities in the market economies higher standards of living and comforts which only the very wealthy enjoyed just a few decades ago. Automobiles, air conditioners, television sets, microwave ovens, personal computers, and hundreds of other "gadgets" have significantly improved human life and widened individual choice for almost everyone. And do not forget, man's inhumanity toward man also declined with the spread of capitalism!

Nevertheless, Engels argued that capitalism had exhausted its vitality in the nineteenth century and this would, he maintained, accelerate the advent of the new socialist order. Obviously, he was not a prophet! His predictions were written before the competitive economy produced the internal-combustion engine, synthetic fibers, plastics, aviation and the thousands of other innovations produced by advances in technology.

Furthermore, according to Marx, any successes under capitalism depend on a class antagonism between "capital" and "labor." For Marx, "no antagonism, no progress." This, too, represents a dogmatic assertion unsupported by the facts. It simly fails to acknowledge the cooperative nature of production under a system of voluntary exchange and private property. The socially beneficial results of the cooperative effort necessary to produce the Sears Tower in Chicago, the new Honda automobile assembly plant in Ohio and the wide-body jet aircraft which transport us in ease and comfort all over the world, to mention just a few of the obvious examples we have experienced under market arrangements, suggests the preposturous nature of the Marxian position.

The cornerstone, however, of the Marxist system is the concept of "surplus value:" The proposition that the worker is cheated because he is not payed the "full value" of his labor and that interest, rent, and profit are simply a form of theft that actually belongs to "labor." For Marx "...the value of commodities is constituted solely by the human labour contained in them," and the important question is: "...how is it possible for the manufacturer to obtain from his commodities a greater value than that invested by him in them." In spite of the attraction which this notion continues to hold on many socialists, the labor theory of value, as we have already illustrated, is simply false. Even Saint-Simon, who was revered by Marx and Engles, recongized the necessity of a reward to the entrepreneur who "directed" production. The profits to entrepreneurs follow from the uncertain and therefore risky nature of the production decision. Interest represents the reward for waiting.

The Soviets recognized long ago that a price had to be attached to the value of non-human resouces engaged in particular avenues of production. Labor after all is demonstrably not the only source of value. Indeed, in a more important sense, as we noted earlier, value cannot be measured in this objective or "real" fashion in terms of something called "socially necessary labor." Value is in the eye (tastes and preferences) of the beholder. It is a subjective phenomenon observable only at the moment individuals make choices. Value, in fact, is measured by the alternatives or opportunities sacrificed as a result of making a particular decision.

Given the asserted "exploitation" of the proletariat arising from this erroneous theory of value, Marx claimed the legitimate role of the "dictatorship of the proletariat" to govern the socialist economy. He never did explain why this "class" would be qualified to rule. Needless to say, the justification of this temporary dictatorship seems unimportant in light of the factual character of Marxist governments. The Societ experience and the experiences of the Peoples Republic of China, Cuba, Poland, North Korea, and Cambodia have all shown that the dictatorship of the proletariat has in fact always meant a ruthless and tyranical dictatorship *over* the masses. The bureaucrats who plan these economies and live in very nice apartments have long ago ceased doing the manual work called for in Marxism. Shouldn't the proponents of the benevolent dictatorship of the proletariat be required to provide at least one real world success story under their banner?

Of course, when this new order of pure communism finally appeared, the state would "whither away," and totalitarianism would disappear. In the new classless society of "scientific socialism" there would be no need for government. Unfortunately this is the exact opposite of the true state of affairs. Those nations who have followed the Marxist dogma the closest represent a list of the very countries in which state power is absolute, government power is arbitrary, and the most elementary human freedoms are denied the average citizen. For example, life in the Soviet Union is described by Vladimir Bukovsky in his essay "The Soul of Man Under Socialism" (from his book *To Build A Castle: My Life As A Dissenter*):

> In such a state, the individual cannot have any rights--the least inalienable right possessed by a single individual instantly deprives the regime of a morsel of power. Every individual from childhood on must absorb the axiomatic fact that never in any circumstances or by any means will he be able to influence the regime one iota. No decisions can be made other than on initiatives from above. The regime is immovable, infalliable, and intransignent, and the entire world is left with no choice but to accommodate itself to this fact. You may humbly beg its indulgence, but never demand your due.

In summary, the Marxist system suffers from errors of logic, faulty assumptions, and incorrect conclusions. The model is not supported by the facts of the real world, and indeed those countries claiming an allegiance to Karl Marx are in all cases reactionary and totalitarian. In spite of the weaknesses, even nonsensical character, of the important propositions of the Marxian "theory" and the undesirable consequences of its actual operation, Western Marxist intellectuals, like in the following passage from Michael Lerner's *The New Socialist Revolution*, want us to believe the following scenario for America's future:

> Immediately after the socialists take control of the U.S. economy, a high level of material prosperity will be possible in the United States and much of the rest of the world. Because we are so highly industrialized, it will be possible to decrease dramatically the amount of time the worker spends in work, at the same time producing adequate material goods for ourselves and helping to advance underdeveloped parts of the world...In this situation, it will be impossible for a new ruling class to emerge that encourages people to delay gratification, while itself benefiting from the labor of the majority.

This utopian nonsense from the "left," however, should not dull our senses to the threat from the "right." Fascist solutions to human problems are being proposed by well-meaning people, frequently in order to fight communism, or so the argument goes. Human freedom was crushed in both fascist Germany and socialist Russia.

## ECONOMIC CALCULATION UNDER SOCIALISM

Those who would substitute socialism or fascism and the centralized planning agency for the separate decisions of individual producers and consumers forget that to throw out the market system is to destroy the market generated prices which give us important information about the relative scarcity of things. The impossibility of economic calculation under socialism in its authoritarian and centralized version was demonstrated more than a half century ago by the great Austrian economist Ludwig von Mises. "The problem of socialist economic calculation," according to Mises, "is precisely this: that in the absence of market prices for the factors of production, a computation of profit or loss is not feasible. The paradox of 'planning' is that it cannot plan, because of the absence of economic calculation."

It was Lenin, in the Soviet Union, who took the organization of the government post office as a desirable pattern for the organization of the economic affairs of society. The substitute of the "service principle" for the "profit principle," by creating one massive planning bureau (the "Gosplan" in the USSR), abandons the market and market prices as a crucial and essential institution for making efficient calculations in the production and distribution of goods and services. In circumstances where rulers have succeeded in abolishing capitalism, chaos has been the result. To destroy the market is to short circuit the system by which economic information is gathered in order to obtain an efficient allocation of scarce resources. All of the Eastern European Soviet bloc countries, the Soviet Union, and most recently China have retreated from total centralized planning and have opted for a "mixed economy" format in which, they hope, the advantages of capitalism can be enjoyed while simultaneously protecting the existing totalitarian regimes.

Not only do Yugoslavia and China permit a good dose of capitalism, but they, like other countries committed to "scientific" socialism, have the luxury of using prices established in capitalist markets for their own internal economic calculations. In the 1930's a Polish economist by the name of Oscar Lange, who taught economics in the United States for many years before returning to his native country, prepared a theoretical case where the signals produced by the market could be "artificially" imitated in a planned, socialistic order. He admitted that efficiency required "shadow prices" be used as substitutes for the market prices that would no longer be generated by the outlawed market mechanism. For Lange it was a simple task of creating an artificial market. Socialist managers of factories would be instructed to act as if they were entrepreneurs in a capitalist order. Unfortunately, the problem of discovering the process by which these "as if" prices were to be calculated was ignored and left unanswered!

In other words, a decentralized socialism is proposed to replace the centralized planning bureaucracy. But a very serious problem remains: How is the unanticipated and unknowable change in local circumstances, which decision makers face on a daily basis, to be mobilized and communicated. Perpetual change characterizes real

132

world economies. Nobel Laureate economist Friedrich Hayek reminds us of the highly specialized knowledge of specific time and place which is never available on a timely or predictable basis, but is necessary for executing a national economic plan. This is the "knowledge problem" which dooms the socialist system to a form of blindness. "Progress," Ludwig von Mises tells us, "is precisely that which the rules and regulations did not foresee; it is necessarily outside the field of bureaucratic activities."

The characteristic feature of the economic scene is dynamic change. In the writings of Lenin, the process of production was described as "Auditing of Production and Distribution" and "keeping the records of labour and products." The economy was one great post office, and the entrepreneurial role of anticipating change in an uncertain and everchanging world was relegated to the back burner. The means and conditions under which some industries expand, new industries are formed, and other sectors of the economy fall by the wayside is simplified to a matter of recording and book entry manipulations. The problems of allocating capital among alternative uses in a complex industrial economy are ignored. According to Mises the scientific socialists "...have no greater perception of the essentials of economic life than the errand boy, whose only idea of the work of the entrepreneur is that he covers pieces of paper with letters and figures." Marxist-Leninist advocates have elected to fall back on the proposition that socialism is inevitable and that it will transform the world into a Garden of Eden. Without exception they have been unwilling to face the issue of economic calculation and, therefore, how in fact the truly socialist order would work.

There is, however, a sense of plausibility to the socialist myth which promises so much, including the advantages of a modernity without the asserted exploitation and alienation. Nevermind that the actual socialist systems are great disappointments. Somehow "true socialism" is still in the future.

# CHAPTER 12

## THE INTELLECTUALS AND THE POLITICIZATION OF SOCIETY

> The question remains, how and why that group of people known as intellectuals has for most of this century become alienated from our society and so often attracted to socialist societies that are objectively reprehensible, that deny individuals even the most basic civil liberties and fail to deliver material well-being.
>
> --Edward Crane

Those countries that have adopted socialist institutions have almost always passed through a phase during which their intellectual community had become advocates of collectivist ideals. Dependent as we are on the opinions and teachings of "second-hand dealers in ideas" (the press, clergy and politicians in particular), the intellectual community is the faction that generally determines our view of society and the positions we are likely to take on public issues.

### THE INFLUENCE OF IDEAS

The extent to which ordinary men and women fail to recognize the power of intellectuals in affecting public opinion is more than interesting. The execution of government policy and social change of all kinds is in fact almost invariably in their hands. As John Maynard Keynes reminded us many years ago, "... the ideas of economists and political philosophers, both when they are right and when they are wrong, are more powerful than is commonly understood. Indeed, the world is ruled by little else. Practical men, who believe themselves to be quite exempt from any intellectual influences, are usually the slaves of some defunct economist. Madmen in authority, who hear voices in the air, are distilling their frenzy from some academic scribbler of a few years back...Soon or late, it is ideas, not vested interests, which are dangerous for good or evil." Even, for example, when a newspaper is owned by conservative interests, it is quite frequently the operating personnel that write the editorial page and therefore have the important influence on public opinion. In the twentieth century the advocacy has usually been in the direction of socialism and a further politicization of society. But that should not be surprising.

Those committed to the socialist myth are more often than not alienated by what they perceive to be the undesirable consequences of competitive capitalism, both its processes and results. Although the objective conditions and circumstances of capitalism are rarely repulsive to the ordinary person, it is nevertheless the specific interpretation of reality offered by the men of letters that remains so influential. Intellectuals, here defined, are those members of the community who wield their power through the spoken and written word. Yet, the economist Joseph Schumpeter reminds us, though wielding great power over public opinion, the intellectuals are, interestingly enough, still characterized by an ''...absence of direct responsibility for practical affairs.''

## INTELLECTUALS HAVE A VISION

Why then this emphatic denunciation of competitive capitalism by most intellectuals? Julien Benda in *The Treason of the Intellectuals* observes that: ''This denunciation of (classical) liberalism, notably by the vast majority of contemporary men of letters, will be one of the things in this age most astonishing to history.'' Intellectuals flocked to the banner of Stalinism during the 1930's and 1940's and joined in announcing the great and glorious changes in the Peoples Republic of China in the 1960's. All this in spite of regimes which were in fact the most ruthless and repressive governments history has known. In a recent book by William L. O'Neill, *A Better World: The Great Shism-- Stalinism and the American Intellectuals,* he reveals the disturbing record of how American intellectuals jumped on Stalin's bandwagon, apparently unaware or unwilling to see the millions who were murdered in the name of communism. Paul Hollander in *Political Pilgrims* documents the praise lavished on these brutal regimes. George Bernard Shaw, for example, said: ''We cannot afford to give ourselves moral airs when our most enterprising neighbor (the Soviet Union) humanely and judiciously liquidates a handful of exploiters and speculators to make the world safe for honest men.'' This, apparently, is to serve as a rationalization for the murder of millions of people! ''Maybe it costs a million lives--maybe it will cost five million--there has never been in human history,'' according to Upton Sinclair's defense of the Stalin regime, ''a great social change without killing.'' In the 1960's, the praise turned to the Mao government in China, but this totalitarian government probably was responsible for more deaths than even Stalin or Hitler. There was also the appeal to a collectivist regime of the right in the experiment with ''national socialism'' in Germany and the Italian fascist movement during the 1930's.

Perhaps intellectuals are attracted to socialist thought, versions of the ''left'' and ''right,'' in spite of its depravities, because of its visionary character. The utopian view of socialism, after all, is a great source of strength. As Schumpeter argued decades ago, ''...capitalism creates its own critics from within by generating spiritual possibilities which are never satisfied." In contrast to the intellectual bankruptcy of our "mixed economy," Marx offers a visionary world view. And the rhetoric is appealing: equality, justice, cooperation, public ownership, and sharing.

Furthermore, if man can harness nature to build dams and split the atom, the intellectual can't help but believe that a good dose of "social engineering" would be conducive to the good society. Our ability to build better mouse traps must mean, according to the central planner, that a utopian social order is also possible. A forced transformation in the character and nature of man is viewed as a problem analogous to harnessing the physical environment.

## THE APPEAL OF POWER

Another very important factor in the appeal of socialism for many intellectuals is the power and influence promised them by the state. Many educated individuals are disaffected, dissatisfied and unimpressed by the market means to self-esteem and self-satisfaction. There are now large numbers of people whose positions depend on their education, but who have had little direct experience or involvement in the market economy. Very few understand, and therefore fail to appreciate, the socially beneficial results of competitive capitalism. As Schumpeter reminded us in *Capitalism, Socialism and Democracy*, "...it is the absence of direct responsibility for practical affairs and the consequent absence of firsthand knowledge of them which distinguishes the typical intellectual from other people who also wield the power of the spoken and written word."

In other words, there are good reasons why so many intellectuals have been captured by the collectivist myth and its rewards of power and influence. The system of competitive capitalism treats in an unacceptable manner the disaffected person of letters who makes his living through the written and spoken word. As one critic has observed: "In a truly capitalistic society intellectuals would be paid exactly what they're worth on the free market, which is perilously close to nothing." The British economic historian R. M. Hartwell describes their predicament as follows:

> Is it so astonishing? Are not the actions and beliefs of the intellectuals self-interested in a very obvious way? Intellectuals dislike economic liberalism because the market economy does not reward them according to their own estimation of their obvious social worth. Intellectuals, therefore, prefer economic systems which give them a place in the sun, in which their cash rewards are almost certainly higher, and in which power rewards are undoubtedly higher. Intellectuals play leading roles in the bureaucracies of the state, as advisers, experts, and administrators, and increasing the power of the state means increasing the power of the intellectuals.

Here then we have the conditions for a mutually beneficial political exchange. The state requires the services of the opinion makers to gain legitimacy for government power over the lives of individuals. Unfortunately for government, the masses have never been easily recruited to utopian socialism and big government. Democratizing society by increasing the power of the state (i.e., politicians and bureaucrats) requires a sophisticated presentation and a frequently repeated defense of the virtues of government. Because of self-interest, the intellectual fills that niche. A natural and complementary relationship is fused between the "men of letters" and the politician. Policies which propose in an explicit and above-board manner to place greater restraints and limitations on individuals would rarely succeed. But politicizing everything in the name of democracy and equality provides a useful backdoor approach. By using the term "politicization" we are describing that irresistible tendency to solve all social issues, no matter how personal, with government imposed solutions. Peaceful exchanges between individuals of both things and ideas are perceived to be subject to political, which is to say forceful, intervention.

Nevertheless, while the state needs its intellectual "brain trust," our concern here is why political solutions remain so attractive. Perhaps the libertarian scholar Murray Rothbard says it best:

> We see clearly why the State needs the intellectuals; but why do the intellectuals need the State? Put simply, the intellectual's livelihood in the free market is generally none too secure; for the intellectual, like everyone else on the market, must depend on the values and choices of the masses of his fellow men, and it is characteristic of these masses that they are generally uninterested in intellectual concerns. The State, on the other hand, is willing to offer the intellectuals a warm, secure, and permanent berth in its apparatus, a secure income, and the panopoly of prestige.

Security, power, and more often than not even income are the essential magnets that draw many of the world's intellectuals to government. The federal Civil Service pay scale for a GS-15, not to mention retirement benefits, compares quite favorably with private sector alternatives.

## THE STATE AND INTELLECTUAL FREEDOM

Of course, all intellectuals are not "court intellectuals." There have always been women and men of letters (and hopefully there always will be) who have opposed the power of government and have produced the most eloquent and profound arguments for a society of inalienable rights and limited government. Thomas Jefferson and

Thomas Paine during the American Revolution, John Locke before, and many others since have made the case for the system of natural liberty. But importantly, these defenders of individual liberty and the free society have flourished only in those societies in which a power base independent of the state was available. The implications: the case for freedom can flourish only in those countries with a strong private sector and an independent press in which decentralized and pluralistic souces of power exist. This open environment, of course, does not exist in any of the "peoples' republics," where even the most rudimentary freedoms are denied to individual citizens.

Unfortunately, the great defenders of human liberty have had their efforts eclipsed in the twentieth century. The western democracies have, to one degree or another, fallen victim to the great collectivist dogma of our time: Socialism in its left and right variations. While lip service continues to be paid to inalienable personal rights, there seems to be an unquenchable demand for political solutions to problems and greater government power over our lives. We "...have accepted the state as the reality of society. It is this actual integration, rather than the theory," according to Frank Chodorov, "that marks the twentieth century off from its predecessors."

## THE TECHNOCRATIC ELITE

The boom in the so-called "knowledge industry," in combination with the appeal of technical expertise, threatens to increase our devotion to political solutions for private problems. Consequently, the intellectuals have more influence than ever before. The majority of men and women feel increasingly unqualified to deal with either their institutions or their personal lives. The implications for freedom and individual choice, given the centrality of the technical expert, has been noted by the sociologist Robert G. Perrin:

> The emergence and multiplication of a new variety of 'intellectual' who represents an increasingly serious threat to patterns of free choice in everyday areas of life. They make up what may be called 'practical' or 'technical knowledge elites'--with obvious emphasis on applied knowledge. With good intentions as well as the all-important badge of scientific authority, they are, when attached to governmental bodies, becoming ever more influential in the ultimate substitution of technical 'expertise' for informed free choice.

Almost always with the best of intentions, the experts, usually bringing to bear the police power of the state, tell us what is good and what is not good for the individual citizen. The result is a reduction in the breadth of individual choice below that which is both desirable and necessary in a free society of sovereign human beings.

The present influence of the intellectual expert, usually an employee of a government agency or hired by government from

138

academia, offers little hope that the dominance of the socialist mindset will be reversed in the near future. There is, however, a powerful force at work which is favorable to those still devoted to individual freedom.

## NO ONE DEFENDS SOCIALISM

The socialist dogma, especially its Marxist variation, is rarely defended: "...the myth has become a petrified ornament" in Eastern Europe, the Soviet Union, and even in China. The western intellectual is daily confronted by the contradiction between socialist theory and totalitarian practice. The radical leftist today stands for almost anything but a Soviet-type state socialism. Today the "left" runs the gamut from fairly moderate populists to those who would advocate revolutionary and militant change. In any case, the totalitarianism of "...Soviet Russia is the albatross we all have to bear," asserts one Marxist.

Given the bad press of the more traditional socialist or communist model, intellectuals sympathetic to a utopian socialist view are advocating milder forms of social change. However, it is important to recognize that these less radical models continue to move western society toward greater use of political decisions and, therefore, a significantly reduced role for individual responsibility and human liberty. Three popular variations on the collectivist theme are identified by the terms "welfare state," the "mixed economy," and, the new wave for many intellectuals, "economic democracy."

## THE WELFARE STATE

If socialism means government ownership of the means of production, then Sweden is not socialist. Perhaps three-fourths of Swedish industry is privately owned, yet Sweden is the classic example of the so-called welfare state. For those who would define socialism as the situation in which the results of production are controlled by government, then Sweden would have to be identified as a socialist country. An important Swedish socialist once said: "We don't care who owns the cow just as long as government gets the milk."

Important contributors to the founding of the Swedish welfare state, Gunnar and Alva Myrdal, in a book published in 1932, argued that "...if it (the welfare state) cannot successfully be developed in Scandinavia, given by historical change quite exceptionally advantageous conditions, it would probably not work out anywhere else." The welfare state was to be characterized by a system of taxation and government outlays which produced a radical redistribution and equalization of income. More than sixty percent of the Swedish

Gross National Product in 1980 was devoted to financing these efforts at achieving material equality. Taxes now represent fifty or sixty percent of the typical industrial workers gross income, and this tax bite does not include the additional burdens of the value-added tax. Sweden's present decay and economic stagnation is not surprising in light of their burdensome tax rates. The structure of incentives confronting the more productive segments of the work force (doctors, lawyers, engineers, skilled artisans, etc.) has produced tremendous increases in labor force absenteeism and a strong preference for more leisure and less work. The Swedish illness/unemployment insurance system, for example, pays ninety percent of wages and salaries. It therefore should not be a great surprise that ten percent of Sweden's labor force is absent on any given day, the figure approaches twenty percent on Mondays and Fridays.

Presently, more than one third of the labor force works for government. The adverse implications of this level of public employment for representative political institutions are serious indeed. Ludwig von Mises in his book *Bureaucracy* makes a persuasive case that "...representative democracy cannot subsist if a great part of the voters are on the government payroll. If the members of parliament no longer consider themselves mandatories of the taxpayers but deputies of those receiving salaries, wages, subsidies, doles and other benefits from the treasury, democracy is done for." At long last even Gunnar Myrdal, who is sometimes considered the father of the welfare state in Sweden, has admitted there are serious problems with this version of collectivism: "Swedish honesty has been a source of pride for me and my generation. Today, however, I have an uneasy feeling that, due to bad tax laws, we are more and more becoming a nation of cheats." Given existing tax burdens, what else could be expected? In the United States, with a significantly lower average tax burden, activity in the "underground economy" already totals hundreds of *billions* of dollars each year.

In spite of a state-owned radio and television monopoly which provides "informative" programming on the benefits of welfare state measures, 1976 saw the first non-socialist government elected in Sweden since 1932. Unfortunately, the socialists have since regained the government, and in the name of security, rather than freedom, the Swedish welfare state continues to ravage incentives, discourage production, and perpetuate the growing leviathan state. Roland Huntford in his *The New Totalitarians* has documented the extent to which the "fascist structure" underlying the Swedish economy has broken the spirit and honesty of the Swedish people.

## SOCIALISM AS THE MIXED ECONOMY

The "mixed economy" (Great Britain and increasingly the

United States would be examples) is the intellectual brainchild of the "social democrat." Mainstream economists in both countries have suggested the need for a "mixed economy" of government intervention and private sector market activity. Unfortunately, a stew that is half horse and half rabbit is hardly "mixed." The general trend has been for government and the public sector of the economy to grow relative to the private sector. In the United States this has meant not so much public ownership, but massive interference in private affairs by government. Regulation and regimentation of and intervention in the private sector (e.g., rules, edicts, executive orders, tariffs, taxes, specifications, minimums, maximums, controls, etc.) have made government the coach, referee, rule maker, and quarterback of the "mixed" system. The latest version in the United States is found in the proposals for a "national industrial policy."

The case for government ownership and/or intervention has been based on the "anatomy of market failure," where the spontaneous order and free market fail to produce efficient and/or equitable results. Unfortunately, the alleged failure of the market place is mostly the result of an uncertain world in which knowledge and information regarding the past, present, and future are not free. Like all economic goods, useful information about alternatives is scarce. The problem then, when contemplating government solutions to correct the market's failure, is that planners in government also lack the information necessary to make efficient and equitable decisions. Chances are excellent, overwhelming in fact, that government will be unable to improve the imperfect performance of the competitive market process. The mixed economy, which proposes to correct the imperfections of the self-correcting market process by using government coercion, presumes that government bureaucrats possess, and can process efficiently information which is unavailable to entrepreneurs in the private sector. Again, Ludwig von Mises suggests some modesty in the claims we make for enlarging government's role in economic affairs:

> There are certainly, both in the actions of individuals and in the conduct of public affairs, situations in which the actors may have good reasons to put up even with very undesirable long-run effects in order to avoid what they consider still more undesirable short-run conditions. It may sometimes be expedient for a man to heat the stove with his furniture. But if he does, he should know what the remoter effects will be. He should not delude himself by believing that he has discovered a wonderful new method of heating his premises.

There is, in the mixed economy, an inherent tendency for relentless pressures toward bigger government and a reduced role for voluntary arrangements. There is, indeed, a fundamental defect in the use of politics as a delivery system. Even if it is demonstrably true that everyone would benefit from a reduced role for government intervention in economic affairs, the fact is that particular individuals (i.e., consumers, producers, employees, employers) do benefit from certain government interventions on their behalf. It all becomes a great race competing to obtain material gain at the expense of the general population through the coercive apparatus of government. As Frederic Bastiat once said, the "...state is that great ficticious entity where everyone tries to live at the expense of everyone else."

The mixed economy is neither true to the socialist dream nor is it the answer to a principled committment to individual freedom, private property, and voluntary arrangements. But, unless policies and ideas change, the mixed economy represents a greased slide in the direction of a totally politicized society in which personal freedom and responsibility will one day totally disappear.


## ECONOMIC DEMOCRACY AND FREEDOM

With the Marxist model on the defensive because of poor performance and the welfare state failing in the absence of much intellectual support, the socialist movement in the 1980's is emerging as a call for "economic democracy." The fundamental meaning of this idea was captured in a statement by Sidney Hillman, the President of the Amalgamated Clothing Workers Union, in 1924: "We must realize that the democratic form of government is bound to penetrate our industrial life as well. It cannot be confined merely to our political institutions." Economic democracy represents a claim to "...the transfer of economic decision making from the few to the many." Simply, the fundamental decisions of production in the economy are to be politicized. Martin Carnoy and Derek Shearer, in *Economic Democracy: The Challenge of the 1980's,* maintain that one of the "limitations" of a market economy is that "...investment and production decisions are not made democratically." The answer is "worker-controlled production" which "...would extend democratic choice to work, employment, income, and technology."

The underlying strategy for "reform" would involve the "...transfer [of]...capital from the corporations to the public, so that the people who work and consume collectively and democratically decide what to do with it." And, of course, "...The logical vehicle for that process should be the government." But, how is this transfer to be accomplished by the state? Presumably, existing owners will be less than delighted by the tyranny of this majority which will be mobilized to create these worker-owned enterprises. It would, of necessity, require the coercive use of force by government.

Let there be no misunderstanding on Carnoy and Shearer's point: "...we are not proposing a return to a competitive capitalism of the past." "Today, we are a nation of employees," and the best way to decide what to produce and how to produce it is "...in a democratically planned economy." It would supposedly be

142

accomplished through elected legislatures and executives. But, what is to be said for the rights of minorities? Are there no limits to the tyranny of the majority? In the name of democracy, can "society" do anything it likes to individuals? The fundamental problem with this interpretation of "economic democracy" is that it allows individual rights to be violated for the "public good" as long as simple majorities of those who actually participate in the political process agree. The majority can effectively ban undesirable books by not producing them, and, in the extreme, can decree that a particular group of people are to be enslaved or even gassed. Individual liberty is totally inconsistent with the proposition that a majority can best determine what is good for society. Minorities have, we believe, certain inalienable rights which cannot be violated by the ballot box. Individuals A and B should not be allowed to do anything they want to individual C simply on the argument that D has certain "needs."

Those who champion economic democracy propose a structure of political arrangements which is no less dangerous to the survival of personal freedom than the tyrants who currently govern the Soviet Union, Viet Nam, China or some of the right wing dictatorships. Upton Sinclair, carrying the banner for socialism in the early part of the twentieth century, argued that "...industry must ultimately be democratized" and that "...autocracy in industry is absolutely incompatible with democracy in politics." However, it is in fact just the opposite. To politicize economic life would be to destroy personal freedom; not only the economic freedoms of private ownership and voluntary exchange, but the civil rights of freedom of expression, of the press, and those other rights guaranteed by the Bill of Rights in the United States Constitution.

Adam Smith said that consumption was the sole end of production. Those who advocate economic democracy are concerned with individuals as employees rather than consumers. It is not the quality and quantity of goods and services made available to the consumer which matters to them, but, in fact, the concern is with how things are made, where they are made, and who makes them. Owners would not be permitted to move their plant to another location or to close down an obsolete facility. Economic democracy would bring protective tariffs to protect the jobs of particular sets of employees. Indeed, capital accumulation would be limited because they tell us, it threatens jobs. Surely, it is a misguided interest which keeps industries labor intensive. Inevitably such a policy would lower productivity, standards of living, and the wealth of us all. Or more specifically, the end results would be disastrous.

If "labor" wishes to own, manage and take the associated risks of successfully anticipating consumer wants, Peter Drucker has pointed out how easy it would be. In his discussion of "pension-fund capitalism," he observes that organized labor in the United States already owns, through the assets of their retirement programs, a very significant part of American industry. Labor can take on the entrepreneurial role in the economy anytime it wants. But we believe there are good reasons why labor does not do that. There exists a great gulf between the entrepreneurial function of directing production in a very uncertain world which includes chances for profits but greater probabilities of losses and the salaried employee who takes none of this risk but instead opts for the paycheck each Friday afternoon.

"The present structure of production in the United States," Carnoy and Shearer describe as suffering from "...problems that appear unsolvable by corporate capitalist development." But competitive capitalism has evolved largely through a process of trial and error. It is a system which offers rewards to those who correctly anticipate the wishes of consumers and losses to those who fail to recongize what the consumer wants. Those who efficiently and effectively direct production in accordance with consumer wishes, earn profits. Those who do not go bankrupt. Competitive capitalism is, in fact, a system of profits and losses.

Economic democracy is a framework which assumes that the large modern corporations "dominate" the market place. This is surely a careless generalization when we consider the problems of A&P, W.T. Grant, the Penn-Central, The Penn Square Bank, Osborne Computer, and Harley-Davidson, among others. Bigness does not guarantee success. But, providing the consumer what they want, at the price they want, and at the time they want insures survivability whether large or small. Nevertheless, the proponents of economic democracy are convinced that we must "restrict corporate power." To do so, they ask that we "build a mass political movement" so that majorities can run roughshod over minorities: "The government--at all levels--is the key arena in the struggle for economic democracy," according to Carnoy and Shearer. Majorities once achieved would obtain legislative measures establishing an "economic bill of rights." These "rights" would include mandatory representation of employees and consumers on the boards of corporations.

Surely it is clear to the reader that this kind of a "right" can come only at the expense of the rights of others: for example, consumers and stockholders. The modification of rights would take place through the legislative work of the majority. We believe these kinds of proposals represent a tyrannical use of majority rule and are inconsistent with a free society. The inevitable result would be a leviathan state like that of Nazi Germany, fascist Italy, or a totalitarian leftist regime like those in the Soviet Union and Poland.

The strongest movement for economic democracy is in the State of California with the Campaign for Economic Democracy (CED) headed by Tom Hayden and financed mostly by his wife, actress Jane Fonda. Carnoy and Shearer are confident that the CED would not be "...hindered by the ideological limitations of traditional Democratic

Party liberalism." Or, in other words, there exist no limits to the degree by which society is to be politicized and individual choice is to be restricted.

## THE INTELLECTUAL'S DREAM

In summary, many of our so-called intellectuals are mesmerized by the appeal of collectivist and rational solutions to human problems. They abhor the spontaneous order of the market with its fundamental modesty regarding man's ability to plan the good society. They are utopian, believing with Marx that socialism could produce paradise on earth. Though most do not advocate revolution, they see nothing wrong with using the political apparatus to deprive minorities (i.e., other individuals) of justly acquired rights to property and position. In the name of majorities, they would transform society and make it one big post office. Whatever the merits of their arguments, there can be no doubt that the intellectual community has been a tremendously important force contributing to the decline and fall of the free market order and, therefore, individual freedom.

Fortunately in the last decade, there has been a renewed interest in the idea of liberty and an accompanying flood of written works on the free society. There is good reason to believe that what seems to be an inevitable move to socialism can be slowed and even reversed. The efforts of Milton Friedman, Robert Nozick, Friedrich Hayek, Ludwig von Mises, Leonard Read, Murray Rothbard, Tibor Machan, Robert Ringer, Eric Mack, John Hospers, James Buchanan, William Simon, William Allen, Robert Nisbet, William F. Buckley, Armen Alchian, George Gilder, Richard McKenzie and many, many others (who we might add differ on some of the particulars) have, in fact, generated considerable interest in the restoration of economic freedom. The ideas of liberty and the market economy are once again alive and exciting intellectual issues. The worthy goals of open markets, limited government, and individual freedom are not dead. Ideas do have consequences. The myth of the socialist "Garden of Eden" is proof of that.

145

# CHAPTER 13

## ECONOMIC GROWTH,
## THE BUSINESS CYCLE, AND GOVERNMENT

> Left-liberal intellectuals are often a wonderous group to behold. In the last three or four decades, not a very long time in human history, they have, like whirling dervishes, let loose a series of angry complaints against free-market capitalism...For forty years we have been told, in the textbooks, the economic journals, and the pronouncements of our government's economic advisors, that the government has the tools with which it can easily abolish inflation or recession. We have been told that by juggling fiscal and monetary policy, the government can 'fine-tune' the economy to abolish the business cycle and insure permanent prosperity without inflation.
>
> --Murray Rothbard

For over half a century, one of the most frequently repeated arguments against capitalism involves the systems' asserted case of inherent instability. Both in the long run (the issue of economic growth) and the short term (the business cycle), competitive capitalism has not performed according to its critics' expectations. In the jargon of the economist, the market economy is subject to macroeconomic instability and, therefore, requires for its survival a massive increase in government intervention. Whether called government fine tuning, centralized planning, or economic democracy, the end result is the same: government control over markets, production, incomes, and consumption; a control which is more specifically socialism. It does not seem to matter that the recommended interventions call for contradictory government policy. The one constant is the asserted proposition that only government action will suffice.

Yet, interestingly, the swings in the business cycle are mild compared to the oscillating socialist prescriptions. Karl Marx, for example, thought the inherent problem with capitalism was a continuously declining rate of profit (or "surplus value"). After a long wait and no such happening, the Marxists Paul Baran and Paul Sweezy in their *Monopoly Capitalism* reversed course and maintained the fundamental problem with the capitalist order was that the profit rate was always on the *rise*. Whether too little or too much, profit for socialists has always been a dirty word. Nevertheless, those who advocate collectivist solutions to the imperfections of capitalism have, especially since the onset of the Great Depression of the 1930's, found what they perceive to be their most fertile areas of attack: the question of economic growth and the problem of the business cycle.

Upon examining the issue of economic growth, the recommendations of the left regarding the merits of growth and rising living standards have been, to say the least, inconsistent. The irony here seems to be that the "left" can be *for* growth or *against* it. But either way, the solution is greater government involvement, less individual choice, and the subsequent decline in human freedoms. It seems that massive government intervention is always required to rid us of the business cycle, and this can be accomplished through the use of so-called "fine tuning" by government spending and taxing policies. In fact, much of the instability in the aggregate performance of the American economy, especially with respect to the Great Depression, has been caused by government itself.

## ECONOMIC GROWTH AND GOVERNMENT POLICY

Over the past fifty years in the U.S., those who have advocated an enlarged role for government in controlling the pace of economic growth have either done so because growth was too slow or, interestingly, because economic growth was too fast. During the decade of the Great Depression, for example, Harvard economist Alvin Hansen wrote that the American economy suffered from an inevitable tendency toward "secular stagnation." When the private sector, especially investment spending on capital goods lags, there is a tendency for private sector spending to fall short of the level required to generate adequate employment opportunities for all those wishing to work. Long-run stagnation, according to Hansen, was the result of declining population growth, the disappearance of the frontier and new areas of development, and a slowing in the rate of invention and innovation in the economy. Hansen proposed what he called "compensatory finance" as the solution to the asserted failure of the private sector. Compensatory finance simply meant an enlarged level of government spending in the economy, and this spending should be financed by budget deficits rather than taxes.

In his presidential address to the American Economic Association in December, 1938, Hansen justified his call for the leviathan state: "We are passing, so to speak, over a divide which separates the great era of growth and expansion of the nineteenth century from where which no man, unwilling to embark on pure conjecture, can as yet characterize with the clarity or precision." By all means, let us call on government to stamp out this uncertainty and keep the ship of state on course.

Alvin Hansen, through his expressions of confidence in government intervention, had an enormous influence on economics and economic policy in the United States for more than three decades. He is universally recognized as the person who brought "Keynesian economics" to the United States from John Maynard Keynes' native England. Hansen's students at Harvard include a Who's Who of left-liberal economists: Paul Samuelson, James Tobin, and the Marxist

Paul Sweezy. Many of these men served in the Roosevelt administration and some, including their students, would later serve in the Kennedy/Johnson administrations. The formulation of economic policy in the United States since World War II has been dominated by those who were influenced by Keynes through the writing and teaching of Harvard's Alvin Hansen.

Earning his doctorate in economics at the University of Wisconsin in 1918, Hansen was strongly influenced by the institutional economist John R. Commons. At that time, when the free-market, limited government model was still clearly dominant in the fraternity of economists, Commons was already arguing for a significant expansion in the functions of government. Commons did not believe that the market system would work very well and proposed a "partnership" between government and the market. Alvin Hansen, who was to have such a great influence in expanding the role of government in society after World War II, accepted the views of John R. Commons early in his career. With the publication of *Fiscal Policy and Business Cycles* in 1941, Hansen took his place as the leader of that group of economists who would continue to recommend more government for problems which were frequently the result of prior government actions. Henry Simons, a free-market economist at the University of Chicago, viewed the book's appearance with alarm, and in his review recognized Hansen's influence:

> Now, from the ranks of older, distinguished economists, comes Professor Hansen to argue their [Keynesian] case and to espouse their cause...His book is the academic apology par excellence for the inner new deal and all its works. It may well become the economic bible for that substantial company of intellectuals, following Keynes and recklessly collectivist, whose influence grows no less rapidly in academic circles than in Washington.

In any case, the fundamental problem with capitalism was supposedly its inability to generate jobs and continue to increase living standards. Stagnation, they argued, was the inevitable consequence of a market order. But, watch this one for a quick switch! In the late 1950's a disciple of Hansen's, John Kenneth Galbraith, tells us in *The Affluent Society* that capitalism has been too successful. In particular, there is too much private oppulence. Americans were consuming wastefully at the behest of the large American coporations which controlled consumer habits through advertising. Alvin Hansen jumped on this Galbraithian bandwagon. The American economy, according to Hansen in 1960, now suffered from a "social imbalance" which meant: "Our budgets, far from being too large, have been too small--too small in terms of needs, too small in terms of growth, and too small in terms of pushing the economy towards full employment and the most economical utilization of capacity." You guessed it, the answer to this new problem of too much affluence was for more government intervention by increasing govern-

148

ment spending on "social" needs through higher taxes. It would appear that whether the problem be stagnation or affluence, the collectivist's answer is always more government. According to Hansen, the problem in the late 1950's was a "composition" of output issue: "A not inconsiderable part of our productive resources is wasted on artificially created wants...a great waste of productive resources on things that have little or no inherent value." And, Galbraith could hardly agree more.

In the midst of this concern with affluence, however, socialist Michael Harrington in *The Other America* was telling us that the real issue was poverty. Presumably, the poor wanted a larger share of these "artificially created wants." It does get rather confusing, but one thing is certain: Hansen and Galbraith had tastes which were different from the American people. Packaged heads of lettuce, metal tennis rackets, tail fins on automobiles and designer jeans are but a few of the thousands of wasteful trinkets demanded by the silly consumer. A chateau in Switzerland for Galbraith apparently did not come under this heading of wasteful consumption.

But, interestingly, the conspicuous consumption gig didn't last very long for the liberals. John F. Kennedy ran for President of the United States on a platform that the economy was growing too *slow*. The 1960 election hinged on the failure of the Eisenhower adminsitration to achieve an "optimum" rate of growth. Walter Heller, University of Minnesota economist and chief economic advisor to President Kennedy, argued persuasively for the need to reduce tax rates in order to eliminate "fiscal drag" and get the economy rolling again. It was recognized later in the Johnson administration that a more rapidly growing economy would generate a "fiscal dividend" which could aid in reaching the collectivist goals of the "Great Society." After all, the "Laffer curve" of the 1980's can be interpreted as a formula for the politician on how to *maximize* tax revenues and the size of government!

The successful tax cut of 1964, desirable as it was, came to be viewed as further justification for a much larger government role in the American economy. With the explosion of social welfare expenditures by the federal government in the 1960's and the 1970's, and the large increase in military spending associated with the war in Southeast Asia, federal spending continued to increase in absolute terms and as a fraction of total economic activity. Whatever the problem, government was the answer, even when the problem was itself the result of some past government policy error.

The growth cult of the early 1960's, however, was to be short-lived. The socialists and their fellow travelers rediscovered the problem of too much growth. In the mid-1960's the "automation hysteria" became the rage. For unexplained reasons, an increased rate of automation of the American economy would cybernate the world and no one would have jobs. Rather than pursue productivity gains

149

through investment in modern plants and new equipment, the goal was to save particular jobs. This issue, interestingly, is currently part of the call for "economic democracy" espoused by Tom Hayden, Jane Fonda and friends. The dire implications for a free society of that idea have already been discussed.

## THE LIMITS TO GROWTH

The most publicized threat of rapid economic expansion, however, involves the proposition of resource limits and the precarious ecological balance of the "spaceship earth." While Rachael Carson's book *Silent Spring* in the early 1960's contributed importantly to the environmental scare, the anti-growth position shifted into high gear with the publication of Jay W. Forrester's *World Dynamics* in 1971 and *The Limits to Growth* by Donella H. Meadows, Dennis L. Meadows, et. al., in 1972. Employing simplistic projections of resource use based on past experience, and not allowing for the conservation which automatically occurs because of rising relative prices, the argument was made that by the second or third decade of the twenty-first century everything would come to a grinding halt.

Using a computer model with dozens of mathematical equations, they forecast a complex interaction between world population growth, the depletion of non-renewable resources, and pollution loads that would produce worldwide scarcity, lower world living standards and mass starvation. Needless to say, the answer required government planning and political action to abolish economic growth. Once again the obvious solution meant more government, more socialization, and increased politicization of our society. Interestingly, many, if not most, of those holding such views were higher income liberals who had already acquired their positons of influence and wealth, and simultaneously could cling to a snobbish dislike of the consumption preferences of the masses.

The collectivists have a phenomenal capacity to argue positions which are essentially contradictory. As the economist Murray Rothbard points out in *For a New Liberty,* these left-liberal types inconsistently maintained, "...at one and the same time that ...we are living in a 'post-scarcity' age where we no longer need private property, capitalism, or material incentives to production; and,...that capitalist greed is depleting our resources and bringing about imminent worldwide scarcity."

Fortunately, the *Limits to Growth* projections involve assumptions about the real world which are far from certain and probably inconsistent with what we might expect from the evidence of history. The model of Meadows and Meadows (frequently called the MIT team or the MIT approach because they were associated with the Massachusetts Institute of Technology) incorporates a Malthusian view of exploding population growth while assuming only a modest increase in world food production. Like Malthus in the early part of the nineteenth century, the MIT model was programmed to significantly underestimate the potential for technological progress. While supporting the notion of exponential population growth, the limits to growth projections failed to grasp the idea that technological progress is only constrained by the imagination of the human mind and the degree of freedom available to exercise that facility. George Gilder provides some feel for this necessarily human process in his book *Wealth and Poverty:*

> Wealth is governed by the mind, but it is caught in matter. The kaleidoscope of shifting valuations (and technology) flashing gains and losses as it is turned in the hands of time, in the grip of 'news', distributes and redistributes the wealth of the world far more quickly and surely than any scheme of the state...The only stable asset among the quakes and shadows is a disciplined brain. Matter melts, but mind and will can flash for a while...inducing their incarnation in silicon and cement...

In other words, technology too can grow exponentially. As a result, Malthus was wrong in the nineteenth century on his predictions regarding living standards and the "iron law of wages." Living standards have in fact risen where economic progress and productivity gains were achieved.

But even if the population problem is solved, according to the "world models" there are other sources of "collapse." Capital accumulation inevitably leads to resource depletion, not only of exhaustible resources but even renewable ones. If the population and resource problems are solved, then pollution loads could still contribute to economic collapse. Or, to paraphrase the MIT team, it is all so complex.

Be that as it may, there were serious errors in these projections. The dynamic computer models of Forrester and Meadows were unbelievably naive with respect to the potential for economically motivated changes in people's behavior. Relative price changes as they affect economic behavior and the potential for rapid and even surprising technological change made their models obsolete before the ink had dried on the computer readouts. Dooms-dayers have predicted the depletion of coal, iron ore, forests, natural gas, oil and all kinds of things for decades, even centuries. But, in fact, an increase in the relative scarcity of a resource raises its price and, thereby, signals consumers to economize and conserve in its use. Furthermore, as we have already suggested, only a slight modification of the assumption regarding the rate of tehnological progress eliminates the dire predictions of these doomsday models.

It is now generally agreed that the *Limits to Growth* conclusions are not substantiated and are subject to very severe criticism. Statements like: "The basic behavior mode of the world system [is the same] even if we assume any number of technological changes in the system;" or: "The limits to growth on this planet will be reached in the next hundred years," are simply inconsistent with the historical record. Further, they are inconsistent with the most realistic assumptions concerning human behavior. Only a very few years after the 1972 publication of their results, Meadows and Meadows themselves published radically softer conclusions regarding the prospects for human life on this planet. The often quoted saying "those who make their living by gazing into the crystal ball must learn to eat cracked glass" haunts yet another group of prolific doomsdayers.

The point of this discussion, however, is to illustrate the way in which the collectivists, the constructivists, and the socialists inevitably call on government to solve problems despite their inconsistent and contradictory recommendations. Too much growth. Too little growth. Too much affluence. Too much poverty. It makes no difference. Government in all of its wisdom (or at least the wisdom of those individuals who happen to command the positions of authority) will save us. There is little recognition of the beneficial role of markets and prices as signals which encourage human beings to change their behavior. Family size, conserving fuel oil and gasoline, and the search for innovations which produce new technologies and result in economizing on a resource that has risen in price, are but a few of the areas where changing relative prices (i.e., the opportunity costs of our actions) motivate individuals to alter their behavior. A system of decentralized and private property ownership in combination with open and competitive markets is much more likely to produce survival and affluence on this planet. We are reminded of Hayek's warning regarding the ability to collect and efficiently utilize the appropriate and desirable kinds of information at a centralized place (i.e., the planning bureaucracy) and on a timely basis. Given the difficulty of dealing with uncertainty and risk by private sector companies like General Motors or Texas Instruments, what makes us think a centralized planning apparatus would improve the situation?

## THE REINDUSTRIALIZATION OF AMERICA

Of course, the latest left-liberal statist plan is to "reindustrialize" America through a cozy "partnership" between government and business. To the extent productivity gains in the U.S. economy have slowed over the past decade, the blame has been wrongly placed on the private sector and not with the acceleration of personal tax burdens and larger government spending which crowds out private investment in research and in new plants and equipment. The Reagan administration's appeal to lower marginal tax rates and slowing federal expenditures--the "supply-side" agenda which attempts to remind us that personal incentives matter for work effort and saving--has, to this point, failed to reduce the relative size of government. Unfortunately, the new left-liberal "partnership" school of thought might gain momentum and carry-the-day in the near term as a result of this continuing growth in government. Federal expenditures represent a larger fraction of the Gross National Product today than when President Carter left office. It is now problematical whether the fascist-type partnership between government and business is avoidable. Nevertheless, there continues to be that one undeniable certainty: the efforts at reindustrialization, like the contradictory no growth nonsense of the 1970's, will demand for the proponents an even larger role for government. What is required, they argue, is a centrally planned economy. Everything we do, individually or cooperatively, must be politicized.

## GOVERNMENT AND THE BUSINESS CYCLE

Politically directed solutions have not been limited to the longer range problems associated with economic growth. The argument is made that intervention by government in the economy is also necessary to protect individuals from the consequences of the business cycle. According to the "fine tuners," severe booms and busts are naturally the fault of competitive capitalism. Although the actions of politicians frequently produce the very instability they seek to correct, for the constructionist and the socialist the only solution is a much larger role for the state.

The intitial shot heard 'round the world' in 1936, and a book that offered an intellectual case for government intervention, was John Maynard Keynes' The General Theory of Employment, Interest, and Money. Unemployment had been at very high levels since the beginning of the decade in the industrial West and the case was being made everywhere that the Great Depression represented the failure of capitalism. Keynes supplied the liberal intellectual community with a theoretical defense for expanding government's role. It made little difference that the General Theory is a ponderous and difficult book to read and that relatively few of those who recommend government intervention had ever read it. Without question, it became the center piece of the "Keynesian Revolution," bringing with it a radical revision of economics and economic policy.

The "Keynesian Revolution" was brought to America by the already discussed influential  economist Alvin Hansen of Harvard University. Keynes himself had received a luke-warm reception when he came to the United States. Roosevelt was not impressed; stating he hardly understood a word the man said. Nevertheless, his book made a break with the prevailing ideas and was very much at odds with what economists of that generation had been taught. It remained for Alvin Hansen, through the publication of his many books, including a volume entitled A Guide to Keynes, to sell Keynes' ideas.

The notions of "discretionary" policy, "pump-priming," "fine-tuning," and "balanced budget multipliers" were first made understandable to economists and then to politicians. The business cycle, especially the contractionary phase of recession, was the result of an insufficiency of private sector spending, Keynes argued. Business investment was woefully inadequate.

The obvious answer for those like Hansen, and, with time, to most of the economists in the United States and Great Britain, was increased government expenditures. "Compensatory finance," for example, meant that government be required to run budget deficits when the economy was soft. As the private sector recovered, the appropriate "fiscal policy" would then be for government to balance its budget or run a surplus to reduce the national debt. However, for Hansen this compensatory finance role would not be just "pump-priming." It would require government's role to be enlarged indefinitely, stemming directly from his infamous secular stagnation thesis. The concept of fiscal discipline, of balanced budgets and fiscal responsiblity, received a blow from which it has never recovered. Herbert Stein in his book *The Fiscal Revolution in America* provides startling documentation of the collapse of government's fiscal responsibility. Current federal budget deficits of more than $200 billion annually and a cumulative national debt fast approaching $2 *trillion* suggest the magnitude of the problem.

## THE CAUSES OF THE GREAT DEPRESSION

Unfortunately, there is one basic problem with this clarion call for government intervention to fine tune the economy. The premise is wrong! The justification for government intervention is based on the proposition that competitive capitalism has an inherent instability. The intellectual defense of a larger role for government in maintaining full-employment, and presumably price level stability, was generated by the actual events of the economic collapse during the early 1930's. For example, the U.S. economy hit bottom in March of 1933 when the unemployment rate rose to about twenty-five percent of the labor force. Industrial production was more than forty percent below its peak of four years earlier and thousands of businesses had failed, including roughly one-half of the banks of the country. But, the fundamental question remains: was it the capitalist order which produced the depression, or did the fault lie elsewhere?

It is our contention that the depression, at the very least its severity and length, was a direct consequence of *government* action and policy. The large and rapid decline in the American economy in the early 1930's was not a failure of capitalism, but indeed was a failure of government. Murray Rothbard, in *America's Great Depression,* makes a very convincing case that government meddling in the

154

1920's contributed importantly to that which followed. He contends that the contraction in the early 1930's followed necessarily from the distortions in the economy produced by the monetary expansion of the 1920's.

But, once the decline was underway, the agency which had been created by Congress in 1913 to take corrective actions, the Federal Reserve System, failed to do so. According to Milton Friedman and Anna Schwartz in *A Monetary History of the United States, 1867-1960,* the Federal Reserve System, charged with the responsibility of avoiding financial panics and business declines, allowed the money supply to decline by roughly thirty percent between 1929 and the spring of 1933. The falling money supply placed great downward pressures on the economy, producing a financial crisis. As thousands of banks failed or were absorbed by other banks, the contraction intensified. In the absence of the false security produced by the existence of the Federal Reserve System, individual banks and bank clearing houses, as they had in previous business declines, would have dealt with the financial crisis in ways which had been used prior to the new government guarantees supposedly provided by the Federal Reserve Act of 1913. Friedman pursuasively concludes, "...it is literally inconceivable that the Depression could have lasted as long as it did, or have been as severe as it was, if the FED had acted early to prevent a decline in the quantity of money." In fact, Friedman observed wisely in another work: "Perhaps the most remarkable feature of the record is the adaptability and flexibility that the private economy has so frequently shown under such extreme provocation."

Superimposed on the monetary contraction of the period, in retrospect a stupendous error by the Federal Reserve System, the United States Congress added its dose of economic lunacy to the times by adopting the Smoot-Hawley Tariff of 1930. This highly protectionist measure increased the average tariff on United States imports to more than fifty percent of the value of dutiable imports. Its severe impact on the exports of other industrial countries into the United States produced an inevitable retaliation. Protectionist measures were adopted by most every country. The resulting "begger-my'neighbor" policies, designed to cope with domestic unemployment, predictably caused a drastic reduction in the volume of international trade. World trade literally collapsed in the decade of the 1930's, falling by more than sixty percent.

Such a decline in trade reverberated throughout the industrial world and contributed importantly to the depth and severity of the World Depression. Once again, government policy and intervention on behalf of special interest groups generated socially undesirable consequences. In the early 1980's, with unemployment at politically unacceptable levels in the industrial world, governments are once again flirting with tariffs and quotas to protect domestic jobs. Unfortunately, there is little discussion of the earlier period when similar pressures produced such expensive and disasterous results.

## CAN GOVERNMENT FINE TUNE THE ECONOMY?

Even if there is a degree of instability in a competitive capitalist order, and unquestionably the market cannot and will not produce perfect stability, the empirical question remains as to whether government intervention and discretionary fine tuning actually reduces the degree of instability. Here again we believe the record is fairly clear. Short run discretionary policy decisions with respect to the federal budget and/or the rate of growth in the money supply do not seem to have played any significant role in reducing the amplitude of the business cycle. In fact, it can be argued that efforts at fine tuning the economy have frequently been counterproductive. Because of time lags in the impact of economic policy, tax cuts have come too late, and jobs bills have been passed *after* recovery is already underway. Expansionary monetary policies by the Federal Reserve System, ostensibly designed to fight a recession, have contributed to making the inflationary pressures worse during the ensuing boom. Those who advocate a discretionary, stop-go, government policy should be required to show where *they* would get the knowledge required to achieve a truly counter cyclical and, therefore, desirable fiscal and monetary policy.

## FISCAL DISCIPLINE AND BUDGET DEFICITS

There is, however, one implication of compensatory financing's role in dealing with the business cycle which stands clear: the government of the United States runs chronic deficits. Fiscal discipline is apparently nonexistent. Before the Great Depression, the United States ran deficits only in wartime. Budget surpluses occurred at least as often as budget deficits. A large national debt was incurred during the Civil War, but by 1893 most of this debt had been eliminated with *twenty-eight* consecutive years of budget surpluses. Following World War I, the national debt was cut roughly in half by eleven consecutive years of budget surpluses during the 1920's. After the Depression and World War II, there still appeared to be some degree of fiscal discipline. Between the years 1947 and 1960, the United States government had seven years of surplus and seven years of deficit. The budget was roughly in balance over this period.

Unfortunately, something went wrong in the 1960's. In the 1930's the United States government prohibited American citizens from redeeming paper money for gold. During the 1960's, the last legal ties between the fiat paper money in circulation and the United

States monetary gold stock was broken. As a result, the constraints on the federal government's issuance of paper money, acting through the assistance of the Federal Reserve System, were significantly reduced. On August 15, 1971, President Nixon closed the "gold-window," and to the relief of the Keynesians, the international monetary system was also now free of the discipline of gold.

The way was paved for larger government spending. Jobs programs, special "needs," and whatever special interest groups could think of were financed through larger deficits and increased doses of money creation. Richard E. Wagner and Robert D. Tollison in *Balanced Budgets, Fiscal Responsibility and the Constitution* have provided an excellent summary of this fundamental change in American politics:

> For the first century-and-a-half of our history, our budgetary policy was influenced by the prevailing belief that budget deficits were proper only during wars or recessions and that at other times some effort should be made to retire national debt through budget surpluses. This ethos can be said to have constituted an unwritten element of our Constitution. It found widespread expression in intellectual discourse. Many economists felt that budget deficits would erode a nation's capital stock, thereby reducing standards of living. They believed that in order to contribute to prosperity rather than to detract from it, government should promote the creation of capital and not its consumption. What was wise for an individual was wise for a nation as well.

Adam Smith had warned in *The Wealth of Nations* that "...what is prudence in the conduct of every private family, can scarce be folly in that of a great kingdom."

The Keynesian onslaught, led by those who wanted greater governmental responsibility for the economy's performance, produced a consensus that a "responsible" budgetary policy by government required deficits. Those like Alvin Hansen who saw a permanent need for "compensatory finance," also visualized a world of perpetual budget deficits. The unwritten constitutional prohibition on budget deficits dissolved slowly between the election of Franklin Roosevelt and the Kennedy/Johnson administrations. Roosevelt had actually proposed tax increases in 1933 in order to balance the budget. In 1964, the famous Kennedy/Johnson tax cut was passed by Congress when the federal budget was already in deficit. A fiscal revolution had, in fact, taken place in America. There were to be no limits to government spending, and the collapse of the budget-balancing ethos has now produced twenty-four federal budget deficits in the last twenty-five years. The cumulative deficit during President Reagan's first administration reached almost $600 billion! Only a determined electorate, bringing the appropriate pressure to bear on the Congress, will be able to turn the lumbering leviathan state around.

157

## THE POLITICAL BUSINESS CYCLE

Unfortunately, in a representative democracy there exists a "political business cycle." Given the modern preference for using government spending increases and tax reductions to stabilize the economy at "full" employment, ignoring for the moment the relevant question of whether it indeed works, the politician interested in generating electoral support tends to favor deficit financing. During periods of rising or unusually high unemployment, the politician will favor increasing spending (jobs bills, public works projects, and the like) and cutting taxes. On the other hand, if inflation is the problem, the rules of discretionary fiscal policy call for spending cuts and higher taxes. However, these contractionary policies reduce electoral support. Politicians find themselves, then, coming down on the side of expansion and increased government spending during recessions, but generally unwilling to take those politically unpopular actions which would thwart inflation.

Budget deficits undoubtedly gain more votes than do balanced budgets, and a balanced budget will generate more political support than a surplus. Therefore, there tends to be a political bias towards deficits and consequently an inflationary bias to federal budgetary policy. For the politician it is easier to fight unemployment than it is to fight inflation. With the unwritten constitutional provision against deficit financing more or less repealed, the "fundamental defect of democracy" with respect to budgetary matters raises its ugly head. In order to retain office, politicians vote for more spending and incur larger deficits.

There are those who believe the only way out of this dilemma is through a constitutional amendment which would limit federal spending and/or require a balanced budget. More than thirty state legislatures have voted in favor of a constitutional convention where the issue of government fiscal responsibility would be addressed. A bill sponsored jointly by the National Tax Limitation Committee and other organizations to amend the Constitution by limiting the growth in taxes and require a balanced budget actually passed the United States Senate in 1982. This proposal would place a ceiling on federal expenditures as a fraction of the national income. The proposed amendment would permit deficits during declared military hostilities, and, whould permit deficits under other circumstances only if approved by a sixty percent majority of both houses.

Unfortunately, just as the Prohibition Amendment to the United States Constitution failed to stop people from drinking, the passage of a spending lid and/or balanced budget amendment would only work if the attitudes of citizens were to change. We must somehow recapture a Lockian/Jeffersonian view of natural and unalienable rights in which the only legitimate role of government is to protect rights. Without a much enlarged, popular support for Smith's "system of natural liberty," amending the Constitution to require balanced budgets would probably accomplish very little. Without ideaological pressures from the electorate, politicians will continue to find the means, for example, through regulation and off-budget spending, to continue to buy votes.

# CHAPTER 14

## THE IDEA OF PROGRESS

> While the twentieth century is far from barren of faith in progress, there is nevertheless good ground for supposing that when the identity of our century is eventually fixed by historians, not faith but abandonment of faith in the idea of progress will be one of the major attributes. The skepticism regarding Western progress that was once confined to a very small number of intellectuals in the nineteenth century has grown and spread to not merely the large majority of intellectuals in this final quarter of the century, but many millions of other people in the West.
>
> --Robert Nisbet

The idea of progress has always been inextricably linked to the idea of human liberty. Herbert Spencer, a student of the human predicament in the nineteenth century, and who more than any other person tied the prospects for freedom to the notion of progress, observed that "progress is difference." If individuals are free to be different in pursuing their own goals, then progress is an inevitable consequence. The sociologist Robert Nisbet in his *History of the Idea of Progress* concludes "...that this idea [of progress] has done more good over a twenty-five hundred year period, led to more creativeness in more spheres, and given more strength to human hope and to individual desire for improvement than any other single idea in Western history." Nobel Laureate Friedrich Hayek believes that "...the preservation of the kind of civilization that we know," meaning one dominated by the spontaneous order of private property and limited government, "...depends on the operation of forces which, under favorable conditions, produce progress." It was Adam Smith in the *Wealth of Nations* who made the very convincing case that larger numbers attain personal success in a society which is experiencing economic growth:

> It is in the progressive state, while society is advancing to the further acquisition, rather than when it has acquired its full complement of riches, that the condition of the labouring poor, of the great body of people, seems to be happiest and most comfortable. It is hard in the stationary, and miserable in the declining state. The progressive state is really the cheerful and hearty state of all the different orders of society. The stationary is dull; the declining melancholy.

### THE LOSS OF FAITH IN PROGRESS

It is interesting to observe the degree to which this faith in progress, cultural and economic, continues to be held by many Americans in spite of the loss of belief among most intellectuals. Nevertheless,

160

opinion setters, the second hand purveyors of ideas, at the very least doubt the efficacy of progress, and their pessimistic views are rapidly being sold to the public. In the past few decades this linchpin of Western civilization, the idea of progress--cultivated and communicated by the great majority of Western intellectuals for more than two thousand years--has seemingly lost its central place in the minds of the intelligentsia. According to Hayek: "Writers nowadays who value their reputation among the more sophisticated hardly dare mention progress without including the word in quotation marks. The implicit confidence in the beneficience of progress that during the last two centuries marked the advanced thinker has come to be regarded as the sign of a shallow mind." Indeed those who do believe in the idea of progress are very likely to be representative of those, especially social scientists, who propose political intervention and socialist solutions to the human predicament. Progress is today an important part of the dogma in those countries which would overthrow Western civilization and all that it has stood for in the past. "This is one more instance," Robert Nisbet tells us, "of the capacity for Western skills and values to be exported, corrupted, and then turned against the very West that gave them birth."

It would appear that we have lost our way. A malaise and ashamedness has set in among the intellectual community in the West, especially, it would seem, among segments of the middle-class young. Like descending fog, a feeling of guilt regarding Western civilization, a general loss of purpose, and an erosion of confidence in traditional institutions has engulfed our country. Forgetting the great intellectual, cultural, and economic accomplishments of the West in the past, and despite the gains in individual human freedom through the Western institutions of private property, constitutions, and democracy, there seems to have occurred an erosion in our optimism about the future. "Manifestly," says Nisbet in *History of the Idea of Progress*, "the power and influence of Western civilization in the world have been declining ever since World War I. All we now know is that the West, still with all its flaws and the major complex of reasonably free and democratic governments, has become, irreversibly one would guess, the object of disdain, contempt, and hostility in the greater part of the world. The West is envied for its material wealth but is no longer either feared or respected, much less regarded as model, in the communist and most of the Third World countries."

Unquestionably, the lost faith in the idea of progress has contributed greatly to the decline in the intellectual's belief in competitive capitalism as a delivery system and source of economic progress. And interestingly, the malaise has even spread to the socialists who in greater and greater numbers no longer believe in the "inevitable" socialist revolution. The idea of progress suffers in both the East and the West.

## THE MEANING OF PROGRESS

What do we mean by progress? Again from his scholarly *History of the Idea of Progress*, Robert Nisbet provides a workable definition: "Simply stated, the idea of progress holds that mankind has advanced in the past--from some aboriginal condition of primitiveness, barbarism, or even nullity--is now advancing, and will continue to advance through the foreseeable future." This progress involves two separate strands of development which are at the same time at least partly complementary. To quote Nisbet, the two "propositions" are as follows:

> First slow, gradual, and cumulative improvement in knowledge, the kind of knowledge embodied in the arts and sciences, in the manifold ways man has for coping with the problems presented by nature or by the sheer efforts of human beings to live with one another in groups.

> The second...centers upon man's moral or spiritual condition on earth, his happiness, his freedom from torments of nature and society, and above all his serenity or tranquillity.

Progress involves a profound respect for the past and a joyous contemplation of the future. The past is crucial. Like beams from a cornerstone, we all stand on the intellectual, scientific, and cultural developments stemming from earlier efforts. Our hope for the future includes both an improvement in man's spiritual well-being as well as material comfort. For those who believe in the value of a free society, it is crucial to remember Hayek's warning that "progress by its very nature cannot be planned." Since change is such an integral part of the future, Hayek insightfully reminds us in his *Constitution of Liberty:* "It would be more correct to think of progress as a process of formation and modification of human intellect, a process of adaptation and learning in which not only the possibilities known to us but also our values and desires continually change. As progress consists in the discovery of the not yet known, its consequences must be unpredictable."

## THE IDEA OF PROGRESS IN THE PAST

Though unknown, unpredictable, and hence unmanageable, the idea of progress has always been deeply embedded in Western intellectual thought. The Greeks believed in progress and forcefully argued its advantages. Likewise for the Romans. Christianity also contributed importantly to the attraction of the idea of progress. Both Christ's parable of the talents and Apostle Paul's admonitions to look to the future point to stewardship, accountability, and progress. St. Augustine wrote passionately about the prospects for progress. Admittedly however, there was a period in the medieval world during which people abandoned reason and turned to mysticism. It is interesting that the views expressed at that dark time are similar in many ways to the loss of confidence which dominates the intelligentsia in the last half of the twentieth century. The historian W. T. Jones in *The Medieval Mind* captures the extent of this malaise in a quotation from the early medieval period:

> You must know that the world has grown old, and does not remain in its former vigour. It bears witness to its own decline. The rainfall and the sun's warmth are both diminishing; the metals are nearly exhausted; the husbandman is failing in the fields, the sailor on the seas, the soldier in the camp, honesty in the market, justice in the courts, concord in friendships, skill in the arts, discipline in morals. This is the sentence passed upon the world, that everything which has a beginning should perish, that things which have reached maturity should grow old, the strong weak, the great small, and that after weakness and shrinkage should come dissolution.

However, a great awakening took place with the Reformation in the sixteenth century. In fact, the renewed attention to the Christian faith in Europe and later in America brought a revival to the idea of progress. The rise of Puritanism, especially in England during the seventeenth century, seemingly unified the two strands of progress: increased knowledge and a spiritual awakening. "Progress in the arts and sciences," according to Nisbet, "is held to be at once a *sign* of the imminence of the golden age of the spirit on earth and a *cause* of this imminence." From the sixteenth century until the early part of the twentieth century the great minds of Western civilization advocated and defended the idea of progress. An example of this faith on the eve of the Industrial Revolution is found in the works of the German philosopher and scientist Gottfried von Leibniz. Leibniz was the founder of the symbolic logic and an important contributor to modern mathematics. Sympathetic to the idea of economic growth, his influence was widespread on those who followed, including Marx, Darwin, and Spencer. Examining the continuity and necessity of progress in his book entitled *On the Ultimate Origination of Things,* he wrote as follows:

> ...To realize in its completeness the universal beauty and perfection of the works of God, we must recognize a certain perpetual and very free progress of the whole universe, such that it is always going forward to greater improvement...Although many substances have already attained a great perfection, yet on account of the infinite divisibility of the continuous, there always remain in the abyss of things slumbering parts which have yet to be awakened, to growth in size and worth, and in a word, to advance to a more perfect state. And hence no end of progress is ever reached.

## PROGRESS, ECONOMIC GROWTH, AND FREEDOM

The idea of progress continued to be an integral part of the mental makeup of most Western intellectuals in the modern period. In the second half of the eighteenth century and during the nineteenth century the idea reached its apex. Intellectuals as well as the masses, embraced progress and its consequences. One important result was a close and complementary relationship between it and economic growth. Voltaire said that "commerce, liberty, and progress were inseparable." Adam Smith in *The Wealth of Nations* believed that progress and economic advance appeared in tandem and wrote about the "progress of opulence" and the "progress of institutions."

The mainspring of human progress for Smith was in "...the natural effort of every individual to better his own condition...to exert itself with freedom and security," and this natural effort is capable "alone, and without any assistance" of producing wealth and progress. In France, Turgot had already pointed out that "self-interest, ambition, vainglory" were sufficient to move "...the total mass of human kind, through alterations of calm and upheaval, good fortune and bad, advances ever, though slowly, toward greater perfection." Borrowing from Turgot and others, Adam Smith combined the philosophy of individual freedom to what he called "the natural progress of opulence." John Adams, one of the founding fathers, in his *Defense of the Constitutions of Government of the United States* summarized what he thought were the implications of the growth of human freedom:

> The arts and sciences, in general, during the three or four last centuries, have had a regular course of progressive improvement. The inventions in mechanic arts, the discoveries in natural philosophy, navigation, and commerce, and the advancement of civilization and humanity, have occasioned changes in the condition of the world, and the human character, which would have astonished the most refined nations of antiquity.

The most penetrating and insightful ideas, however, of the necessary connection between individual liberty and the idea of progress were in the writings of Herbert Spencer in the second half of the nineteenth century. Robert Nisbet persuasively argues in his *History of the Idea of Progress* that: "No one before or since so effectively united the two philosophies of freedom and of progress, or so completely anchored the former in the latter." For Spencer, freedom was a necessary prerequisite to progress. In part, progress itself is to be measured by the extent to which human freedom is realized. In other words, this profound belief in human progress would require Adam Smith's "system of natural liberty," or equivalently, the "spontaneous order" of Hayek, in which individuals would be free to pursue their own goals without the coercive interference of other people or government. For Spencer, progress was literally defined as the path towards greater individual freedom.

Unfortunately, during this same period there was another group who believed just as passionately in the inevitability of progress. But, unlike the others, progress was to be intimately associated with power. August Comte, Rousseau, Hegel, and Karl Marx were unanimous in their acceptance of this definition which emphasized power. To draw the distinction, we offer the following paragraph from J. B. Bury's *The Idea of Progress,* which was published in 1920:

> Theories of progress are thus differentiated into two distinct types, corresponding to two radically opposed political theories and appealing to two antagonistic temperaments. The one type is that of constructive idealists and socialists, who can name all the streets and towers of the 'city of gold,' which they imagine as situated just round a promontory. The development of man is a closed system; its term is known and is within reach. The other type is that of those who, surveying the gradual ascent of man, believe that by the same interplay of forces which have conducted him so far and by a further development of the liberty which he has fought to win, he will move slowly towards conditions of increasing harmony and happiness. Here the development is indefinite: its term is unknown, and lies in the remote future. Individual liberty is the motive force, and the corresponding political theory is [classical] liberalism.

Progress, as power, requires that man be changed. The "scientific reality of human progress" seeks to bend and mold man, a form of progress requiring the creation of a new type of human being. And, of course, the instrument of all this behavior modification is government. Rousseau went so far as to define absolute state power as freedom! The German philosopher Hegel made the point in the following manner: "The state power is...the achievement of all, the absolutely accomplished fact, wherein individuals find their essential nature expressed, and where their particular existence is simply and solely a consciousness of their own universality...it stands as the absolute basis of all their action." This "higher freedom" of Hegel's would be achieved when the individual recognized his or her subsidiary position relative to the absolute, leviathan state.

Karl Marx, a true believer in progress (e.g., "In broad outlines we can designate the Asiatic, the ancient, the feudal, and the modern bourgeois methods of production as so many epochs in the progress of the economic formation of society."), recognized the requirements of power which would be necessary for the achievement of his socialist utopia:

> The question then arises: What transformation will the state undergo in a communist society? In other words, what social functions will remain that are analogous to present functions of the state?...Between capitalist and communist society lies a period of revolutionary transformation from one to the other. There is a corresponding period of transition in the political sphere and in this period the state can only take the form of a revolutionary dictatorship of the proletariat.

As we all know, the totalitarian "dictatorship of the proletariat" in the Soviet Union shows no signs of whithering away. Nor do the dictatorships in Poland, Bulgaria, the People's Republic of China, or Cuba. Rather than freedom and progress (as autonomy) and individual responsibility, the Marxist claims the state must *force* the individual to be free. In summary, the viewpoint associated with the names of Adam Smith and Herbert Spencer is the proposition that freedom is something which adheres to individuals as we actually find them. For Comte, Rousseau, Hegel, and Marx, freedom belongs to some collectivity or state in which government intervention and force is employed to create a new type of human being.

## THE RECENT MALAISE

Although embraced by two drastically different interpretations of the meaning of progress, the idea itself continued to command the attention and conviction of most intellectuals well into the twentieth century. For example, as late as 1927 a respected American scholar could write the following without fear of ridicule or embarrassment:

> The remarkable increase in the efficiency of industry through the achievement of science and the multiplication of tools and machinery seems to justify the belief that the age of plenty has dawned...Such considerations would seem to offer some support to the belief in a natural law of progress, and to strengthen the unquenchable hope that by the gradual evolution of sweeter manners and purer laws, the *Civitas Dei* will ultimately be reached, and the Apocalyptic visions of seers realized.

Even today the social sciences continue to be founded in and subject to the paradigm of progress. After all, the original works of Adam Smith, August Compte, Karl Marx, and Herbert Spencer have shaped the modern disciplines of economics, sociology, political science, and anthropology.

However, encouraged by the economic hardship and intellectual revisions produced by the Great Depression of the 1930's, the idea of progress began to be called into question. Even in the 1920's faith in Western progress was questioned in many literary works, including the writings of T. S. Eliot and James Joyce. Following World War II, but especially in the 1960's, a new kind of radicalism surfaced. Students, faculty, and others on American university campuses were prepared to use violence as a weapon to voice their doubts regarding progress. For these radical-left groups the loss of faith in progress was, according to the political scientist George Reisman, associated with a loss of faith in the inevitability of the socialist revolution. Increasing numbers in the Western community, especially among the intellegentsia, believed with Max Weber that it is "...not summer's bloom [which] lies ahead of us but rather a polar night of icy darkness and hardship." Even those who would advocate the use of power to achieve their notion of progress--through a large interventionist role in society for government--have come to doubt their competence to plan and arrange the lives of every individual.

It is clear to Robert Nisbet the source of this decline in faith:

> Everything now suggests...that Western faith in the dogma of progress is waning rapidly in all levels and spheres in this final part of the twentieth century. The reasons...have much less to do with the unprecedented world wars, the totalitarianisms, the economic depressions, and other major political, military, and economic afflictions which are peculiar to the twentieth century than they do with the fateful if less dramatic erosion of the fundamental *intellectual* and *spiritual* premises upon which the idea of progress has rested thoughout its long history. (emphasis added)

The major intellectual and spiritual premises according to Nisbet are five in number. First, faith in the idea of progress has always included, even for the Greeks, a strong attachment to the past. History does have something to teach us. Second, the superiority of Western Civilization, its institutions, technology, and religion, was taken for granted. Third, there has always been a strong attachment to the "intrinsic importance" and "ineffaceable worth of [human] life on this earth." Fourth, the idea of progress has always been based on the inevitable acquisition of knowledge which stems from man's ability to reason. Faith in progress and the power to reason are synergistically bound together. And fifth, the idea of progress for at least three hundred years has been intimately tied to the desirability and advantages of economic growth and technological advance. Nisbet shows how, to one degree or another, these fundamental premises have been and are being challenged by the intellectual community, especially in the West.

## LIMITS TO GROWTH AND PROGRESS

Given the major theme of this book, that the Great American Experiment is hinged on the close and complementary relationship between human liberty and the nature and causes of the wealth of nations, we choose to focus on the question of the desirability and possibility of economic growth. One of the most important reasons for the decline in faith regarding progress in general, among many if not most intellectuals and opinion makers follows from their loss of confidence in the benefits associated with technological progress and economic growth. For example, Ezra J. Mishan, a British economist, argued in his *Costs of Economic Growth* and a number of books since 1967, that economic growth will necessarily result in a deterioration in our physical environment and thereby drastically lower the quality of human life on this planet. As already noted, the Club of Rome's *Limits to Growth* in 1972 projected the collapse of our eco-system and therefore the end of human civilization. While others, like Fred Hirsh in *Social Limits to Growth*, argue the gradual erosion of moral values will spell the end of capitalism, most proponents of the "no growth," "Age of Environmentalism" movement stress the *physical* limitations to economic progress.

Nisbet has provided an excellent summary of this no-growth mentality:

> With steadily enlarging sectors of Western and particularly American society, a disenchantment with or more ominously an outright hostility toward economic growth is to be discerned. There is rising fear that we and our planet are doomed unless we bring this growth to halt, unless we drastically curtail our use of fuels and minerals, unless we renouce all nuclear power, unless we declare vast areas of land and water to be eco-system off limits to any kind of economic or technological use...Rarely has human society been without doomsday predictions based upon some kind of belief, but what we are experiencing today in the West is without precedent in kind of volume.

Herbert E. Meyer in *The War Against Progress* shows how the no-growth position involves hundreds of "battles" that, while seemingly unconnected, throttle economic progress and in total represent a powerful force. Delaying the Alaskan pipeline for over a decade, stopping a billion dollar hydroelectric project because of the snail darter, refraining from drilling for oil because of the strutting sage grouse, *ad infinitum*. Although each is combatted with great sincerity from the specific interest group, the end result has been a dismantling of the economic engine and consequently curtailed material progress. Perhaps, as Meyer suggests, it is analogous to a man bleeding to death from a thousand small cuts.

On "Earth Day" in 1970, for example, a group of students in California buried an automobile to demonstrate their opposition to materialism and economic growth. Understandably, the event was picketed by black students who believed that the buried automobile might have been of some use and value to the poor. Though much of the opposition to material progress is in the name of "saving" the environment, there appears to be other important considerations. William Tucker, in *Progress and Privileges*, makes a very important point: "What is being purveyed...is a view of the world in which human activity is defined as 'bad' and natural conditions as 'good.' The Sierra Club's definition of a 'degraded environment' is an environment that shows evidence of human habitation." The opposition to economic growth stems from an environmental movement represented by "preservationists," not conservationists.

Gifford Pinchot, in many respects the father of the conservationist movement in America, captured the natue of this distinction: "The object of our forest policy," he declared at a meeting of the American Society of Foresters, "is not to preserve the forests because they are beautiful...or because they are refuges for the wild creatures of the wilderness...but the making of prosperous homes." The Age of Environmentalism is in fact an elitist movement, which according to William Tucker, "...favors the affluent over the poor, the haves over the have-nots." He continues: "Sitting at the top of the economic heap, aristocracies naturally do not want to see too much economic or social rearrangement. Having made it to the top, they become far more concerned with *preventing others from climbing the ladder behind them,* than in making it up a few more rungs themselves." Bayard Rustin, the veteran civil rights leader, has appropriately called the radical environmentalist "...self-righteous, elitist, neo-Malthusian who call for slow growth or no growth...and who would condemn the black underclass, the slum proletariat, the rural blacks, to permanent poverty." The black economist Thomas Sowell has observed that "you don't see many black faces in the Sierra Club." We are in fact dealing with what William Tucker appropriately calls the "politics of aristocracy."

In a very important article in *The American Spectator* Robert Nisbet has characterized the limits to growth movement very clearly. Namely, its strength rests mostly with its potential for facilitating and encouraging a political and social revolution. Its mild version would politicize the state. The next step would be complete socialism and undoubtedly totalitarianism. According to Nisbet:

> In its more militant and agressive manifestations environmentalism has become a social movement devoted increasingly to political, social, and economic ends. More and more, in both structure and aim, environmentalism resembles other fundamentally revolutionary movements in Western religious and political history.

Another strand of this commitment to what John Stuart Mill called "the stationary state" is the notion of eliminating risk from the human environment. The proposition that if economic growth and change is stopped the dangers and risks can somehow be eliminated. Mary Douglas and Aaron Wildavsky in *Risk and Culture* argue that this attempt to "obliterate" all "evils and risks" is analogous to primitive peoples who "demand an autopsy for every death." This in part represents a "revolt against science." Remember that there actually were attempts to *outlaw* the steam locomotive and the use of alternating electric current among other interesting examples of wrongheadedness. The scientist Robert L. Sinsheimer illustrates the nature of the pessimism regarding the productive acquisition and use of new knowledge which is currently quite fashionable:

> For four centuries science has progressively expanded our knowledge and reshaped our perception of the world. In the same time technology

169

has correspondingly reshaped the pattern of our lives and the world in which we live. Most people would agree that the net consequence of these activities has been benign. But it may be that the conditions which fostered such a benign outcome of scientific advance and technological innovation are changing to a less favorable set.

In summary, the idea of progress is on the defensive. We seem to have lost our confidence, and the loss of confidence in economic growth derives its sense of moral force from those who want a great deal more than a healthy environment. The "Age of Environmentalism" in large part is a political and social movement for revolution in order to make *all* things political. "The conservation movement that began to flourish at the turn of the century under men like Theodore Roosevelt and Gifford Pinchot was a movement in prudence and efficiency, designed to increase and prolong economic growth," Nisbet reminds us in his *American Spectator* article. "What it has become in organizations like the Friends of the Earth is a sectarian struggle to abolish economic growth as far as possible, to preserve the wilderness at whatever cost to economy and democratic society."

## REASONS FOR OPTIMISM

In spite of this elitist opposition to economic growth and material progress, many thoughtful individuals have raised an important question: Can we stop the striving for economic progress even if it was somehow desirable? We all experience the benefits of growth, but often we are forced to share the costs associated with change. There are those among us who view economic progress to be more of a curse than a blessing. Nevertheless, most of the world's population are still engaged in the fight to eliminate hunger and disease and recognize the potential for higher material standards of living. It would seem that the world's poor will not and cannot be denied. Given the high rates of population growth in many parts of the world, a decline in our rate of material advance might indeed be a disaster for tens of millions or even hundreds of millions of people. In his discussion of the idea of progress in the *Constitution of Liberty*, Friedrich Hayek recognized the implications of the West's demonstrated success, through the institutions of competitive capitalism, in raising living standards and increasing human choice:

> We must take into account the fact that the consequences of past progress--namely, world-wide extension of rapid and easy communication of knowledge and ambitions--have largely deprived us of the choice as to whether or not we want continued rapid progress. The new fact in our present position that forces us to push on is that the accomplishments of our civilization have become the object of desire and envy of all the rest of the world. Regardless of whether from some higher point of view our civilization is really better or not, we must recognize that its material

results are demanded by practically all who have come to know them.

Therefore, if the world's people do in fact demand economic growth, the truly important question becomes the degree to which the case made by the no-growth movement has factual merit. Are circumstances such as environmental decay, resource exhaustion, population growth and limits to technological change likely to curtail the possibilities and prospects for continued economic growth? What is the future of progress? Forutnately, many important voices are saying, and we agree, that the idea of progress is not dead. Responding to the doomsday predictions and dissaster lobbyists, there have appeared in recent years many articulate and persuasive arguments on behalf of continued economic growth. For the world's poor, that means hope.

An early critique of the Club of Rome's *Limits to Growth* appeared under the title of *Models of Doom: A Critique of the Limits of Growth.* This was a collection of studies edited by the eminent economic historian H.S.D. Cole. Though relatively mild in their criticism of the "world models" of Forrester and Meadows and Meadows, these studies nevertheless demonstrated the many unwarranted assumptions regarding the prospects for economic growth on the "spaceship earth." Ernest Beckerman, in his *In Defense of Economic Growth* provided a very believable scenario regarding the long-run prospects for continued economic expansion supported by readily available resources and food supplies. As George Reisman has pointed out: "While the total volume of chemical elements in the world has remained the same, the volume of *useful* elements and compounds *at the disposal of man* has been enormously *increased.*" The problem is which deposit to exploit first, and that is best decided on economic efficiency grounds.

While in our opinion Alvin Toffler failed to comprehend the Lockian tradition of individual freedom, he presented in his book *The Third Wave* a truly exciting glimpse of an exciting future. Possibly making use of his "Electronic Cottage," and surely supported by the development of the microprocessor and other technological breakthroughs, progress is surely possible. Rising living standards are almost inevitable for Toffler. The best-seller, *Megatrends,* by John Naisbitt also points to a rosy future, predicting a greater decentralization of society and more numerous power centers. Unfortunately, *Megatrends* fails to recognize the role that a market system of private property and limited government must play. His optimistic conclusions, based on tens of thousands of newspaper clippings which identify trends, will hardly occur if statism and government growth continue unabated.

The late Herman Kahn and his research team at the Hudson Institute have produced a powerful argument for an almost unlimited potential for rising standards of living. In *The Next 200 Years,* the case was persuasively made that world population might increase by a factor of ten and the world's production of goods and services increase by a factor of two hundred "...without exceeding the intrinsic carrying capacity of the earth." At the same time they "...believe that the population and gross world product are likely to stabilize well below these levels." The opening statement of *The Next 200 Years* summarized the forecast by Herman Kahn and the Hudson Institute:

> Two hundred years ago almost everywhere human beings were comparatively few, poor, and at the mercy of the forces of nature, and 200 hundred years from now, we expect, almost everywhere they will be numerous, rich, and in control of the forces of nature.

In Kahn's more recent book, *World Economic Development: 1979 and Beyond,* he reaffirms that "we still believe in that prediction--barring (an essential *caveat*) bad luck or bad management." The book was required, according to Kahn, because "the desirability of increasing economic affluence and technological advancement is under such broad and intense attack today that some defense seems necessary." Unfortunately, they also tell us that the growth "trip" will require "skilled guidance and direction," presumably from the center; a point of view in sympathy with the rational constructionist model. We have already found this model of centralized planning of limited value and inevitably dangerous.

In any case, there are really no limits to economic growth. "Indeed," according to Kahn, "we expect both the technology and the opportunities for rapid growth to become so available and so relatively easy to exploit that many of those societies that today find it most difficult to make this kind of [growth] adaptation will do so." If economic growth should slow in the presently industrialized West, it will not be because it has to, but because society has so decided. In *World Economic Development* Herman Kahn summarizes his case for economic progress:

> If this book has made a persuasive case for the *feasibility* of world economic development, we believe this also constitutes an argument for the desirability and morality of such development. To introduce the words *desirability* and *morality* is, of course, to make the argument for economic development turn explicitly on questions of values. I believe that the arguments in favor of continued world economic development-- given all the likely human, ecological, environmental, and material costs and risks--are close to, if not fully overwhelming.

Economic growth is not inevitable, but a convincing case can be made that it is surely desirable. Kahn continues: "To attempt to stop economic development and to contend that the world is already rich enough when this is patently not true is to assert what has always been described in Western history as an immorally conservative position."

While the work of Ernest Beckerman, Alvin Toffler, Herman Kahn, and others have argued the desirability *and* possibility of economic growth, Julian L. Simon's book, *The Ultimate Resource,* seems to be the best documentation of those possibilities. With respect to the assertion that we are running out of resources, Simon defends the proposition that natural resources have not become less abundant, but that "if the past is any guide, natural resources will progressively become less scarce, and less costly, and will constitute a smaller proportion of our expenses in future years." Popular myth to the contrary, per capita food production has continued to rise and "there is strong reason to believe that human nutrition will continue to improve into the indefinite future, even with continued population growth." Even the current energy crisis is shown by Simon to be a case without merit: "Grab your hat again--the long-run future of our energy supply is at least as bright as that of other natural resources." Concerning the environment, he makes a persuasive case that pollution levels are below what they once were, and population growth over the past centuries has been consistent with a better environment. "The key trend is that life expectancy, which is the best overall index of the pollution level, has improved marketly as the world's population has grown."

Agreeing with the conclusions of the English economist P. T. Bauer in *Dissent on Development,* Simon also makes a powerful case for the net benefits which are associated with a growing population: "In the long-run...per capita income is likely to be higher with a growing population than with a stationary one, both in more-developed and less-developed countries." For Julian Simon, *The Ultimate Resource* is people:

> Contrary to common rhetoric, there are no meaningful limits to the continuation of this [economic growth] process. There is no physical or economic reason why human resourcefulness and enterprise cannot forever continue to respond to impending shortages and existing problems with new expedients that, after an adjustment period, leave us better off than before the problem arose. Adding more people will cause us more such problems, but at the same time there will be more people to solve these problems and leave us with the bonus of lower costs and less scarcity in the long-run. The bonus applies to such desirable resources as better health, more wilderness, cheaper energy, and a cleaner environment.

The idea of economic progress is far from extinguished. The growth in world population has gone hand-in-hand with rising standards of living in those nations devoted to the market system. Greater wealth has invariably been accompanied by declining real prices for raw materials and a generally cleaner environment. And, this combination has produced better health and greater longevity.

In spite of the important arguments and profound contributions made on behalf of economic progress by these students of the subject, the majority of intellectuals refuse to recognize the validity of such an optimistic scenario. Some, like the sociologist Robert Nisbet, blame our malaise on the loss of faith in religion: "There is one generalization that can be made confidently about the history of the idea of progress, it is that throughout its history the idea has been closely linked with, has depended upon, religion or upon intellectual constructs derived from religion." Whatever the responsibility for the current lack of confidence in the idea of progress, a rejuvenation of belief in a free society and the market economy will have to have its philosophical or moral component. As Friedrich Hayek has observed: "The main lesson which the true [classical] liberal must learn from the success of the socialists is that it was their courage to be Utopian which gained them the support of the intellectuals." Peter Berger tells us that a broad-based revival and belief in individual freedom and the economic system of competitive capitalism "...will be ineffective unless they can be fueled by the power of mythic plausibility." Something analogous to a religious commitment will be required if we are to restore our faith in private institutions. Hayek has provided (and it is repeated here again) a most insightful summary of our predicament:

> Unless we can make the philosophic foundations of a free society once more a living intellectual issue, and its implementation a task which challenges the ingenuity and imagination of our liveliest minds, the prospects of freedom are indeed dark. But if we can regain that belief in the power of idea which is the mark of [classical] liberalism at its best, the battle is not lost.

Progress *is* being made on the restoration of a free society and the market economy. There has, in fact, been in the past quarter century a tremendous outpouring of scholarship and evidence on the beneficial results of private, market solutions to individual problems, the incompetence of government as a "delivery system," and the adverse and necessarily coercive results of political solutions.

From HISTORY OF THE IDEA OF PROGRESS by Robert Nisbet.
© 1980 by Basic Books, Inc., Publishers.
Reprinted by permission of the publisher.

# PART
# III

*THE RESTORATION OF FREEDOM AND THE MARKET ECONOMY*

# CHAPTER 15

## THE COUNTER REVOLUTION IN ECONOMICS

> We may ask ourselves, then, whether the growing influence of the messages of the new economists in certain political and intellectual circles is initiating a political process somewhat analogous to the process set in motion over two centuries ago by the publication in Britain of the works of Adam Smith.
>
> --Henri Lepage

To this point, we have noted the most important factors contributing to the decline of economic freedom in America. The understanding of and commitment to competitive capitalism--what Adam Smith called the simple system of natural liberty--has substantially deteriorated during the first seven decades of the twentieth century. Ideas do have consequences, and the majority of intellectuals have for many years pressed for social arrangements and policy prescriptions involving political solutions to human problems. The private sphere of human action has been reduced far below what many of us believe is necessary for the restoration of the market system in America. Today, the dominant view believes that the good society can be constructed and planned by government in spite of the insurmountable knowledge problem this point of view presents. In the name of equality and justice, it is argued that we must rob Peter in order to pay Paul his just due. The Marxist movement and its many variations try to convince mankind of an inherent contradiction in the institution of private property in spite of the abject failure of Marxism everywhere. Even the U.S. Constitution, which the founding fathers hoped would limit the power of government and preserve human freedom, has been interpreted by the courts in a manner which permits the federal government, always in the "public interest," to do almost anything it pleases. And as noted, the very idea of human progress has come under intense attack. The earlier view, from the period of John Locke, Thomas Jefferson, and Adam Smith, believed progress almost inevitable under a system of individual liberty, private property, and the market economy.

It is clear that socialism and the politicization of society have been the dominant characteristics of human institutions in the twentieth century. While a third of the world's population live in totalitarian states which claim an allegiance to communism, another third have announced some type of commitment to socialism. The essential characteristic of such systems is a large and coercive role for government in economic and social life. Nations committed to competitive capitalism, on the other hand, account for less than one-fourth of the world's people. The prospects for individual freedom on this planet,

177

if viewed in sheer numbers, are not encouraging. The most important remnant of competitive capitalism is the Unites States of America. But even here the prospects for liberty are anything but bright.

## THE PLAIN INTELLIGIBLE LAW OF THINGS

Encouragingly, all is not lost. In fact, a very strong case can be made that a major intellectual revolution has been taking place both in the United States and in other parts of the world. This renaissance in thinking about the issue of human freedom and private ownership may very well turn the tide and bring us back from the brink of totalitarian collectivism. We hope to show that this intellectual revolution and the philosophy of a free society have the same taproot. The ideas formulated in the seventeenth and eighteenth centuries by the defenders of liberty may once again be followed in our time.

During competitive capitalism's darkest hour, the decades of the 1930's and 1940's, there were still a few vocal proponents of individual freedom and the market economy. As the intellectual case for socialism reached its zenith (exemplified by the rave reviews given Joseph Stalin's socialization of the Soviet Union) and while the growth of government's role in Western society was expanding considerably, there remained a few scholars who refused to bow to socialism, the omnipotent state, and the end of individual freedom. As Albert Jay Nock in *Our Enemy the State* pointed out: "In every civilization, however generally prosaic, however addicted to the short-time point of view on human affairs, there are always certain alien spirits who, while outwardly conforming to the requirements of the civilization around them, still keep a disinterested regard for the plain intelligible law of things, irrespective of any practical end." Impressed by " the august order of nature," there were, fortunately, certain intellectual giants who kept the fire of liberty burning "...even in circumstances where its operation is ever so manifestly unfavourable to their best hopes and wishes."

## BEGIN THE COUNTER REVOLUTION

The current revival of interest in the ideas of liberty and the socially beneficial implications of private property, the market system, and limited government stems, in large part, from two small but powerful and important books. Following a decade of the "New Deal" in the U.S. and the massive growth in government's role in economic life in Europe, Friedrich A. Hayek's *Road to Serfdom* was published in 1944. This volume provided a grave warning to those who would follow the Soviet central planning model. Directed at the socialist intelligentsia in England, Hayek, reminded his audience--those calling for a large increase in government's role in economic affairs--that a totalitarian regime, whether of the left ("communism") or the right ("fascism"), necessarily must utilize brute force. In the *Road to Serfdom*, Hayek persuasively presented the adverse implications of an "...organized movement toward a deliberate organization of economic life by the state as the chief owner of the means of production." Assisted by the publication of the condensation of the book in the *Reader's Digest*, it sold extremely well in the Unites States and has undoubtedly had an important influence on American thought.

In a sense Hayek's book was just the opening salvo. By the time of the publication of Milton Friedman's *Capitalism and Freedom* in 1962, the counter revolution in economic thinking was well underway. Friedman told us that "the preservation of freedom is the protective reason for limiting and decentralizing governmental power," and "viewed as a means to the end of political freedom, economic arrangements are important because of their effect on the concentration or dispersion of power." Friedman continued: "The kind of economic organization that provides economic freedom directly, namely, competitive capitalism, also promotes political freedom because it separates economic power from political power and in this way enables the one to offset the other." In the years following the publication of *Capitalism and Freedom*, there occurred a veritable flood of scholarly books, essays, and other materials on the beneficial implications of a market order which continues to this day. The research of this counter revolution documents the wealth creating potential of private and voluntary arrangements and at the same time, illustrates the important limitations of government as a delivery system.

## THE CHICAGO SCHOOL OF ECONOMICS

While these two small but powerful books by Hayek and Friedman bound a period representing the beginnings of a counter revolution, it is important to remember that during the dark days of socialism's ascendency in the 1930's in the United States and even earlier in Europe, there were many "classical liberals" who, in spite of poor odds and little reward, continued their writings and faith in freedom. The University of Chicago in the United States and the Austrian School of Economics of Vienna, Austria, both represented critically important sources of study and scholarly activity on the benefits of private arrangements and the competitive market process. Ideas and traditions were passed to a generation of young scholars, and then again to their students who, in the 1960's and 1970's, would lead the counter revolution in favor of competitive capitalism. It is important that we briefly trace these movements, given the influence they were to have.

First, and most important for the study of economics in the United States, the University of Chicago is responsible for training a large number of economists who have articulated the case for private property and market arrangements. The important influence of the University of Chicago is largely explained by the arrival at Chicago in 1927 of two economists, Frank H. Knight and Henry C. Simons. While neither Knight nor Simons published as extensively as other leading economists of the day, their impact on a whole generation of students at the University of Chicago was nothing short of remarkable. As William Breit and Roger L. Ransom in *The Academic Scribblers* point out: "Knight was to the students of economics at Chicago in the 1930's...the father image and social philosopher, whose seminars and classrooms were attended with reverence and who awakened within some of the best young minds of a generation the excitement of the intellecutal quest." About Knight's friend and colleague Henry Simons, Nobel Laureate economist Milton Friedman, one of their students at Chicago, has said: "No man can say precisely whence his beliefs and values came--but there is no doubt that mine would be different than they are if I had not had the good fortune to be exposed to Henry Simons."

If the idea of a free society once again becomes an important and exciting intellectual issue, and it would seem it has become just that, a significant part of the credit must go to Frank Knight and Henry Simons. They made competitive capitalism come alive at the University of Chicago, and their influence has truly been staggering. A list of the students and junior faculty in economics at Chicago between 1927 and 1950 represents a major portion of those influential American economists who speak and write on behalf of the market system.

The fundamental message at Chicago during this period, running counter to the conventional socialist dogma of the time, included a demonstration of the socially beneficial results of voluntary arrangements and private property in combination with a recommendation to limit government's responsibilities in the economic sphere of human action. In his book *Economic Policy for a Free Society*, Henry Simons summarized his general views regarding the relative roles of the market and politics:

> The [classical] liberal creed demands the organization of our ecomonic life largely through the individual participation in a game *with definite rules*. It calls upon the state to provide a stable framework of rules within which enterprise and competition may effectively control and direct the production and distribution of goods. The essential conception is that of a genuine division of labor between competitive [market] and political controls--a division of labor within which competition has a major, or at least proximately primary place.

During his career at Chicago, Simons especially studied the issues of unemployment, depression, and the appropriate government policies for dealing with America's economic problems during the Great Depression. Simons was greatly concerned with the potential for a totalitarian outcome from John Maynard Keynes' *A General Theory of Employment, Interest and Money;* a book which was the beginning of the so-called "Keynesian Revolution," and argued for a drastically enlarged role for government in the economy. Simon was a most vocal opponent of the proposals of America's leading Keynesian, Alvin Hansen.

Frank Knight's contributions and influence on the students at Chicago were mostly concerned with microeconomic issues of market performance and efficiency. In his classic volume *Risk, Uncertainty and Profit,* the nature and determination of profits in a market system were systematically analyzed, and the crucial role of entrepreneurial activity under competitive capitalism was demonstrated. A major contribution by Knight was his revelation of the adverse implications of failing to assign property rights to particular owners. Treating scarce resources as if everyone had a right to use them would necessarily mean inefficiency and waste. From this early insight in an article by Knight in 1924, a host of economists have been motivated to study in great detail the implications of the establishment and enforcement of private property rights. In a related matter, with its own famous history, Thorsten Veblen's attack on the notion of consumer sovereignty brought Frank Knight's biting criticism. "Improper" consumption, Knight pointed out, could only mean consumption "...of which he (Veblen) disapproves." Knight added a challenge: "If he (Veblen) has an objective test for distinguishing between valid and false aesthetic values...he does a grievous wrong in withholding it from publication."

The counter revolution in economics over the past twenty years stands literally on the shoulders of economists like Knight and Simons at Chicago. The impact of the "Chicago School" was realized in large part because of the brilliant and ambitious students who attended their seminars. Milton Friedman, without question the most articulate defender of a free society in the post-World War II period, earned a masters degree from the University of Chicago in 1933 and, as we have already indicated, was greatly influenced by Knight and Simons. Friedman later returned to Chicago to teach and has in turn had a tremendous influence on another generation of doctoral students.

James Buchanan, the co-founder of the Center for the Study of Public Choice, an organization dedicated to studying the limits of government as a delivery system, earned his Ph.D at Chicago in 1948. Beginning with *The Calculus of Consent,* written with Gordon Tullock in 1962, Buchanan, his students and colleagues have produced an enormous scholarship demonstrating the limitations and failures of government interventions. G. Warren Nutter and Roland McKean earned their doctorates from Chicago in the late 1940's, and, along with Leland Yeager, have made the University of Virginia an important source of learning with regard to the beneficial results of private market arrangements. George Stigler, the 1983 recipient of the Nobel Prize in economics, earned his Ph.D. at the University of Chicago in 1938 and as a faculty member at Chicago continues to be an important spokesman for the limits of political solutions. Yale Brozen, another persuasive defender of competitive capitalism earned his Chicago doctorate in 1942 and now teaches in the School of Business at the University of Chicago. The students of these remarkable economists, and many other colleagues not mentioned here, are now teaching and doing research at universities and private research organizations around the world.

Of course there have been important contributions to this counter revolution in economics at universities other than Chicago. Influential ideas favorable to the market economy have been developed at UCLA, the University of Washington, Virginia Polytechnic Institute, George Mason University, Texas A&M, Montana State University, Brown University and a number of other institutions. Armen Alchian and William Allen at UCLA, in their *University Economics,* have provided an articulate defense of private property and voluntary exchange. Richard Stroup and James Gwartney of Montana State and Florida State synthesize many of the Chicago and VPI insights in their best selling book on introductory economics. Harold Demsetz, Benjamin Rogge, John S. McGee, William Niskanen, Richard McKenzie, Murray Weidenbaum, and Henry Hazlitt are just a few of the many economists who have contributed to the restoration of the market system. But without a doubt, during freedom's darkest hours, it was Frank Knight and Henry Simons who maintained the lonely vigil for free market institutions.

## THE AUSTRIAN SCHOOL

The second prong of the attack on socialism and the politicized society was headquartered in Vienna, Austria, and was later transplanted first to London and then to the United States during World War II. Known as the "Austrian School," its brightest and most articulate leader in the first few decades of this century was Ludwig von Mises. The Austrian School was in effect founded with the publication in 1871 of Carl Menger's *Principles of Economics (Grundsatze der Volkswirtschaftslehre)*, but for our purposes the most imposing figure was Mises. In turn, one of Mises' prize students in Vienna was Friedrich A. Hayek who would later win the Nobel Prize in economics. A number of Mises' students in Vienna later emigrated to the United States before World War II. These included a number of economists who would become influential names on the American scene: Fritz Machlup, Gottfried Haberler and Oskar Morgenstern. Hayek, who much later, following the death of Ludwig Mises, would assume the nominal leadership of the Austrians, moved to the London School of Economics during the period 1931-1950 and influenced a whole generation of British economists, including respected economists like Lord Lionel Robbins, Sir John Hicks, Ludwig Lachmann, G. L. S. Schackle and G. F. Thirlby.

Von Mises meanwhile migrated to the United States in the 1940's and proceeded to hold his famous seminars at New York University from the 1950's until his death in 1973. Many of his students have made important contributions to our understanding of the private property, free market system, especially Israel Kirzner and Murray Rothbard. Other Austrian economists would include Dominick Armentano, Gerald O'Driscoll, Walter Block, Roger Garrison, Walter Grinder and Edwin Dolan.

The migration of the Austrian School to the United States was finalized when, following his stay at the London School of Economics, Friedrich Hayek accepted an appointment at the University of Chicago. While not directly associated with the Department of Economics, and writing mostly on philosophical issues about the nature of a free society, his influence was also felt at Chicago. David Friedman, the son of Milton Friedman and an important economist in his own right, was just one of many moved by Hayek's scholarship.

The point of this discussion, like the role of Knight, Simon and the Chicago School, centers on the sophisticated defense of a spontaneous order of private action by Mises and Hayek during the interwar period when socialism was being advocated everywhere. Ludwig von Mises in his many books, such as *Socialism, Bureaucracy, Liberalism: A Socio-Economic Exposition,* and the great treatise *Human Action,* provided a profound defense of free institutions and the competitive market process. Hayek too, in works such as *Individualism and Economic Order, The Constitution of Liberty* and in the 1970's the three volume study *Law, Legislation and Liberty,* demonstrated the severe limitations government faces when attempting to plan and coordinate economic life; an environment which necessarily involves the desires and actions of many millions of distinct and separate decision makers.

An essential ingredient of the Austrian economic view is found in their emphasis on the limitations humans face in mobilizing information for centralized decision making. The great advantage of the market system is its ability to collect usable information for human actors as reflected in competitively determined market prices. The difficulty of collecting in a useful form information at a central location--the problem, as Hayek reminded us, of the importance of special knowledge of specific time and place--provides the underlying argument against centralized planning. Actual results in the centrally planned economies of the world have proven the importance of this valuable "Austrian" insight. Hayek in his Nobel memorial lecture beautifully summarized this fundamental point:

> The recognition of the inseperable limits to his knowledge ought indeed to teach the student of society a lesson in humility which should guard him against becoming an accomplice in men's fatal striving to control society--a striving which makes him not only a tyrant over his fellows, but which may well make him the destroyer of a civilization which no brain has designed but which has grown from the free efforts of millions of individuals.

Austrian economic analysis is founded on the purposefully acting individual which both defines the basic approach to economic inquiry, "methodological individualism," and the underlying source of value which is the "subjectivism necessarily associated with the act of individual human choice." In a fundamental departure from a "real" (or labor) theory of value expounded by Marxists, the Austrians rightly identify the subjective nature of valuation. Irrespective of the number of necessary labor hours embodied in a new rock-and-roll song, if the young people don't like it, its value will be negligible in the only meaningful sense of that term. Subjectivist cost theory literally makes a shambles of Marx's theory of value (which he borrowed from the British economist David Ricardo).

The Austrians stress the importance of the competitive *process* as a vehicle of discovery (the generation of useful knowledge of alternatives) and through which market coordination is facilitated. One interesting implication of this process approach to competition is a quite distinct and more realistic interpretation of the so-called monopoly problem under capitalism. The Austrian theory of the business cycle, especially through the writings of Hayek and Murray Rothbard, emphasize the distortions in the structure of production between consumer goods and producer (capital) goods which arise from manipulation of the money supply by government. It follows that the Austrians have a very pessimistic view of the potential for beneficial, fine tuning by government monetary and fiscal policies. And finally, but of great importance, Mises and Hayek have shown the impossibility of economic calculation under a full-blown socialist economy. The case for the market means, private property and competitive capitalism is, in fact, an affirmation of the proposition that nothing even closely compares if we want progress, economic efficiency, and freedom.

In summary, and following the theme of a recent book by Henri Lepage, *Tomorrow, Capitalism*, there has been "...a major intellectual and scientific renaissance" in economics, and the authors of this book agree with Lepage when he tells us it is "...one of the great intellectual events of the century." A rigorous comparative analysis of market solutions and government solutions as alternative delivery systems has been undertaken in the past two decades, and the political mechanism has finished a distant second.

# THE MARKET FOR IDEAS ON THE MARKET SYSTEM

A separate but obviously related illustration of the counter revolution in ideas can be found in the growth of private "think tanks" and research organizations devoted to explaining the positive characteristics of private property and a free society. An early example of this type of effort, when socialism was still in its ascendency, involved the formation of the Foundation for Economic Education by Leonard Read in 1946. Influenced by the regular visits of Ludwig von Mises, the Foundation kept freedom's light burning during the watershed years of the 1950's. FEE's journal *The Freeman* continues to offer important statements on the socially beneficial implications of the private property, free-market system. Leonard Read, founder of FEE and a great champion of human liberty, died in 1983.

The institute for Humane Studies in Menlo Park, California, which matured under the wise and intelligent leadership of F. A. "Baldy" Harper, has also effectively communicated freedom's message to the people of this country and the world. Founded by Anthony Fisher in 1957, the Institute of Economic Affairs in London has published and reprinted a number of influential studies on market ideas in Great Britain. Economists such as Arthur Seldon, Ralph Harris, Arthur Shenfield, S. C. Littlechild, and Jack Wiseman, among others, have been important contributors.

Private organizations have proliferated in recent years, and they seem to be making a great deal of difference in the debate on socially desirable economic institutions. They include, naming just some of the better known organizations, The American Enterprise Institute for Public Policy Research in Washington, D.C., the CATO Institute now also located in Washington; the International Institute for Economic Research in Los Angeles; the Center for Political Economy and Natural Resources at Montana State University in Bozeman, Montana; the Fraser Institute in Vancouver, British Columbia; the Center for Education and Research in Free Enterprise in Texas; the Center for Libertarian Studies in New York; the Council for a Competitive Economy in Washington, D.C.; and the Reason Foundation in Santa Barbara, California. A number of individuals have played essential roles in the evolution and success of these organizations, including Leonard Liggio at the Institute for Humane Studies, Edward Crane at the CATO Institute, Robert Poole at the Reason Foundation, William R. Allen at the International Institute for Economic Research, Murray Rothbard at the Center for Libertarian Studies, Sheldon Richman and Richard Wilcke at the Council for a Competitive Economy, and Terry Anderson, John Baden, Richard Stroup and P.J. Hill at the Center for Political Economy and Natural Resources.

## PHILOSOPHY AND THE OTHER SOCIAL SCIENCES

It is exciting that the counter revolution in economic science complements and is supported by the changes taking place in philosophy and the other social sciences regarding the relative merits of voluntary versus forced arrangements when dealing with social problems. We have already made extensive use of the important writings of the sociologist Robert Nisbet. Political scientists like Robert Perrin and William Mitchell have contributed to our understanding of a market order in which government's role is limited. Psychologists like Nathaniel Branden and psychiatrists Thomas Szasz and Peter Breggin have focused our attention on the nature and character of individuals which make up the human community. Unfortunately, it is beyond the scope of this book to discuss the many contributions from these other fields on the nature and benefits of economic and political freedom.

While the practical advantages of freedom and private property continue to be studied by members of the social science fraternity, it has been important that philosophers have also experienced an important revival in their study of human liberty. Ayn Rand, novelist and philosopher, has been an important influence for many. Her book *Atlas Shrugged* has been a significant force in gathering converts to the idea of individual freedom. A watershed contribution in this renewal was the powerful book by Harvard's Robert Nozick, *Anarchy, State and Utopia,* which made a philosophical case for human liberty and the limits to government in a just society. Two years earlier John Hospers, a philosopher at the University of Southern California, published his *Libertarianism,* an important statement regarding the attributes of individual freedom. In 1975 Tibor Machan, another philosopher, published *Human Rights and Human Liberties* and defended the importance and value of the notion of "natural" rights. There has been a veritable explosion of interest, especially since Nozick's book, among philosophers on the nature, attributes and implications of individual freedom. Eric Mack, John O. Nelson, James Sadowsky and many young philosophers have taken up the challenge associated with restoring the free-market economy; humanity's last great hope for the protection of human liberties.

## THE RESTORATION OF THE FREE MARKET ECONOMY

From the universities and policy research and publication organizations already mentioned have come a whirlwind of scholarly activity in defense of what Adam Smith more than two hundred years ago called the system of natural liberty. The weight of this scholarship and evidence being provided on the beneficial results of free institutions by the counter revolution in economics has brought to an end, at least at the level of ideas, the decline of the free market order. The intellectually exciting work today is making the case for the market means and against the political means. The documentation of government's failure to work efficiently or ethically has belatedly shown the emperor has no clothes. Making all issues political and therefore public is now thought to have been a mistake by a growing number of scholars and opinion makers. An intellectually powerful case for private ownership of the means of production, voluntary exchange relationships, and therefore the restoration of the competitive market system is being made.

# CHAPTER 16

## THE ANATOMY OF GOVERNMENT FAILURE

The contrasts between the ostensible objectives of government programs and their actual results...is so pervasive, so widespread, that even many of the strongest supporters of big government have had to acknowledge government failure--though their solution almost always turns out to be still bigger government.

--Milton and Rose Friedman

We no longer expect results from government. What was a torrid romance between the people and government for so long has now become a tired middle-aged liaison which we do not quite know how to break off.

--Peter F. Drucker

By any objective standard, government's performance as a delivery system, regulator or economic fine tuner over the past two decades has been demonstrably atrocious. Great expectations for government programs have repeatedly produced pathetic outcomes. Yet, as the political scientist William C. Mitchell has noted: "Somehow...people believe that 'collective choice' through governmental institutions can supplant the market and replace its alleged vices with sweetness and light. Politicians will not be stupid or corrupt; bureaucrats will not be officious and tyrannical; and citizens will not be apathetic, alienated, and selfish." It is comparable to the judge who awarded the prize to the second singer after hearing only the first contestant.

The standards for evaluating the socially beneficial results of the free market must be a comparison of the market means and the political means as we actually find them in the real world; not by some ideal, mystical view of government manned by omniscient and altruistic men and women. For as we now know--knowledge painfully gained from the growth of government over the past half century--government involvement in economic affairs more often than not either fails to deliver the anticipated outcome, accomplishes its task very inefficiently, or creates consequences opposite of those intended. Like dawn piercing darkness, people are slowly realizing that no matter how noble the motivations or humanitarian the principles guiding politicians and bureaucrats, the political means have failed miserably.

### THE THEORY OF PUBLIC CHOICE

An important part of the counter revolution in economics involves the analysis of government as a delivery system. Led by James Buchanan, Gordon Tullock, Anthony Downs, Mancur Olson, William Niskanen, Richard McKenzie and other economists and political scientists, the study of "public choice" has become an important part of economic science. Summarizing this development of the public choice model, Henri Lepage in his book *Tomorrow, Capitalism* defines its basic approach: "The market's great rival, government, has been brought under the economic microscope..." Rather than study what government *should* do, many economists in the past twenty years have come to analyze and document what government *does* do. Actual outcomes are contrasted with rhetorical hopes and initial expectations. The theory and the evidence overwhelmingly support the summary judgement of Milton Friedman: "The contrasts between the ostensible objectives of government programs and their actual results...is so pervasive, so widespread, that even many of the strongest supporters of big government have had to acknowledge government failure."

Literally volumes of empirical research have now revealed that special interest groups control the apparatus of government at the expense of the individual taxpayer. At one and the same time, government creates miracles for one group (entitlements, price supports, exclusive franchises, import restrictions, etc.) while taxing others (the anti-miracle) to pay for it. Concentrating enormous benefits on a special interest group while distributing the costs thinly over all taxpaying citizens, government would have us believe in the tooth fairy. But unfortunately, as the late Senator Dirksen used to tell us: a billion dollars here and a billion dollars there adds up to real money! And, not surprisingly, the taxpayer has begun to howl.

Representative political democracy has a profound defect: inevitably there are special interests who place great value on particular political outcomes and are prepared to provide vote gaining resources to political candidates who sympathize or can be made to sympathize with their objectives. At the same time, most voters have a small personal interest in most issues and are not going to be politically active in opposing special interest legislation. The net result is that the process responds more favorably to special interest groups than it does to the taxpayer/consumer. Government programs with immediate, concentrated benefits and widely dispersed costs, especially if those costs are borne later, are likely to be approved. On the other hand, politicians find it much more difficult to vote for programs with readily identifiable and concentrated costs and with benefits realized only after a significant passage of time.

The politician's goal must be to win the election. Entrepreneurs all, they must obtain more votes than their opponents. To remain in office, according to the theory of public choice, they must sell favors to individuals and groups who are prepared to deliver votes at election time. Sugar beet growers promise to deliver votes and make contributions to the politician's campaign war chest in exchange for quotas on sugar imports and price supports. The National Education Association endorsed President Carter in 1976 in order to obtain a new U. S. Department of Education. The American dairy industry makes large contributions to politicians who are expected to support the dairy price support programs. The AFL/CIO provides financial support for congressional candidates who will maintain the federal minimum wage law and enforce the Davis-Bacon Act. The American Medical Association, one of the largest campaign contributors, lobbies heavily in Congress for legislation which would limit the ability of foreign trained physicians to practice medicine in the United States. A whole book could be devoted to the special interests who have politicized their industries by currying favor with government bureaucrats and elected politicians. Taxes now represent about 35 percent of the national income in the United States in order that the special interests can keep their bounty. Nevertheless, the politician, ever alert to taxpayer rebellion, constantly harps on the need for lower taxes, but seldom reveals the actual tax burden. As J. B. Colbert, a famous minister to the King of France pointed out with great candor: "The art of taxation consists in so plucking the goose as to obtain the largest amount of feathers with the least possible amount of hissing."

Logrolling coalitions of special interest groups, finessed into electoral majorities by entrepreneurial politicians, continue to produce larger and larger government. But interestingly, this fundamental defect in democracy contains a startling paradox: while government continues to grow and political solutions multiply seemingly without limit, simultaneously there is a growing recognition by the American people, regardless of ideological persuasion, of government's failure. Public opinion polls continue to reveal that people want smaller government. A Harris survey in 1981 found that 59 percent of an adult sample agreed with Thomas Jefferson's statement that "the best government is the government that governs least." Only 32 percent had agreed with that sentiment in 1973. Another query found that 53 percent of respondents believe that big government is the greatest threat to well-being in this country. Yet, the Census Bureau reported that in the 1980 Census, one-third of all American households made use of at least one of the following five federal benefit programs: Medicare, Medicaid, food stamps, subsidized housing, and school lunch aid. Clearly a significant fraction of these households were not in the ranks of the poor!

In spite of President Reagan's election in 1980 in the name of reducing the size of government, total federal spending in fiscal year 1983 exceeded 25 percent of the Gross National Product; an *increase* of more than two percentage points from President Carter's last year in office. Political noise to the contrary, income transfer programs were also a *larger* fraction of the GNP in 1982 than they had been in

1980. Indeed, in fiscal year 1983 total federal transfers to persons, the so-called safety-net programs, exceeded $400 billion, an increase during the first three years of the Reagan administration of more than $120 billion. The political process has produced massive increases in government spending in recent decades. The 1985 fiscal year federal budget will be more than three times larger than the $268 billion federal budget in 1974! Yet, there is a mounting body of evidence--widely shared among conservatives, neo-conservatives, libertarians, and even many if not most liberals--that government as a delivery system has failed to efficiently and effectively do what we have asked it to do. Or, as the sociologist Robert Nisbet has said: ''By every serious reckoning the spell of politics and the political is fading. It is not simply a matter of growing disillusionment with government and bureaucracy; fundamentally, it is declining faith in politics as a way of mind and life.'' This distrust and lack of confidence in government to solve individual problems bodes well for the restoration of the market system of private property and mutually beneficial voluntary exchange.

## THE POLITICAL MARKET PLACE

The Congress has been likened by an economist to a ''...general store whose inventory includes monopolies, preferences, and concessions'' all to be bought in the political market place by interested parties. The service purchased is necessarily the government's monopoly right on the use of force, the essential attribute of sovereign governments. The tariff or the subsidy, for example, requires that government, by force, modify or restrain voluntary trades which would have otherwise taken place. The freedom of some persons is limited in order to materially benefit others.

Furthermore, when particular goods, for example education, mosquito abatement, surface transportation, or tennis courts are provided by government, the individual voter has little say about the amount purchased. In addition, the person is required, through taxation, to make a payment for government supplied goods and services irrespective of individual preferences. The provision of goods and services through the political market is an all-or-nothing proposition. Inevitably the ''consumer'' gets too much or too little. Some are required to buy more national defense than they would like; others are getting less. As an illustration, in our local government school districts we must accept an educational package determined partly through the voting process but mostly through the wishes of the educational bureaucracy. In contrast, the private market permits decisions to be made by individuals regarding the exact amounts they would want.

Bowling, for example, is invariably in the private sector while

191

tennis courts are usually provided "free" by government. We would imagine that bowlers are not at all thrilled by the fact they are subsidizing the tennis players! There surely exists a fundamental defect in the political sphere. We pay taxes for a bundle of publicly provided goods and services but are not permitted to express our individual preferences for the specific items which make up the total government budget. In the political arena, more often than not, votes are cast against a legislator, who in turn approves a package of government programs which citizens are required to support with their taxes.

The most serious limitation of government as a delivery system, however, is the bias in the structure of personal incentives confronting special interest groups in comparison with the average citizen. The benefits and costs of understanding and participating in the "mysteries of political processes" are determined by the value of the interest at stake. It is no accident, as already suggested, that the benefits government bestows by warping the market's outcome are invariably concentrated among a few potential beneficiaries, and the costs are usually widely distributed across the population. The trucking industry and the teamsters union receive billions of dollars of benefits from price fixing agreements and entry restrictions enforced by the Interstate Commerce Commission. These costs, in turn, are distributed through higher shipping costs and therefore higher prices for more than two-hundred and twenty-six million Americans. Encouragingly, this particular intervention has been significantly reduced with the passage of the Motor Carrier Act of 1980. The U. S. merchant marine, peanut and tobacco growers, the wheat and corn producers, Chrysler, Lockheed, small commercial banks, Continental Illinois, and many other special interest groups receive sizeable subsidies and/or protection from the rigors of competition. Yet the costs of these interventions in the free market mechanism are paid, a few dollars at a time, by consumers and taxpayers who are very likely unaware of their price.

Special interests do in fact devote time and money to "buy" protection, franchises, licenses, concessions, certificates or other forms of subsidy from the politicians who are prepared to sell. The purchase price is determined by an interplay of the various groups seeking special government favor and the politicians who are in the position to supply these favors. The massive increase in the number of Political Action Committees (PAC's) over the past decade is one indication of the scope of "political entrepreneurship" in the United States. And, unfortunately, these political incentives have partially replaced or distorted market incentives.

The politician, in turn, is prepared to supply those favors desired by those holding the most votes. Walking an interesting tightrope, the politician must appeal to individuals and groups on issues that matter enough to obtain their financial support in the political campaign.

Candidates hope majorities are formed from disparate coalitions of interest groups who can produce enough votes to win the election. Yet at the same time the truth must be kept from the average voter regarding the facts of this monstrous ripoff at his expense. What is the ultimate outcome of this asymmetry between beneficiaries of government favor and the costs borne by those who pay? The public choice model predicts larger government and a relentless politicization of society; an outcome that very few would desire, but whose adverse consequences nevertheless continue to multiply. The implications have been summarized by Milton Friedman, Nobel Prize winning economist, in an interesting reversal of Adam Smith's statement on the benefits of market arrangements. There is an all too *visible* invisible hand in politics: "Individuals who intend only to promote the *general interest* are led by the invisible political hand to promote a *special interest* that they had no intention to promote."

The invisible political hand, operating through pork-barrel majorities, inappropriate political incentives, and the monopoly character of government action, has produced rather perverse outcomes in the public sector. The economic theory of democracy, however, reminds us that they are both predictable and expected. Legislatures will pass bills which offer obvious short-term benefits and deferred costs. Attempts to abolish government programs, on the other hand, are unlikely to succeed given the current system of political entrepreneurship. Government programs which explicitly identify beneficiaries of public subsidy are less likely to be approved than policies which hide benefits under the claim of protecting the "public interest."

The predictions of this public choice model of political behavior are invariably verified by the facts of the real world. The evidence is that government, as a delivery system, rarely promotes the "public good," but indeed serves politically powerful interest groups. In fiscal 1983, for example, federal farm programs cost the American taxpayer about $21 billion, yet the poor are supposed to be grateful that government provides "free" surplus cheese and butter. Unfortunately, the poor eat more than just cheese and butter. For other food purchases they pay more than they would have had government stayed out of the agriculture price support/subsidy business. The "voluntary" quotas on Japanese steel and automobiles have raised prices to consumers on a long list of products, thereby imposing a burden of billions of dollars on American consumers. The beneficiaries are those individuals having a personal stake in the industries directly affected by the import competition. Those bearing the costs are the consumers, especially the poor, as they are more likely to buy four cylinder Japanese subcompacts than are the rich.

Tariffs on foreign textiles and clothing continue to provide a sizeable subsidy to the relatively inefficient American textile industry, thus raising everyone's clothing bill. Textile industry officials confirm that they will get their representative in the White House, a special presidential aid dealing with textile trade, if they support Commerce Secretary Baldridge's idea for a new Department of International Trade. President Reagan's promise of a tightened import quota system for textiles was an ominous sign indeed. While a few get the lemonade, the many get the squeeze. The American manufacturer of Harley-Davidson motorcycles, really its parent corporation, was successful during 1983 in "buying" from government a *forty-nine* percent tariff on large Japanese motorcycles, an increase from the previous four percent.

For more than 20 years, the three major television networks have, through the good offices of the Federal Communication Commission and certain key federal legislators, used the political market place to suppress new technologies in the broadcast media (e.g., cable television and low power transmission stations), restricted competition, and therefore reduced the variety of entertainment available to the consumer. These are just a few examples, among hundreds, of government responding to a special interest group's demand for forceful intervention in the market. The protected industries receive significant monetary benefits, while the costs to consumers in the form of higher prices, fewer alternatives, and higher taxes tend to be widely dispersed and consequently less objectionable. Nevertheless, the aggregate cost is very large indeed.

## THE MYTH OF THE PUBLIC INTEREST

One of the most fascinating dimensions of this discussion of government's role in economic life is the often repeated assertion that it is all being done in the "public interest." The jargon of the political market place necessarily includes terms like "overall good," "general welfare" and "public good." Notwithstanding the popularity of these terms when defending larger government appropriations, it remains, unavoidably, the nature of government action to choose between competing interests. Government intervention is a zero-sum game, frequently a negative-sum game, in which the existence of winners requires that there be losers. Government, with its monopoly on the use of force, must worsen someone's material situation in order to provide benefits to others. Higher safety-net expenditures require that others pay higher taxes. Minimum wage laws prevent teenagers and prospective employers from freely negotiating a mutually beneficial employment opportunity. Dairy price support programs raise the price of milk and other dairy products to the poor. *Ad infinitum.*

It appears that another term has been discovered to be empty of meaningful interpretation. Similar to the earlier conclusion that the concept of "social justice" or "distributive justice" was meaningless, the concept of the "public interest" or "general welfare" again exposes an emperor without clothes. The economist M. Bruce Johnson concisely summarizes the point:

> The *public interest* (or the common good) is an empty phrase unless it is interpreted literally to mean an unambiguous improvement in the situation of each and every member of society or, on a weaker criterion, to leave no one any worse off. Since it is difficult to even imagine any (government) activity that does not hurt someone, let alone uniformly increase the lot of everyone, the concept is empty--a piece of rhetoric used to persuade others through the political process. In fact, public interest arguments usually mean that the good of some men takes precedence over the good of others. In certain cases the common good appears to mean the good of the majority versus the good of the minority or of the individual.

Human welfare is an individual matter where gains or losses are to be personally evaluated, rather than measured by those who think they know what is best for others. Unfortunately, the political means --the use of government to affect economic conditions--is necessarily coercive and either uses force or the threat of force to gain compliance. It is our judgement that the good society should seek to minimize the number of involuntary transactions and strive to maximize the social sphere for voluntary arrangements among free individuals. Appeals to the meaningless notion of the public interest to justify state intervention in the private lives of free men and women are without merit and indeed morally reprehensible.

## THE ECONOMICS OF BUREAUCRACY

The anatomy of government failure does not stop with the misguided incentive structure confronting the *elected* politician. The problems associated with legislated intervention represent but the tip of the proverbial iceberg. Legislation authorizes government action, but the day-to-day operations of government are carried out by bureaucrats. The economics of public bureaucracy, in contrast to private bureaucracy, suggests that the "public servant" is not much concerned with efficient economic outcomes. We should not be surprised by the cliche: "Old bureaucracies never die; rather, they just grow larger and more oppressive." William A. Niskanen, in his book *Bureaucracy and Representative Government,* made the convincing case, supported by a number of other studies, that the provision of a good or service by a government agency would, on average, be roughly twice as expensive than if the provision were accomplished by the private sector. Many economists refer to this phenomenon as the "rule of two."

This "fifth estate," the government bureaucracy, or as Robert Nisbet has said, the "New Despotism," necessarily increases the distance between a citizen and his elected officials. Most readers have their own story about an unpleasant encounter with an unresponsive member of this caste. The massive public bureaucracies in the American government--the alphabet agencies-- have forged a wedge between the electorate and their elected representatives. And sadly, our frustration with the bureaucracy continues to grow.

The bureaucrats continue to multiply and have become a crucially important special interest group in their own right. Government employment, at all levels, represents one out of every seven or so workers in the United States. Interested in their own well-being, government employees have a strong incentive to exercise their franchise and vote themselves payraises and other perks. Have we reached the ultimate terror? The situation where elections are determined by those with an overwhelming *personal* interest in larger government! Given the low participation rates in elections, public servants of the "new class" might be pushing the Republic in a direction that few would wish to go.

Our argument here is not that government bureaucrats are disreputable people, or even that they are motivated by ulterior goals. Government employees are, with few exceptions, well-meaning, devoted public servants to *their* view of the public interest. The economics of bureaucracy, however, suggests the structure of incentives faced by the typical bureaucrat leads to inefficiency with relatively little attention devoted to the agency's purported goal.

As already indicated, private bureaucracies are usually more cost efficient than their public counterparts. The private business faces the continuous threat of competition in the market place, unless protected by government franchise, where it has an easily measured test of its success. Profits and losses (i.e., "the bottom line") communicate important information on whether consumer wishes are being served. Government bureaucracies, on the other hand, usually have complex sets of objectives, most of which are difficult to measure. As a personal example, President Lyndon Johnson, through executive order, required in the mid 1960's that all federal agencies submit Planned Programming Budgets in which agency objectives were identified and the means to their efficient achievement demonstrated. Suffice it to say, in the Bureau of International Commerce of the U. S. Department of Commerce it was literally impossible to judge whether objectives were being reached (assuming they were identified correctly), let alone whether our efforts were cost effective. There was simply no way to know how well we were serving our "customers."

Another complication is the fact that government agencies, as a result of providing services "free" to consumers, find it extremely difficult to acquire objective measures of effective demand. With no immediate, out-of-pocket outlay, individuals can be expected to demand or "need" more tennis courts, more medical services, or more whatever. Is it any wonder, for example, that university presidents plead for more money for buildings and professors from the state legislatures? Economics is very clear on the proposition that resources priced as if they were free stimulate demand. Since the students of government colleges and universities pay a very small share of the direct cost of their education, should it surprise us that the admission lines are long and college administrators continually "need" more money?

In addition, the bureaucrat usually benefits personally when his agency grows. Service to the public is often secondary. For example, have you stood in line at your local post office lately? The government bureaucracy's sugar daddy, the legislature, usually knows very little about the cost of providing a particular service. In combination, these factors suggest that public bureaucracies are too large and predictably getting even larger.

Consequently, most models of government bureaucracy predict that the agency will be governed by "size maximizations," "waste maximization," or a combination of both. Profits and losses are unavailable as a guide to the success or failure of the organization. The size maximization model suggests that the public provision of police and fire protection will all too often mean more police patrols and firemen than necessary for efficient protection. There is a good bit of evidence that this is in fact the case. The waste maximization model provides convincing evidence that the provision of services by government is almost always more expensive than the equivalent service being provided in the private sector. Illustrations of such waste are legion. The evidence from studies on public versus private garbage collection, public versus private maintenance of highways, the delivery of packages by the U. S. Postal Service in comparison with the United Parcel Service, and others, suggest the degree of inefficiency associated with government production. Even inner city private schools (parochial in most cases) are apparently providing an equivalent or even better educational product than the predominant government owned school systems, and at a significantly lower cost.

The fundamental problem with the public bureaucracy is the fact that those responsible for the agency's actions have no residual claim on improved productivity. Bureaucrats do not share in the "profits" which would arise from improved efficiency. The government bureaucrat's well-being is simply not closely tied to how efficiently the service is provided. Yet, following what we have called the economic theory of democracy and the economics of bureaucracy, it is recognized that the government bureaucrat is motivated by the same kinds of goals and desires as the employee in the private sector. Salary, working conditions, job security, retirement benefits, personal reputation, and other private amenities of the position determine the employee's behavior. When the chips are down, and without the discipline associated with obtaining resources in a voluntary manner as in the free market, is it all that surprising to discover that the devoted, well-meaning public servant will act in his or her own self-interest? That is, of course, exactly what the model suggests. In the private sector the penalty for not serving one's customers is lower profits, losses, and even bankruptcy. The public sector bureaucrat simply has no comparable discipline. The civil servant just digs a little deeper into the taxpayer's pocket, defending the need for more money in order to serve this mythical thing called the "public interest."

Only market arrangements--on private property, voluntary exchange, and entrepreneurship for profit--can improve upon the inefficiencies associated with government as a delivery system. Our faith must lie in the socially beneficial system of competitive capitalism. The choice is between the political means in which we have lost all confidence and the market means which seeks to minimize the use of force in society. Both in the United States and around the world, as we choose between these imperfect alternatives and prepare to live with the consequences of our decision, it is worth reciting the famous statement by Pierre Joseph Proudhon on the nature of government and what it can and does do to us:

> To be governed is to be watched over, inspected, spied on, directed, legislated, regimented, closed in, indoctrinated, preached at, controlled, assessed, evaluated, censored, commanded; all by creatures that have neither the right, nor wisdom, nor virtue...To be governed means that at every move, operation, or transaction one is noted, registered, entered in a census, taxed, stamped, priced, assessed, patented, licensed, authorized, recommended, admonished, prevented, reformed, set right, corrected. Government means to be subjected to tribute, trained, ransomed, exploited, monopolized, extorted, pressured, mystified, robbed; all in the name of public utility and the general good. Then, at the first sign of resistance or word of complaint, one is repressed, fined, despised, vexed, pursued, hustled, beaten up, garroted, imprisoned, shot, machine-gunned, judged, sentenced, deported, sacrificed, sold, betrayed, and to cap it all ridiculed, mocked, outraged, and dishonored. That is government, that is its justice and its morality!...O human personality! How can it be that you have cowered in such subjection for sixty centuries.

# CHAPTER 17

## THE COMPETITIVE MARKET PROCESS AND MONOPOLY

Competition is that no less indomitable humanitarian force that wrests progress, as fast as it is made, from the hands of the individual and places it at the disposal of all mankind.

--Frederic Bastiat

The adequacy of an economic system is judged not by the efficiency with which it allocates given resources at a point in time, but by the speed with which it discovers and responds to new opportunities over time.

--S. C. Littlechild

As already discussed, there is a subtle but important reason why many people attach great significance to a "mixed" economy with considerable government intervention. Namely, that special interest groups can use government to protect themselves from the rigors of competition. Therefore, politicians, acting as political entrepreneurs, are more than willing to offer the coercive power of the state in exchange for assistance from special interests in the quest for political office. There is, however, another popular argument often used to defend a larger role for government. The growing complexity of modern economic life, some would say, requires that government be involved in correcting the market's mistakes and directing economic traffic. The problem is analogous to a busy intersection in New York City without traffic lights; government intervention simply helps to coordinate a very diverse and undirected process. But this confuses enforcing the rules of the game with the separate and difficult problem of directing the game itself. Unfortunately, this case for intervention and planning makes a demonstrably false assumption; to whit, that the individuals implementing governmental actions have the *knowledge* to both discover and correct the so-called failures of the competitive market process.

As a matter of fact, the realization that information and knowledge are so widely dispersed and expensive to acquire represents a quite profound argument in favor of the market means and against government. The complex nature of the institutional characteristics of modern capitalism, arrangements which have produced the high standards of living we know in the West, occurred mainly because of the *spontaneous* nature of the market order. Central direction by government would have failed for the U. S. as it fails now for those countries committed to socialism. Israel Kirzner, economist and author of *Competition and Entrepreneurship,* argues that "...this discovery of the inherent regularities that emerge spontaneously from free society interaction represented the major scientific breakthrough in the history of social understanding."

The central planners under socialism, as illustrated earlier, presume that the knowledge of alternatives, relative scarcities, tastes, ambitions, and the cost conditions necessary for the execution of their plans are already possessed. But in fact they are not. It is indeed the central role of an economic system to generate and mobilize this information to achieve the coordination of individual plans. The debate over the "political means" and the "market means" is concerned with the question of the comparative ability of government versus the market to produce the socially necessary knowledge to coordinate individual decision making in a socially beneficial manner. The economic system which aspires to allocate resources efficiently in response to consumer wants must provide socially useful information regarding the benefits and costs of employing resources in alternative uses.

In addition the system also must provide an incentive structure to motivate individuals to take advantage of this information. Success in economic matters can best be evaluated by the capacity to coordinate over time the innumerable plans and actions of decision makers in a community or nation. Our defense of the price system and competitive capitalism rests upon the "economy of knowledge" by which it operates. The complexity of the modern economic world requires a decentralized market system of private property and voluntary exchange. At least that is true if the ultimate purpose of social institutions is to maximize individual opportunities for higher living standards and to sustain individual liberty.

## THE KNOWLEDGE PROBLEM

Those who would politicize our economic system apparently presume that the information necessary to its working exists in the minds of those who would plan the system. Unfortunately, it does not. Central repositories of socially useful knowledge and its ready accessibility are illusions and impossible. The willingness of buyers and sellers to produce and trade are forever changing. Tastes and preferences are fickle and subjective. The relative scarcity of particular resources is also subject to change. No person or committee can possibly know all the relevant conditions necessary to achieve an efficient allocation of resources. The problem indeed is to discover that set of institutions which will in fact make such knowledge "constantly communicated and acquired."

Friedrich A. Hayek, a Nobel Prize recipient in ecomonics, wrote a relatively short, but profound, article in 1945 entitled "The Use of Knowledge In Society." In that piece he summarized the necessary conditions for an efficient and socially beneficial economic system:

> The peculiar character of the problem of a rational economic order is determined precisely by the fact that the knowledge of the circumstances of which we must make use never exists in concentrated or integrated form but solely as the dispersed bits of incomplete and frequently contradictory knowledge which all the separate individuals possess...It is rather a problem of how to secure the best use of resources known to any of the members of society, for ends whose relative importance only these individuals know. Or, to put it briefly, it is a problem of the utilization of knowledge which is not given to anyone in its totality.

While Adam Smith characterized the division of labor as the centerpiece of the economic problem, Hayek suggests that it is the "...problem of the division of knowledge." This is a fundamental point in the comparison of alternative economic systems.

How do individuals and people within hierarchial organizations produce, transmit, and utilize knowledge? And just as important, how can specialized information be coordinated to produce socially beneficial outcomes? It is crucial to note that technical knowledge or book knowledge, while obviously important, is not at issue here. We are referring in fact to a special kind of knowledge which is often largely ignored. In Hayek's words we mean "...the knowledge of the particular circumstances of time and place." Those people intimately familiar with the unique circumstances surrounding any given situation can best make the appropriate decision.

The competitive market's price system represents an incredibly valuable process by which the fragmented and widely dispersed kinds of knowledge of specific circumstances are made available to an ever widening circle of buyers and sellers. Understanding this fundamental role of the competitive market process has been a powerful contribution of the Austrian School of Economics. The Austrian economist Ludwig Lachman reminds us that the kind of knowledge we are talking about "...is an elusive concept...it cannot be quantified, has no location in space." With the passage of time, objective as well as subjective circumstances change; or for the economist the conditions of demand and supply are altered. But if this is so, what then prevents chaos? Why do the right amounts of things--lettuce, shoes, plastic pipe, and personal computers--arrive in New York City each day? Why don't we all move to golden California, sunny Arizona, or all become dentists, teachers, or truck drivers? How can a country possibly direct resources to their highest valued uses without a plan? The answer is prices; or more precisely the structure of *relative* prices. Prices convey objective information on the subjective attitudes and feelings of buyers and sellers and the trade-offs available. As relative prices change, options are altered; perceived benefits and costs are continuously affected by changes in an individual's objective circumstances.

An interesting demonstration of the existence of this knowledge problem, and Hayek's emphasis on the "...special knowledge of circumstances of the fleeting moment not known to others..." is illustrated by the way centrally planned and supposedly socialist and non-market economies rely on price information generated in Western markets. The impossibility of economic calculation under a truly socialist regime was demonstrated more than fifty years ago by Ludwig von Mises. The ability of the Soviet or Cuban economy to fumble their way along in years past has depended crucially on historical price relationships and currently available world market prices generated in the market economies. Viewed differently, the planned economies have had to relax their totalitarian grip and permit the market and capitalism to creep in the back door. British scholar John Gray makes the point beautifully: "Planning policies in socialist economies are only shadows cast by market processes distorted by episodes of authoritarian intervention."

**THE PRICE SYSTEM AND ECONOMIC COORDINATION**

Buyers purchase. Sellers sell. Buyers prefer to buy low. Sellers want to sell high. The market is the arena in which all these interacting decisions take place; a continuing process with an overall tendency towards coordination. It is a process for the discovery of error and the behavioral changes by decision makers to increase social harmony. Everyone acts on their best information, but that information is necessarily imperfect and incomplete. Because information is scarce and therefore costly, and the future cannot be known with any certainty, mistakes are bound to be made. Disappointments compete with successes. Market opportunities are lost by some, while others experience entrepreneurial success. Some decisions involve monetary losses and bankruptcy; others produce profits. But that is the nature of a world where resources are limited and people must operate in partial ignorance of their circumstances. Changes in the underlying conditions of supply and demand represent a never ending, on-going process of generating price, wage, and interest rate signals for market participants. This is the language of the competitive market process; a form of communication which economizes on the specialized knowledge of particular time and place. Even the Marxist Frederick Engels was unequivocal on the necessary role of relative prices: "Only through the undervaluation or overvaluation of products is it forcibly brought home to the individual commodity producers what things and what quantity of them society requires or does not require."

Impediments to the market process, especially government intervention that restricts private action, prevent such coordination of the plans of buyers and sellers. The essential function of changes in relative prices after all is to provide information on relative scarcities. Resource endowments, consumer preferences, technology, and a thousand other things are continually changing and thereby producing altered circumstances. The price system represents the *only* reliable and efficient system of allocating resources to their most productive uses, especially if consumer wishes are deemed paramount. Market prices generate information about changes in personal tastes, of the relative availability of different raw materials, and of the comparative expense of capital and labor, to name but a few. In turn, they signal the reactions of market participants to these changes. For example, an increase in housing costs induces the consumer to reduce the amount of housing the family will purchase. Significantly lower prices for personal computers, on the other hand, would increase the number being bought. Higher oil and gas prices in the late 1970's signaled those who search for new energy sources to increase their efforts, but when oil prices leveled and even declined in the early 1980's, the number of new wells drilled decreased. Indeed, the market system even acts as a window on the future by permitting individuals to register their expectations about tomorrow's relative scarcities. If a frost destroys a part of the Brazilian coffee crop, the price for the future delivery of coffee on the Chicago commodities market immediately rises.

Prices are the language of the market economy; a summation of a great amount of knowledge and information necessarily not known to most market participants. As the price of bauxite rises, the producer of aluminum may not know why. But, nonetheless, it is clear that the real cost of an important input has risen and production plans will be altered. If the going wage rate for unskilled labor rises relative to the wage rate for unskilled labor, an employer's hiring practices will probably change, but he need not know anything at all about why this change in relative wages has occurred. Nothing conveys information faster than prices. Blind to race, sex, and religious preference, the price system is an incredibly efficient way to implement the rationing function required of all economic systems. While explicit price tags do not hang from everything people want, there is always an implicit price which is reflected in the necessity of foregone alternatives. Objects of our desire require sacrifices, which is to say they have prices.

Kirzner writes in *Competition and Entrepreneurship* that those who propose the use of the political means--government intervention in resource allocation decisions--"...calmly assume that the critically important task of making all the scattered bits of information available to those making decisions has already been performed." The popular misconception is that knowledge of relative scarcities, consumer tastes, production costs, and the most recent technologies are immediately and inexpensively available to most anybody. However, the problem in fact is our ignorance of what we would like to know. And as a matter of utmost importance for living standards, it is the competitive price system which offers the best opportunity for maximizing the quantity and quality of information made available to purposefully acting individuals.

Many educators, writers, spokesmen for the broadcast media, and others have indicated that they think competition a dirty word. Preferring terms like cooperation and sharing to competition and self-interest, they believe it more noble to focus on man's higher instincts. Though the ideas of cooperation and sharing are salutory, we believe there exists a fundamental misunderstanding of the word competition. Is there really a difference between cooperation and competition? Could it be that competition in fact encourages, nay requires, cooperation? The members of families, businesses, churches, clubs, and countries cooperate because to do so places them in the best position to compete. The concerted efforts between "labor" and "management" to increase productivity and quality in the American automobile industry in order to compete with the Japanese producer is a classic illustration. And we might add that this interplay between cooperation and competition also brings higher quality automobiles at lower prices to the American consumer.

In turn, competition generates untold examples of socially beneficial cooperation. The voluntary nature of exchange in the market system guarantees that both parties benefit; that in the language of the mathematician, trade is a positive-sum game. In this fundamental sense then, the market system produces a rivalry among buyers and a rivalry among sellers which results in cooperative trade and therefore personal fulfillment. Competition requires cooperation, and cooperation encourages competition. When the consumer chooses between Sears and K-Mart for a new washing machine, the decision to buy produces a mutually beneficial exchange with the successful seller. Hayek tells us in "The Meaning Of Competition" that competition, in the production and distribution of useful information for reaching mutually beneficial exchanges, creates a mosaic of "unity and coherence" in the spontaneous order. Consumers find out what is best and cheapest, while producers discover lower cost resources and more efficient production processes. The end result is a greater range of choice and increased opportunities for people to improve their lives.

The much older idea that human wisdom is possessed by a very few who in turn must direct the masses dies hard. It is admittedly not an easy task to understand the remarkably beneficial nature of the free market system and to appreciate the nature of a competitively determined structure of relative prices. And yet, capitalism, neither created nor planned by mortals, and evolving over many centuries, has produced a high degree of social coordination and fantastic increases in standards of living where it has been allowed to operate. As the economist Thomas Sowell has said: "Individually we know so pathetically little, and yet socially we use a range and complexity of knowledge that would confound a computer." It is the price system in the market economy which makes all this possible.

It is a testimonial of the competitive market system that those societies which have rejected market incentives and the price system in total (for example, Russia following the Revolution of 1917 and the People's Republic of China in the period of the Cultural Revolution) eventually returned to the efficiency and safety of market signals in response to the abject failure of their planned, non-market arrangements. In the last decade or so the centrally planned economies have moved toward decentralization and a relatively greater reliance on market incentives. In the early 1980's capitalism seems to be emerging everywhere in the Peoples Republic. Sooner or later, it would seem reality prevails.

## ENTREPRENEURSHIP AND THE COMPETITIVE PROCESS

While we have discussed the central role of private property and voluntary exchange in the maintenance of individual freedom and the efficiency of the market system, the driving force of competitive capitalism is, of course, the entrepreneur. It is the entrepreneur who, as the quotation at the head of this chapter says, ''...wrests progress, as fast as it is made, from the hands of the individual and places it at the disposal of all mankind.'' The short but spectacular history of the Apple Computer is suggestive of the speed at which new ideas are made available to the general public. The entrepreneur attempts to read the market's signals, anticipate previously undeveloped consumer demands, and take risks usually with his own money; and then, if the effort is successful, earns a profit. The media can be counted on to bring attention to the winners. However, the more numerous entrepreneurs who incorrectly anticipate consumer preferences are little nor long remembered.

For Joseph Schumpeter, a dominant figure among economists in the twentieth century, entrepreneurship involved a process of "creative destruction." The entrepreneur disturbs the tranquility of economic life by innovation and discovery which radically modifies the past and creates new opportunities for the creation of wealth in the future. While emphasizing the equilibrating and coordinating role of entrepreneurship in contrast to Schumpeter's disruptive force, the Austrian economists, drawing on the original insights of Ludwig von Mises, define entrepreneurship to be ''...the alertness that human beings...display toward potentially worthwhile goals hitherto unnoticed, as well as toward potentially valuable, available resources.'' Restated by the contemporary Austrian economist Israel Kirzner, ''...entrepreneurship does not consist of grasping a free ten-dollar bill which one has already discovered to be resting on one's hand; it consists in realizing that it is in one's hand and that it is available for the grasping.''

205

The competitive process then involves a continuous sequence of adjustment arising from unforeseen changes in the particular circumstances of market participants. The market system produces socially beneficial results, as if by an invisible hand Adam Smith told us, when entrepreneurs alertly respond to newly discovered opportunities for gain. Their profits are made by moving resources from lower to higher valued uses. In the process of recognizing an unrealized opportunity for personal gain, the alert individual responds to demand by moving resources in the direction of consumer preferences. Examples abound: the McDonald's hamburger, Wendy's, and now Burger King's charbroiled Whopper; the Apple personal computer caught the attention of IBM, AT&T, and others (notice how prices continue to fall!); designer jeans; quick stop automobile tune-up outlets; the Xerox copying machine and its many competitors; and the list is endless.

In other words, the essential nature of entrepreneurship is the *alertness* to new information and opportunities. Profit is a necessary consequence of the imperfections in the knowledge held by consumers and businesses. When profits are made, other competitors are attracted. Burger King, Wendy's, and Whataburger were initially attracted by the success of McDonald's. Colonel Sanders Kentucky Fried Chicken generated dozens of imitators. "It is," Kirzner tells us, "this entrepreneurial element that is responsible for our understanding of human action as active, creative, and human rather than as passive, automatic, and mechanical."

## THE ROLE OF PROFITS (AND LOSSES)

If entrepreneurs represent the engine of the competitive market process, then profits and losses are the accelerator and brake. In the absence of perfect coordination of the independent plans of decision makers, where knowledge is always widely dispersed and expensive in its acquisition, opportunties for moving resources to higher valued uses are always present. Entrepreneurial alertness to opportunties for greater social coordination are stimulated by "the heady scent of profits." Capitalizing on profitable opportunities represents a capitulation to consumer demands. Losses, in turn, strongly suggest that resources are being used relatively inefficiently. Though painful, losses are as necessary as profits. Cleansing an economic system removes what consumers do not want and signals producers to either change, improve, or else fail. The entrepreneur, therefore, is constantly attentive to consumer preferences. The reward of profits and penalty of losses provide powerful incentives to be alert to new opportunities and individual wants.

Entrepreneurial profit is the carrot which permits us to believe, with a good deal of confidence, that market forces can be relied upon to coordinate the disparate plans of individuals. In contrast, for those advocating the political means, there is no similar incentive, yardstick, or objective test to gauge success. Simply, there is no bottom line. The presence of entrepreneurial alertness to serve consumers can be illustrated by comparing the United Parcel Service (UPS) to the U.S. Postal Service, private schools to public schools, Disneyland to Yellowstone National Park, and private garbage collection to govenment garbage collection. Kirzner has provided an excellent summary of the distinction between the market and political means:

> It is solely because of the desire to obtain profits that we can, in any degree, rely on entrepreneurial discovery of where profits are to be had. Under government direction, it is not at all clear what substitutes for the profit incentive are available, in the absence of omniscience--not merely to spur the exploitation of socially desirable opportunities, but to direct attention to their very existence. Only if we ignore the role played in the market by this entrepreneurial element can we fail to raise the question of a corresponding role in the government directed economy.

## RISK TAKING AND ENTREPRENEURSHIP

Under the market system entrepreneurial alertness to opportunity is demonstrated daily. Whenever a difference exists between prices paid for a bundle of resources and the price obtained in the relevant product market, the possibility of profit exists. Modern industrial societies are continually engaged in the process of coordinating resouce markets with product markets. Imperfect coordination (i.e., profit potential) means there are unnoticed opportunities to buy resources, transform them into a good or service, and then sell them at a price which more than covers the costs of acquiring the inputs. The best-seller *In Search of Excellence* documents important examples of this kind of alertness.

Of course entrepreneurship is risky. There are no guarantees. The mere passage of time, with changing tastes and preferences, often turns anticipated profits into agonizing losses. Hundreds of thousands of new businesses are started each year in the United States but only one of three survive as long as five years. In the past decade, over 200,000 firms have gone out of business each year. Nevertheless, risk and uncertainty serve a crucial function in the competitive process. As George Gilder pointed out in *Wealth And Poverty*, "...such waste and irrationality is the secret of economic growth. Because no one knows which venture will succeed...a society open to the future rather than planning it, will call forth an endless stream of innovation, enterprise, and art." The more common view today is that risk is a four letter word. Many believe that government can minimize or even eliminate uncertainty and risk. But such a tidy, predictable, and riskless society is illusionary and, fortunately, neither possible nor desirable.

If entrepreneurial incentives are to benefit society, which is to say coordinate individual plans and maximize wealth, then rewards for this alertness must be available to those who perceive and act on opportunities. As Walter Wriston, Chairman of Citicorp, has said: "The driving force of our society is the conviction that risk-taking and individual responsibility are the ways to advance our mutual fortunes." But America seems hell-bent in another direction. In the name of equality of outcome, the entrepreneurial role--so necessary to the social benefits which are expected from the competitive market process--is being suppressed. Public policy, which imposes taxes in direct proportion to entrepreneurial success (higher incomes and profits means higher tax rates), is bound to discourage the kinds of economic activity that have in the past secured our high standards of living. Combined state and federal personal and corporate tax rates in the United States (for marginal dollars earned) are in excess of fifty percent for even fairly moderate incomes. There is indeed something to the supply-side agenda which proposes a significant reduction in marginal tax rates! They have jolted us from our slumber by reviewing what Adam Smith and others long ago told us about the role of incentives in the creation of wealth.

## THE QUESTION OF MONOPOLY

Arising in part from the confusion over the role of profits in the free market system and the large size of many American corporations, it is frequently asserted that American industry is characterized by monopoly. The Marxist economists Paul Baran and Paul Sweezy have written of "monopoly capitalism" as if they have identified the essential character of our economic environment. But their view is both factually wrong and influenced by an inappropriate interpretation of the competitive process. In the market economy, whenever competitors are not restricted from offering more attractive opportunities to other buyers or sellers, competition is potentially present. From this perspective, monopoly power can arise only if entry barriers are erected which prevent market transactions between consumers and producers. As the entrepreneurial process is inherently competitive, limits or restrictions to market exchange must be imposed externally. In fact, these outside impediments to the competitive process invariably originate in government. Government, employing its monopoly on the use of force, is the source of monopoly power.

Therefore, from our perspective, the market process is always competitive unless government barriers to entry are enacted. If follows that the number of sellers in a particular industry provides little reliable evidence on the degree of rivalry in a market. Size, or what economists call industrial concentration, is a poor indicator of monopoly power. Harold Demsetz, Yale Brozen, Dominick Armentano, J. Fred Weston, and John S. McGee are just a few of the contemporary economists whose scholarship documents this proposition. There are essentially two ways to restrict entry and curtail the competitive process. First, monopoly positions can be held if the control and ownership of an important resource is necessary to a particular activity. This might involve the exclusive ownership of a mineral resource and/or the possession of a patent or secret technology unavailable to potential competitors. Luciano Pavorotti, the great tenor, in this sense has monopoly power as a result of "owning" those remarkable vocal cords. However, resource monopoly tends to dissipate through time when new production processes, substitutes, and technologies are discovered.

Second and by far the most important source of protection from competition involves the barriers to market entry enforced by the power of government. Examples are the granting of an exclusive franchise such as for intercity truck routes, garbage collection services, cable television, the licensing of professions and taxicabs, and other government interventions used to prevent competition. Even our so-called antitrust laws have impeded the competitive market process and encouraged monopoly. More specifically, *government* is the source of monopoly in the American economy! It follows that the most effective way to deal with the "monopoly problem" would be to eliminate government imposed barriers to participation in the market process.

## THE ANTITRUST LAWS AND COMPETITION

Perhaps the most unfortunate, but we believe predictable, implication of government monopoly laws is the extent to which they protect *competitors* rather than the competitive process. As already demonstrated, the competitive market is inherently risky. From the community's point of view it is desirable that there be both winners and losers, both profits and losses. Competitive capitalism is a great "flushing system" through which scarce resources are inevitably withdrawn from lower valued uses and mobilized for higher ones. Therein lies one of its great values. A necessary consequence of this rivalrous process is the disappointment and financial loss of those who fail to correctly anticipate consumer preferences or underestimate production costs. Thomas Sowell, in his book *Knowledge And Decisions* has summarized the essential character of a truly open competitive process:

> The advantages of market institutions over government institutions are not so much in their particular characteristics as institutions but in the fact that people can usually make a better choice    out of numerous

options than by following a single prescribed process. The diversity of personal tastes insures that no given institution will become the answer to a human problem in the market...Responsiveness to individual diversity means that market processes necessarily produce 'chaotic' results from the point of view of any single given scale of values...People who are convinced that their values are best--not only for themselves but for others--must necessarily be offended by many things that happen in a market economy...The diversity of tastes satisfied by a market may be its greatest economic achievement, but it is also its greatest political vulnerability.

As already noted, federal antitrust legislation has more often than not been a government enforced device to restrict competition and protect competitors from more efficient rivals. The argument and evidence for this point of view has been forcefully made by the economist Dominick Armentano in his book *Antitrust and Monopoly*. This startling and radical indictment of American antitrust is described by Armentano:

> The general public has been deluded into believing that monopoly is a free-market problem, and that the government, through antitrust enforcement, is on the side of the 'angels.' The facts are entirely the opposite. Antitrust, therefore, whatever its intent, has served as convenient cover for an insidious process of monopolization in the marketplace. Such is the deeper and more subtle meaning of antitrust policy.

A good example of legislation which protects particular competitors from the rigors of the competitive process is Section II of the Clayton Act (1914) as amended by the Robinson-Patman Act (1936). In this instance an overwhelming majority of economists generally agree on the undesirable consequences of the so-called price discrimination laws. Passed to protect small, independent businesses from "unfair" competition of the large regional and national chains evolving during the early part of this century, this legislation in fact suppressed price competition. In the name of "unreasonable" economic power, and of course always in the "public interest," special interest groups used government to obtain protection from the rigors of the market. Naturally, political entrepreneurs were prepared to sell these favors for campaign money and votes. Robinson-Patman is quite explicit in its intentions. Certain parts of Section II in law suggest that price cuts, even when justified by cost differences, are not defendable and, therefore, price competition is illegal *per se*. As Armentano points out: "At least the price discrimination law is refreshingly honest concerning its intent to limit price competition and restrain the rivalrous process of an open market."

Among the many court cases on this issue was the much publicized complaint brought by the Federal Trade Commission in the early 1960's against the Borden Company. Accused of selling its own brand of evaporated milk at a higher price than its private label milk, a complaint was brought against Borden. The law suit charged that

Borden's private label business had "...placed *severe competitive pressures* on the entire unadvertised brand of private label milk structure and that has...largely been felt in the way of *lowered market price*" (emphasis added). Incredibly, we have turned the whole notion of free market competition upside down! Borden was condemned for offering a product to the public at a lower price which in turn stimulated competition among rivals. As one witness before the FTC complained: "The competition has forced our prices down from the level we had previous to that...and it is made highly competitive because of these factors."

The good news is that a brave hearing examiner for the FTC was unwilling to accept the idea that the law's intention was to protect competitors. Armentano quotes the examiner's recommendation which provides an eloquent statement of the benefits to be expected from the competitive process:

> These competitive advantages which council supporting the complaint would have us condemn as unlawful are the accumulated benefits of that private initiative, industry, and business acumen which our system of free enterprise is designed to foster and reward.

The bad news, however, was that the Federal Trade Commission reversed the hearing examiner's decision and found Borden guilty of an illegal price discrimination. Finally, and unfortunately for economic efficiency and a free society, the U. S. Supreme Court in 1966 upheld the FTC ruling. In a powerful dissent, Justice Stewart of the Court tried in vain to defend the competitive market process:

> In the guise of protecting producers and purchasers from discriminatory price competition, the Court ignores legitimate market preferences and endows the Federal Trade Commission with authority to disrupt price relationships between products whose identity has been measured in the laboratory but rejected in the marketplace. I do not believe that such power was conferred upon the Commission by Congress.

The Borden case, in our view, represents the "climax of absurdity" in a long list of price discrimination suits. Space does not permit an enunciation of the anti-competitive implications of other cases like Morton Salt, Minneapolis-Honeywell, Sun Oil, Standard Oil of Indiana, and many others. Suffice it to say that a number of prestigious committees in recent years have condemned the suppression of the competitive process through the Robinson-Patman Act. To summarize, from Armentano's excellent analysis of this issue in *Antitrust and Monopoly:* "The economic nightmare that is Robinson-Patman is working exactly as it was intended to work back in 1936 when the important amendments were drafted. The law, through the threat of enforcement or actual enforcement, can make serious price competition almost impossible, and that may have been exactly the purpose of the statute."

There is little debate among informed observers concerning the socially undesirable consequences of price discrimination laws. Unfortunately, there is much less unanimity of opinion regarding the consequence of the other major monopoly laws: specifically the Sherman Act (1890), the Clayton Act's other major provisions, and the Federal Trade Commission Act (1914). A majority of economists continue to believe that the Sherman Act and the others have, on balance, been socially beneficial. However, we believe, following the important studies by Armentano, Richard Posner, Donald Dewey, Harold Demsetz, Robert Bork, Wesley Liebeler, Yale Brozen, J. Fred Weston, John S. McGee, and others, that important reservations are appropriate regarding the likelihood that the antitrust laws have increased economic efficiency and served the American consumer.

An excellent illustration of the relevance of this "new learning" is found in the classic case of "witch-hunting for Robber Barons," the Standard Oil of New Jersey Supreme Court case of 1911. Supported by the highly biased and incomplete work of writers like Ira Tarbell in *The History of the Standard Oil Company,* it was argued that this was a classic example of "monopoly" power. This conventional view was roughly as follows: through predatory pricing and restrictions of output, monopoly profits were achieved by the Standard Oil Company. The Company was accused of monopolizing the petroleum industry and therefore deserving of government dissolution. According to a noted historian: "He [Rockefeller] iron-handedly ruined competitors by cutting prices until his victim went bankrupt or sold out, whereupon higher prices would be likely to return." In another textbook two historians maintain that "...Rockefeller was a ruthless operator who did not hesitate to crush his competitors by harsh and unfair methods." However, this conventional point of view is simply inconsistent with the facts!

More than a quarter of a century ago economist John S. McGee, after reviewing more than 10,000 pages of the Standard Oil trial record, demonstrated on both theoretical and empirical grounds "...that Standard Oil did not systematically, if ever, use local price cutting in retailing, or anywhere else, to reduce competition. To do so would have been foolish; and, whatever else has been said about them, the old Standard organization was seldom criticized for making less money when it could readily have made more."

The rapid increase in Rockefeller's share of total refining capacity in the United States (from 4 percent in 1870 to more than 80 percent in 1880) resulted from a combination of influences. Economic efficiency, entrepreneurial management, the generally depressed conditions during the 1870's, and the excess capacity in refining which had appeared following the Civil War were the most important factors. Rockefeller's acquisitions, an exchange of money for assets agreed to by all parties, were evidently favorable to the sellers, especially when the generally low market values of the depressed times are

212

considered. Some refineries were anxious to be purchased, and frequently Standard Oil thought the asking price "outrageous."
Furthermore, the techniques of production were changing during this period, and the economically efficient scale of refinery output was increasing rapidly. Larger capital requirements meant that bigger firms had advantages not available to small producers. Most important of all, however, the Rockefeller organization exhibited the classic attributes of entrepreneurial alertness which are the fundamental source of new ideas, products, production techniques, and over the long-haul, rising real standards of living for the population. Armentano's summary description of those momentous events of the 1870's captures the exciting flavor of the competitive process at work in this important industry:

> Efficient operations in the 1870's meant tank cars, pipelines, adequate crude sources, cheap barrels, huge storage facilities, and export capabilities, all of which the Standard Oil Company had invested in heavily, and most of which the smaller competitors had not. The Standard Oil Company has often been criticized for the fact that its competitors could not enjoy the efficiencies of a tank car fleet, access to cheap pipelines, and large storage facilities. But, surely, the fact that competitors would not or could not be as efficient as Standard in these areas was not Standard's responsibility. Was it unfair to buy or build pipelines and then employ them to obtain lower rates for railroad freight? Was it unfair to own tank cars and use them efficiently? Was it unfair to invest millions in storage facilities to take advantage of slight variances in the demand and supply of crude or refined petroleum? And was it unfair for Rockefeller to surround himself with singular men of exceptional 'brainpower, astuteness, and foresightedness'? While competitors that could not or would not do these things might have regarded these activities as unfair, the ultimate justification of these policies was proven again and again in the market place: they lowered the costs of production and the price of the product and raised the profits of the Standard Oil Company.

Economists are in general agreement with the textbook argument against monopoly: barriers to market entry permit the restriction of production levels, facilitate a higher "monopoly price," and therefore permit higher profits and an inefficient allocation of resources. Presumably the Supreme Court, in ruling that Standard Oil was in violation of the Sherman Act, interpreted this to be the case. Again, however, the facts run contrary to the Court's decision. Between 1870 and 1885, the period during which the Rockefeller organization reached the zenith of its "power," refined kerosene prices *fell* from 26 cents per gallon to just 8 cents. Average costs per gallon were reduced by a factor of six. From 1880 to 1897, when Standard Oil supposedly possessed this monopoly power, or more than 90 percent of refinery capacity in the United States, the price of refined oil per gallon in barrels *declined* from 9.33 cents to 5.91 cents. At the same time the quality of petroleum products was being significantly improved. Furthermore, the volume of production increased rapidly throughout the period; a performance which directly contradicts the traditional case against monopoly.

In fact, the history of Standard Oil represents an important example of the power and socially beneficial implications of the competitive process when barriers to market participation are absent. Long before the breakup of the Standard combination, according to one student of this period, "...the process of whittling Standard Oil down to reasonable size within the industry was already far advanced." While Standard's volume of refined production increased from 39 million barrels in 1892 to 99 million barrels in 1911 (hardly a monopolist output!), its share of the petroleum product's market had *declined* to 64 percent in 1911 from almost 90 percent in 1890. With the expansion of the industry and newly discovered crude oil supplies in the West and Southwest, new companies were formed including the Pure Oil Company, Texaco, Union Oil, and Gulf Oil Company. On the eve of the Supreme Court's verdict against Standard there were at least 147 independent refineries in the United States. In conclusion, and once again quoting Armentano in his profound book *Antitrust and Monopoly:* "To seriously maintain that Standard was increasingly monopolizing the petroleum industry at the turn of the century, or that the antitrust suit against Standard...was a legitimate response to almost complete monopolistic control, is patently absurd."

It is interesting that in recent decades the coercive power of government *has* been used to erect barriers to competition in the petroleum industry and thereby protect certain sectors from the rigors of competition. Through import quotas, restrictions on well-head production, and more recently in the government intervention which came out of the "energy crisis," the federal government has in effect cartelized the petroleum industry in a manner which had been found to be impossible for Rockefeller and his powerful combination. Once again the hard facts of reality must be recognized: government has invariably been the source of long-lasting monopoly power. The competitive process can only be surpressed by a force external to the market.

Our conclusions regarding the Standard Oil example are generally applicable to the other cases brought under the Sherman Act and the Clayton Act. Almost without exception the record shows that government intervention is brought to bear *against* businesses which are *increasing* output, innovating, *reducing* costs and *passing these lower costs along* in large part to the ultimate consumer. For example, part of the brief against the Aluminum Company of America (Alcoa) in the antitrust suit before the special federal court in 1945 was that the company continued to research, innovate, lower their costs, and pass these savings on to the buyer in the form of lower prices, thereby precluding profitable entry by potential competitors. Alcoa had no competitors in the production of primary aluminum ingots because potential entrants simply could not match the company's economic efficiency. Appeals Court Justice Learned Hand seemed totally confused about the nature of competition and its benefits when he concluded that Alcoa "forestalled" competition by encouraging the consumption of aluminum and then "doubled and redoubled" its refining capacity to meet that demand. Striving for more business and increased economic efficiency, their actions were interpreted as *restraints* of trade. Antitrust had literally been turned on its head, penalizing what it allegedly was designed to promote.

The Sherman Act provides that "...every contract, combination, or conspiracy, in restraint of trade is hereby declared to be illegal;" that *restraint* of production and trade is a violation of the law. Like Standard Oil, Alcoa, U. S. Steel, Brown Shoe Company, and many others, the evidence of actual behavior contadicts the indictments. Du Pont is a case in point. In the 1970's the Federal Trade Commission charged that Du Pont's new low-cost method of producing titanium dioxide pigments had enabled it to gain forty percent of the domestic market. Not only had they acquired a larger share of the market through increased efficiency, but their new, efficient plant in Mississippi also increased their capacity to serve even more customers. University of Chicago economist Yale Brozen identified the fundamental point: "Can you imagine that any enterprise would engage in such a nefarious activity? It should, according to the FTC, behave like a monopolist. It should restrict its output, instead of expanding, and charge higher prices." Examples of this confusion between protecting *competitors* from the market process and the desirable goal of encouraging entrepreneurial rivalry could fill volumes.

Armentano has summarized the role "anti-monopoly" statutes have played in actually suppressing the benefits derivable from the market process:

> The most important conclusion is that the entire antitrust system--allegedly created to protect competition and increase consumer welfare--has worked, instead, to lessen business competition and lessen the efficiency and productivity associated with the free-market process. Like many other governmental interventions, antitrust has produced results that are far different from those that were allegedly intended...In each and every case the indicted corporations were engaging in an intensely competitive process; yet in each and every case, such behavior was condemned, by the FTC or by the Justice Department, as a 'restraint of trade' and as an alleged violation of the antitrust laws...In the vast majority of...private cases, it is perfectly clear that the legal concern is not monopoly or resource misallocation at all, but an obvious and blatant attempt by the plaintiff to restrain and restrict the competitive rivalry emanating from the more efficient defendant company.

To reiterate the fundamental point on the question of monopoly, the only long-lasting and meaningful source of monopoly power in the economy stems from the advantages and protection granted to market participants by government. The state frequently suppresses the competitive process, thereby contributing to inefficiency and a loss of wealth which would otherwise be generated by an open and competitive market environment.

## THE MARKET MEANS VERSUS THE GOVERNMENT MEANS AS DELIVERY SYSTEMS

It is crucial to demonstrate the fundamental problem encountered by all economic systems: the efficient communication and coordination of knowledge that is widely dispersed and not possessed by any single individual or small group of individuals in its entirety. Following the analysis of the market means by the Austrian School of Economics, the price system makes massive amounts of fragmented but important information available, inexpensively, to the buyers and sellers in a competitive market economy. A structure of competitively determined and ever-changing relative prices generates the knowledge by which the separate plans of individual are reconciled and coordinated. In fact, a strong case can be made that without market prices economic calculation and relative scarcities would be impossible to calculate. Or, according to Hayek, "...if we agree that the economic problem of society is mainly one of rapid adaptation to changes in the particular circumstances of time and place, it would seem to follow that the ultimate decisons must be left to the people who are familiar with these circumstances, who know directly of the relevant changes and of the resources immediately available to meet them." Indeed, the complexity of the modern economic world demands less, not more, government intervention. Only through decentralized market arrangements can we hope to solve the economic problem efficiently and honestly.

It is totally inappropriate to evaluate the competitive market process in terms of some hypothetical, ideal, and all-knowing government. Government simply cannot efficiently correct the mistakes which necessarily appear in an uncertain and therefore risky world. The relevant comparison is with alternative institutions realistically available to mortal men. The planned economies of the world have been infamous for their demonstrated inefficiencies. It is irrelevant for the human predicament to compare the market means with an ideal standard which is unobtainable. Indeed, as we have already shown, the market usually fails to recognize available opportunties because government has prevented entrepreneurs from acting. The Federal Trade Commission suppressed cable television for twenty years. Competition in long-distance telephone communications was prevented by government until just recently. Improved air service and lower fares were suppressed by the Civil Aeronautics Board prior to deregulation in 1978. And the list goes on and on.

Another Nobel Laureate in economics, Milton Friedman, writes insightfully about preserving the beneficial implications of competitive capitalism in his proposed amendment to the U. S. Constitution: "The right of the people to buy and sell legitimate goods and services at mutually acceptable terms shall not be infringed by Congress or any of the States." The stark realities of the options available when choosing between competition and government monopoly where poignantly identified a number of years ago by the late comedian Lenny Bruce:

Capitalism is the best. It's free enterprise. Barter. Gimbels, if I really get rank with the clerk, 'Well I don't like this,' how I can resolve? If it really gets ridiculous, I go, 'Frig it, man, I walk.' What can this guy do at Gimbels, even if he was the president of Gimbels? He can always reject me from the store, but I can always go to Macy's. He can't really hurt me. Communism is like one big phone company. Government control, man. And if I get rank with that phone company, where can I go? I'll end up like a schmuck with a dixie cup on a thread.

# CHAPTER 18

## ECONOMIC REGULATION
## AND GOVERNMENT MONOPOLY

There have been more serious studies made of government regulation of industry in the last fifteen years or so, particulary in the United States, than in the whole preceeding period. These studies have been both quantitative and nonquantitative...The main lesson to be drawn from these studies is clear: they all tend to suggest that the regulation is either ineffective or that when it has a noticeable impact, on balance the effect is bad, so that consumers obtain a worse product or a higher-priced product or both as a result of the regulation. Indeed, this result is found so uniformly as to create a puzzle: one would expect to find, in all these studies, at least some government programs that do more good than harm.

--Ronald H. Coase

During the 1976 Presidential campaign candidates Gerald Ford and Jimmy Carter ran on a platform which promised to reduce the scope of government regulation. In 1980 President Reagan did the same, and in the administration's "Program for Economic Recovery" they proposed "a far-reaching program of regulatory relief" for the American people. The rhetoric was appealing. As the above quotation by Ronald Coase proclaims, economic regulation has invariably stifled competition, increased costs, reduced consumer choice, and in general protected existing suppliers from potential rivals. Yet, in spite of the overwhelming case against government regulation, certain segments of the federal regulatory octopus continue to expand. While the old-style economic regulation has been slowed, even cut back in important industries, the new social regulation has continued its phenomenal growth. It has been recognized that economic regulation of industries like trucking and broadcasting has, almost without exception, increased the monopoly power of existing sellers and reduced consumer choice. Yet the relentless drive to politicize job safety, protect the consumer, and insure a pristine environment continues. Senator Ted Kennedy can lead the fight to deregulate the American airline industry, but simultaneously lobby for expanded social regulation and increased government intervention, failing to recognize that limits to the one apply equally to the other.

The political means of forceful intervention in voluntary economic arrangements is invariably both inefficient and immoral. Government intervention is inefficient because it reduces consumer choice. By denying peaceful human action in which participants in the market produce and exchange, we prevent mutually beneficial trade. Personally beneficial behavior is sacrificed and economic efficiency suffers.

218

In general, government's use of force to prevent economic specialization and exchange on a voluntary basis denies individuals that personal autonomy which is a prerequisite to a moral human life. In our agenda for the restoration of economic freedom and therefore personal liberty, the case is made for a "far reaching program of regulatory relief for the American people."

## THE NATURE OF GOVERNMENT ECONOMIC INTERVENTION

The competitive market process involves the voluntary exchange of private property rights in an environment where artificial impediments to these kinds of mutually beneficial actions are absent. This process, following the categories of the German sociologist Franz Oppenheimer, is called the use of the market means. On the other hand, the forceful interference with or intervention in these voluntary arrangements through the police power of the state is called the political means. Murray Rothbard, in his book *Power and Market,* identifies three general types of government intervention in peaceful social interaction. First, there is what he calls "autistic intervention." This category includes both permissible government actions which protect individual rights and impermissible autisitc acts. Government, for example, is charged with preventing, and needless-to-say it should not itself instigate, murder, assualt, fraud, or any forceful denial of speech, assembly, or religious observance. Autistic intervention involves the unilateral use of force or violence by one individual or by government upon another individual or group of individuals. There is no exchange; simply a command to do as the intervener demands through the threat of force. As John Locke and Thomas Jefferson told us, governments are supposedly instituted among men to protect citizens from this kind of autistic invasion of their individual rights. Unfortunately, governments are themselves notorious for committing this type of intervention into private circumstances.

The second type of (potentially) violent intervention involves an exchange which is forced on an unwilling party. Rothbard has labeled this type of interference "binary intervention." Prime examples of binary intervention originating in government would include military conscription and taxation. These are situations in which a "coerced gift" or "coerced exchange" between an individual and government takes place. It is taken for granted that individuals cannot coerce exchanges from other individuals. Any violent or potentially violent invasion of one's right to refuse a coerced exchange offered by another individual, for example robbery ("your money or your life"), is precisely the kind of binary intervention which government is charged with preventing. Unfortunately, government is now so busy doing other things, it frequently fails to perform these more obvious functions which are necessary to a free society.

However, it is Rothbard's third category of government intervention into private economic relationships which has captured the attention of economists when analyzing the implications for economic welfare in the use of the political means. "Triangular intervention" involves the use of government force or the threat of force to compel, prohibit, or alter the particulars of an otherwise voluntary exchange between two individuals. It includes those situations where the police power of the state is used to define permissible transactions between consenting adults. Most of the intervention under this triangular category takes place in the market where money is exchanged for a good or service. The intervention by government, as Rothbard reminds us in *Power and Market*, "...signifies *per se* that the individual or individuals coerced would not have done what they are now doing were it not for the intervention."

Of profound importance is the recognition that government interference in private and voluntary transactions in the market must of necessity involve the assignment of gains in the form of wealth and income to one party at the expense of another. For example, the monstrous increase in the tariff on large Japanese motorcycles in 1983 generated a windfall gain for the suppliers of American made motorcycles (Harley-Davidson) and came at the expense of American consumers of motorcycles who are paying higher prices and having fewer choices. In contrast to the political means, voluntary exchanges occurring in the competitive market process, as we have already shown, are always mutually beneficial to the trading parties.

## REGULATION AND THE SUPPRESSION OF SOCIALLY USEFUL KNOWLEDGE

While it is morally wrong to forcefully deny individuals the freedom to undertake voluntary and, therefore, mutually beneficial trades, there is also Friederich Hayek's concern with the "knowledge problem." The suppression of socially useful knowledge about alternative opportunities and relative costs through government intervention in the market process is economically inefficient and destructive. The great advantage of the market in a world of scarcity is the proposition that the competitive process generates information and useful knowledge for market participants about the existence and terms of mutually beneficial trades. Triangular intervention by government, which suppresses entry by potential competitors into particular markets and/or constrains the communication of prices, has the definite consequences of reducing the quantity and quality of useful information available to consumers and producers alike.

In summary, the suppression of market signals by force is not only circumspect on moral grounds, but can also produce cumulative distortions in the prices and other objective facts that it is the purpose of the market process to discover. Price controls, for example, prevent the appearance of the relative terms under which mutually beneficial cooperation and coordination might otherwise take place. The answer for economic efficiency and progress then is the elimination of such artificial distortions. Government price controls, licensing requirements and a myriad of other interventions in the market process by government must be eliminated.

## CONTROLS: PRICE CEILINGS

The restoration of economic freedom and therefore the maintenance of economic progress depends on our ability to eliminate government imposed maximum and minimum price laws which suppress and distort the efficiency characteristics of free and open market competition. Rent controls, usury laws, and natural gas price controls are existing examples of legislated price ceilings which reduce the ability of the market to allocate resources to their most efficient use. And, of greater importance, these market interventions almost invariably produce results opposite of that which the politicians had intended.

### Rent Controls

In recent years there has been a veritable explosion of ways to politicize housing markets in the United States. There have been clarion calls for rent controls and increased regulation in the construction and geographic distribution of housing. Equity and justice are the terms used to justify such actions. Unfortunately, as Charles W. Baird has conclusively demonstrated in *Rent Control: The Perennial Folly*, actual experience with rent control legislation has produced both unanticipated and undesirable consequences for the quality and quantity of housing in America.

The imposition of government enforced rent controls holds the rental price of housing below the price which would have been established in the free market. One of the most powerful and empirically verified propositions of economic analysis is that effective price ceilings will produce shortages. And they do! Therefore, some form of non-price rationing must be used to allocate existing supplies. The evidence of shortages is startlingly demonstrated by the experience of New York City where rent controls have been in effect since the 1940's. Owner landlords, limited by law in the rents they may collect, are motivated to postpone and reduce maintenance expenditures. Expectedly, they disinvest, finding far more remunerative places to put their money. The effects, observed only after an extended period of time, are the destroyed and abandoned buildings which so sadly characterizes New York City. Eric Hemel captures the flavor of the disasterous consequences of government intervention in New York:

> The effect of rent control most obvious to the casual observer is deterioration of older housing. The New York streets described so movingly in Alfred Kazin's *A Walker in the City* and Betty Smith's *A Tree Grows in Brooklyn* are now littered with the wreckage of broken buildings. Some blocks look as if they had been bombed by B-52's.

One of the cruel ironies of the New York experience is the fact that the monstrous destruction of rental housing came at the expense of the very people it supposedly was designed to protect. The empirical evidence of rent controls on the poor is uniformly the same. The Fraser Institute in Vancouver, British Columbia sponsored a study in 1975 detailing the rent control experiences of the United States, France, the United Kingdom, Sweden, and Austria. The universal outcome in these countries has been summarized by the Scottish economist F. G. Pennance:

> It is that in every country examined, the introduction and continuance of rent control/restriction/regulation has done more harm than good in rental housing markets--let alone the economy at large--by perpetuating shortages, encouraging immobility, swamping consumer preferences, fostering dilapidation of housing stocks and eroding production incentives, distorting land-use patterns and the allocation of scarce resources, and all in the name of the distributive justice it has manifestly failed to achieve because at best it has been related only randomly to the needs and individual income circumstances of households.

A few years ago the president of the American Stock Exchange, hardly a person on welfare, was living in an apartment in which the controlled price was $660 a month and the fair-market value of the apartment was between $850 and $1200. In the late 1960's more than forty percent of the rental units subject to rent control in New York City were inhabited by households with incomes at or above the national average.

In summary, legal price ceilings on rental housing units have created shortages, prevented market adjustments to changing circumstances, destroyed housing, and finally, have come largely at the expense of the poor. The 200 or so cities currently constrained by rent control legislation, including large metropolitan areas like Los Angeles, Baltimore, and Miami Beach, can predictably expect to experience the same results as New York City. Rent control has been tested and found lacking. The restoration of economic freedom and justice demands that the appropriate political pressures be brought to bear to repeal this misguided policy.

## Usury Laws

Laws that limit the rate of interest charged on credit transactions, known as usury laws, have also produced results which harm the very persons they are designed to assist. Like effective price ceilings on rents, usury rate ceilings, if effective, create artificial shortages of loanable funds. Credit granting financial institutions discover an excess demand for the limited funds available at the ceiling interest rate. Nevertheless, the problem of scarcity is not repealed by the imposition of a law. Credit must still be rationed, and if not by the interest rate, then by some other non-price rationing device. As one would expect, financial institutions will tend to ration loan funds to their most credit worthy customers in order to reduce risk, lower costs, and increase profits. Individuals with poor credit ratings, usually the poor and often times minorities and other disadvantaged groups, will be denied access to the credit market. Once again an example of the use of force by government in the name of assisting the less advantaged produces results diametrically opposed to those intended.

## Energy Price Controls

It would be remiss to leave the topic of price ceilings without at least some mention of the so-called "energy crisis" of the 1970's which was the direct consequence of the U. S. government's imposition of price ceilings on petroleum and petroleum products. Government policies meant shortages and misallocations were unavoidable. Instead of rationing by price, gasoline was rationed by long lines and restricted hours at the pump. By maintaining artifically low prices, the government encouraged "wasteful" consumption of petroleum products and simultaneously discouraged the search for new energy sources. Furthermore, as a result of the actual implementation of federal regulations and ceilings, including the so-called "entitlements" program, the United States actually encouraged imports from the OPEC cartel and other foreign countries while at the same time pronouncing a program of "energy independence" for the United States. It is no accident that with the deregulation of petroleum prices the mysterious "energy crisis" has disappeared. Hopefully, the Congress will recognize the market's efficiency and completely deregulate the natural gas industry.

## CONTROLS: PRICE FLOORS

The costly, disruptive, and generally negative implications of maximum price legislation is repeated with similar results in the case of minimum price controls. They are wrong not only because they deny individuals the opportunity to freely enter into what they perceive to be beneficial transactions, but also because they distort market signals and prevent scarce resources from being allocated to their most productive uses. Import tariffs on foreign goods forcefully deny individuals the opportunity to obtain products at a lower cost and in addition generate higher prices in the domestic market. Like most examples of triangular intervention by government into economic life, there are important changes in the distribution of income and wealth. In the example of tariffs, it is almost invariably a transfer of wealth from consumers to the domestic producers in the protected industry. For example the politically motivated program to subsidize the domestic sugar industry through a combination of import duties and quotas (on purpose with regard to beet and cane sugar, but an inadvertant by-product with respect to fructose) has cost the American consumer about $1 billion a year.

## Agriculture Price Supports

U. S. Government intervention in agricultural markets over the past half century has largely occurred through the mechanism of minimum agriculture price supports for a number of commodities. In a short but excellent summary of government involvement in American agriculture, Clifton B. Luttrell in *Down on the Farm With Uncle Sam* has documented the waste, distortions, and injustices perpetrated by the use of the political means in support of some parts of American Agriculture. The most conspicuous characteristic of price supports (price floors) is the appearance of surpluses. Legislated prices above the market clearing price encourage production and discourage consumption: the U. S. government has acquired mountains of wheat, corn, cheese, butter, dried milk, etc., to hold prices up. For example, at the end of March 1983 the Commodity Credit Corporation of the U. S. Dept. of Agriculture owned 1.2 billion pounds of non-fat dry milk, 758 million pounds of cheese, and 415 million pounds of butter. Annual storage costs for just these dairy products was $56 million. To lower government owned stocks federal authorities have been giving "free" cheese and butter to the poor. But the dairy industry is now complaining that they are losing cheese sales. A new government program to discourage milk production presently offers dairy farmers roughly $1,000 per cow for milk not produced. That, of course, means that beef producers are now faced with more red meat competition. To say the least, the beef industry is unhappy.

The issue of justice also must be recognized in the equation. Under the existing Department of Agriculture programs, the price support payments and income support payments accrue overwhelmingly to the owners of the big farms, and relatively little of the billions of dollars end up in the hands of the truly needy rural resident or small farmer. If the farm programs exist to produce "fairness," it is certainly difficult to identify the socially beneficial results.

But things get worse. Surpluses, created by government price supports, require additional government intervention to get rid of the surplus commodities. In addition to giving away "free" cheese, the U. S. has other important food distribution programs both at home ("food stamps") and abroad (Public Law 480 - "Food for Peace"). Production is discouraged through output controls which have included acreage restrictions, "soil banks," and finally in 1983 the ultimate outrage: the Payment-In-Kind (PIK) program in which the federal government pays farmers not to produce, and the payment to the farmer takes the form of commodities taken out of government owned surpluses. In the first year of the PIK program it is estimated that as much as $12 billion of surplus commodities were given to America's farmers for not producing. In fiscal year 1983, the total cost of the traditional price and income support programs which subsidize American agriculture was about $21 billion, almost as much as total farm income in the United States in the same year. If we also consider subsidized lending and other programs which indirectly assist agriculture, the total subsidy from all sources approached $50 billion in 1983. We simply do not believe that the American people, both as taxpayers and consumers, will tolerate the continuation of such a misguided and expensive public subsidy.

One of the tragic ironies of U. S. price support programs in agriculture is the fact that they raise world prices as a result of the American dominance (as residual supplier) in many of these export markets. Unfortunately for American markets abroad, higher world prices for wheat, corn, and soybeans encourage foreign producers like Canada, Argentina, Australia, Brazil, and France to increase their acreage. Each of these countries has profited from the farm price support programs implemented by the American government at the instigation of the agricultural community.

Government has also used American grain exports as a foreign policy tool; another form of market intervention ending in folly. For example, in 1980 the U. S. imposed a grain embargo on exports to the Soviet Union for its invasion of Afghanistan. To make a long story short, the Soviets continued to obtain their grain from other sources; they stayed in Afghanistan (their Viet Nam); and the American grain farmer's share of the Soviet market fell from 70 percent to 20 percent in one year. To rectify the government's success in destroying our export markets, that very same government now proposes to subsidize U. S. agriculture exports.

Government intervention in American agricultural markets has been demonstrably unsuccessful. Average farm incomes remain low; the problem of surpluses continues; scarce resources continue to remain in the low productivity farm sector; and the great majority of those classified as farmers benefit very little from the billions of dollars annually pumped into agricultural subsidies. At the same time, these programs have been horrendously expensive. Between 1929 and 1982 total budget outlays by the U.S. Department of Agriculture (USDA), excluding the food stamp and nutrition programs, increased from 1 percent of net farm income to 160 percent of net farm income. While the significant decline in the number of farms and farm workers in the United States since the Great Depression suggests that fewer USDA bureaucrats are needed, the number of employees at the Department actually grew from 24 thousand to 85 thousand during the same preiod. Total USDA expenditures in 1982 were more than $45 billion, roughly twice as large as total farm income in the United States. In 1929 there were 67 USDA employees per million acres harvested; by 1982 the figure had risen to 346.

The "farm problem" remains: we simply have more farmers in the United States than can successfully compete in an open market. Price supports encourage excess production and simultaneously generate misleading signals regarding the need for farmers. The result, as we have shown, is commodity surpluses which in turn produce government programs in which the police power of the state is employed to reduce production. All this occurs while governments claim massive famines are on the horizon if something is not done immediately. A restoration of economic freedom in agriculture is in the interest of the American farmer, and it is in the interest of the poor and hungry of the world. The wheat, corn, and soybean producers in the United States have a higher level of productivity than any farmer in the world. U.S. farmers continue to be an important force in world grain markets *in spite of* government programs which significantly reduce the ability of the American farmer to compete in foreign markets.

An important implication of government price controls is the adverse impact on the poor. It has been estimated that during the 1960's price and income support programs for American agriculture raised the nation's food bill by about 7 percent. While this figure was around 2 percent during the 1970's when agriculture was relatively free of support programs, it has probably risen to the 7 percent figure in recent years as USDA expenditures have skyrocketed. Support levels in 1981 increased the food bill of the intermediate budget family in the U. S. by $409. The burden is proportionately greater for lower income families than higher ones. The American government may be giving away "free" cheese, but the poor have already paid for it. And, as we have already pointed out, it is the higher income farmer who benefits from the support programs. The small, marginal farmer has benefited relatively little from the massive increase in agriculture subsidies.

However, there is another beneficiary of these programs: namely the people employed by the Department of Agriculture. In 1980 there were *thirteen* assistant secretaries of agriculture, under-secretaries, or equivalent level titles in the USDA and numerous civil service employees in pay scales above the GS-12 rank. For all these reasons, the American people should demand a gradual phase-out of price and income support payments to American agriculture over a reasonable period of adjustment, say five to seven years. The whole thing is frightfully expensive and has generally failed to realize its announced objectives.

## Minimum Wage Law

Although government intervention in American agriculture has been wasteful and in large measure counterproductive, a persuasive argument can be made that the social and economic costs are relatively unimportant when compared with the federal minimum wage law (a price floor) which condemns large numbers of young and unskilled Americans to a second class status with respect to employment opportunities. Economist Walter Williams in his book *The State Against the Blacks* clearly documents the adverse implications of the federal minimum wage for young blacks. As in the case of agriculture price supports, or for that matter any effective minimum price, a minimum wage law tends to create surpluses. But in this situation the surpluses consist of unemployed teenagers and other unskilled workers, especially blacks and other minorities. A wage rate held above the market clearing wage simultaneously discourages hiring--reduces the number of employees demanded--and encourages a greater desire to participate in the labor force by low productivity workers. Unemployment is the necessary consequence. Some economists have called the federal minimum wage law the most anti-minority piece of legislation ever passed by the U.S. Congress. Nevertheless, it goes on.

The efficiency or productivity of individuals differs greatly. Relative wage rates among skill groups in the labor force reflect these differential efficiencies. A legislated minimum wage requiring an employer to pay the least efficient worker more than the relevant differential in productivity condemns that least efficient worker to unemployment. The unskilled worker, frequently a teenager, is literally made unemployable. The worker with the lowest productivity is employable only if the wage differential is at least equivalent to the productivity differential between the least efficient and the more efficient members of the labor force. While the announced purpose of the minimum wage law is to raise the income of the least efficient workers, presumably the poor, the result is in fact precisely the reverse: there are fewer jobs available at the higher than market clearing wage.

But, that's not all. If market determined wage rates are not to be

227

permitted to ration jobs, some sort of rationing of the less numerous jobs as a result of the minimum wage must still take place. Discrimination now takes place, not by price, but through nepotism, income class, religion, ethnic background, or the color of one's skin. In the late 1940's, the unemployment rate among black teenagers was actually lower than the unemployment rate among white teenagers. Today, the unemployment rate among black teenagers might be as high as fifty percent, while that of white teenagers is about fifteen percent. The repeated increases in the minimum wage have literally cut off the bottom of the economic ladder for Blacks and Hispanics. Prior to the Great Depression, a world essentially without minimum wage laws and occupational licensing, the Italians, Jews, Germans, Poles, and the Irish who migrated to this country, though discriminated against, could at least grasp the bottom rung of an economic ladder that inevitably went up. The story of this comparative performance of the earlier migrants to the U.S. and the black migration to the North after World War II has been eloquently told in a book by economist Thomas Sowell entitled *Race and Economics*. Once again the restoration of economic freedom and the establishment of simple justice demands the repeal of government enforced minimum wage laws. They not only distort the efficiency signals of the market place, but indeed are counterproductive with respect to their impact on the economically disadvantaged.

Price controls, maximum or minimum, as a form of triangular government intervention, are inefficient, constrain the mutually beneficial implications of the competitive process, and most importantly, invariably fail to produce the sought-after outcome. The restoration of economic and personal freedom in general requires that all of these examples of triangular intervention, and the many others which space does not permit us to analyze, be rejected and eliminated. To ease the burden of adjustment for those who have been the recipients of subsidies at the consumer and/or taxpayer's expense, a transition period of a few years is proposed during which all legislated price ceilings and price floors would be repealed.

## OCCUPATIONAL LICENSING

Special interest group propaganda notwithstanding, occupational licensing deliberately seeks to reduce the supply of competitors (i.e., to restrict entry and to benefit those already licensed). Triangular intervention, in this case, establishes the amount to be supplied which in turn raises the prices at which trades will take place. Special interests demand that politicians suppress competition by restricting entry into an occupation in exchange for election assistance. For example, the most effective "labor union" in the United States is probably the American Medical Association. Unquestionably a large part of its success stems from licensing requirements for physicians required by laws the medical associations actively supported. In an important article written by economist Rueben Kessel, "Price Discrimination in Medicine," he argues with impeccable logic that the AMA has been a cartel for the provision of physician services in the United States. The success of a cartel with hundreds of thousands of members, however, could only be successful with the assistance of the police power of the state. Early in this century, organized medicine successfully lobbied government for legal restrictions on the entrance into the practice of medicine.

The practice has continued. In 1983, for example, the Missouri state medical association brought suit against certain nurse practitioners who were "practicing medicine" in Missouri without a license. "Unorthodox" medicine continues to be suppressed by the tremendous political power of the medical societies in the United States. It is no accident or mere coincidence that the AMA and its local counterparts are some of the largest campaign contributors to federal elections. In a similar attempt, the Airline Pilots Association threatens to shut down commercial air transportation in the United States unless the Congress restores the cartel which, prior to 1978, permitted their monopoly salary scales.

Although the AMA would have us believe they have the public interest in mind when suppressing competition in their fiefdom, it is invariably the case that restrictions on the practice of medicine in the United States have never come at the behest of an aroused public but in fact from the pressures arising within the medical profession from the fear of "excess" competition. Even alternative organizational structures for the provision of orthodox medical care, for example prepaid medical plans in lieu of "fee for service," have been fought to the death by organized medicine. This sad history is documented in a John C. Goodman's *The Regulation of Medical Care: Is the Price Too High?* and in an article by Elton Rayack, "The Physicians Service Industry." Naturally, other professions are not exempt from this propensity to protect their own turf. Dentists have also been known to restrict competition by bringing the police power of the government against denturists who would dare to manufacture and install false teeth for forty percent less than the licensed dentist.

Occupational licensing has also had an important impact at the lower end of the economic ladder. Lower income groups in society are adversely affected by the licensing which exists in the provision of services requiring fewer skills. Taxicab licensing in large American cities, for example, restricts entry, increases fares, and limits consumer choice. New York City and Philadelphia have had very restrictive licensing practices with regard to taxi drivers. The nation's capital, Washington, D.C., by contrast, has for all practical purposes had unrestricted entry (personal bond, insurance, appropriate drivers license, an automobile, and you are in business). Which of the cities has more frequent service and lower fares? Which city offers more employment opportunities for lower income and minority individuals? You're absolutely right if you said Washington, D.C. Licensing provides a tremendous bias in favor of those who are already practicing a trade. Escalating standards for admission impose additional costs on those who would compete with existing practitioners. The beneficial effects of open markets, which is to say, no artificial barriers to the entry of potential competitors, include the predictable consequences of the competitive market process at work: higher production, lower prices, rapid innovation, and resources being used in their highest valued uses.

There are numerous occupations in which licenses are required and, therefore, there are the predicted implications of higher prices and less competition. Licenses are frequently required for peddlers on city streets, barbers, auto mechanics, hair dressers, lawyers, veterinarians, tree surgeons, and the list goes on and on. Economic freedom, let alone the requirements of a moral order, requires that government mandated occupational licensing be eliminated. The criticism of this point of view is the claim that the poor, uneducated, uninformed consumer would be at the mercy of charlatans and quacks of every sort. Yet, the very same people who insist the consumer is too ignorant to shop in the private sector will simultaneously defend and expound on the competence of that same individual to participate in the political process where the issues are far more complex and comprehendible only through considerable effort. Concerning the relative merits of the MX missile, the Trident submarine, and agriculture subsidies, we are asked to pull a lever or punch a voting card. But in Missouri individual consumers were deemed incapable of deciding which medical services should be obtained from a nurse practitioner and which services froma licensed physician!

## GOVERNMENT FORCE AND EMINENT DOMAIN

Government not only intervenes in the terms and conditions of private exchange between consenting individuals and specifies those suppliers with whom we may trade, but in addition suppresses and prevents voluntary exchange through outright confiscation of property. Through the state's power of eminent domain, government implements what we have defined to be "binary intervention." Employing the police power of government, private property is purchased from frequently unwilling sellers at "fair market value." Similar to the military draft in which the individual makes an exchange with the government at a price determined by that government, eminent domain permits the government to dispossess individuals from their property on quite arbitrary terms from the original owner's point of view. Urban renewal programs represent classic examples of the

230

"taking" which occurs under this power. Seldom do these "planning projects" using government's power of eminent domain work out. Quite often these amputated areas develop galloping cases of gangrene. Pushed around by the hex of a planners "design," thousands of individuals and businesses are condemned, expropriated, and uprooted against their wills, and inevitably they are conquered and destroyed. These *involuntary* exchanges, wracked from the powerless, make a mockery of efficiency and justice.

In most cities, urban renewal programs displace the poor. Moreover, the new users of the land are usually beneficiaries of subsidies, thanks to the taxpayer and involuntary enforcement. Almost without exception "urban renewal" has destroyed more low income housing than it has created, and the new owners are almost invariably from higher income groups. The Bunker Hill area in downtown Los Angeles, for example, is now the home of very expensive condominiums, fancy office towers, and performing arts centers for the generally well-to-do. At one time this area was an important source of housing for lower income groups. This experience of redistributing wealth from poor to rich has been repeated in almost every large American city. Cutting freeway systems through the middle of ethnic neighborhoods and destroying the continuity of communities so that upper income groups might have easier access to their offices is surely a questionable use of the taxpayers money.

## OLD STYLE ECONOMIC REGULATION

Unfortunately, government regulation mandating a maximum price for rental units in an apartment complex or the requirement of a government granted license to cut hair is but the tip of the iceberg. Agencies of the federal government have in fact been created to regulate most all aspects of whole industries. Beginning with the Interstate Commerce Commission (ICC) in 1887, and usually referred to as old-style economic regulation, the U.S. government has sought to regulate certain industries in the "public interest." Usually in the name of combating the adverse consequences of "natural monopoly" or the existence of market "externalities," the "public interest theory" of regulation required that government intervention correct for the failures of the market place.

However, there is an important problem with this interpretation: it simply fails to square with the facts. The old-style regulatory agencies --the ICC, the Civil Aeronautics Board (CAB), the Federal Communications Commission (FCC), the Federal Reserve System, and the Food and Drug Administration (FDA)--control industries which, in large measure, do not exhibit the characteristics of natural monopoly or even signal market failure. There is another interpretation of the existence of these alphabet agencies and the intimate relationship which usually exists with the industries they regulate. Drawing on the "public choice" model of government action, economists George Stigler and Sam Peltzman pioneered another explanation of the widespread existence of "public interest" regulation. Namely, that politicians, acting as entrepreneurs who wish to remain in office, are prepared to offer (sell) protection from the rigors of competition through government regulation in exchange for election support from the beneficiary groups. Existing competitors, fearful of new competition, are prepared to seek (buy) the suppression of competition by offering election support to the political candidates prepared to do their bidding.

In other words, the regulation and regimentation of particular industries has not been to correct for imperfections in the working of the market process but have served as a vehicle by which competition is suppressed; the political means is employed to short-circuit the competitive process and create government enforced monopoly power. The socialist historian, Gabriel Kolko documents the extent to which the Interstate Commerce Commission was created at the behest of the eastern railroad interests in order to restrict entry and enforce price fixing agreements which the railroads themselves had been unable to maintain and enforce without the police power of the state. Similarly, in the 1930's when the widespread introduction of trucks to ship goods destroyed whatever argument there might have been for the existence of natural monopoly conditions in railroading, the ICC did not call for its own abolition. Instead, Congress proceeded to bring trucking under the regulatory umbrella which enforced the existing cartel in transportation. The public interest theory would supposedly have predicted the end of the ICC. The economic theory of regulation, however, which proposes the existence of a market for political regulation, correctly predicted the actual outcome. Increased competition in surface transportation in the United States as a result of the new trucking mode produced *more* not less regulation!

In the past decade or so the record of the vast inefficiencies of U. S. government regulation of industry (the increased costs being paid by American consumers in the form of higher prices, lower quality service, and fewer choices) has come to be appreciated by spokesman from almost all political persuasions. The liberal U. S. Senator Ted Kennedy and "consumer advocate" Ralph Nadar agree with the great majority of market economists that the costs of economic regulation have been high. The regulation of the railroads, trucking, the merchant marine, airlines, telephone communications, broadcasting, even the drug industry has cost the American consumer and taxpayer literally billions of dollars each year in higher prices, suppressed competition, and, importantly, caused a slower rate of technological change and innovation in these regulated industries. The inefficiencies arising from the regulation of industry have been documented in a volume of studies published in 1975 by The

Brookings Institute and edited by economist Almarin Phillips entitled *Promoting Competition in Regulated Markets.* Fortunately the case for deregulation is so obvious that progress has been made in recent years to restore the competitive market process in the affected industries. Another very important book was published in 1982 which offers additional evidence and recommendations concerning the dismantling of inefficient and very costly regulation of the aforementioned industries. In Robert Poole's *Instead of Regulation: Alternatives to Federal Regulatory Agencies,* scenerios are provided by a blue ribbon list of economists on restoring the Great American Experiment in competition and, therefore, progress in these hamstrung industries.

**Transportation**

A giant step in ending regulatory monopoly and restoring competition in an American industry was taken in 1978 with the passage of the Airline Deregulation Act. This law has resulted in a substantial dismantling of the regulations which had made the American airline industry a cartel enforced by the Civil Aeronautics Board (CAB). Price competition has been restored and entry restrictions on behalf of existing competitors have been eliminated. In fact, the CAB will cease to exist in 1985 unless we have a senseless political relapse. Prior to deregulation, the extent of the suppression of competition was illustrated by the fact that the CAB had not permitted one new trunk carrier like United or American Airlines to enter the industry in the first 38 years following its creation in 1938. The airlines, with the passage of the Civil Aeronautics Act, were successful in achieving their objectives: to reduce competition and erect barriers to new competition. The outcome was quite similar to the earlier experiences in railroading and trucking under the ICC. If you couldn't obtain from the CAB a ''certificate of convenience and necessity,'' then you were not going to be in the business of flying passengers on a regularly scheduled basis.

Economist Richard Caves more than two decades ago demonstrated the expensive nature of airline regulation. CAB policies restricted the choices available to the consumer among types of air service, raised significantly the cost of air tranportation, produced wasteful non-price competition, and prevented new competitors from entering the interstate market. Important evidence of the monopoly power and waste contained in CAB regulation was provided by the competition offered by the *intrastate* carriers, especially in California and Texas. Not subject to CAB fare regulation, these intra state carriers were offering frequent and reliable air transportation between Los Angeles and San Francisco and between Dallas and Houston at fares which were twenty to fifty percent lower than comparable interstate, and therefore regulated flights. The CAB was in fact "owned" by the existing trunk carriers and was costing the American people dearly. The important lesson in air transportation is a recognition of the socially undersirable consequences of a government enforced monopoly in what is basically a competitive industry: higher prices, reduced consumer choices, and a generally wasteful and inefficient allocation of scarce resources.

Deregulation has produced a veritable whirlwind of change in the airline industry. There have been numerous new entrants into the industry, and competition is intense. Prices have been generally lower, especially when account is taken of the increase in fuel prices which took place in 1979 and 1980. Important monopoly labor groups, their privileged position protected by the barriers to new competitors before deregulation, have had their wings clipped: the pilots, flight attendants, mechanics, and other ground personnel have had to make wage and salary and work-rule concessions in the new competitive environment. Similar concessions have been made by the Teamsters as a result of the partial deregulation of trucking. These wage and salary rollbacks are a result of the artificially high pay scales which could not be obtained in the regulated environment where new competitors (like Muse, U. S. Air, People's Express, and many new trucking firms) were prohibited. One new carrier in Arizona advertised for 29 pilots and received over four thousand applications. The new non-union carriers are paying their flight crews far lower salaries than the six-figure salaries paid pilots prior to the deregulation of 1978. The Airline Pilots Association admits to the existence of a "tremendous pool of pilots out there." Those who would re-regulate the airline industry are simply ignoring the lessons of competition.

One of the most frequently repeated arguments against deregulation has been the proposition that smaller communities would lose their air service. The evidence on this issue suggests otherwise. Many small communities, through the proliferation of commuter carriers, have better service. In any case, it is not at all obvious why small, rural towns and cities should be subsidized by larger high density markets. As the CAB expiration date nears, it is apparent to most that the U. S. is moving in the direction of having a more efficient and responsive air transportation industry. Fare increases have been significantly lower since 1978 than the increases in the consumer price index. In spite of higher fuel costs and the long recession of 1981-1982, the number of domestic flights at the end of 1982 was four percent higher than in 1978. Seat mile costs of the new carriers like Southwest and People Express are five or six cents, while at TWA seat mile costs are ten to thirteen cents. The old cartel trunk carriers have a long, tough road ahead of them, and only the more efficient will survive. For example, Northwest Orient Airlines has greater revenue ton mile productivity and lower labor costs as a percentage of revenues than most of the other major carriers. Continental and some of the others have higher than average costs. But that is what the competitive market process is all about.

Progress has also been made in the restoration of competition in surface transportation industries in the United States. During the 1970's, it was estimated that a combination of factors, including restrictions on entry of new competitors in specific trucking markets, ICC regulations requiring trucks to "back-haul" empty (35 percent of truck capacity according to the ICC in 1976), and price fixing regulations which allowed carriers to set rates collectively, were costing the American consumer at least $1 billion and maybe as much as $3 billion a year. And this was a result of regulating *just* the common carrier segment of trucking.

The Motor Carrier Act of 1980 produced at least a partial deregulation of trucking. The legislation provided for the deregulation of rate setting, reduced the barriers to entry, and removed other restrictions on operations. The early results are encouraging, if a competitive and economically efficient trucking industry is the goal. Rates have been cut by 5 to 20 percent on different routes to meet the new competition. Applications for grants of operating authority increased by a factor of five following its passage, despite the recession of 1981 and 1982. While trucking deregulation has only been partial in scope, the new operating authorities granted by the ICC generally contain fewer geographic and commodity restrictions than in the past. Another encouraging dimension of deregulation is the fact that organized labor, represented by the Teamsters, have moderated wage demands and relaxed work rules which will assist unionized trucking companies in competing more effectively with the new non-union carriers. But, as one might imagine, the Teamsters have not supported deregulation.

There has been an infusion of smaller companies who are holding their own against the industry giants (trucking is definitely *not* a natural monopoly). The complaint, as with air service, that smaller communities would suffer as a result of deregulation does not appear to have been an important factor. A study by the Interstate Commerce Commission suggests that there has been little, if any, adverse affects in the quality and availability of trucking services to small communities. Prior to deregulation, the American Trucking Association had estimated the monetary value of operating rights on protected routes at 15-20 percent of annual revenues on those routes. For the shipper and consumer's sake, those days are hopefully gone forever. During the final months of 1983, the ICC sought public comment on proposals to lift the antitrust immunity of truck companies to fix their own rates (a protection from the competitive process which has been provided by the ICC for more than 35 years). But, of course, the American Trucking Association continues to argue in favor of "collective rate action." Unfortunately, as 1983 came to a close, the Reagan adminsitration seemed to waver on its committment to deregulation in trucking.

There has also been a degree of deregulation in interstate bus transportation and the moving industry. Previously prevented by the ICC, new bus companies are forming to offer competition to Greyhound and Trailways. Both bus companies are concerned with labor costs in the context of the new competitive environment. Rates on the moving of household belongings have also fallen as competition intensifies in this industry. Unfortunately, the battle is not won.

The railroad industry, while experiencing some piecemeal deregulation, still finds itself locked by regulation into outmoded technology and limited in the extent to which innovative and new technology can be introduced. The deregulation under the Staggers Rail Act of 1980 has been helpful, but much remains to be accomplished. Railroad legislation in 1971 that created Amtrak, the Railroad Revitalization and Regulatory Reform Act of 1976, and a 1973 piece of legislation providing for the public ownership of railroads (Conrail, for example), have increasingly collectivized America's railroads under government ownership. There is little reason to believe government ownership in the United States would be any more efficient than in Japan, Germany, or France where quite massive subsidies are required of the taxpayer.

## Banking

The passage of the Depository Institutions Deregulation and Monetary Control Act of 1980 and the Garn-St. Germain Act of 1982 has caused a wholesale deregulation in the markets for financial services. Fundamental changes in the number and kinds of institutions that provide credit to consumers and business and attract loanable funds into deposits are taking place. Barriers to competition between geographic regions and different product lines have also been significantly reduced and continue to fall. The restrictions on competition which were initiated during the Great Depression in the name of preserving the "soundness" of the financial system, were, in fact, devices to suppress competition between financial institutions and segments of particular markets for financial products. The prohibition on the payment of interest on checking accounts, the imposition of interest rate ceilings (the Federal Reserve System's infamous "Regulation Q"), the suppression of competition among geographic territories through restrictions on charters granted by the Comptroller of the Currency and state finance departments, and the prohibition on interstate banking have all secured a significant degree of monopoly protection to existing competitors. Once again the police power of government, both federal and state, was used to protect existing deposit taking institutions from the threat of new competition.

Encouragingly, the "pillars" of monopoly support for commercial banks and savings and and loan associations are being eliminated. Ceilings on interest rates paid on deposits have been partially removed and will be totally eliminated by 1986 under existing law. Mutual savings banks and savings and loan associations have received authority to broaden the kinds of assets they may hold, including the authority to make consumer loans and business loans. The prohibitions on interstate banking have been reduced through 1970 amendments to the Bank Holding Company Act which permit a holding company to own and operate "bank related businesses" across state lines. This authority includes finance companies, mortgage companies, leasing companies, loan production offices, and other devices by which commercial banks are attempting to provide financial services on an interstate basis.

The opposition to deregulation obviously has come from those banks and other thrift organizations who hope to maintain the restrictions on competition that characterized the protective legislation of the 1930's. But it appears there is no turning back. The argument that the little guy, the small entrepreneur, will be eliminated doesn't seem to be supported by the evidence. In California, home base for four or five of the largest banks in the United States, charter applications for new banks and S & L's skyrocketed in 1983. These entrepreneurs, and the other 250 plus banks in California, seem to be telling us that they can prosper, if efficient and well run, right alongside the Bank of America. This is encouraging for economic freedom, the system of competitive capitalism, and ultimately for human freedom in general. The agenda for the restoration of the market system must include actions which continue to eliminate laws and regulations that suppress competition, provide monopoly protection to special interests, and therefore produce economic inefficiency.

**Communications**

Like the ICC and the CAB, the Federal Communications Commission (FCC) has acted on behalf of those it supposedly regulates in the "public interest." Thereby, it has encouraged inefficiency, a reduced range of consumer choice, higher prices, and discouraged innovation and new forms for serving the consuming public. The federal regulation of communications and broadcasting has produced some of the most startling and undesirable consequences imaginable. In the case of broadcasting, one long-time student of regulation has asserted that "spectrum management is so bizzare that none of us can even imagine what efficient utilization of the frequency spectrum [for radio and television] would look like."

In a study by the Federal Communication Commissions own staff in 1980 the point was made that: "Consumers may be better off with a monopoly price based on efficient technology rather than a regulated price based on obsolete facility costs." From within the FCC itself, we have the proposition that the regulation of communications has not served the public interest. The evidence seems clear that FCC regulation suppressed the expansion of both broadcast and telephone service, slowed innovation in these industries, and delayed the introduction of new services and technologies for many years. For example, cable television was suppressed by the FCC for close to twenty years on behalf of the major television networks. Just as the CAB prevented entry of competitors into the airline business, the FCC obstructed the introduction of new forms of competition in broadcasting. The degree of competition associated with some of the new technologies is illustrated by micro wave broadcasting. The applications for new Multi-Point Distribution Service filed with the FCC through September 1983, numbered more than sixteen thousand and included telephone companies, broadcasters, cable operators, major newspapers, a major league baseball team, and thousands of smaller concerns. Ida Walters, in a survey of the regulatory quagmire, which appears in the volume *Instead of Regulation,* summarized the current state of the debate: "The old arguments supporting regulation of communications are admittedly bankrupt and are seldom even heard anymore, except when they are useful in attempting to resist changes that affect the fortunes or power of blatant special interest."

Unfortunately, as documented in an article by Tom Hazlett in *Reason* magazine, cable television continues to be suppressed by the politicians and the special interests who wish to protect their turf. The newest objection is to claim that cable television is itself a natural monopoly and therefore individual cable operators deserve the monopoly protection afforded by the police power of the state. Or, as Tom Hazlett reports: "Confusing as the game becomes, the joust of cable television franchising amounts to this: who promises the biggest buffet..." to the relevant local politician.

As FCC procedures change and new broadcast tehnologies appear and are permitted, a revolution is simultaneously taking place in telephone communications. The courts have broken AT&T's monopoly over the Bell System and its research and manufacturing subsidiaries. Competition is now pervasive in long-distance service, prices have fallen, and the consumer has choices formerly unavailable. The great public debate is whether local service should pay its own way, or whether, on political grounds, the long-distance rates should continue to subsidize local telephone service. Cross-subsidization has always been an important objective of government regulation and ownership. The U.S. Postal Service subsidized third class rates with higher first class rates, and the CAB used to subsidize short-haul flights at the expense of long-distance flights. In the name of both efficiency and justice, open competition should be the order of the day. Consumers ought to pay the full fare for services provided. Sadly, the local telephone issue is quite likely to be settled politically. Politicians and public utility regulators recognize all too clearly where the votes are; indeed, who butters their bread. Consequently, the inefficiencies and injustices of the existing system are likely to continue.

## THE NEW SOCIAL REGULATION

Progress is clearly being made in the restoration of economic freedom and competition in those industries which have traditionally been subject to the old-style economic regulation; more than imagined possible just a few short years ago.

Nevertheless, as one cancer is being partially removed, a new sickness of an over-governed society is being experienced. Especially in the decade of the 1970's, there occurred an explosive growth in what most people call "social regulation." In contrast to the traditional economic regulation where a regulatory agency controlled most aspects of a single industy, the new social regulation involves the creation of a regulatory body which seeks to protect the public from a single problem. Its responsibility in this single area covers all sectors of the economy. In contrast to the CAB's broad responsibilities in air travel, the Environmental Protection Agency (EPA) is charged with protecting the public from environmental abuses, the Consumer Product Safety Commission (CPSC) with the safety of products, the Occupational Safety and Health Administration (OSHA) with work place safety, and the Equal Employment Opportunity Commission (EEOC) with discrimination in employment.

There are important and undesirable economic implications of the new federal bureaucracies. Their responsibilities are broader than the old agencies in that they are given jurisdiction over all sectors of the economy. The ICC continues to be, with allowance made for the partial deregulation, responsible for the trucking industry's objective: to provide tranportation services to the public. The ICC therefore has a broader view of the mission and health of the industry it regulates. On the other hand, the EPA or the CPSC is concerned with only one aspect of a business's responsibilities. While this certainly means it is unlikely that any particular industry, say steel, will "capture" the EPA on its behalf, it also suggests that the EPA will not have much interest in the overall performance, efficiency, and provision of the industry's products to the consumer. As Murray Weidenbaum has suggested in his comprehensive study of the new social regulators, *Business, Government, and the Public,* "...little attention is given by the regulators to the *basic* mission of industry, to provide goods and services to the public."

The meteoric rise in the new social regulation since the amendments to the Food and Drug Administration in 1962, has been both startling and costly. There were more than 40 major pieces of federal regulatory legislation between 1962 and 1978 including the Equal Pay Act, Water Quality Act, Child Protection Act, Traffic Safety Act, Consumer Credit Protection Act (Truth-in-Lending), National Environmental Policy Act, Occupational Safety and Health Act, Noise Pollution and Control Act, Highway Speed Limit Reduction, Department of Energy Organization Act, and Saccharin Study and Labeling Act. There can be no doubt that this massive legislative exercise reflects real issues, and the goals of our political representatives may have been well-intentioned. The relevant question, however, is whether we have been getting our money's worth in terms of tax burdens, compliance costs, higher consumer prices, and loss of personal freedom which necessarily accompanies the forceful government intervention mandated by these laws.

The direct cost to the taxpayer of more than 130 federal regulatory agencies has almost tripled since 1974 to about $8 billion. These agencies employed more than eighty thousand inspectors and other regulators in 1979; total employment exceeded 140,000. Forty-one of these agencies at least doubled their budgets in the four year period ending in 1979. The growth in the regulatory bureaucracy has taken place mostly among these newer agencies. While employment at the CAB, ICC, and FCC remains about the same as in years past, employment at the EPA and EEOC has shown a significant increase. In 1970 the *Federal Register,* which identifies compliance requirements for federal regulations, had 20,000 pages, but by 1979 it was up to 77,000 pages. The direct tax-burden costs of the regulatory agencies, while important, are relatively small when compared to the compliance burdens placed on the private sector. It is generally agreed that these costs to the American economy, and therefore the American consumer, easily exceed $100 billion per year. The chief executive officer of a fairly large bank has disclosed that eighteen linear feet of shelf space is required to house the regulations and explanations of these regulations to which the bank must comply.

**Food and Drug Administration**

Probably the most controversial policy issue in the area of government regulation is the role and impact of the Food and Drug Administration (FDA). Most of the so-called social regulation of the past two decades improved the health and/or safety of some individuals without harming the health and/or safety of anybody else. The cost is usually very high and, based on efficiency criteria, demonstrably not worth it. But the EPA and OSHA do help some people. On the other hand, the FDA, the oldest of the new agencies, in the process of regulating the admission of new drugs to the market for the benefit of one group simultaneously endangers the health or shortens the life of other individuals. Amendments to the FDA in 1962 significantly increased the time between the discovery of a new drug and the authorization needed to place it on the market. David Weimer has summarized the implications of this delay in *Instead of Regulation:* the system of "premarketing clearances," as it has operated for the past two decades has unquestionably slowed the rate of innovation and delayed the appearance on the market of beneficial drugs. Needless to say, this has also reduced the individual's freedom of choice with respect to the drug or medicine of choice.

Sam Peltzman, David Seidman, and others have documented the extent to which drugs available in Europe and Latin America but not available in the United States have, as a consequence, produced higher death rates, shortened life spans, and/or permitted greater pain and suffering than would otherwise have been the case in this country. While the thalidomide tragedy remains on all of our minds, it remains true that the FDA has held drugs off the market which consequently have caused thousands of deaths in the United States that were otherwise unnecessary. As David Weimer has pointed out: "those who suffer because some drug that would have been beneficial to them has not been approved by the FDA often do not even know they have been harmed."

It is interesting that during the 1970's three successive FDA Commissioners simultaneously denied the existence of this delay in the introduction of new drugs while claiming, however, they were in the process of abolishing it. The structure of personal incentives facing the FDA physician or chemist who must make decisions on the release of a new drug is biased against the premature marketing. If a bad drug is permitted to be marketed, the FDA employee's career is ruined. However, if a good drug is delayed, there is little impact on the examiner's personal fortunes except to the extent it might lengthen his tenure and keep him busy. The extent of this bias in the procedures and politics at the FDA is illustrated by former FDA Commissioner Alexander Schmidt's recollection: "In all our history, we are unable to find one instance where a Congressional hearing investigated the failure of FDA to approve a new drug." Congressional pressure has always been on the side of disapproving new drugs.

Government intervention in this area has been extremely costly, especially for those who failed to receive treatment from a drug with beneficial properties. Economist Sam Peltzman, the leading scholar in the study of these drug issues, has summarized the implications of past governmental intervention by the FDA in his *Regulation of Pharmaceutical Innovation: The 1962 Amendments:*

> In a wider perspective, any attempt to minimize risk in the area [of drug development] has costs which [according to the history of drug development] far exceed the benefits: those who will suffer death and disease while a potential drug therapy is evaluated will suffer no less than the

victims of a drug disaster, but their number is likely to be much larger than the number of victims of the disaster...The unequal emphasis placed on the benefits and cost of risk taking may be explained, if not excused, by the contrast between the anonymity of the beneficiaries and the visibility of the victims.

A fairly drastic overhaul and reduction in the scope of FDA regulation is necessary. The current regulatory environment and the mandated procedures for the introduction of a new drug should largely be replaced with a commitment to strengthening the laws of liability. Strict liability laws would require that drug makers be responsible for their actions. If drug manufacturers promote their products in a misleading manner, then the solution is to strengthen the laws against fraud. What is required is a restoration of the idea that individuals are responsible for their own actions; that in a free society violent invasion of a person's rights (for example the dissemination of a dangerous drug) is not to be permitted; that under the common law, avenues for the restitution of the infringement of rights are available and should be nurtured by the courts.

**Federal Trade Commission**

The perception of benefits to be gained from government regulation of food and drugs contributed importantly to the expansion in the responsibilities of the Federal Trade Commission (FTC) in the area of consumer protection. If drugs, why not tricycles? Both the American Bar Association and Nadar's Raiders concluded in the late 1960's that the FTC was simply a mess: inefficient and seemingly without direction or purpose. Unfortunately, the answer in the ABA study was to "...re-create the FTC in its intended image" by recognizing "...the great potential of the FTC in the field of antitrust and consumer protection."

The antitrust economists and lawyers became very active. In April 1972, the FTC filed an antitrust complaint to break up the cold cereal industry. It was asserted that four producers had a "shared monopoly." A decade later this suit was dropped in large part because of the flimsy and unsupported case. Later, a suit against the large petroleum firms was launched which threatened to destroy the economies of scale associated with the vertically integrated nature of the industry. The generally counterproductive results of FTC antitrust enforcement have already been discussed.

The real growth area at the FTC, however, was in "consumer protection." The Bureau of Consumer Protection was established in the FTC as a result of the proposals in the fall of 1969 by the Nixon administration to reorganize the agency. The FTC's responsibilities in the area of consumer protection were greatly enlarged. During the 1970's, numerous new laws were passed to regulate American business, and in the 1980's the FTC is responsible for the enforcement of more than 30 statutes, including the Bureau of Consumer Protection, Fair Packaging and Labeling Act, Truth in Lending Act, Fair Credit Reporting Act, and Federal Cigarette Labeling and Advertising Act. The consumer protection efforts of the FTC include the regulation of advertising; the requirements that certain product information be disclosed, products modified, contracts rewritten; the regulation of consumer credit practices; the scrutinization of licensed occupations; and numerous additional responsibilities which have quite radically altered important aspects of consumer-business relationships. Unfortunately, as one student of consumer protection has pointed out, the FTC compares an imperfect market with a romantic and idealized view of government's ability to correct, let alone understand, an asserted threat to consumer safety.

After more than a decade of expanded FTC authority in the area of consumer protection, the evidence seems overwhelming that the agency's performance continues to be as poor as that characterized by the American Bar Association in the late 1960's. But today its budget and the compliance costs imposed on business and therefore the consumer are much larger. The one group in society who *have* benefited from the FTC's expanded authority in antitrust and consumer protection are the employees of the agency, especially lawyers and economists. It has proven to be an important stepping stone to other more rewarding positions in the private sector for many professionals. By the late 1970's, the FTC was operating in such disarray that there was an open rebellion in Congress against the free-wheeling, power-grabbing activities of the FTC.

The existing mandate of the FTC and the Bureau of Consumer Protection which prohibits ''unfair or deceptive acts or practices'' could just as well be carried out in the market place. This would require a proper definition and protection of property rights, the prohibition of the violent invasion of one's person, and in turn an appropriate utilization of the laws which prohibit fraud. The protection of consumer interests can be achieved by an appropriate use of the common law stand on fraud and misrepresentation, with complementary statutory standards for deception and unfairness. Given the current interpretation by the courts of strict liability under the law, which has if anything gone too far in the granting of compensation to so-called consumer victims, the competitive market process can protect the consumer from dangerous and harmful products. Finally, replacing the FTC and its absolute standards with the market process, where the consumer is protectd by existing legal safeguards, would preserve freedom of individual choice, a neccessary ingredient in the restoration of personal and economic freedom.

## Consumer Products Safety Commission

The Federal Trade Commission's expanded mandate in this area was not enough. In 1972 the U. S. Congress passed the Consumer Product Safety Act which created the Consumer Product Safety Commission (CPSC). The CPSC, after notice is provided in the *Federal Register,* may establish requirements and standards concerning "performance, composition, contents, design, construction, finish, or packaging of a consumer product." If a product fails to conform to the announced standards and is deemed to present "an unreasonable risk of injury," it may be banned from the market by the CPSC. In its authority to collect, analyze, and disseminate data on injury, death, and illness related to consumer products, the CPSC discovered what most ten year olds could have told them: bicycles, footballs, baseballs, basketballs, and playground equipment are associated with the highest injury rates. One would suspect that parents and others are aware of the greater risks associated with these kinds of activites. Generally, they are also more fun! Irrespective of the value of this kind of information, the most important activity of the Commission is the regulation of consumer products and not the provision of information to the consumer.

Roger E. Meiners, in an article in the collection of studies entitled *Instead of Regulation,* summarizes a number of important examples of consumer protection in which the costs of the commission's actions were far greater than any benefits that would accrue from greater safety. The CPSC found that lawnmowers were the cause of a number of different kinds of injuries. Estimates of the annual accident costs of these kinds of injuries, including estimates for pain and suffering, had a median figure of $234 million. However, the annual compliance costs of the lawnmower standards in the form of higher prices to the consumer and reduced revenues to the industy was $383 million, and this estimate assumed there would be no loss of sales due to the higher prices. Not only were the costs of the regulation much greater than the benefits to be realized (estimates suggested injuries would fall by 50 to 75 percent and the benefits in reduced injuries would range from $117 to $175 million), but the costs imposed on the industry of $383 million represented almost a third of the industry's annual sales of $1.2 billion. Furthermore, the producers who would most likely be driven out of business were the smaller companies, therefore having an unfortunate side-effect on the competitive nature of the industry.

Another classic example of waste, which is to say too much safety, involves the proposed safety rules for matchbooks. The Council on Wage and Price Stability (COWPS) estimated the proposed safety regulations would roughly double the production costs of matchbooks and consequently cost the American consumer $70 million a year, again assuming no loss in sales from the higher prices.

It was also estimated that one-half of the existing producers would fail and, like the lawnmower producers, the smaller manufacturers would be eliminated. Another example of government's inability to recognize the indirect effects of their actions: the safety standards for matchbooks would increase the use of butane lighters which also pose safety hazzards. This independent study by COWPS estimated that the standards would cost $240,000 per injury if all injuries involving hospitalization were eliminated. The benefit/cost calculation didn't appear to be very favorable. Yet, the Consumer Protection and Safety Commission introduced part of the recommendations. However, in 1978, the U. S. Court of Appeals struck down all but the reverse-side striking surface regulation on the grounds that the CPSC had not demonstrated a connection between injuries and the proposed safety standards, and the expected benefits were quite small in comparison to the costs imposed on the industy and consumers.

An important but often neglected aspect of consumer safety regulations is their impact on product variety in the market. Greater product safety almost of necessity means the products at the lower end of the price schedule are squeezed from the market due to higher costs. Product safety, therefore, necessarily discriminates against lower income families and individuals who want to maintain their freedom of choice to sacrifice some safety in order to have more of other goods and services. The very costly standards imposed on the manufacture of bicycles to be sold in the United States has undoubtedly been borne much more heavily by the poor than by the rich. Product safety, like everything else, has a price; there are no free lunches. Automobile producers can produce a much safer automobile at $50,000 a copy than $10,000, and automobile accidents and injuries can be reduced by lowering the speed limit from 55 MPH to 10 MPH. But these examples should demonstrate to everyone that there is an optimum amount of safety and it is *not* infinitely large. Another little discussed cost of greater consumer product safety standards is the artificial restraints placed on individuals as they attempt to choose, as free individuals, favorable combinations of consumption and risk. Freedom itself is a risky business.

Studies have shown that a realistic use of the rule of strict liability would produce an economically efficient amount of safety. The efficiency criteria simply asks that product safety be increased as long as the benefits in the form of fewer injuries, less pain, lost time, etc., are greater than the costs of producing the additional safety. A great deal of safety has been built into the market system over many centuries through the common law system of torts and contracts. The implications of the choice between regulation and strict liability for human liberty are concisely summarized by Roger Meiners: ''In products-liability law, the government acts as a referee, enforcing the rule of the game. With direct regulation, however, the government tells all participants how they must play the game. The latter method stifles innovative competition and excellence; the former method does not."

Unfortunately, the courts have taken the concept of strict product liability far beyond that which is necessary for reasonable product safety. A tort, under the law, arises out of wrongful conduct. The courts, however, are placing the burden of responsibility on manufacturers even in those cases where the consumer could rightly be held responsible for "foreseeable misuse" of the product. Compensation is being granted for injuries without any demonstration of causation between the product's defect and the injury. The sad implication of this revolutionary interpretation of strict liability is captured by Meiners in his study of these issues: "...the courts may be on the verge of destroying the common-law system of products liability in favor of regulatory solutions."

One final thought on consumer protection regulation. It is frequently argued that the comprehensive regulation included under the mandate of the Federal Trade Commission and the Consumer Products Safety Commission is required to protect the uneducated, unsophisticated, and helpless consumer. The fact of the matter is that the competitive market system has an incredibly important built-in protection for the uninformed consumer. Competitors, hoping to increase market share and make greater profits, must appeal to the undecided or marginal buyer. They must capture the attention of the consumer who is still wavering. The businesses that gain the attention of these buyers will prosper. Those of us already committed to a particular product or producer benefit from the extra attention this unknown consumer devotes to the acquisition of product safety information. The percentage of American consumers who spend a good deal of time and effort in acquiring safety information is normally quite small. Nevertheless, the marginal buyers have a disproportionate impact on the results we see in the market place. The circulation of *Consumer Reports* is remarkably small, but the impact on safety, product quality, and competition is exceedingly great. Frankly, those who tell us we need these massive public bureaucracies to protect the American consumer already have, as the great economist Joseph Schumpeter once said, the guilty verdict for the market economy in their back pocket, despite the profound evidence of the system's benefits.

The final irony to the more than $100 billion per year price tag on federal regulation--and space simply does not permit us to analyze the costly burden of OSHA, the EEOC, and all the rest--is the clarion call in recent years for a super Consumer Protection Agency in Washington, D.C., which would be asked to protect the American consumer from all the other protective agencies! A national survey in 1979 reported that 75 percent of the respondents thought we should have a consumer protection agency to promote the interests of consumers. But, presumably they were not told that one of the important arguments in favor of the agency by its leading proponents was to correct the abuses and problems already present because of the other federal agencies currently "helping" the consumer. Regardless of the results of a survey, madness is madness. Why should we expect that an agency designed to protect us from other agencies with similar mandates will act any different or produce different results than those already in existence? The economic theory of public bureaucracy tells us we should expect the very kinds of behavior on the part of commissioners, directors, and bureau chiefs as we currently observe in the existing alphabet agencies. It is sheer folly to expect a new super-consumer protection agency to protect the American people from older agencies when it is subject to the same influences, incentives, and problems inherent to government bureaucracy.

## SOCIAL REGULATION AND THE ISSUE OF MONOPOLY

It is rather easy to understand why Greyhound would petition the ICC to prohibit the entry of new competitors in the business of transporting passengers by bus. Likewise for the behavior of United and Eastern Airlines before deregulation in 1978. However, a more interesting phenomenon is the stony silence of certain segments of American industry, or indeed outright support, for some of the new so-called social regulation. Or, put another way, why have important sectors of industry done so little to relieve the excess burdens which have been the result of the generally ill-conceived or overly costly regulations put into law during the 1970's? There is indeed an answer. Certain parts of American industry *benefit* directly from the new social regulation. The obvious example is the producers who supply the control equipment for environmental protection and workplace safety. Older producers in the northcentral states benefit from regulatory burdens which make it more costly to introduce new plants in the sun-belt states.

Frequently big business gains at the expense of small businesses in terms of the relative burden of regulatory compliance costs. The monstrous increase in the cost of developing new drugs as a result of the FDA's procedures has undoubtedly made it more difficult for smaller drug firms to compete relative to the big four or five. Therefore, we have an important side effect of the alphabet agencies, like the EPA, CPSC, OSHA, FDA, etc.: they are not equally or universally burdensome to the business community. "Perhaps most troubling of all," according to Robert W. Crandall in his Brookings Institite study, "is the failure of the [Reagan] administration's business constituency to press for substantial reform of the health, safety, and environmental policies that have grown almost without control in the past decade." Crandall raises the very important issue of why would we expect the efforts at acquiring monopoly power with economic regulation by the airline or trucking industries to be any different than the use of the police power of the state by the beneficiaries of social regulation. Crandall has provided a concise summary of the point:

> Is it possible, for instance, that the federal regulation of safety in small nonunion plants serves as a barrier to competition with larger unionized plants? That the much-maligned 'drug lag' created by the Food and Drug Administration's safety and efficacy regulation is of benefit to pharmaceutical concerns that have large numbers of drugs already on the market? That tight environmental standards imposed on new plants in Texas and Louisiana serve as a barrier to entry in such industries as chemicals, paper, and steel?

To politicize economic activity means to make all questions subject to a political solution. Voluntary exchange of private property in an environment of strict liability is replaced with binary and triangular government intervention which sets standards, restricts entry, suppresses competition, and in general brings the coercive power of the state to bear on what are otherwise private actions.

# CHAPTER 19

## PRIVATIZING THE FEDERAL GOVERNMENT

> It is one of the finest problems of legislation--what the state ought to take
> upon itself to direct by the public wisdom, and what it ought to leave,
> with as little interference as possible, to individual discretion.
>
> --Edmund Burke

> In the absence of an unquestionable yardstick of success and failure it is
> almost impossible for the vast majority of men to find that incentive to ut-
> most exertion that the money calculus of profit-seeking business easily
> provides.
>
> --Ludwig von Mises

The restoration of economic freedom in the United States, and therefore the resultant economic efficiency and justice generated by the competitive market process, requires a radical reduction of government "owned" and operated economic activity. Though governments are noted for their proficiency at raising money through the power to tax, they cannot succeed as well as the private sector in providing goods and services to the consumer. The private sector is invariably more efficient, more responsive to changing consumer demands, and demonstrates a greater flexibility in discovering and activating innovative ways of providing better service. In addition, justice and equity are better served because beneficiaries pay for what they get. Compare this to government provision where some individuals pay for the benefits received by others through imaginative schemes of cross-subsidization. Utilizing the efficiency and equity arguments developed earlier, we believe a powerful case can be made for privatizing many, if not most, of the services currently provided directly by government.

### THE GENERAL CASE FOR PRIVATIZATION

Governments, at all levels, are notoriously bad at business. Political solutions to provide goods and services are inherently limited and critically flawed. Simply put, with the "political means," there is no readily identifiable "bottom line." Enterprise becomes politicized and the most successful managers resemble politicians, not managers. As the great Austrian economist Ludwig von Mises pointed out over a long and illustrious career, "...in the absence of an unquestionable yardstick of success and failure," government agencies are incapable of being operated on an efficient basis. Without the test of profit and loss, the government enterprise will fail to husband scarce resources and thereby prevent resources from moving to more productive uses. When supported by tax revenues obtained from the general taxpayers, special interests necessarily receive a free ride. Invariably government provision of a service, from the delivery of the mail to the assignment of a landing slot at a busy airport, subsidizes one group at the expense of another.

In contrast, a private business must obtain its revenues voluntarally from its customers. The private entrepreneur is forced to continually monitor revenues and costs. Whenever private firms serve their customers in an unacceptable manner, business is lost. A business either controls costs, at least as well as its competitors, or it is forced out of business. It is no accident that the glaring examples of inefficiency and cross-subsidization in government operated enterprises represent situations in which competition is prohibited by an exclusive franchise or rivalry is suppressed by a special law. The postal service, urban transportation systems, government schools, and municipal garbage collection are just a few examples.

Even when government operated enterprises are profit-oriented, the nature of the political process suggests that bureaucratic rules and regulations will compromise attempts to achieve greater efficiency. Fire supression services by government, for example, have unquestionably slowed the introduction of innovative technologies in fire fighting. The U. S. Postal Service is justifiably famous for its inefficient mail delivery. Can there be any doubt that the "public school" system in the United States suppresses innovation in teaching and learning modes? The fact is that rarely do the direct beneficiaries of services provided by government pay full fare. Landing fees for small private aircraft at FAA controlled airports, for example, pay about twenty percent of the full cost. Third class mail is highly subsidized. The poor help the rich by paying for the "free" access to books in our public libraries. Those whose recreation preferences are bowling or minature golf subsidize through property tax payment the "free" tennis courts provided by the city parks department. Those advocating more government solutions might be queried as to the fairness of the distorted pattern of government production already in place.

Before analyzing the more obvious candidates for privatization, there is a related issue of great importance to the survival of representative political institutions and human liberty. The case against government business is more than just its demonstrated inefficiencies and forceful transfer of income from taxpayers to favored beneficiaries. Another concern is the growth in the number of individuals employed either directly or indirectly by government. After all, employees of the state have a vested interest in larger government and higher taxes. Being "tax consumers," they are more concerned with the outcome of elections and therefore can be expected to be more active participants in the election process than the average citizen. According to economist Ludwig von Mises: "Representative democracy cannot subsist if a greater part of the voters are on the government payroll. If the members of [Congress] no longer consider themselves mandatories of the taxpayers but deputies of those receiving salaries, wages, subsidies, doles, and other benefits from the treasury, democracy is done for."

Early in 1983 all levels of government in the United States employed almost 16 million people, representing roughly one out of every seven workers in the labor force. The voting strength of those with a vested interest in larger government is obvious. The political influence of "public employees" in a system of representative institutions, when most elections are won by a plurality or at most a simple majority of the votes cast, fuels government growth despite the popularity expressed in public opinion polls on the threat of big government to human freedom. Even if government businesses were as efficient as private firms, and even if the beneficiaries of government services did pay full cost, there still remains a serious threat to representative political institutions from the magnitude of government employment. The Hatch Act which prohibits political activity by federal employees is an imperfect reflection of this concern. In general, state and local governments have few restrictions on the political activity of government employees. Witness the militant actions of unionized government school teachers, police and firefighter unions, the defunct air traffic controllers' union, and the postal unions in recent years if you doubt the implications for democracy and freedom of larger government!

The efficiency case for the restoration of a private sector provision of current government activity has recently been the subject of a great deal of theoretical and empirical investigation. Privatization through government withdrawal in favor of the competitive market process has numerous possibilities. Contracting of services to the private sector by government invariably lowers costs, increases consumer choice, and produces innovational ways of delivering services. Why? Because the competitive market process disciplines inefficient producers. Government provision of services, on the other hand, is usually protected from competitive pressures. Those who manage a private company invariably have a personal stake in the financial implications of their decisions. Public bureaucrats, however, almost never share in the rewards associated with greater efficiency or the losses arising from stagnation and high costs. And, as already noted, the private firm is relatively free of the political constraints which normally accompany governmental provision of goods and services. Fairness in the market process suggests that those who acquire benefits must pay for those benefits. "Fairness" in the government sector however, inevitably spawns special interest groups running through the corridors of the nation's capital, state houses, and city halls lobbying for benefits paid for by taxpayers' dollars.

Given the almost infinite variety of consumer wants, "voting" in the market place with our own money is surely more sensitive to what people want than the political process which requires an all-or-nothing voting mechanism. Further, when government "sells" services below cost, excess demand and wasteful consumption inevitably result. Citizens' "needs" for access to tennis courts, fire prevention, urban transportation, better schools, additional landing slots for aircraft, medical care, ad infinitum, are obviously going to be greater when supplied "free" or at taxpayer subsidized prices. College presidents, for example, are forever making the case for more buildings and professors because of the "great demand for education." One wonders what would happen to the demand for food and automobiles if they too were provided "free" and subsidized by taxpayers. Just as poverty figures continue to climb because it is subsidized, so too is the demand for any scarce resource elevated when costs are not fully borne by the user.

Another undesirable consequence of artificially low prices is congestion and crowding. The government freeway is "free" to drivers at rush hour, and, as expected, there are horrendous traffic jams. The National Park Service charges just a couple of dollars a night at Yellowstone and Yosemite National Parks, yet people are surprised at the congestion and inevitable destruction of the scenic beauty. The "free" provision of fire *suppression* by local government encourages consumption and therefore discourages private expenditures on fire *prevention* which, studies suggest, would lower the societal loss from fire.

The equity or fairness case for privatization depends on whether beneficiaries of government services can be readily identified. Is it fair that urban dwellers subsidize the delivery of first class mail to rural residents? Where is the justice in the subsidy provided by the airline passenger in the Boeing 727 to the pilot of the Cesna 182 as they both vie for a landing slot at a major metropolitan airport? Should the average property taxpayer subsidize the bus fare of the upper middle income person who, except during rush hour, rides a mostly empty municipal bus but pays directly only thirty to fifty percent of the total cost of the trip?

An important irony in these government induced schemes at cross-subsidization is the fact that the redistribution of income and wealth frequently flows from the poor to the rich! Who will argue for the justice of a low income family paying local taxes to finance the provision of "free" tennis courts to the upper middle class? The provision of goods and services on a user-pays basis in accordance with a benefits received principle of justice represents an important advantage over "free" government provision. Poverty and a concern with the poor is a wholly different issue. The argument that many goods and services must be provided "free" by government in the name of the poor and social justice is absolutely unsupportable. The proposition that some people cannot afford a particular service is manifestly *not* an argument for subsidizing *everybody*. As economists Burton Weisbrod and W. Lee Hansen demonstrated years ago, the provision of tuition-free education in government colleges and universities is simply a giant welfare program favoring the middle class and rich largely at the expense of the poor. We believe this to be a far cry from justice!

Before analyzing specific services currently provided by the federal government, and the efficiency and equity problems inherent therein, we must reiterate the fundamental issue: human liberty. Increasingly, people want to be left alone, to get government off their backs. Interestingly, these expressions of concern for personal space and freedom have been heard from most all ideological persuasions. The tax revolt of the late 1970's reflected the people's concern with the striking growth in the size of government, where larger tax burdens are rarely matched with proportional benefits. The restora tion of human freedom requires that we take advantage of those opportunties in which the private sector will not only be more efficient than government and more consistent with sound principles of fairness and justice, but will also sustain the individual liberty envisioned by the founding fathers. Privatization is a legitimate alternative to existing arrangements in a number of industries. Private alternatives to existing inefficiencies under government ownership are feasible in the areas of tranportation, including railroads, airports, and air traffic control; the production of weather information; energy markets, including federal power projects, nuclear power, and fossil fuels; mail delivery; the social security programs; and federal involvement in the housing industry. The list is not exhaustive of the federal government's involvement in the economy, but it does provide a useful catalog of the potential for privatization.

## TRANSPORTATION AND THE FEDERAL GOVERNMENT

Comparable to government ownership and operation of transportation industries all over the world, the U. S. government's involvement in transportation has been very expensive to the taxpayer and almost always generates an inequitable distribution of costs.

### Railroads

To begin, the federal government should get out of the railroad business. Since its inception in the early 1970's as the government's answer to the Penn Central failure, the Consolidated Rail Corporation, familarly known as Conrail has already cost the American taxpayer more than $7 billion. With $3 billion in government loans outstanding to Conrail, the company's prospects are not very bright. After cutting the work force of the six bankrupt railroads preceding Conrail (including Penn Central) by sixty percent and cutting track mileage by fifteen percent, the federal operation still remains inefficient and politicized. Fortunately, plans are being considered to sell Conrail to the private sector. Among other possibilities, there are three popular options. Either have the operation be acquired by an existing railroad, for example Santa Fe Industries; allow the employees to buy the corporation; or conduct a public offering of stock in Conrail. Hopefully, by the mid-1980's Conrail will be returned to the private sector where the bottom line demands efficiency for survival.

Unfortunately, while the federal government apparently sees the wisdom of getting out of the freight business, Amtrak continues to cost the taxpayer billions of dollars. Always in the name of assisting the poor and on behalf of the public interest, Amtrak provides large subsidies to segments of the middle-class and the rich who ride these expensive trains at prices which seldom cover even half the cost of providing the service. As one commentator pointed out a few years ago, it would be cheaper to buy an economy ticket on a commercial airline for the poor and disadvantaged who ride these trains than to continue the Amtrak boondoggle. Both economic efficiency and justice would indicate that tax-supported passenger rail service should be phased out and returned to the private sector where its economic feasibility will be determined by market forces.

## Airports

The same problems associated with rail transportation in the United States also occur with government's involvement in civilian aviation. As an example, the Federal Aviation Administration (FAA) in the U. S. Department of Transportation owns and operates both Washington National Airport in the District of Columbia and Dulles International Airport in nearby Virginia. With the Baltimore-Washington International Airport in nearby Maryland, inefficiencies and excess capacity abound. Due to the proximity of National Airport to the Washington, D.C. hub and the much lower cost of ground transportation to the center of the nation's capital (the taxicab fare from Dulles is more than $35), travelers naturally prefer National. Dulles was built at a cost of about $108 million in the early 1960's, so it was argued, to provide greater airline capacity in the area around Washington. In addition, a 17-mile, four-lane divided highway was built exclusively for transporting people to and from the District of Columbia. As it turned out, the forecasts for airport useage were significantly overestimated. The Baltimore-Washington International

Airport alone has the capacity to handle twice as many passengers as currently use it plus current traffic at Dulles International. Simply put: Dulles is a white elephant.

Like most government businesses, cross-subsidization occurs for political reasons. Beginning in 1982, the Department of Transportation treated National and Dulles as a "single costing unit." User fees at the two airports are the same. Hence, passengers using National Airport subsidize those travelers using Dulles International. Paul Feldman estimates the subsidy at Dulles to be about $4 per passenger. The problem of rationing the limited landing slots at crowded National Airport exists due to its convenience to downtown. Though various bureaucratic and political rationing devices have been used, price has not been one of them. Consumer valuations are thereby ignored. Furthermore, in an operation relying on the political means and caring little about economic efficiency, airplanes operated by users other than scheduled airlines, in the name of fairness, demand their share of landing slots. In 1983, 23 of the 60-per-hour landing and takeoff slots at National Airport were reserved for these non-airline operators. As a result, the bizzare situation needlessly occurs in which 130 passengers on a Boeing 727 fly into Dulles so that a private Cessna might land at National.

The U. S. government's operation of National and Dulles exhibit many other examples of economic inefficiency. Suffice it to say, there is not a private operator in the world who would allocate landing slots in such an arbitrary and costly fashion. The FAA's use of fees at both airports based on average costs guarantees both an inefficient and inequitable operation. A private firm, operating for profit, would divorce the allocation of landing slots from politics and encourage user based fees. A study in 1981 by the Civil Aeronautics Board estimated that travelers would be prepared to pay as much as $16.50 extra per passenger for the convenience of using National Airport. Under the current politicized system of allocation, small, private aircraft are charged a landing fee of just $4. It can be assumed that one of the scheduled airlines would be willing to pay more for that slot! In addition to an efficient allocation of landing and takeoff spaces, a private, for-profit operator would also be financially motivated to design systems of capital improvements, parking, and better navigation and instrument landing systems. Presently the Department of Transportation must compete with hundreds of other federal spending bills for easier access and improved safety systems.

In contrast to the congestion at National, the current political system finds Dulles International "underutilized." Travelers simply refuse to fly into such a time-consuming and expensive alternative. It is very likely that with privatization Dulles would close down, and much of the remaining air traffic would go to the Baltimore-Washington Airport. Another cost advantage of the closure of Dulles would be the utilization of the nearly empty Dulles Airport Road which could be opened up to local traffic to ease traffic congestion in the Virginia suburbs. Drew Lewis, former Secretary of Transportation, when asked about his largest problem in that position, responded that the Washington airport problem was his most time consuming responsibility.

The obvious answer on both efficiency and equity grounds is the privatization of both National and Dulles airports. As a result of the non-economic character of the government's operation, National Airport is costing the American taxpayer, according to Paul Feldman, $225 million per year in subsidies to commercial air travelers and operators of other private aircraft. Bureaucrats answer that privatization is impractical. Nevertheless, the bureaucratic rules and political pressures which characterize government enterprises condemn these "nationalized" airports to high-cost, inefficient operations, and never ending confrontations over the question of "fairness."

At the absolute minimum, airport operations should be contracted out to private, for profit organizations. The municipal airport in Westchester County, New York, for example, turned to the private firm Pan American World Services in 1977, converting a losing operation into an annual profit of $1 million. Lockheed Air Terminal, Inc. owned and operated the Burbank Airport in the Los Angeles area for 40 years until the local competing and subsidized government airports eroded profits and forced Lockheed to sell to a group of municipal governments. Now under contract to these governments, Lockheed continues to operate Burbank at a profit. There exists little justification for local governments to own and operate commercial airports. Though complete privatization is the ultimate goal, contracting operations to the private sector, as is currently done at Burbank, is an essential first step if we are to lighten tax burdens and require individuals to pay for benefits received. Hopefully, the privatization process has only just begun. All major airports in the United States are owned and operated by government or an agency of government, mostly state and local political jurisdictions. Local property taxes and other levies, borne in part by lower income groups who rarely fly, subsidize the more frequent flying done by higher income families and the business flyer. Privatization would guarantee that those who do fly, the readily identifiable beneficiaries, pay their way.

## Air Traffic Control

A strong case can also be made that the U. S. government should remove itself from the air traffic control business. Since the air traffic controller union (PATCO) strike in August 1981 and the ensuing problems and publicity, many observers would argue that air traffic control would be both cheaper and probably safer if private, profit making operators were in charge. In a study by John Doherty, the important arguments for privatizing air traffic control centers have been summarized. Doherty found that the average cost of operating and maintaining a Level I tower (the lowest FAA rating in terms of the volume of air traffic) was $96,000 per year by the private sector compared to the average FAA cost for government operated Level I towers of $294,000 per year. The construction cost of a new Level I tower for the FAA has been in the range of $1.4 million. Private operators, on the other hand, conscience of the need to monitor costs, have taken advantage of existing structures to minimize the cost of the tower facility. FAA towers are equipped with amenities most would characterize as plush, but political agencies financed with taxpayer money have no bottom line. High cost service to a select group continues to be subsidized by the general taxpayer.

Concerning safety, there is no evidence that private towers are less safe than those operated by the FAA. Two of the largest firms operating air traffic control towers, Midwest ATC and Barton ATC, Inc., have had, respectively, no FAA "violations" in four years of operation and only one controller violation in fourteen years of operation, a nearly perfect record. Though the current government system is financed both out of general federal revenues and user fees, the user fees cover only a fraction of the true cost of the traffic control service. As already noted, the small private aircraft pays a much smaller fee than the large commercial airliner at an FAA installation, though requiring roughly the same equipment and controller services. A U. S. Department of Transportation study found that commercial airlines were covering 95 percent of their share of costs via the user fees, but general aviation was covering less than 20 percent of its allocated costs. Is it any wonder that local governments, which generally own and operate the airports, and the private aviation lobby wish to retain the relatively "free" control towers?

Like all government businesses, with revenues obtained largely from the unwilling taxpayer, efficiency suffers and the FAA bureaucrats have little incentive to please the customer. The militant confrontation between the FAA and the PATCO union, it seems clear, stemmed in large part from the politicized nature of the air traffic control business. It is encouraging however, that Senator Pete Domenici sponsored legislation in 1982 which would permit the spending of federal funds on contracting with private firms to operate air traffic control facilities. Privatization, with its significantly lower cost structure, promises that many Level I airports which lost their FAA operated towers in the aftermath of the PATCO strike are likely to be the beneficiaries of privately operated control towers. In summary, and quoting from the director of the FAA's Southwest Region on the privatization experiment by the FAA in Farmington, New Mexico: "What's going on in Farmington is a good demonstration of why air traffic control should be a business, and not the function of government." Unfortunately, the FAA perceives this movement to efficiency and lower cost service as a threat to their bureaucratic empire. Nevertheless, we are confident that private, for-profit operations will someday prove their superiority over government towers.

## WEATHER AND THE MARKET

The federal government is also intimately involved in the production and distribution of weather information. Flying requires detailed and up-to-the-minute weather information for safety. The aviation industry is in fact one of the more important "consumers" of specialized weather data. Here again, the government owned and operated weather forecasting business burdens all taxpayers so that special interests may be subsidized. The U. S. government spent more than $1 billion in 1983 to gather, analyze, and disseminate weather information. The National Oceanic and Atmospheric Administration (NOAA) collects and distributes meteorological and climate information to a number of important consumers of weather information, including aviation, the maritime industry, and agriculture, as well as the media for distribution to the general public. Much of this weather data is wholesaled "free" to private organizations which in turn make the information available to various users. Patrick Cox, in an important article, makes a persuasive case for the privatization of the weather forecasting business. While asserted to be "frivolous to propose charging users," according to a 1982 study by the National Advisory Committee on Oceans and Atmosphere, the NOAA spends about $1.2 million per year to save $750 million for American agriculture. Who indeed should pay for that kind of service? The farmer or the taxpayer?

Economist Steven Hanke, when a senior staff member of President Reagan's Council of Ecomonic Advisers, proposed a complete privatization of the government's weather system. Early in 1983 the administration announced a plan to sell the government owned weather satellites to commercial interests. Unfortunately, in November 1983, the Department of Commerce, as a result of Congressional politics, had to abandon its plan. On another front, the Communications Satellite Corporation (Comsat), a quasi-private institution created by Congress in 1963, proposed that it assume operation of the Landsat program which takes orbital pictures of crops and other relevant targets. A number of private firms plan on entering the weather business including RCA, the Environmental Satellite Data Corporation, and American Science and Technology Corporation. In addition there has been an explosive growth in recent years in the private provision of weather forecasts for interested consumers. As an example, MacLaren Plansearch, a Toronto based company, provides important weather reports to companies operating ocean-based oil drilling rigs. These private firms take the data provided by NOAA and the National Weather Service and sell it to interested groups. Unfortunately, the great bulk of special weather information provided by NOAA continues to be provided "free." The principle argument against user fees, or outright privatization for that matter, is the incorrect assertion that forecasting the weather is a "public good." That is, the market, without government involvement, would fail to produce the socially desirable quantitiy of weather information. However, it is clearly a product in which specific beneficiaries can be identified, and therefore prices for the service can indeed be charged. There is, in fact, no reason why the free market would not provide such information. Not only would privatization achieve greater efficiencies, but taxpayers too would benefit from reduced taxes. Clearly, both economic freedom and justice demand, at the very least, an honest debate on the merits of removing the U.S. government from the weather business. In any case, a story written by Jack Williams in USA Today reported a "boom" taking place in private weather companies. He reports that in 1949 there were 12 private weather forecasting firms, in 1975 there were 64, and at the end of 1983 there were 97.

## THE POLITICIZATION OF ENERGY MARKETS

The history of government involvement in energy markets is one of suppressed competition, missed opportunities, and inefficiencies galore. Government ownership and regulation have produced, it is generally agreed by economists, undersirable consequences.

### Tennessee Valley Authority

Created in 1933 for promoting flood control, river navigation, and "social progress" in southern Appalachia, the federal government's Tennesse Valley Authority (TVA) is now the largest electric utility. Presently it operates five nuclear, twelve coal-fired plants, and thirty-eight dams which produce electric power. A three-member board appointed by the President of the United States runs this giant bureaucracy that controls nineteen billion dollars in assets. Created during the Great Depression, critics then argued that it represented but another example of the "creeping socialism" occurring in the United States. In spite of the gains in per capita income in the region since TVA's inception, stemming in part from taxpayer subsidies to this particular area, criticsm continues to swirl around the TVA.

Critics, as we would expect from our earlier analysis of political competition and the anatomy of government failure, argue that the TVA has become a bloated, inefficient, and insensitive bureaucracy. Consumers of TVA power are enraged over rapidly rising electricity bills because of TVA's vast expansion into high-cost nuclear power plants. Partially built nuclear plants now seem destined for the scrap heap due to the lower rate of growth in the demand for electricity. Without the massive regional consolidation represented by this government monstrosity, the mistaken estimates of power needs in the 1980's would never have been pyramided into the billions of dollars spent on partially completed nuclear plants no longer needed. A similiar political fiasco is currently making headlines in the Pacific Northwest with the Bonneville Power Administration and the Washington Public Power Supply System's (WPPSS) multi-billion dollar boondoggle.

The TVA has experienced problems other than money. The Tellico Dam project in eastern Tennessee has driven many people from 16,000 acres of farmland flooded by the dam. Unfortunately, the industrial develoment promised by the politicians has not materialized. The dam itself cost significantly more than projected because of delays associated with the famous 3-inch fish called the Snail Darter.

Environmentalists also complain that the TVA is one of the worst air and water polluters in the country. One such environmental group has suggested that TVA stands for "Tennessee Valley Arrogancy." Government ownership provides few guarantees regarding the quality of the physical environment. Politically motivated goals are hardly the answer. The decision by the Roosevelt administration in 1933 to tax the American people for the benefit of this relatively poor region in Appalachia was scarcely the first and quite clearly wasn't the last time the federal government, through regulation or ownership, would "take" from one group of citizens for the benefit of another. And like most efforts at using the political delivery system, the customers are inevitably disappointed with the service. The historian North Callahan documents the many problems and conflicts in his *TVA: Bridge Over Troubled Waters.*

Perhaps the final irony is that just fifteen percent of the power generated by TVA comes from hydroelectric dams. Economies of scale, natural monopoly, or other economic arguments cannot possibly justify the monopoly ownership and operation of the five nuclear and the twelve coal-fired power plants. In fact, most economists now agree that the production of electric power is consistent with a multi-firm, competitive rivalry between power plants. The potential for private power generation, however, has been sacrificed to the political needs of the massive public bureaucracy. Interestingly, Callahan also notes the TVA's paternalistic attitude toward the people living in the region.

Both economic efficiency and justice support the gradual privatization of the electric power portion of TVA. Allegiances are fading. As one public relations official with the TVA in Knoxville was quoted as saying: "The older ones will always love us, because we emancipated them from the drudgery they knew before. But for a lot of the

younger ones, we're just the power-and-light company--that's all."
But we must remember that it was the American taxpayer who emancipated the region's poor. It is not at all clear whether the citizens of
Iowa, Wisconsin, Oregon or Texas, if put to a vote, would have
volunteered the necessary tax subsidies.

## Washington Public Power Supply System

Many of the same kinds of interest group politics, inefficiency,
waste, and bureaucratization of the electric power industry have
been taking place in the Pacific Northwest. Awarded an operating
license from the Nuclear Regulatory Commission, the debt ridden
Washington Public Power supply System (WPPSS or "Whoops")
began testing commercial operation of nuclear plant Unit 2 in July
1984. One of five nuclear plants planned by WPSS for the Pacific
Northwest, the unit will begin operations seven years after its
scheduled completion and $2.7 *billion over* budget. The total cost of
Unit 2 is expected to reach $3.2 billion, more than six times the
original estimate of $500 million! Construction on Unit 1 at Hanford,
Washington, which is 63 percent complete, and Unit 3 at Satsop,
Washington, which is 75 percent complete, has been halted indefinitely. Nuclear Unit 4 at Hanford and Unit 5 at Satsop were terminated in 1982. The cost of finishing these two plants was originally
estimated at $3.3 billion, but when work was halted in 1982 estimates
on the cost of completion had risen to $12 billion. Between 1973 and
1980 WPPSS had sold $5.1 billion in bonds, and as the woeful story
winds down, WPPSS is holding a fire sale on $462 million worth of
machinery, tools, and hardware intended for units 4 and 5. News
stories report that the sales were earning between 2 and 37 percent
of the equipment's original cost. In July 1982, "Whoops" defaulted
on $2.25 billion in revenue bonds, the largest municipal default in
U.S. financial history.

The history of the Washington Public Power Supply System
represents a profound example of government planning gone awry.
In 1957, 23 publicly owned utilities joined together to form a
"municipal corporation" in the State of Washington. Powers were
granted to the corporation to finance, construct, and operate power
plants in order to keep electricity rates down. By the early 1970's, the
federally owned Bonneville Power Administration (BPA) and other
utility companies in the Northwest were forecasting power shortages
in the 1980's. BPA and WPPSS developed an ambitious plan to deal
with the projected shortage: five massive nuclear power plants. As
James T. Bennett and Thomas J. DiLorenzo have shown, WPPSS
utilized what has become a very popular vehicle for raising money
for "off-budget" government enterprises. Revenue bonds are floated
to raise funds, in lieu of taxes, and therefore citizens and taxpayers,

due to the implied government guarantee, did not closely scrutinize the projects. Not only is the profit motive and the need to monitor costs absent, but even normal political constraints are ignored. The predictable outcome includes cost overruns, construction delays, shoddy workmanship, and continually revised budgets and completion dates. For example, in 1980 WPPSS was fined $59,500 by the Nuclear Regulatory Commission for faulty construction and record keeping on Unit 2.

The lawsuits brought by holders of the defaulted bonds and Chemical Bank of New York, trustee for the bonds, have revealed additional gory details. As early as 1976, WPPSS probably realized its power-demand forecasts were "unreliable" and the power from the five nuclear plants would not be needed. Four years before the first WPPSS bonds were sold, Oregon utilities raised the question regarding the authority of public utilities to sponsor the plants. The Washington State Supreme Court has since ruled that the utilities in fact did not have the authority to participate and therefore could not be compelled to pay off the WPPSS bonds. According to WPPSS studies, it was concluded very early in the venture that the ability to complete the plants within the announced cost estimates was questionable. From beginning to end, the great power plan for the Pacific Northwest assumed a capacity for forecasting, organizing, engineering, and constructing plants which Hayek warned is beyond the knowledge of mortal men.

Unfortunately, the implied solution of less government involvement and a greater reliance on decentralized, private decisions is not on the agenda of the bureaucrats. In the late 1970's, the Pacific Northwest Power Council was established which threatens the complete politicization of energy markets in the Pacific Northwest. The Northwest Regional Power Plan established by the Northwest Power Act of 1980 promises, ironically in response to the outcry over the financial debacle of WPPSS, to solve all problems. There are a few worthwhile recommendations in the Power Plan, for example the use of the price mechanism to ration electric power among competing users in light of the incremental cost of new production facilities. Sadly, the Northwest Regional Power Plan is yet another layer of government developed to supposedly correct the previous government fiasco.

Finally, as expected, the various interest groups are screaming for a "bail-out" to save them from their mistakes. The management of WPSS, the public utilities, labor unions, and suppliers have all proposed various "rescue" plans. Senator James McClure of Idaho introduced a bill in Congress which would create another off-budget enterprise to float bonds to pay off the defaulted WPPSS bonds. It would be affiliated with the federal Bonneville Power Adminsitration which must shoulder a good part of the blame for the original WPPSS project.

Rather than assigning responsibility to those who created the problem, the rescue plans propose giving WPPSS a blank check to spend even more billions of dollars. Fortunately, the bail-out proposals have received little support in Congress. As Bennett and DeLorenzo have pointed out, the proposal of an off-budget government enterprise to funnel money to WPPSS is practically identical to the creation in New York of the Municipal Assistance Corporation ("Big Mac") in the mid-1970's to save New York City from its fiscal irresponsibility. The effect of Big Mac was to have the taxpayers of New York State pay part of the bill for negligence of New York City. Just as Big Mac issued revenue bonds to pay off the city's debt, "Whoops II" would have the purpose of retiring existing WPPSS debt. Enough is enough. It is high time to cut our loses and get government out of the energy business.

## Nuclear Power

Not content to own, operate, and regulate these bloated and inefficient regional bureaucracies for the production and distribution of electric power, the U.S. government, beginning shortly after World War II, began to subsidize and, for all practical purposes, financially guarantee the nuclear power industry. It is safe to say that there is not a private risk-taker in the world who would have built today's nuclear power capacity without the aid and protection of the federal government. Cost-plus construction contracts, government subsidies of all kinds, and the Price-Anderson Act limiting the private liability of a nuclear power accident have produced a truly dismal situation. Proposals are now surfacing which would have the U.S. government buy all existing and future nuclear power plants and lease them back to the utility companies at subsidized rental prices. The American taxpayer would once again pick up the bill for government mismanagement and extravagance.

Caroline and Richard Hellman's book, *The Competitive Economics of Nuclear and Coal Power*, documents the "lousy economics" of nuclear power. They estimate that electric power from a nuclear facility would be at least twice as expensive as the power generated by a new coal-fired plant. When nuclear reactor plant orders peaked in the mid-1970's at 236 units, with an estimated cost of $400 billion, the evidence was already apparent. Rushed by the Nuclear Energy Commission, the Department of Defense, and the Nuclear Regulatory Commission, the commercial generation of nuclear electric power overwhelmed management in the utility companies. Nuclear technology was prematurely adopted with inadequate study of costs, operations, and safety. As a result, construction times and non-fuel operating and maintainance costs were underestimated, while capacity operating ratios and the assumed life of a plant were overestimated. In addition, the unreliability of nuclear power availability (the so-called yo-yo factor) has in practice meant utilities needed even greater reserve capacity. The end result is very expensive electric power. And, we might add, these higher costs relative to coal-fired plants hold true even when account is taken of the environmental problems associated with the burning of high-sulphur coal. Finally, the problems of radioactive-waste disposal and the necessity of decommissioning old nuclear plants must be considered as an important issue without obvious solution.

Yet, this government miscarriage rolls on. Partially completed nuclear plants in the TVA region, in the Pacific Northwest, and other locations lie as idle tombstones to another misguided federal adventure. Taxpayers, rate payers, and bond holders naturally feel betrayed. Many in the private utility business demand federal bailouts in spite of their own culpability a quarter of a century ago. Their solution now is to nationalize. Or, as the Hellmans summarize: "The industry has been its own worst enemy in refusing to recognize that nuclear power is uneconomic and getting worse. To this day, the Tellers, the Weinbergs, the Atomic Industrial Forum, and the Edison Electric Institute are leading the industry down a path of fool's gold." If we are to have nuclear power, then permit the market to determine its efficiency and safety. Repeal the Price-Anderson Act which guarantees limited liability to the industry, and stop all the government subsidies. The evidence suggests, in the absence of govenment subsidies, that economically viable nuclear power lies in the next century, if ever. Risk takers rather than taxpayers is where the responsibility belongs.

If serious questions exist on the grounds of efficiency and equity regarding the desirability and economic feasibility of nuclear power- then the case for the Clinch River breeder reactor project also deserves examination. On October 26, 1983, the United States Senate voted 56-40 to deny further funds to the research program. Senate Majority Leader Howard Baker of Tennessee, the "principal patron" of the project (the Clinch River project is in Oak Ridge, Tennessee), naturally regreted the loss. An interesting coalition had opposed the breeder reactor project, including the fiscally conservative National Taxpayers Union and the liberal Natural Resources Defense Council. Efficiency, cost, safety, and the environment were all cited as reasons for opposition. The cost of the experimental reactor plant was $4.5 billion of which $1.5 billion had already been spent when it was terminated. Unfortunately, the Reagan administration was disappointed at the loss of the program according to President Reagan's Energy Secretary Donald Hodel. This is, of course, the same Donald Hodel who so infamously engineered the WPPSS mess in the Pacific Northwest before becoming Secretary of Energy.

The Clinch River plutonium fuel plant was approved by the Nixon administration in 1972 mainly because of increasingly scarce supplies of uranium as a power source for nuclear power plants. But similar to the Soviet five-year plans which are revised on an annual basis, this plan too went awry. The uranium shortage never appeared, the growth of energy consumption slowed significantly in the late 1970's, and construction costs had to be revised continually upward. The Three-Mile Island nuclear accident and other reports of safety problems have clearly soured Congress on nuclear power. It hasn't helped to find the world awash in oil and therefore stable or even falling oil prices! As the National Taxpayers Union and many other observers have noted, the private electric power industry, relying on its own resources, would have been prevented from undertaking these wasteful adventures into nuclear power by the factual realities of the market place. Political solutions, where politicians and bureaucrats are presumed to have better knowledge than does the market, rarely have happy endings.

### Fossil Fuel Energy

Seemingly unable to learn from the nuclear power fiasco, the federal government in the decade of the 1970's proceeded to complete the politicization of the fossil fuel energy markets begun decades earlier. In 1980 Congress passed legislation creating the Synthetic Fuels Corporation (SFC). In particular, the Corporation would foster "commercial" production of synthetic fuels within the United States, including liquid, gaseous, or solid fuels produced from non-conventional raw materials. The government corporation would provide incentives including purchase agreements, price loan guarantees, and ultimately joint government-private ventures with the SFC as a minority shareholder. The case of government intervention was partly based on national security and partly on the assertion that government subsidies to the private sector might accelerate the commercial success of synthetic fuels. The United States, it was argued, must reduce its dependence on foreign oil.

Unfortunately, the reality was that government imposed price ceilings and petroleum allocation schemes, vis-a-vis the "entitlements" program, were actually subsidizing the importation of foreign oil and therefore making the U. S. *more* dependent on imported oil. When the synfuels legislation was passed, U. S. oil imports peaked at eight million barrels of oil per day or about 42 percent of our total petroleum requirements. In late 1983, following the deregulation of price ceilings on oil in 1981, imports were closer to three million barrels per day. Government planners, in all their wisdom, were again terribly wrong.

The chairman of the Synthetic Fuels Corporation announced a $15 billion taxpayers obligation to synfuels projects by the end of 1983. The original authorization, unbelievably, was a mind-boggling

$83 billion through 1988. The underlying claim, of course, was that the market price system would not achieve an efficient and timely development of alternative energy sources. Ignored by the politicians, most economists warned of the problems associated with government mandates replacing the price signals generated by the market. Would $83 billion in taxpayer subsidies produce the right amount of synfuels production by the target date of 1995? Or more realistically in light of energy conservation and the abundance of oil and natural gas predicted for the future, is it in fact another government rathole? Since the passage of the Synfuels Act, projections of demand, costs, and oil import requirements have all proven to be far different than anticipated. The legislated target reduction in oil imports of 1.5 million barrels per day has been significantly exceeded by the energy conservation associated with the deregulation of oil prices. Oil imports, as already noted, are currently about half of their peak in 1980.

Tragically, as a former economist with the Synthetic Fuels Corporation, Elena Folkerts-Landau, noted a number of months ago in the *Wall Street Journal*: "The SFC appears oblivious to these lessons..." from the free market. Private investors in shale oil projects are solicited with price guarantees of up to $67 per barrel, while world petroleum prices average $28 per barrel. For natural gas derived from synthetic sources, the SFC offered to pay $11 per thousand cubic feet of high-BTU gas that had a market price of slightly more than $4. In spite of these horrendously high prices, subsidized by the taxpayer, the chairman of the Corporation said that the American people "...have got to go ahead and bite the bullet." Both the chairman and the president of SFC assert that the federal government must be active in the ownership of the project, presumably because they are so inefficient. As the bureaucrats dream on, the combination of moderating oil and natural gas prices and the incredibly high cost of synthetic fuel development has caused private energy companies to reject and withdraw, except for basic research, from this economic fantasy.

Yet the economic analysis of public bureaucracy suggests the SFC will unidirectionally pursue its course despite the inefficiencies of government regulation and ownership and valuable lessons learned from allowing the price system to operate. The limited number of bureaucrats appointed by President Carter has mushroomed into a staff of 150 civil servants and energy planners. As former government employees and consultants, their very livelihood depends on the continued and costly role of the federal government in energy issues. The SFC justifiably earned the golden fleece award from Senator William Proxmire in 1982. Apparently undaunted, the chairman of the Corporation in 1983 told us that an expenditure of $15 billion was justified, Alice in Wonderland like, because there no longer was an energy crisis: "I think that now, when we don't have a crisis...we

266

must go ahead to show the rest of the world that we can..." develop synfuels. It is scarcely possible to imagine a more obvious case in which government should get out. If Synfuels are someday economical, let the private sector, not the taxpayer, risk its money. Is it criminal or just outright madness to spend $15 billion on synfuels to obtain, at inflated prices, less than two percent of the estimated 1987 U. S. oil consumption?

## GOVERNMENT AND THE MAIL

In 1977 a report by the U. S. Department of Justice, entitled *Changing the Private Express Laws,* confronted by the inefficiency of the United States Postal Service (USPS), made what to many seemed a startling statement: "Given the tremendous problems that now confront the Postal Service, it is not irresponsible to argue that things are now so bad that any change can only be for the better." The USPS believes more money is the answer. As 1983 ended the board of governors of the Postal Service proposed a $3.5 billion package of rate increases, representing a fifteen percent average increase in rates. The first class postage would rise to 23 cents from 20 cents, and taking into consideration the two rate increases in 1981, the entire package represents nearly a fifty percent increase over a four year period ending in 1984. The increase is required, according to the Postal Service, because of projected operating losses of $800 million in fiscal year 1985. The monopoly post office is in trouble, and many informed observers are suggesting private competitive solutions.

The federal Constitution in Article I provides that: "The Congress shall have Power to establish Post Offices and Post Roads." However, it said nothing at all about a *monopoly* on mail delivery. Admittedly, the postal monopoly preceded the Revolutionary War period in the colonies. As early as 1692 the British crown granted one Thomas Neale an exclusive franchise on letter delivery in the colonies. In 1792 the U. S. Congress passed the first of the Private Express Statutes which to this day support the postal monopoly in the United States. For most of our history the post office represented a political plum permitting politicians to reward friends and gain political support. One of the most desirable Congressional committee assignments use to be the House Post Office and Civil Service Committee. The patronage system began to unravel, however, as a result of rising costs, deteriorating service, and shockingly the complete breakdown of major postal operations in Chicago during the 1966 Christmas season. President Johnson appointed a postal reorganization commission from which came the Postal Reorganization Act of 1970.

The post office, according to the new legislation, was to be run like a business and without political involvement. All postal services were to pay their own way. Unfortunately, the new United States

Postal Service lacked one fundamental ingredient: the profit motive was missing. President Johnson's Commission, chaired by Frederick R. Kappel, who not surprisingly would become the first chairman of the board of governors of the USPS, recommended the retention of the Private Express Statutes. Competition was thus suppressed, and the monopoly power of the postal service continued. Throughout the decade of the 1970's postal service deteriorated and rates continued to rise. In 1978 a study by the American Conservative Union's Education and Research Institute asserted: "Observers of all persuasions agree that the Postal Reorganization Act has been a failure. The two main goals of the act--efficient management and self-sufficiency--remain unachieved." A former chairman of the Postal Rate Commission insightfully suggested: "The only solution to the problem of adequate mail service is competition and is to do away with the Private Express Statutes."

Early in 1983 Ralph Nader's Center for the Study of Responsive Law produced a study indicating the gravity of the situation. They too asked whether "...the U. S. Postal Service [can] survive." Nevertheless, given the ideological bias of the Nader people against the socially beneficial implications of the competitive market process, their answer was not competition and privatization. Rather they proposed that "...private citizens must form a national consumer action group to force accountability on the service." In other words, they wanted even more politicization. The author of the study, Kathleen Conkey, believed the partial privatization under the Reorganization Act "...was a serious mistake." She maintained the Congress had two choices: it could solve "...the very real financial, labor and modernization problems of the post office" or it could "...wash its hands of the postal headache through an expedient reorganization." Both avenues represent political solutions. Heaven forbid that we would permit the fresh winds of competition to play a role. Not surprisingly, the postal labor unions "commended" the Nader study "...for recognizing that the Postal Service should expand services...and that the Private Express Statutes must be maintained for the Postal Service to continue to fulfill its constitutional obligations." Nader supported the study's recommendation of spending $2 or $3 billion a year over the next five years to guarantee the bloated postal bureaucracy's survival.

As one might guess, the answer is *not* more government. The provision of an efficient and innovative mail delivery system requires the repeal of the Private Express Statutes. Competition must be allowed to replace monopoly. Self-serving postal officials repeatedly claim that the loss of their monopoly franchise would seriously erode the revenues required to subsidize other mail services. Free competition would encourage "skimming the cream" of the most profitable deliveries and thereby leaving rural residents and the second and third class mail users unsupported. Sadly, the courts continue to accept this argument.

Many researchers, however, disagree. As John Haldi of the American Enterprise Institute pointed out: "In a competitive market, cream skimmers are the good guys who protect consumer interests by keeping other suppliers honest." Economist Alan Reynolds in the *Harvard Business Review* made a telling point with respect to the misplaced emphasis on cream skimming. Anytime a company "...is compelled by the state to engage in activities that are not economically justifiable," higher prices must be charged elsewhere to subsidize the mandated service. Yet, private firms do in fact profitably provide second, third, and fourth-class carrier services. The United Parcel Service, for example, delivers packages at lower prices and reduced likelihood of enroute damage than does the parcel post delivery of the U. S. Postal Service. The country's largest newspaper, the *Wall Street Journal*, seldom relies on the Postal Service for its distribution. The relevant point is summarized by Alan Reynolds: "The fact that competitors can profit from a service that is unprofitable for the tax-exempt and subsidized USPS suggests that the USPS may simply be inefficient. If so, the monopoly rates on first-class mail actually subsidize inefficiency; this seems at best, a dubious policy objective."

In those circumstances, however, where competition for the postal monopoly has been permitted by law or encouraged by tehnological change, the Postal Service miraculously discovers numerous ways to cut costs, improve service, and innovate. With increasing competition in the delivery of packages, magazines, newspapers, and books, the Postmaster General recently confessed: "There are literally hundreds of other regulations that we are scrutinizing. Many of these date from the beginning of this century and bear no relationship to the way the Postal Service and its customers today do business." There can be no more profound indictment of monopoly than this admission! In contrast, the competitive market process demands that the bottom line be profitable to determine whether a service is "worth" providing. The obvious answer is competition. The electronic revolution in the transmission of information not only threatens this government monopoly, but in fact may eventually destroy it. Jeff Sampson's study points out: "Safely behind the Private Express Statutes, the Postal Service can afford to watch and wait for a sign from above." Unfortunately, this luxury continues to cost the American consumer/taxpayer dearly.

Realistically, the issue of privatizing the Postal Service is politically unpopular. Congress is literally scared to death of the implications of a truly competitive environment for the communication and delivery of information. The idea that rural residents be subsidized by urban residents and that first class mail should subsidize the delivery of magazines and "junk mail" is well entrenched in the political market place. Though most independent studies of the monopoly situation conclude that repeal of the Private Express Statutes would lower costs, spur innovation, and improve mail delivery, Congress continues to recommend further study.

Needless to say, the postal lobby is effective and powerful, based mainly with the American Postal Workers Union and the National Association of Letter Carriers. Indeed, in the early 1970's the union itself went to court to enforce and maintain their monopoly power associated with the Private Express Statutes (*National Association of Letter Carriers vs. Independent Postal System of America, Inc.*). Like the airline pilots and teamster truck drivers mentioned earlier, the postal unions have a very large stake in the suppression of competition. These two postal unions alone, representing more than 650,000 members, have obtained highly inflated wage settlements because of minimal competition and the deep pocket of the taxpayer/consumer. The lines at the postal stations when an examination is announced for prospective postal employees substantiate this assertion. Thousands of would-be mail carriers and postal workers actively pursue these limited but high paying jobs. It is no accident that the resignation rate for postal workers is far below the average for comparable positions in related fields. Unfortunately, the postal service's only competition is between those already employed with their high paying jobs and liberal benefit programs and those who would like to secure such attractive positions.

Once again both economic efficiency and justice require privatization and competition. Far from destroying America's first class mail service, it would in fact produce lower costs, better service, and insure the rapid introduction of new technology. According to Sampson: "Competition makes the Postal Service work better, not worse." The monopoly pillar of support is the suppression of competition through the Private Express Statutes. We urge the repeal of this legislation over an adjustment period of perhaps five years. This would allow the Postal Service and its unions time to prepare for a competitive environment and in turn would signal private entrepreneurs that competition in price, quality, and service is now open for entry.

## SOCIAL SECURITY

During 1983 the federal government paid more than $170 billion to 38 million beneficiaries of the various programs known as "social security" (not including Medicare and Medicaid). Officially known as Old Age Survivors, Disability, and Health Insurance (OASDHI) and created by the U.S. Congress in 1935, it is a government operated system which, funded by payroll taxes, simultaneously attempts to provide an insurance program and a welfare program on behalf of the American people. In 1982 the combined tax rate on employees and employers was 13.4 percent on the first $31,800 of earnings. Without further modification in benefits and/or taxes, by 1987 the combined tax rate will be 14.3 percent and will apply to the first $42,600 of earnings. By comparison, in 1950 the tax rate was 3 percent, and in 1960 the combined tax rate was 6 percent. The maximum tax payment by the employee and employer together in 1950 was $90 per year. For 1982 the comparable figure was $4,262. The majority of American tax payers now pay more in social security taxes than they do federal income taxes!

Despite the explosive increase in the system's tax revenues, the social security system continues to have serious budgetary problems. Most observers agree that unless something quite drastic is done, the existing "pay-as-you-go" system will collapse. The mish-mash of programs amounts to one of those fraudulent pyramid schemes which asks that newly attracted participants make financial payments to previously enrolled beneficiaries. In this pyramid scheme, however, government forces everyone, with the notable exception of federal employees, to participate. A few years ago Social Security Commissioner Sanford G. Ross warned that the American people must forget the "myths" about contributing to their own retirement programs under social security. The myth is the assertion that families are making premium payments when they are simply paying another tax. There are no trust funds accumulating the specific annuities which would be associated with a private program. It is simply a system of taxing those currently in the labor force for the benefit of system recipients. Commissioner Ross said that the insurance idea "...proved valuable in the early days of the program, but...is helping to confuse the debate over Social Security today." Believe it or not, the U. S. government currently has *unfunded* obligations in excess of $5 *trillion* under the existing social security and related programs.

There are two important reasons for the near collapse of the system, in addition, that is, to the underlying problems which accompany the government created monopoly provision of any good or service. First, in recent years the number of people receiving benefits has risen substantially relative to the number of workers paying the tax. Longer life expectancy coinciding with declining birth rates since the late 1950's means there are now barely three workers paying social security taxes for each retiree. While in 1950 there were sixteen workers per beneficiary, it appears that this ratio will fall to two workers for each retiree by the year 2010. Secondly, the increase in benefit payments has risen much more rapidly than the earned income from which the taxes must come. During the peiod from 1970 to 1979 the *real* (i.e., after account is taken of inflation) average monthly benefits of social security beneficiaries increased by about forty percent while the average real gross earnings in the private sector of the economy actually declined by two percent. In 1972 benefit payments were "indexed" to the consumer price index (CPI) in order

271

to protect their purchasing power. Unfortunately, the formula had benefits rising faster than the CPI. Compounding the problem, the CPI itself actually overstated the increase in the cost of living for most beneficiaries during this period, thereby producing an additional upward bias in benefit payments. The net effect was larger real payments taken from a reduced economic base.

The smaller real income base in the private sector of the economy, to add insult to injury, is itself partially the result of the adverse impact that social security taxes have had on private saving and investment in new and more productive capital. As a result of the pay-as-you-go system, mandatory tax payments for retirement are immediately dispersed to social security retirees. In contrast to private retirement programs, payroll taxes do not enhance private saving, but overwhelmingly are tansferred to recipients who consume goods and services rather than save. In a 1974 study, Martin Feldstein, past Chairman of the President's Council of Economic Advisors estimated that the existing system reduced private saving approximately fifty percent below what it otherwise would have been. The reduced rate of capital formation, which necessarily follows the decline in personal saving, naturally slows the rate of increase in labor productivity and thereby contributes to smaller real incomes. Nevertheless, larger benefit payments must still be paid from the smaller economic pie. Economist Ronald J. Vogel offers this advise to the "baby boom" generation: "Start saving money...now, to take care of ourselves, because it looks as if Uncle Sugar isn't going to do it for us, like he did before." His statistics indicate that while the number of people age 65 and over will increase by 120 percent between 1980 and 2030, the general population will grow by only 35 percent during the same period. According to Vogel, there is an irreconcilable conflict between the prospects of too many people depending on too few.

Unfortunately, the system also perpetuates the myth that the employer pays half of the social security tax. However, when the employer pays social security taxes, most of that money is now unavailable for wages, salaries, and other fringe benefits. Most recognize that both halves of the payroll tax are in fact being paid by the worker. Even worse, as we have already suggested, there is absolutely no connection between individual social security tax burdens and the structure and amount of benefits. In the past, Congress has levied taxes to obtain enough revenue to meet benefit "entitlements" determined by earlier votes. Higher benefits mean more votes today. Consideration of how to pay for such beneficence comes later. But, lest we forget, in spite of the rapid increase in taxes, the government can also decide to cut benefits.

When compared with private retirement plans, the social security program falls short on other counts. Private plans are tailored to individual preferences and lifestyles. Social security has but one plan. Strings and restrictions attached to social security are numerous and often arbitrary. The system limits outside earned income; it pays benefits only on a monthly basis; widows lose survivor benefits if they remarry; *ad infinitum*. Is it any wonder that federal employees, through their benefactors, the Congress, have opted to remain outside of the social security system? They apparently understand this Ponzi scheme for what it is.

The fundamental problem is again monopoly. In the absence of competition, few choices exist. Furthermore, the Old Age Survivors, Disability, and Health Insurance system does not have a "bottom line." Actuarial soundness is non-existent. The Social Security Administration can, in effect, ignore its "customers." In contrast, if retirement plans in the private sector fail to meet the requirements of individual preferences, consumers take their business elsewhere. Personal contracts with Prudential or Northwest Mutual Life are voluntary. But with respect to social security, consumers are compelled to buy a product universally known for having a lousy, noncompetitive rate of return. Peter Ferrara, in his book *Social Security: The Inherent Contradiction,* documents the irrationality of the existing system. And there are cruel ironies. The regressive nature of the social security tax structure, Ferrara tells us, "...is hurting most of all the poor who most need the higher benefits of the private system and who could help their children and grandchildren break out of poverty with the larger amounts of assets they could leave them."

As an absolute minimum, individuals should not be required to purchase a retirement plan from the federal government. The goal should be eventual privatization. Though some believe this solution to be politically unrealistic, existing proposals are merely bandaids attempting to stop a major hemorrhage. Yes, Congress has approved proposals raising the eligibility age above 65 and to a very limited extent reducing certain benefits. But their main solution entails higher and higher taxes for a system which denies individuals freedom of choice. Ed Clark, in a marvelous book entitled *A New Beginning,* offers what in the long term is the answer for the restoration of economic and personal freedom. He proposed that all individuals below a certain age (forty years, for example) be permitted to leave the system immediately. These people would do better under a private system than remaining under social security. At the same time benefits to those over forty would be guaranteed by the federal government, but paid from general revenues. The social security tax on both employees and employers would thus be repealed, and over a period of twenty-five years the rigid, inefficient, and morally repugnant government enforced monopoly would be dissolved. The rapid growth in private retirement programs would channel tens of billions of dollars into saving and therefore new capital formation. The modernized physical plant in the economy would raise productivity and income for all Americans. In this more properous economy those truly in need would be assisted by private charity and what

Richard Corneulle, in his book *Healing America*, calls the independent or third sector of the economy. We are confident that philanthropy and independent organizations would grow apace with the reduction in federal spending and commensurately lower tax burdens.

If such a program is not adopted, the young of America will be at war with the elderly. Tax rates paid just to support social security will be so high that saving, investment, and productivity will falter. The ultimate risk of this scenario is the total collapse of the social fabric of society and perhaps the loss of democracy and human liberty. In summary, and drawing from the final paragraph on this issue in Ed Clark's book, *A New Beginning:*

> Only a fundamental reform like this can avert the otherwise inevitable consequences of today's Social Security problems: higher taxes and bankruptcy. Any politician who says we don't need such fundamental reform is seriously irresponsible. The reform presented here is absolutely necessary. The liberty and prosperity of the American people depend on it.

## HOUSING AND THE FEDERAL GOVERNMENT

Since the passage of the Housing Act of 1949, which established government responsibility to insure "...a decent home and a suitable living environment for every American family," there has occurred a colossal increase in the government's role in the housing market. "Public housing" projects, owned and operated by local authorities and financed by securities guaranteed by the federal government, cost taxpayers more than a billion dollars each year. Subsidies are provided under a bewildering variety of federally supported programs. It is estimated that more than 30 million households, or roughly forty percent of all households in the United States, are eligible for housing subsidies under one or more of the existing programs.

Superimposed on these programs, which directly subsidize rent payments, mortgage payments, and/or interest rates, are the alphabet agencies that subsidize the credit markets' financing of construction and loans for new housing. The Federal National Mortgage Association (Fannie Mae), the Government National Mortgage Association (Ginnie Mae), and the Federal Home Loan Mortgage Corporation (Freddie Mac) together borrow more of the nation's capital funds than any single borrower other than the federal government. During the decade of the 1970's these and other government-sponsored institutions financed almost one-fourth of all home mortgages. By year end 1982, Ginnie Mae had outstanding obligations of $120 billion, Fannie Mae's liabilities were $22 billion, and Freddie Mac had debt obligations outstanding of about $53 billion. The federal government, as the numbers indicate, has a fairly significant involvement in the housing market! Needless to say, home builders' associations, private lending institutions, the real estate industry, and construction unions spend tens of millions of dollars in lobbying activity to insure the continuation and expansion of these many programs.

In addition, there are many provisions of the tax laws which subsidize home ownership. Mortgage interest payments and property taxes are deductible for tax purposes, and capital gains on the sale of a home are not subject to tax if another home is purchased within a specified period of time. In recent years Congress has approved an additional subsidy which permits the home-owner, after reaching a certain minimum age, to avoid paying any taxes on the proceeds from selling a home valued less than $150,000. Given the inflationary spiral of the past two decades, home owners have been able to pay off the principle and interest on their mortgage notes in depreciated dollars. And in spite of the repeated assertions about the high cost of housing and the high mortgage interest rates, the "real" cost of owner-occupied housing has undoubtedly declined since the late 1960's. By December of 1980 the number of occupied housing units *per capita* was at an all-time high. Americans owned more housing on the average than they did in 1970, and their homes on the average had greater floor area, more bathrooms, bedrooms, garage space, and central air conditioning. In summary, Americans were buying more housing because its real price was falling, a phenomenon economists call the "law of demand."

This massive federal intervention in the housing market occurs in spite of the inherently competitive nature of the construction, real estate, and finance industries. There is absolutely no reason why, on economic grounds, that a free market cannot produce the "right amount" of housing. Why is housing such a "sacred cow?" The Housing Act of 1949 declared that it was the purpose of public housing to insure, through the police power of the state, "adequate" housing for all Americans. Since the "public interest" is at stake, government, through its power of taxation, requires that some individuals pay for the housing of others. It is this same government, however, which destroys tens of thousands of housing units through the power of eminent domain. It would seem that this kind of "taking" is incompatible with a just society in which individual rights, including property rights, are protected and enforced. But even on their own merits, an analysis of the programs subsidizing housing markets suggests they frequently fail to realize their legislated objectives. On the dark side, they encourage graft and illegality. But economically, they devote a dangerously large fraction of the capital funds in the American economy to this industry favored by political gift-giving.

The alphabet agencies, like Fannie Mae, have been charged with the responsibility of increasing the *level* of housing starts to meet the Housing Act goals and also to reduce the cyclical *volatility* of the construction and housing industries. Unfortunately, while the housing market becomes more dependent on federal subsidies, economists and others who have studied the situation question whether either of these objectives is in fact being accomplished. Nevertheless, there is *certainly* one area where these federal programs have been "successful": the coercive power of government to direct and allocate America's limited savings to the "favored" and "more deserving" housing sector.

Studies on the question of government's impact on the level of housing starts are about evenly divided. There are those that find a positive contribution of the federal credit programs and those that find either no effect, or indeed, even a negative impact. In a study by the Federal Reserve Bank of Dallas, economist Sydney Smith Hicks found that the positive impact was in the short run as a result of lower interest rates induced by additional credit flows to housing, but that in the long run most of the studies were uanble to find any significant impact on housing starts. This is a startling conclusion when the tens-of-billions of dollars of federal funds and guarantees are considered.

Government programs have apparently not been very productive in reducing the volatility of the housing/construction cycle either. In general, the evidence seems to suggest that federally sponsored agencies have not accomplished a reduction in the cyclical swings in housing construction. For example, during the recession year of 1975, when housing starts had fallen to less than one million units per year, Fannie Mae's net borrowing remained negligible. In reviewing the role of Fannie Mae, Ginnie Mae, Freddie Mac, and the Federal Home Loan Banks in the housing sector since the mid-1950's, the evidence that the selective provision of federally backed credit contributes to a less volatile housing market is weak.

Far and away the most productive action government could take would be a sound policy of monetary restraint and therefore less inflation and lower interest rates. The high cost of mortgage credit and construcion loans over the past two decades is a direct result of the acceleration in inflation in the United States. Invariably, high rates of inflation are associated with high market rates of interest. Lower long term rates of inteest will happen only if we reduce the rate of inflation. Inflation in turn will come down only if the Federal Reserve System implements a believable monetary policy which achieves money growth rates roughly in line with the capacity rate of growth in the economy.

The problem, however, is even bigger than the inefficient and costly use of taxpayers' money to subsidize housing. As a result of the pronounced decrease in the rate of growth in labor productivity since the early 1970's, fundamental questions are being asked regarding the economy's allocation of capital funds. The popularity of supply-side economics, the notion of "reindustrialization," and many other proposals suggest, as economist Anthony Downs has reported, that too much capital is going to housing, probably at the expense of industrial modernization. The important question according to Downs and many others is whether subsidized financing of housing is diverting too many resources from other investments which, if larger, would counteract the recent decline in labor productivity gains? Have the tax structure, the inflationary environment, and all of the other programs subsidizing housing drained funds from projects which otherwise would have contributed to the modernization and productivity of our economic system? Evidence has already been cited which supports the proposition that Americans in the past two decades have significantly increased the amount and quality of housing they buy. The tax breaks, subsidies, and guarantees have produced an imbalance in the allocation of the necessarily scarce pool of saving in the economy which must be allocated among competing uses.

Government subsidized housing seems clearly to have crowded out other kinds of investment which would have otherwise ensured greater productivity and hence higher standards of living. Economist Downs noted that during the period 1966-1971, the fraction of all capital raised in the nonfinancial sectors of the American economy devoted to home mortgages was about sixteen percent. In the late 1970's the figure had risen to more than twenty-eight percent. Though driven by the desire to limit tax liabilities and to hedge against inflation, the fact remains that monies going to housing are not available to modernize Chrysler facilities, the Bethleham steel plant, or the textile mill in South Carolina. Rather than government allocation of credit, the competitive market is much more likely to identify the highest valued use of scarce capital. The "credit allocation" schemes proposed by politicians, using the political system to allocate money to "productive" instead of "speculative" purposes, are necessarily subject to interest group pressures. Once again, political solutions are found to be very inequitable.

Comparative rates of return in alternative employments of capital, determined through an open and competitive process, have always produced efficient outcomes over time. And if you believe that individuals should get what they pay for and nothing more, market solutions are also synonymous with just solutions. Unfortunately, government induced inflation and intervention in the housing market have produced inequitable outcomes. A growing social and economic disparity between individuals who already own homes and therefore benefit from the numerous tax breaks, and those who cannot afford to become homeowners, especially the young, threatens irreparable damage to the social fabric. By the end of the 1970's the percentage of buyers purchasing their first home fell to less than twenty percent, less than half of what it had been earlier in the decade.

The answer is lower mortgage rates which would contribute

significantly to lower monthly housing payments. Both the size and volatility of the housing market stem directly from the instability of government monetary and fiscal policies. Stop-and-go monetary policy, massive federal budget deficits, and an irresponsible Congress have jointly produced a roller coaster which rewards some, penalizes most, and assuredly reduces the longevity of the free market economy.

In addition to sound economic policy on the question of inflation and fiscal responsibility, economic efficiency and justice demand a gradual weaning of the building industry, real estate industry, and lending institutions from the federal trough. For the sake of productivity and therefore rising standards of living, the relative tax advantages of investment in housing as opposed to other forms of investment must be eliminated. Federal policies which provide "in-kind" subsidies to housing, including public housing, rent supplements, or subsidized mortgages, must be phased out over a period of time. If complemented by a non-inflationary package of economic policies, there is no reason why the six percent conventional mortgage cannot reappear just as fast as the acceleration of inflation produced higher rates. Since the financing of housing for the American people is a very competitive industry with literally thousands of existing firms prepared to provide credit at non-subsidized market terms, the inequities in housing would gradually be eliminated. And the protective blanket subsidizing the special interest groups would be removed. A secondary market in mortgage paper can profitably exist in the absence of the guarantees associated with the alphabet agencies. If Fannie Mae, Ginnie Mae, Freddie Mac, the Federal Land Bank system, and other agencies which provide subsidized terms to real estate purchases are to continue, they must do so without the explicit or *implicit* protection of the federal treasury. Housing requires a large dose of privatization in combination with a politically courageous decision to deal with inflation.

## SUMMARY

The case for privatization rests on the socially beneficial implications of the competitive market process and the observation that the functions government can do well are, as James Madison told us long ago, limited in number. Thomas Jefferson, Adam Smith, Friederick Hayek, and many other observers of the human scene have warned us repeatedly of the limits to the use of force in the implementation of social arrangements. We believe that the scope of government is currently far larger in the United States of America than is consistent with maximum individual liberty and economic freedom.

Many other examples, in addition to those discussed, where federal ownership and/or operation is economically inefficient and generally inequitable could have been cited. R. Joseph Monsen and Kenneth D. Walters' book, *Nationalized Companies*, contrasts the efficiency of nationalized and private enterprises in Western Europe. They found sales per employee lower for nationalized firms, profits per employee lower, physical production per employee lower, operating expenses and wages higher, sales per dollar of investment lower, and with the exception of nationalized oil companies, almost all government owned companies generate accounting losses.

The President's Private Sector Survey on Cost Control, or the "Grace Report" for J. Peter Grace the survey's chairman, was submitted to President Reagan in January 1984. Numerous opportunities for privatization in programs currently operated by the federal government were discovered. Appointed in early 1982 and staffed by some 2,000 executives from industry, finance, and accounting, the Grace Report recommended privatization of Veteran's Administration hospital management and construction, Defense Department commissaries, Coast Guard rescue activities, NASA's space shuttles and launch vehicles, the federal government's vehicle fleet, and the government's marketing of electric power among many other possibilities. The privatization task force estimated that their recommendations could "result in cost savings, revenue enhancements, and cost avoidances" of billions of dollars over a three-year period. Federal insurance programs abound and should be eliminated. And, the Corp of Engineers and its work deserves a critical review with an eye to reducing the agency's authority to build and build, usually at taxpayers' expense.

The point has been made. The ownership and operation of "business" by government seems everywhere and always to be relatively inefficient when compared with the private sector. But of even greater importance, as government involves itself in economic affairs, usually in the name of "social" justice and /or the "public interest," it also fails to produce equitable results. Economic intervention by government is inevitably a zero-sum game of both winners and losers. The essence of government involves its police power to require some individuals to subsidize others. Whether it be the poor subsidizing the airfares of the rich, the urban dweller paying part of the first-class postage on a letter to the rural resident, or the general taxpayer subsidizing the development of synthetic fuels, it is difficult to discover principles of "fairness" which justify these kinds of legislative and judicial interventions in people's lives.

# CHAPTER 20

## THE TRAGEDY OF THE COMMONS

> What is common to many is taken least care of, for all men have greater regard for what is their own than for what they possess in common with others.
>
> --Aristotle

> While it may be emotionally or philosophically pleasing to conservationists and environmentalists to believe that wildlife belongs to everyone or that the oceans and their resources belong to mankind as its common heritage, the inevitable results of such a system is the opposite of what they desire.
>
> --Robert J. Smith

Why do Rhode Island Red and Leghorn chickens multiply in great profusion and the Atwater's greater prairie chicken remains an endangered species? Why is there graffiti on the walls of public restrooms but not in our homes? Where do we find more litter and garbage: the city park or at Disneyland? Is sewage dumped in the backyard swimming pool or in the creek? What was the main contributing factor to the overgrazing of the western Great Plains and the resulting "dust bowl?" Why did the Buffalo almost become extinct, yet the Hereford multiply and become an important source of protein for the American people? Why, in a more fundamental sense, do plants and animals grown on private lands survive and prosper while common property resources, supposedly in the custodial care of government, suffer from excess use and dwindling supplies? The answers to all of these questions are found in what the biologist Garrett Hardin called "The Tragedy of the Commons." Following the case for privatization, the current debate on environmental issues stems from the differential effects of private versus government ownership of resources. Although the issues are usually posed in terms of whether one is for or against forests and wildlife, the truly fundamental question is whether the environment is ultimately safer in the hands of private owners or safer when treated as a "commons" held in trust by government in behalf of everyone.

### THE LOGIC OF THE COMMONS

There are two crucial attributes of a property right: the power to exclude others from using it and the ability to transfer title. Private property allows individuals to have control, with rights that are legally transferable and exclusionary. A common property resource, on the other hand, is owned by no one. Unfortunately, the invariable interpretation is that everyone "owns" the communal resource and, therefore, it can be used by anyone. Whether the commons is unowned or government controlled, a perverse structure of incentives motivates individuals to excess exploitation, waste, and political conflict. Almost all environmental problems result from resources being held in common.

If property rights to grazing lands do not permit exclusion, then every stockman is motivated to graze as soon as possible before the grass is gone. If salmon are believed to be a "common pool" resource without well defined private property rights, then the basic motivation is to immediately harvest as many fish as one can before someone else does. The decimation of whale populations stems from the common property treatment of the oceans. The buffalo was effectively removed from the Great Plains because of the difficulty in assigning private property rights to this fugitive animal. Water and air resources are used as waste dumps because they are considered common property resources. In the absence of an institutional arrangement which says "that body of water is mine and I will not allow you to dump your chemicals in it," excess exploitation and environmental degradation will continue.

The inevitable consequences of resources held in common--the proposition that everyne owns the forests, ranges, oceans, and wildlife--are excessively rapid and inefficient exhaustion of the resource, deterioration of the environment, and social conflict among those who compete for their use. As the quotation by Robert J. Smith at the head of this chapter observes, the environmentalists might be emotionally and philosophically buttressed by the notion that everyone owns a share of the forest, whales, or Grizzly bears; nevertheless, the inevitable consequences of a common property approach are the deterioration and exhaustion of the very resources they hope to preserve. Allow Garrettt Hardin, in his pathbreaking article, describe the logic of common "ownership":

Picture a pasture open to all. It is to be expected that each herdsman will try to keep as many cattle as possible on the commons...As a rational being, each seeks to maximize his gain. Explicitly or implicitly, more or less consciously, he asks, 'What is the utility *to me* of adding one more animal to my herd?' This utility has one negative and one positive component. (1) The positive component is a function of the increment of one animal. Since the herdsman receives all the proceeds from the sale of the additional animal, the positive utility is nearly + 1. (2) The negative component is a function of the addtional overgrazing created by one more animal. Since, however, the effects of overgrazing are shared by all the herdsmen, the negative utility for any particular decision-making herdsman is only a fraction of − 1. Adding together the component partial utilities, the rational herdsman concludes that the only sensible course for him to pursue is to add another animal to his herd. And another; and another. But this is the conclusion reached by each and every rational herdsman sharing a commons. Therein is the tragedy. Each man is locked into a system that compels him to increase his herd without limit--in a

281

world that is limited. Ruin is the destination to which all men rush, each pursuing his own best interest in a society that believes in the freedom of the commons. Freedom in a commons brings ruin to all.

The recommended solution for most environmentalists is to assign government property rights to the common pool and/or migrating resources. According to the argument, public ownership is required so that government can utilize regulations, standards, and other controls to prevent the tragedy from working its ways. Unfortunately, the government or, more realistically, the bureaucrats who manage these resources do not "own" the capital value of the trees or the body of water, and therefore will have little incentive to conserve the resources and maintain their market value to potential users. Only private property rights of exclusion and transferability guarantee that managers of scarce resources will maintain them in their highest valued uses. The inevitable result of a communal use of natural resources is overexploitation and eventual exhaustion or extinction.

## PROFIT VERSUS PEOPLE

For most environmentalists, government must conserve natural resources and protect the environment because the market system focuses on profits, not people. The competitive market process is blamed for "raping the land," and therefore government must rescue our natural environment from the greedy capitalist. But this is a case of mistaken responsibility. It is not the market means working through the profit motive which has defiled the environment and produced wasteful resource management. Rather, goal oriented individuals have been given faulty signals and inappropriate incentives as a result of our failure to carefully define and enforce private property rights.

It is not a failure of capitalism then, but in fact represents the difficulty and sometimes inability to assign property rights to specific resources; that is, to give exclusive control of valuable resources to individuals who will have the motivation to conserve and protect them in their own self-interest. As economists Richard Stroup and John Baden have observed in their book, published by the Pacific Institute For Public Policy Research, *Natural Resources: Bureaucratic Myths and Environmental Management:* "In the private sector, the asset value of the land is the voice of the future. It holds the owner's wealth hostage to good management...Land values--that is, the present capitalized value to *all* future services from the land-hold the owner accountable." In contrast to the government manager who has a minimal personal stake in the stand of Douglas Fir trees or the politician facing re-election in less than two years, the private owner can transfer title to the trees in the market by being alert to maximizing the present monetary value of the timber stand. The ability to exclude others and the fact that they are transferable (can be sold) guarantees that the private forester will act *as if* he was interested in the uses to which others might put the timber. It is not a question of profit versus people or profit versus nature; the problem is the failure to assign property rights and remove the resource from the commons.

A related argument is the proposition that the market process fails to heed the demands of "posterity" producing too much for today's generation and thus leaving a smaller legacy to "future generations." It is asserted that we are going to "run out" of fossil fuel energy sources, forests, and other flora and fauna, and therefore government must appropriate resources to guarantee their conservation. Unfortunately, this argument is basically wrong. Since politicians face frequent elections, if they wish to remain in office, the long run gets scant attention while "yes" votes on particular issues produce immediate electoral support. So much for posterity. In contrast, a system of well defined private property rights with effective markets in natural resources and wildlife produces individuals who do indeed look to the future and are motivated to conserve simply for the possibility of profit. In the market, according to Stroup and Baden, "...farsighted outcomes are made possible through the activities of speculators who have an incentive to protect resources for future sale and use because such preservation may benefit them...The speculator thus acts as a middleman between the present and the future." When property rights are transferable, "...the speculator can do well for himself while he does good for future resource users...This incentive to look to the future contrasts sharply with the incentives faced in the public sector."

It is the *private* forest of Georgia-Pacific or Weyerhaeuser that gets special care, while the National Forests in the Rocky Mountain area are raped by the harvesting of timber whose market value is less than the cost of cutting access roads and the resulting erosion in the watershed of these semi-arid timber stands. No matter how high the price of cattle, the private owner would never slaughter all of his breeding stock. Herefords and Black Angus are conserved on private ranches, while the inevitable logic of the commons destroys the salmon run, the green sea turtles, and the public grazing lands in the American West.

There remains another fundamental point with regard to posterity. Why does present society supposedly owe so much to future generations? The current generation will leave a vastly enlarged stock of knowledge and *useful* resources to future generations. Why, in addition, should the living suppress consumption and give the future an even greater advantage than it already will undoubtedly possess? Note the profusion of inventions of the nineteenth century available to the current generation. Anthony Scott, in his classic volume

*Natural Resources: The Economics of Conservation,* reminds us that "...most of [our] progress has taken the form of converting natural resources into more desirable forms of wealth. If man had prized natural resources above his own product, he doubtless would have remained savage, practicing 'conservatism'." The tranformation of minerals, timber, and energy into more useful forms transmits a very valuable legacy to our children and grandchildren. As Harold J. Barnett and Chandler Morse noted in their book *Scarcity and Growth: The Economics of Natural Resources Availability:* "By devoting itself to improving the lot of the living...each generation...transmits a more productive world to those who follow."

The process of transforming minerals and other natural resources into higher valued uses more or less guarantees future generations a preferred position. Julian L. Simon, in his challenging book *The Ultimate Resource,* provides an excellent summary of why the environmentalist's concern with the future is essentially misguided:

> [The existing generation provides for future generations]...by accumulating real capital to increase current income, by adding to the stock of useful knowledge, by making its own generation healthier and better educated, and by improving economic institutions. This is why the standard of living has been rising with successive generations. Because we can expect future generations to be richer than we are, no matter what we do about resources, asking us to refrain from using resources now so that future generations can have them later is like asking the poor to make gifts to the rich.

If natural resources are held in the form of transferable private property rights, selfish capitalistic speculators will indeed, as we have shown, act *as if* they are interested in the value that future generations might place on particular resources. It is in the commons where individuals are motivated to exploit the resource before someone else, who *also* "owns" the resource, exploits it. The inevitable outcome is environmental degradation and the depletion of a valuable resource.

Finally, the debate between profits and people also rests on the desire of preservationists to maintain a pristine environment, frequently meaning to be seen or touched by few if any humans. According to this view and irrespective of the potential success at conserving resources and protecting the environment, profits are morally repugnant. Environmental control then is a people problem, and its solution lies in changing human nature. As Stroup and Baden have noted: "Environmentalists are sensitive to the problems caused by governmental management of the land. But they...confidently attribute the causes of the problems to 'bad' administration and 'bad' people." The answer is to "re-work" human beings so that they will acquire the *appropriate* respect, or the particular preferences of the hard-core preservationist, for the environment. Then it would simply be a matter of placing better government managers, those who have acquired the right environmental ethic, in charge of the pollution and conservation issues.

## ELITISM IN THE AGE OF ENVIRONMENTALISM

The modern environmental movement already possesses a verdict on the social and economic implications of a *commerical* social ethic. In the years since the publication of Rachael Carson's *Silent Spring* in 1961, which marks the beginning of the new environmentalism, a significant segment of the upper-middle class has advocated an "aristocratic conservatism" which would stop economic growth and "preserve what we have." As Wiliam Tucker observes in his book *Progress and Privilege*, "environmentalism has...entwined itself with the protection of privilege. In the end, it has become an extremely conservative doctrine--fearful of the future, despairing of human effort, worried about change, and wed to the status quo." The new "aristocratic elite," *their* material well-being now guaranteed, oppose further economic growth and progress. This characterization of the new environmentalism had been summarized by long-time environmentalist Robert J. Smith in his *Earth's Resources: Private Ownership and Public Waste:*

> Clearly, much of the environmental and preservationist movement consists of an elite new class of mandarins, and this is especially true of the movement's leadership. they are generally quite well-to-do, secure and smug in their comfortable niche in the establishment, and somehwhat isolated from the pressures of taxation and inflation. Much of their time is spent honing their refined esthetic sensibilities, expressing dismay, shock and even outrage at the fact that trees are being chopped down--all from the comfort of their expensive redwood and glass ranch-style home...

This newly arrived and privileged minority advocate a "stationary state" economy in which economic advance is stopped in its tracks to preserve the environment. And the great mass of the people, the middle-class to the very poor, are asked to approve of this elitist preservation ethic which would deny them the opportunity to push their way up the economic ladder. "Why is it," asks William Tucker in *Progress and Privilege*, "...that some people should actually take a kind of grim pleasure in the idea that it may be impossible to provide ourselves with energy without doing irreparable damage to the landscape, or that trying to feed the world's people may be a hopeless undertaking?" It is in large measure a thinly veiled effort to impose hardship on the blue-collar, urban dweller in order to provide exclusive playgrounds for a generally high-income and aristocratic elite. Vernon Jordan, former Director of the Urban League, once offered what he believed to be the response of his constituents to the conflict between economic progress and preservationism:

Walk down Twelfth Street [in Washington, D.C.] and ask the proverbial man on the street what he thinks about the snail darter and you are likely to get the blankest look you ever experienced. Ask him what he thinks the basic urban environmental problem is, and he'll tell you jobs. I don't intend to raise the simple-minded equation of snail darters and jobs, but that does symbolize an implicit divergence of interests between some segments of the environmental movement and the bulk of black and urban people...[Environmentalists] will find in the black community absolute hostility to anything smacking of no-growth or limits-to-growth. Some people have been too cavalier in proposing policies to preserve the physical environment for themselves while other, poorer people pay the costs.

The bumper sticker: "If You're Hungry and Out of Work, Eat an Environmentalist" expresses a message which is thoroughly understood by the great majority of the American people. The proposition eminating from the leadership of the Sierra Club, National Audubon Society, and the Wildlife Federation that economic growth and security is an irrelevant and vulgar nuisance doesn't sit well with most Americans. Robert J. Smith has astutely noted the implicit unwillingness of the aristocratic minority to subject their preferences to a popular referendum: "It is ironic that the very people who constantly refer to wilderness and wildlife values as part of the common heritage and a birthright of all the people are never willing to let all of the people put the provision of these resources to a market test." At work in the modern environmental movement is another classic example of a special interest group: environmentalists who employ the coercive power of government to transfer wealth and influence from the majority of the American people to themselves. Wilderness designation simply transfers control of certain kinds of resources to an elitist minority.

Rising standards of living in recent decades, partially reflected in improved transportation networks, have made scenic forests and mountains available to more people and have lowered the cost of spending time in wilderness type areas. At the same time, the value of this experience has probably been lowered for some people. Nevertheless, a crucial question is: to what extent is a small minority prepared to sacrifice its isolation in the wilderness so that others, like the urban working class, can also participate in the outdoor experience? The elitist attitude in this age of environmentalism follows the line of defense offered throughout history by the aristocracy: privilege and preservation for the new mandarin class. In his book *The Ultimate Resource*, Julian Simon captures the distinction:

Of course, one may look upon the increased numbers of visits as an indication that the wilderness is not so isolated anymore, and hence that it is less desirable. But that is the point of view of an eighteenth-century prince who wished to enjoy the entire forest all alone and could afford to do so...The imperial view differs from the basic democratic view that more people sharing in the enjoyment of something is a good thing even if the experience is not perfect for any one of them.

286

In fact, the upper-middle class preservationist would do well to review the number of vehicle registrations for campers, pickup trucks, off-road vehicles, snowmobiles, and other kinds of recreation vehicles--and especially the number of votes they have--before making a final commitment in favor of government ownership in order to preserve the wilderness.

The virtuous actions of the new environmentalism on behalf of "everyone" to protect "our" common natural heritage, in fact means very little to the automobile mechanic in Dallas, the fry cook in Camden, the beautician in Baltimore, let alone the inner city black or hispanic whose greatest ambition is to grasp the bottom rung of the economic ladder. It is an elitist movement which protects privilege and provides playgrounds and esthetic benefits to mostly the rich generally at the expense of those who have yet to "make it." Simply stated, the suppression of economic progress in the name of the environment favors the haves over the have-nots.

## GOVERNMENT OWNERSHIP: GOOD INTENTIONS, POOR RESULTS

Self-interest aside, the environmental movement has appropriately focused our attention on environmental degradation, excess exploitation of valuable resources, and the importance of our natural surroundings in general. The issue, however, is not whether conservation and pollution are important; but the crucial problem is how to develop institutional arrangements to protect our planet's physical and social habitability in the most efficient and equitable way. In that discussion, environmentalists, with very few exceptions, have assumed government to be the necessary custodian of the natural environment, since capitalism, in the name of profits, will exploit the minerals, forests, wildlife, and other natural values to the detriment of the environment. As noted earlier, the idea that self-interest and the market economy are at fault has been shown to be in error by the biologist Garrett Hardin in his classic description of the environmentally destructive implications of the commons. The promise that government will manage the natural environment in the "public interest" remains to be challenged.

In contrast to the private sector of the economy, where the quality of managerial decisions are brought to light by the signals of profit and loss, managers in the public sector are seldom totally accountable for their decision. When resources are not held privately, and therefore are not transferable to others by those in control, the public bureaucrat is rarely held accountable for any wasteful and exploitive use. Efficient resource allocation in the government sector requires informed voters and legislators. Unfortunately, existing political institutions guarantee neither. Good intentions and good people are not enough. The problem is not one of bad people running the Bureau of Land Management,the U.S. Forest Service, or the National Parks Department. Natural resource economists Richard Stroup and John Baden have identified the fundamental dilemma: "Even with good intentions and expertise, public servants are likely to generate environmental problems because they lack the feedback and reality checks inherent in the price system and markets."

Government stewardship of natural resources guarantees bitter conflict over the use of the "public domain." As the mountain valley, lake, river, forest, or desert become popular due to rising incomes and growing population, a politicaL struggle is the inevitable consequence of public ownership. Irresolvable conflict among competing users leaves the government bureaucrat in the middle of the argument. Hearings are held, special interests lobby their legislators, but almost inevitably good intentions produce poor results. One group lobbies to save the wild horses in the American West; consequently the horses multiply in great numbers and consume the forage which supports other wildlife species dear to the hearts of other special interest groups.

Bureau of Land Management grazing policies, determined in the political arena by special interests, destroy the land. Federal irrigation projects subsidize farmers at the expense of free flowing rivers. "Multiple use" policies guarantee political confrontation over access to "public lands" and necessarily produce inefficient results. Quality in the management of natural resources, whether in the public or private domain, is largely determined by the structure of the property rights in force. When resources are treated as common property, the tendency of fast depletion and environmental destruction is assured. However, when resources are exclusively under the control of a private owner who has an absolute right to the capital value of the assets, the owner will have a direct interest in conserving and protecting those values. In addition, the profit motive assures that the resources will be moved to their highest valued use.

Stroup and Baden in *Natural Resources* persuasively argue that an efficient management of natural resources involves three interrelated issues. First, the authority to control resources must be coupled with the personal responsibility for actions taken. Decision makers must have a personal stake in the consequences of their decisions. The public sector inevitably breaks this link and therefore inhibits accountability. Second, it must be recognized that we live in an imperfect world, and while the market system is not ideal, it does not follow that government solutions are preferrable. The competitive market process, even when not operating perfectly, has otherwise unobtainable beneficial effects. Finally, it must be recognized that individuals respond to the incentives they face. Unfortunately, institutions in the past have encouraged wasteful exploitation of the commons, and for emotional and philosophical reasons the assignment and enforcement of private property rights have been falsely condemned as a surrender to "big business" and the profit motive.

The fact of the matter is that individuals conserve, husband, save, protect, and expand their stocks of valuable resources *if* they have exclusive claims on the proceeds resulting from their sale. Black Angus cattle on private ranches thrive, while the wolf nears extinction. Lion populations in private game reserves flourish, while their numbers are threatened in the wild. Hawk populations on public lands dwindle, but domesticated chickens, turkeys, and geese are harvested in great numbers in the private sector. Forest economist Barney Dowdle has documented how the private forests in the Southeastern United States are much more productive than the public forests in the Pacific Northwest. The contrast has been starkly stated by Stroup and Baden:

> Private ownership allows the owner to capture the full capital value of his resource, and thus economic incentive directs him to maintain its long-term capital value...In contrast when a resource is owned by everyone, the only way in which individuals can capture its economic value is to exploit the resource before someone else does.

A profound illustration is provided by the National Audubon Society's management of its privately owned Rainey Wildlife Sanctuary in Louisiana where environmental values of preservation and wildlife protection exist in harmonious partnership with gas wells and grazing cattle. Nevertheless, in stark contrast to their practice at Rainey, the Audubon Society continues to advocate public ownership of federal lands to prevent mineral exploitation and development. At Rainey, "reality checks" that produce management decisions in which opportunity costs must be squarely faced are available to the Society. In the political arena the bureaucratic manager, faced with ill-defined multiple use mandates and without a personal stake in decisions, produces outcomes which are pleasing to no one.

The environmental movement's preference for government ownership of natural resources has the potential of producing results opposite of what they desire for yet another reason. Government can both give and take away. The reliance on government for environmental protection is a double edge sword which can just as easily swing in the direction of environmental destruction. The election of President Reagan in 1980 and his appointment of James Watt as Secretary of the Interior should remind us of how rapidly political circumstances can change and how the reigns of government power can be shifted to those who would oppose our favorite interest. Given the speed and degree by which governments can change their mind, depending on which individuals occupy power, the ultimate security for places of beauty rests with secure and enforceable *private* property rights.

There are many examples of how the environment can be sacrificed on short notice because of emergencies declared by government. For example, the oil embargo by the OPEC countries in November 1973, quickly produced a suspension of the National Environmental Protection Act by a Congressional vote so that the Alaskan Pipeline might be built. The Wilderness Society's court action was quickly circumvented. And this was the same government which held energy prices *down* during the 1970's and thereby stimulated energy use in the U. S. While spending billions to encourage energy conservation with their right hand, government simultaneously "encouraged" consumption, through price controls, with their left hand through price controls.

In the summer of 1979, largely as a result of the government created "energy crisis," President Carter and important members of both parties in Congress advocated a new Federal Energy Mobilization Board which would have had broad powers to override all existing environmental legislation. A little emergency here, another there, and the political atmosphere shifts to a stance which argues that the environment must be sacrificed to the latest *political* difficulty.

The essence of politics is compromise, which hardly assures confidence that environmental concerns will have priority. The same government that limits the liability of private power companies from nuclear accidents under the Price-Anderson Act, and thereby contributes to the proliferation of nuclear power stations like the Diablo operation on the coast of California, is the very *same* government that most environmentalists wish to assign the responsibility of conserving, preserving, and protecting our physical environment. To a degree, fortunately, the environmental movement is coming to recognize the risks associated with government's stewardship of the land and wildlife. Audubon's experience with the Rainey Wildlife Sanctuary is difficult to ignore. Nature Conservancy and Ducks Unlimited have demonstrated their recognition of the importance of private ownership and, therefore, control of valuable wilderness and other environmental treasures.


## LAND CONSERVATION THROUGH PRIVATE ACTION

In spite of the evidence on the undersirable implications of public ownership, the U. S. Congress passed the Federal Land Policy and Management Act of 1976 which declared that "it is the policy of the United States to retain its public lands in Federal ownership." The Act represented the culmination of efforts which began in the Progressive Era of Theodore Roosevelt, and it completely reversed the practice of land disposal to the people dating from the American Revolution. In contrast to the principles embodied in the Homestead Act of 1862, the law now declares that the federal government is to hold stewardship in perpetuity over roughly a third of the land mass of the United States. Given the competition for access to these resources, history suggests that wasteful outcomes and environmental decay will follow. If a renewed commitment to private ownership is to be achieved, and a "moral consensus" for economic progress through private development of resources is to be found, it will happen because the benefits of private property rights are clearly demonstrated.

The phrase "Land Conservation Through Private Action" is the motto of the Nature Conservancy, an environmental organization which has purchased hundreds of thousands of acres of wild and scenic lands. John Baden and Richard Stroup, in their controversial article "A Radical Proposal: Saving the Wilderness," quote a fundraising effort by Nature Conservancy:

> We don't sue or picket or preach. We simply do our best to locate, scientifically, those spots on earth where something wild and rare and beautiful is thriving, or hanging on precariously. Then we buy them. We're good at it. In less than three decades we've acquired--by purchase, gift, easement and various horse trades--Rhode Island, twice over.

Examples of Nature Conservancy owned lands are the 55,000 acres of Santa Cruz Island in the Channel Islands off the southern California coast and the 33,000 acre Virginia Coast Reserve which includes 13 barrier islands stretching 60 miles along a natural seashore on the Atlantic coast. These valuable natural resources are preserved privately without the coercive intervention of government.

Another remarkable example of privatization in the name of wildlife preservation was the purchase many years ago of the land creating the Hawk Mountain Sanctuary in eastern Pennsylvania. Encouraged by government bounties for killing hawks, hunters used to kill hundreds, sometimes thousands, of migrating hawks. The private sanctuary for these birds is now world famous and many visitors gather in the fall to watch thousands of hawks, safe from extinction, migrating down the Appalachian mountain range. As environmentalist Robert J. Smith has observed: "This single piece of private action has probably done more to preserve the birds of prey and change public attitudes than all the subsequent legislation against killing them." As another example, Ducks Unlimited maintains over 1500 water management projects providing over 3 million acres of habitat for waterfowl and other wildlife. While condemned for their interest in hunting by some environmentalists, the fact remains that the rest of us have the opportunity to see and hear the waterfowl preserved by this private effort.

Privatization of resources also resolves the "multiple use" problems traditionally associated with government controlled lands. Preserving the capital value of renewable or nonrenewable resources requries that the profit-oriented capitalist consider the value that consumers and producers place on privately owned property. In light of competing demands on the acreage in the Rainey Wildlife Sanctuary, for example, the Audubon Society wisely perceived that multiple use, determined mostly by market values (i.e., its profitability), could be safely undertaken while avoiding "measureable damage to the marsh." Or, as Baden and Stroup have observed: "The inherent contradiciton between the situation at Rainey and the pleas of environmentalists to maintain an increasing amount of pristine wilderness is sharply defined." The revenues earned from the gas wells and the cattle which graze in the sanctuary are resources the Audubon Society can employ to acquire additional environmental treasures that they in turn can conserve.

## THE COMMON POOL AND FUGITIVE RESOURCE PROBLEMS

Conservation and environmental protection is relatively easy where property rights can be readily established. The tragedy of the commons works its inevitable logic in those circumstances where it has been difficult to enforce, control, and exclude through the use of private property rights. The logic of the commons worked unmercifully toward the near extinction of the Buffalo in the last century, as both the Indian and the white man "hunted" the sad beast. And this in spite of the Plains Indians' respect for their natural environment. Ideology notwithstanding, in the absence of enforceable private claims to particular animals on specific pieces of ground, when dealing with this kind of common pool environment and the fugitive nature of the Buffalo's migrating instinct, each Indian hunter is isolated from the total consequences of his actions. The inevitable outcome in this example was the slaughter of millions of animals, frequently just for the horns or a single cut of meat.

Today, important examples of the common pool problem are the unowned world's oceans and the related fugitive nature of the whales, seals, and other aquatic life which frequently migrate over long distances, making ownership difficult to establish. In the absence of enforceable rights to exclude others, whalers from many nations have exploited the whales close to extinction. The salmon runs in the Pacific Northwest and Alaska exhibit the same unfortunate characteristic of migrating in the great ocean commons. The delicacy of the meat from the green turtle also threatens to disappear, as hunters exploit the animals before their inevitable competitors do. However, the answer isn't a United Nations conference to declare these species as the "common heritage of mankind." The survival of wildlife in the commons depends on the extension of private property rights into the oceans, not on government prohibitions.

Technology now permits the electronic "fencing" of sea life and therefore the establishment of property rights in Abalone or turtles. Bays, inlets, and estuaries can and are being privatized. In the case of migrating animals like whales, the fugitive nature of these species makes it more difficult to establish private property rights. But homesteading, herding, and patroling by boat offers significant prospects for privatization even for the whales. Private efforts on the West coast in breeding salmon and other valuable fish, and the private property rights established in Norway's spawning fish populations, suggest that privatization is indeed the ultimate solution to exploitation and eventual extinction.

Rather than trying to find workable solutions to the commons problem, most environmentalists favor the prohibition of hunting endangered species. Harvesting rare land and sea animals is made a crime, and legal impediments are established against domestication, private trading, farming, and breeding. As the world's sea turtles are found to be either threatened or endangered, a direct consequence of their living in the commons, environmental groups simultaneously attempt to place legal roadblocks in the path of the Cayman Turtle Farm's captive breeding program which is trying to save the green turtle from extinction. This philosophical and emotional rejection of private property and the market economy threatens the very survival of those values which the preservationists wish to sustain. Sadly, the prohibitions on killing these threatened species leads predictably to black markets, illegal raids on the wild populations, smuggling, high prices, and, as night follows day, declining numbers.

In contrast to policing the commons, ultimately the survival of common property resources in the oceans, rivers, jungles, forests, and mountains, including the plant and animal life inhabiting these areas, depends on the extension of private property rights. If not, the logic of the common will work its disasterous ways.

## HOMESTEADING THE PUBLIC DOMAIN

In 1980, more than 760 million acres or 33 percent of the total amount of land in the United States was owned, regulated, or controlled by some agency of the federal government. Including land owned by state and local governments, the state at all levels owns roughly 40 percent of the nation's land. Most of the federal lands are in the western states. For example, 95 percent of Alaska, 86 percent of Nevada, 66 percent of Utah, 64 percent of Idaho, 52 percent of Oregon, 45 percent of Arizona, and 44 percent of California are owned and controlled by the federal government. From the beginning of the Republic, it had been the goal of the American government to dispose of the public lands for economic development by individuals. The crowning achievement of this policy was the Homestead Act of 1862 which opened vast areas of opportunity to the American people.

In 1976, Congress passed the Federal Land Policy and Management

Act (FLPMA) which formally reversed the historic practice of getting potentially productive resources into the hands of people. It explicitly repealed the Homestead Act. Given the growing dependence of the United States on minerals from abroad and the importance of upward economic mobility for the poor, it is imperative that the FLPMA be repealed and that the nation's natural resources be opened to environmentally sound exploration and production. Consistent with environmental safeguards, including the avoidance of pollution through the enforcement of property rights in clean water and air, the public domain must be reopened and transformed in ways which will continue to support the rising material standards of living desired by the overwhelming majority of the American people.

Serious consideration, then, needs to be given to the privatization of the nation's forests and the lands managed by the Bureau of Land Management, the Bureau of Reclamation, and other federal agencies. For twenty years forestry professor Barney Dowdle, at the University of Washington, has made a persuasive case for privatizing the national forests. A proposal by economists Richard Stroup and John Baden of the Center for Political Economy and Natural Resources at Montana State University to sell the national forests to correct for inefficient timber production, environmental costs, and subsidies to private lumber companies under existing arrangements should be adopted. Simultaneously, they see a possible solution to our social security system by using the proceeds from forest privatization to assist in the privatization of the social security retirement program. In an interesting chapter entitled "Timber Beasts, Tree Huggers, and the Old Folks at Home" from their book *Natural Resources*, they have summarized the essence of their proposal:

> We suggest that a realistic solution to the forest productivity problem as well as a major attack on the labor productivity and the Social Security deficit problems would be possible if the national forests were sold. At the same time, the federal Social Security program could be made voluntary, permitting carefully monitored private alternatives. Existing Social Security obligations could be met largely from proceeds from the forest sale. Both the weight of theory and the bulk of available evidence suggest that the interests of those desiring maximum production of material goods from the forests, those concerned with amenities in the environment, and those demanding that we keep promises to older citizens could all be advanced considerably.

In 1981, the Reagan administration proposed selling a portion of the govenment's 107 million acres of timberland, but the plan encountered stiff political opposition. the Sierra Club, for example, labelled the proposal a "master plan for government giveaways." Not surprisingly, important segments of the timber industry also registered their opposition. Subsidies stemming from U.S. Forest Service policy and paid for by the taxpayer are not easily relinquished. Nevertheless, Bruce Ramsey, in his article "Forest Socialism," drawing on the work of Barney Dowdle and other economists, convincingly reminds us that to grow and harvest a commercial crop of trees is much the same as growing commercial crops of wheat, cotton, or grapes. The evidence is overwhelming that privately owned land, where the existing timber can be sold, is managed more intensively and productively than are govenment forests.

Economist Steven Hanke has shown that federal timberlands produce a cash flow deficit of more than $1 billion a year, and the taxpayer picks up the tab. Current estimates are that federal timber lands would generate more than $200 billion of revenue, probably a good deal more, if the sales were judiciously spread over time to avoid a temporary timber surplus. Georgia-Pacific, Weyerhaeuser, and hundreds of small owners would conserve these forests because *it would be in their interest to do so!* The fact is that under existing political control, in the absence of market prices and incentives derived from private ownership, rational "multiple use" policies for competing users are impossible. Decisions are made by government managers as a result of pressure group influences in which powerful minorities with political clout (i.e., environmental groups, ranchers, timber companies) impose higher taxes and more costly homes on the vast majority of the American people. Surely the present system is no way to run a forest.

The so-called "Sage Brush Rebellion" is not the answer with respect to Bureau of Land Management (BLM) lands. It simply proposes to transfer title from federal control to the separate states so that the special interests, generally commercial interests, can more easily get their way. Analogous to the Homestead Act of 1862, BLM lands should be opened to private owners through homesteading. It would be imperative to encourage economically viable acreages (generally much larger than 160 acres in the semi-arid West), and assuredly conservation and wilderness groups could and would homestead some of these lands. The conservation record of the BLM is a sad one, and private ownership, as history invariably demonstrates, produces better results.

Finally, why not think the unthinkable? Given the superiority of private resource management where the manager has a personal stake in the outcome, why not privatize the National Parks, National Wildlife Refuges, and other similar govenment owned resources? Nobel Laureate Milton Friedman made the argument for privatization more than twenty years ago in his powerful book *Capitalism and Freedom*. Robert Smith, Richard Stroup, John Baden, and other natural resource economists maintain that with fee simple title to National Parks, Bird Refuges, and other valuable wilderness areas, the Sierra Club, Wildlife Federation, Audubon Society, and other established environmental groups would necessarily be held accountable for their stewardship and would have to take the costs of *total* nondevelopment into consideration. Stroup and Baden have summarized the environmental and economic implications of privatization:

> It would be especially beneficial if areas with both ecological and economic importance were managed by groups with the expertise to weigh the potential damage to the environment against the potential profits. Making environmental groups owners (residual claimants able to garner any benefits they generate via added resource values) of the holdings would accomplish this end. Under these conditions, it is likely that other environmental interest groups would emulate the Audubon Society on the Rainey Reserve.

Like the multiple use revenues that accrue to the Audubon Society at the Rainey Wildlife Sanctuary, private owners of wilderness areas could generate funds to buy additional wilderness. Economist Edwin Dolan, in his book *TANSTAAFL: The Economic Strategy for Environmental Crisis,* points out that preservationist groups could employ the practice of "excess taking" in which additional land bordering the valued wilderness or scenic area is purchased and in turn helps, through commercial uses, to support the maintenance of the unique sight. Edwin Dolan has identified the benefits this practice might bring to environmental groups wishing to save esthetic values:

> The practice of 'excess taking' [is] frequently used in New England to finance such establishments as ski slopes. If you want 1000 acres to build a ski run, you buy that 1000 acres *and* the adjoining 1000 acres. As soon as the facility is built, the surrounding land is sold off at several times its purchase price as homesites and commercial properties to those who are attracted to the area by the available recreation. Conservationists have spent much time fulminating against speculators and developers, yet isn't it obvious that wherever a park is built, land values will inevitably go up and speculative profits will be made? So why not get a piece of the action and put these profits to work in a good cause?

Robert J. Smith cites the famous resort development at Hilton Head Island in South Carolina as an example of excess taking to maintain environmental preservation. Even Disneyworld in Florida exhibits this process to a degree.

In the name of harmonious reconciliation of esthetic environmental values and material progress, let's put the National Parks and other wilderness areas now "owned" by the federal government into the exclusive control of qualified environmental groups such as the Nature Conservancy or Sierra Club. Competing demands on the Superintendents of the National Parks, political and otherwise, have, as admitted by the National Park Service, produced a decline in the environmental quality of a visit to Yosemite National Park and Yellowstone National Park. Under private ownership, the capitalized value of these national treasures would be maintained. A profit orientation recognizes that there are trade-offs and that the market generates prices which permit us to know the opportunity costs of our choices. Fee simply ownership for qualified preservationist groups would bias the subjective evaluations in the direction of the physical environment and esthetic values.

## POLLUTION AND THE ENVIRONMENT

Pollution is largely the consequence of treating air and water as "free" goods. Similar to the preceding analysis of conservation and wildlife issues, air, rivers, lakes, and oceans are unowned, common property resources used as "sinks" for the disposal of waste and effluents. Businesses and individuals are thus given inappropriate incentives when making cost calculations on the disposal of environmental pollutants. However, as previously observed, this is not a failure of capitalism, but represents a failure to protect individual rights because of an absence of recognizable and enforceable private property rights.

Individuals have inalienable rights to the protection of their lives. Pollution represents an invasion of individual rights, and over the past century and a half, as Morton J. Horwitz documents in his book *The Transformation of American Law, 1780-1860,* human rights to environmental protection have been violated in the name of industrialization, economic progress, and the "public interest." The courts have permitted a deterioration in environmental quality in the name of "progress," yet the blame is inappropriately placed with the profit seeking capitalist. The ultimate solution to the pollution problem is a *restoration* of the common law protections offered by nuisance law, the law of trespass, and the general law of torts. The violation of rights to one's health and property by noxious odors, dangerous chemical, smoke, and excessive noise is a crime and should be protected by access to legal recourse. Robert Poole, Jr. has summarized the rights violating nature of environmental pollution:

> When a factory discharges a great quantity of sulfur dioxide molecules that enter someone's lung and cause pulmonary edema, the factory owners have aggressed against him as much as if they had broken his leg. The point must be emphasized because it is vital to the...laissez-faire position. A laissez-faire polluter is a contradiction in terms and must be identified as such. A libertarian society would be a *full-liability* society, where everyone is fully responsible for his actions and any harmful consequences they might cause.

On a moral basis, individuals have inalienable rights to their lives and property which are not subject to compromise. Justice requires that the emission of harmful chemicals into the air be treated in the same manner as if someone physically attacked another person. Pollution is health or life threatening aggression and therefore violates individual rights.

Essential to the protection of individuals from pollution is the development of private property rights in common pool resources like moving air masses and bodies of water. Because the environment is unowned, pollution is the inevitable consequence. Individuals are motivated by false signals to treat environmental sinks as free disposal sights. Responsible behavior will be encouraged, even required, when property rights in these resources enable individuals to prevent the dumping of effluents. The fact that the market process is *not* at fault is easily verified by the magnitude of *government* caused pollution. Municipal sewage systems, military establishments, and public construction projects continue to be among the most environmentally destructive sources of pollution.

Unfortunately, federal legislation concerning environmental pollution has almost always adopted absolute emission standards rather than taking advantage of the signals generated by self-interest, private property, and the market process. Amendments in 1970 and 1977 to the Clean Air Act of 1963 mandate that the federal government establish and enforce ambient air quality standards and enforce strict emission standards for automobiles. The Water Pollution Control Act of 1956, and amendments, established similar pollution standards for water resources. The government has placed primary reliance on direct regulation of particular sources of pollution. Regulators identify the best available technology for controlling emissions, and then polluters are required to adopt that technology. This approach has proven to be incredibly time consuming and requires government regulators to gather and interpret large quantities of complex information about different kinds of sources and alternative technologies. This direct, source-by-source regulation by standards requires superhuman knowledge of particular circumstances and thus is very inefficient. The gains in environmental quality have been increasingly costly.

Absolute standards for each emission source have been inefficient for a number of reasons. First, the uniform application of source-by-source regulation discourages the reduction of pollutants by the least costly method. It ignores the fact that the cost of reducing emissions at one source will be different than the costs at another source. Therefore, the uniform reduction of pollution, say sulphur dioxide, at all sources fails to minimize the costs of a given reduction in emissions. Yet, to assign by government decree a program of differential pollution reduction by source requires government regulators to have more knowledge of industrial costs and pollution technologies than is available to mortal men and women.

Second, direct standards for all sources discourage innovation in pollution abatement technology. Businesses are discouraged from adopting more cost-effective pollution controls by the bureaucratic redtape associated with replacing the mandated technique under existing standards. It seems probable that the firm's own engineers have the requisite knowledge to adopt innovations in emission controls, especially in comparison with government's outside technical people.

Finally, direct source-by-source standards restrict industrial development and therefore economic progress. Amendments to the Clean Air Act prohibit the construction of new pollution sources in regions which do not satisfy ambient air quality standards. Equal reduction in pollution by all sources restricts the possibilities of voluntarially trading "rights to pollute" and consequently slows the rate of economic advance below that consistent with a particular air quality standard.

As a result of these obvious limitations of past regulation standards, there have been experiments in recent years that relax the direct standards and introduce incentives which make it profitable to control pollution in more efficient ways. Each of these experiments uses the market process. Federal regulators, for example, are experimenting with "bubbles": an entire plant or geographic area is treated as a single pollution source, and within that plant or area managers and firms are free to allocate emission reductions among different sources as long as the quality standard for that bubble is met. However, "Quality standards" should be established at levels consistent with the individual's right to be free to health threatening emissions.

There in now an "offset" program that permits new industrial activity in a region and therefore new emissions if they are *more* than offset by reductions in emissions from existing sources. Offsets not only permit economic development in areas with pollution problems, but also encourage the most efficient reduction in existing effluent sources. Businesses wishing to build in the region are motivated by the urge to maintain profits to obtain their offsets from existing firms with the lower pollution control costs. There is also, as another example, an experiment with an emission "bank" program which extends the possibilities for the offset program. Under the bank program a pollution source which reduces its emission levels below government mandated levels can "bank" those reductions for an offset trade at some future date.

Unfortunately, experiments with these controlled-trading options are more cosmetic than substantive in their effects. Federal regulations continue to rely on source-by-source direct standards which have the undesirable consequences already enumerated. Mandated technologies for particular pollution sources remain in force, and the massive bureaucratic maze remains in place. The basic unwillingness of government regulators and bureaucrats to accept a property rights/market solution to the pollution problem rests, in large part, on the fear that they will be expendable if the market process is permitted to do the job! Environmentalist opposition notwithstanding, the most cost-effective means of dealing with environmental pollution is to establish property rights in pollution or, depending on relative prices, the absence of pollution. Following the lead of J. H. Dales, in his 1968 book *Pollution, Property, and Prices,* a number of economists have shown the potential for a market in rights to pollute.

Air and water quality regions with quality standards would be established by government, persumably *in a manner consistent with individual rights to be free of* noxious gases, chemicals, and the like. Permits would be distributed to pollution sources which authorize the emission of pollutants such that the standards are not exceeded. Firms are free to choose their own pollution control program which, in light of the profit oriented nature of the business, will be the most efficient available. Soruces are permitted to buy and sell permits to meet abatement costs most efficiently. The volume of pollution at a particular source is limited only by the permits it holds. If new industrial firms wish to enter the air quality region, permits must be bid away from existing owners. In a growing region, an excess demand for pollution permits will raise their price and induce some businesses to increase their own control effort and sell permits to new pollution sources.

The market in permits-to-pollute would encourage technological change and innovation in pollution abatement because, potentially, firms could *profit* from the sale of permits to sources of pollution that are less efficient in control efforts. Emissions would be reduced most where it was least costly to do so thereby meeting pollution standards in the most efficient manner. Federal regulations would no longer need to monitor for mandated technologies since the allocation of emission reduction efforts would be handled by the market process. In summary, the market in "pollution permits" automatically, via Adam Smith's "invisible hand," directs polluters to the desired level of emission control by the economically most efficient methods.

Economists propose another variation on the market solution to abatement control: the use of "effluent charges" or taxes on pollution. Effluent fees generate the same kinds of incentives as pollution permits; however, the effluent tax rate must be continually adjusted for changes in the objective facts regarding business expansion and the quality of the air or water. With permits, the market clearing price is automatically determined by the interplay of demand and supply of permits. Once again, less is asked of the government regulator as a result of the efficiency of the market mechanism.

Either effluent fees or a market in permits-to-pollute are preferred to the inefficiencies which have been associated with the direct source-by-source standards approach to environmental control. The essential ingredients in the issue of pollution, and, as it is for resource and wildlife conservation, entail the enforcement of the existing laws of nuisance and trespass to protect people's rights *and* the assignment of private property rights, where possible, to fugitive resources in the commons. If not, the logic of the commons will inevitably produce the tragedy of which Garret Hardin warned.

## THE ENVIRONMENT UNDER SOCIALISM

Capitalism and the profit motivated capitalist are *not* fundamentally to blame for the various classes of environmental decay witnessed on spaceship earth. Indeed, private ownership for profit generates an incredibly powerful incentive to conserve and cultivate resources in order to increase their value to other users. The final documentation of the roll that the commons plays, even when the common pool resource is supposedly protected by the state, is illustrated by the environmental problems encountered by the nations which have committed themselves to government control of almost all resources. Government ownership is no guarantee of environmental purity, and this assertion is easily documented by looking at the actual experiences of the socialist states.

The Soviet Union's record on environmental matters is demonstrably bad. Economists like Marshall I. Goldman, an expert on the Soviet economy, and other scholars have recorded the extent to which environmental issues are neglected in the U.S.S.R. Public ownership of resources has clearly not been for the purpose of protecting the environment. The lakes, seas, and rivers of the Soviet Union have suffered greatly from pollution. The magnificent Lake Baikal in Siberia, treated as part of the commons, is being destroyed. Both the Aral and Caspian Seas are despoiled by the rivers which are, for all practical purposes, open sewers. Hydroelectric projects and massive irrigation have produced declining water levels and increased salinity. Even the mighty sturgeon is threatened, causing a precipitious decrease in caviar production. Their rivers are treated as dumpsters for industrial effluents and municipal sewage. The result is massive fish kills. The air pollution situation is comparatively better primarily because the autombile is so scarce. However, as Robert J. Smith observes in his survey of pollution in the Soviet Union, "...clean air through poverty is hardly praiseworthy!"

The situation with respect to conservation and wilderness is even worse. The Soviet Union, according to Robert Smith, "...has the lowest percentage of total land set aside for preserves and parks of any developed country in the world." The fundamental point involves the implications of government ownership of land and other resources when government's objective is industrial development and not preservation of the environment. The same government that in the United States is asked to conserve and protect the environment is essentially the same state apparatus which exploits the environment unmercifully in the name of economic progress in the Soviet Union. Ultimately, the environment is safe only if it is held in fee simple ownership by individuals who have the *private* property right to exclude unwanted users. The "power" referred to in the following quotation from Marshall Goldman's book *The Spoils of Progress:*

*Environmental Pollution in the Soviet Union* stems in the final analysis from the enforcement of private property rights.

In the Soviet government's drive toward industrialization and economic growth all too often there has been no person or group around with any power to stand up for protection of the environment. Until the point is reached when environmental disruption causes other state interests, especially manufacturing and agriculture, to lose as much as those in favor of greater exploitation of the environment stand to gain, environmental quality in the U.S.S.R. is in a very fragile condition.

The evidence is the same everywhere. In the People's Republic of China and the rest of Eastern Europe, as well as the Soviet Union, wherever government ownership of the means of production is the characteristic mode of economic organization and wherever totalitarian political regimes control events, the very idea of an environmental movement separate from the state is out of the question. So much for government and the political establishment as guardians of posterity and future generations! It is our conviction that the best hope for the long run conservation of natural resources and the environment rests with privatization and the enforcement of private property rights in a free-market setting.

# CHAPTER 21

## PRIVATIZING LOCAL SERVICES

It is time to disabuse ourselves of the notion that local governments are somehow 'better' than the more visibly obnoxious state and federal levels. Coercive local government, by design and by failure, is responsible for fostering and managing, but seldom *resolving*, the conflicts which we perceive as 'local problems'.

--William D. Burt

While public attention has been riveted on the rapid growth in federal spending and the growing involvement of the federal government in our individual lives, we must also recognize the explosive growth in state and local government. The taxpayers in California in 1978 finally indicated through Proposition 13 that enough was enough; and the California revolt was not an isolated phenomenon. For example, in 1979 twenty-two states cut property taxes, eighteen states cut income taxes, fifteen states reduced the sales tax, and eight states adopted spending limits of one kind or another. This nationwide rebellion followed a very rapid growth in the size of state and local governments and the taxes required to finance that growth. Although federal employment increased by 19 percent between 1960 and 1975, the number of local government employees increased by 114 percent during the same period. In fiscal year 1980 total state and local government expenditures reached $434 billion, almost *triple* what they had been just a decade before. In the decade ending in fiscal year 1980 property taxes had doubled, sales taxes had almost tripled, and individual income taxes at the state and local level had quadrupled! The most startling increase, however, in state and local revenues represented the transfer of federal tax revenues to state and local government. Similarly, state taxes were being transferred to the local level. In fiscal year 1970, for example federal intergovernmental transfers amounted to about $22 billion. By 1980, these revenues to state and local governments had reached $83 billion, a level four times higher than just ten years earlier. As Robert Poole, Jr., observed in his book *Cutting Back City Hall*, ordinary citizens want change: "...it means an end to business as usual for local governments." Unfortunately, in the early 1980's a number of states have once again started raising tax rates.

The irony in the explosive growth of state and local government spending over the past few decades is the simultaneous discovery, through numerous scholarly investigations, that the provision of goods and services by government is quite inefficient when compared to private market solutions. As a delivery system for what people want, state and local government bureaus, offices, and agencies have done a poor job. It is not a question of just trimming the "fat," but rather it involves a willingness to entertain a "mood of experientation" in which we recognize the importance of cutting the "lean" out of government. Government provision of goods and services is not only economically inefficient, but it also requires the police power of the state to collect the money needed to pay for its "free" services. Relying on the important studies of Robert Poole, William D. Burt, E.S. Savas, and others, we will show both from efficiency and equity considerations, that the privatization of local government services is desirable. Unfortunately, many people simply take for granted that municipal services must be government's responsibility. Although change is always controversial, we believe that there are peaceful solutions to local issues which bypass forceable government taxation. Nevertheless, progress will probably be slow. As the great socialogist Herbert Spencer reminded us in *Social Statics:* "...in the majority of men, there is such a love of tried arrangements, and so great a dread of experiments, that they will probably not act upon this right until long after it is safe to do so." Slow or not, the agenda is quite clear.

## PUBLIC OR PRIVATE: CUTTING BACK CITY HALL

Repeatedly we have emphasized the fundamental distinction between the "political means" and the "market means." The market means, which is to say the competitive market process, is characterized by a "selective access" to goods and services. That is, if an individual wishes to have a pair of shoes or see a movie, the person must provide something in exchange. In contrast, when goods or services are provided by government, "equal access" is usually guaranteed. The direct, out-of-pocket cost of using municipal tennis courts, public libraries, highways, neighborhood police patrols, or the city park is zero. The good or service is provided "free" to all comers, and the cost is covered by the taxpayer. Those who "use" seldom have to pay, and those who pay often do not use. No attempt is made to match benefits and costs. In the case of the market place, however, the benefits of a new stereo album or a new dress are tied directly to a purchase price or the potential consumer is excluded from the enjoyment of that good.

Providing something for "free" has another important implication. Inevitably, it means cross-subsidization. Those who use the city parks or the municipal transit system are subsidized by those who pay their local taxes but use and financially support a private park or drive their automobile to work. The gross mismatching of consumer benefits and tax costs in these situations generates both an efficiency and equity argument in favor of a system in which those who benefit from a service should be those who pay for it. In the following discussion of private alternatives to government provision of local services, it is crucial that beneficiaries be identified and appropriately charged for the service provided. The fundamental issue, after all, is freedom of choice. Individuals must be permitted to choose the services they want and therefore determine the ways in which they wish to spend their money.

This is not to suggest an immediate and wholesale curtailment of the services currently provided largely by state and local government. It is, however, a plea for the privatization of most of these services to achieve economic efficiency and fairness. Where possible, selective access to goods and services should be of highest priority, and individuals should pay for the benefits they receive. Given the inherent inefficiency of government operated businesses, a point we have already made, privatization should be considered when beneficiaries can be identifed. Even in those situations which suggest government may continue to be involved (for example, police protection and municipal courts) local government should begin to implement "user fees."

An unfortunate limitation in providing things for "free" (i.e., equal access for everyone) is the false economic information given to the elected officials concerning the intensity of demand for municipal services. The function of price is to ration goods, services and resources. Most people would prefer to drive a Mercedes until they see its sticker price. A $30,000 price tag convinces them a Ford or Honda will do. Price not only measures the cost of acquisition, but it also indicates the intensity of demand. Goods and services provided "free" encourage "wasteful consumption." Grocers would hardly be astounded to see their shelves emptied quickly if food prices were zero. Yet, government officials are quick to ask for larger budgets, whether for bridges, highways, education, tennis courts, or whatever, citing the "intense demand" or "need" for the good or service in question. Providing things "free" will always encourage people to want more.

Rather than business as usual with respect to the growth of local government, the analysis which follows proposes an agenda which, through privatization, will stop the upward trend in local government spending and, with time, reduce the burden of state and local taxes.

## URBAN TRANSPORTATION

The history of government involvement in transporting people within metropolitan areas vividly illustrates the failure of the political means. Most of the urban areas in the United States are currently limited to two kinds of transportation: large 50-plus passenger buses and an exclusive taxi-cab service. There are a few cities with heavy

305

rail mass transit (for example, New York and Chicago), but they represent the exception. Other technologies are by and large outlawed by local ordinance. A past chief of federal mass-transit and manager of the Washington, D.C., Metro System, Richard Page, agrees that "...we need public transportation and whoever can offer it in the most efficient way ought to provide the service, whether it's a transit system, private firms, local government, or inter-city bus lines." Although he recognizes the growing interest in "para-transit" in the form of vans, jitneys, and taxi-cab sharing, and is supposedly interested in competition, Mr. Page was opposed to the Reagan administration's plan to gradually eliminate federal operating subsidies for mass transit. Why? Because, "...it is too important to too many communities." In the same *Wall Street Journal* article, Page is quoted as being pleased about "...what's come on the books in the way of tax support for transit in the last 10 years." His enthusiasm for tax finance is understandable. The Metro System in Washington, D.C., will cover, at most, about 45 percent of the systems' operating expenses from rider fares. Here is an example of one of the most respected administrators of public transportation in the United States who continues to believe that urban common carrier transportation *must* be a losing proposition and, therefore, should be run by government and subsidized by the taxpayer.

Federal government largess to provide up to 50 percent of a transit company's operating costs stems from fares well below the cost of service and hence produces large operating deficits. In 1975, for example, capital grants totaled $1.28 billion and operating grants about $140 million. But by 1981 these numbers had skyrocketed to nearly $3 billion and $1.1 billion respectively. In other words, local mass transit is made to appear inexpensive to local politicians. According to Gerald Miller, acting director of the transportation program at the Urban Institute, a Washington, D.C., based think tank, "...you can put up a couple of hundred million dollars and get billions back." Baltimore received $640 million from the federal government for the $800 million cost of their system's initial eight mile leg. Atlanta, unbelievably, received nearly $1 billion in federal planning and capital assistance for the Metropolitan Atlanta Rapid Transit System. And, the 55 percent *operating* subsidization of the District of Columbia's transit system totaled almost $61 million in 1983 alone. Public transportation for the relatively few who use it costs taxpayers billions (half a billion in Pittsburgh, another half billion in Buffalo, $300 million in Portland, and $200 million in Miami). Or, repeating Senator Everett Dirksen's famous comment: " A billion dollars here and a billion dollars there adds up to real money."

Urban transportation systems, however, do not need to be owned and operated by government. And more importantly, there is every reason to believe that the competitive market process can generate viable, efficient, and *profitable* private transportation networks

306

in our cities.

Had it not been for past government intervention in the business of transporting people across urban areas, the United States would quite likely have an efficient private transportation system. During the last two decades of the nineteenth century, the electric streetcar was developed. By the turn of the century this electrically powered machine was nearly universal in America's cities. Systems were consolidated to take advantage of the efficiencies associated with the central generating plant for the production of electricity. Electric railway systems were quite profitable through World War I. However, ridership began to fall in the 1920's due in part to the appearance of the inexpensive family automobile and the improvement in roads. As transit company charges for the electric transit system were generally flat rates, regardless of the distance traveled, short-haul passengers were in fact subsidizing long distance riders. Comparable to the practice of subsidizing local calls by maintaining an artificially high price for long distance telephone service, there appeared a growing competition for the short-haul streetcar business. Given the relatively high fares for the shorter ride on the electric railways, which were subsidizing the riders going to the growing suburbs, the "jitney" became a viable substitute form of transportation.

The jitney, a word meaning nickel or the price of a ride, is an automobile, van, or small bus employed either part-time or full-time to transport people in urban areas. By World War I, and before government restrictions were imposed against them, there were 60,000 jitneys on the city streets of America. Unfortunately for the future of urban transportation, a momentous decision outlawing the jitney was made by local governments, mostly at the behest of the electric streetcar companies. As reported by William Burt in his analysis of this issue, "...the response of local governments at this crucial junction set the mold for much of our modern urban transportation." This economically viable, relatively inexpensive, and convenient service was eliminated in favor of fixed route electric rail systems. The American people were literally forced to choose the private automobile as an alternative to streetcars and, later, large buses.

The railway and bus systems began a decline which continues to this day. Barriers erected by municipal government to suppress competition for the fixed route systems were not enough. The rigid rail systems, according to economist George Hilton, "...produced an organization so inferior to the automobile in speed and comfort that the transit monoplies could only decline." The results are clearly visible. In 1955, fourteen percent of urban travel was still by streetcar, bus, and subway. By 1979, the figure had fallen to just four percent. The industry's *Transit Fact Book* reported a few years ago the inevitable result under existing arrangements: "The private transit company is today all but extinct."

Local governments have, through their police power of licensing and granting of franchises, prevented a smooth integration of the various technologies which are available. Small towns, large cities, and most urban places in the United States have restricted consumer alternatives to just two: the large bus on high-density fixed routes and the taxi-cab which in almost all cases is precluded by law from carrying riders with multiple destinations.

Fortunately, most of the world, especially the less developed countries, have recognized the viability and flexibility of the so-called "para-transit" systems. In their book *Free Enterprise Urban Transportation,* Gabriel Roth and George Wynne document the socially beneficial results of the competitive market process in urban transportation. They describe systems of "informal public transport" which offer low-cost, frequent, and reliable transportation. It turns out, not surprisingly, that the viable system centers around the jitney.

The success of these private systems for profit, Roth tells us in a summary of this issue in *Reason* magazine, depends on the existence of four factors. First, private ownership and the profit motive encourages cost cutting and efficient operation. In Australia where private bus systems are quite numerous, unit costs for private firms are substantially lower than those of the public companies. The ratio of total employees to buses owned is 1.0-1.5 for private bus companies, and 2.0-2.5 for the government owned firms.

Second, the private transportation firms frequently operate smaller vehicles which seem to have lower total costs per seat, contrary to the arguments one hears for larger vehicles due to high labor costs. Roth cites the example of San Juan, Puerto Rico, where a 17-seat minibus purchased from a mass-production assembly line costs $17,000, in contrast to a full-size bus with 50 seats costing $140,000. Furthermore, if one takes into consideration the quality of the service being offered to the consumer, which a private firm would of course have to do, the smaller vehicles provide more frequent service and, therefore, less waiting time.

A third factor contributing to the success of para-transit is the size of the firm. The jitney and shared taxi-cabs of Ethiopia, Nairobi, Kenya, Bangkok, Thailand, Kuala Lumpur, Malaysia, etc., are frequently one vehicle companies. Although the evidence is admittedly mixed on the effect of fleet size on efficiency, there is an abundance of evidence that small owner-operators of mini-buses and jitneys can and do earn profits in circumstances where large bus fleets incur losses.

The final factor contributing to the success of the "informal public transport" systems involves voluntary arrangements in which small owners form cooperative ventures to insure reliable service over a broad area. "Route associations" are formed that assist in providing schedules and frequency of service which the consumer can anticipate will be delivered as promised.

Given the evidence concerning the viability of private transit alternatives in urban areas, why do city governments continue to suppress these para-transit alternatives? Burt, Hilton, Poole, Roth, and the others who have studied the issue tend to agree on three factors. First, there seems to be an unbreakable political attachment to cross-subsidization. Poliliticians and special interest groups in a natural alliance continue to subsidize one class of customers by taking money from the pockets of others. Just as profitable long distance air travel was forced under the authority of the Civil Aeronautics Board to subsidize the short-haul traveler, municipal governments force "good" bus routes to subsidize low volume routes.

A second factor contributing to the status quo pertains to entrenched interest groups who currently profit from government monopoly transit systems. Wage levels are notoriously high in many government operated municipal transit systems when compared with similar work in the private sector. In New York City, for example, transit workers earn $16 per hour with very attractive fringe benefits. Competition would of course mean the end of these inflated wage schedules. Taxi-cab drivers, in turn, also oppose the entry of jitneys, vans, or provisions for shared taxi-cabs because of the monopoly position they too enjoy. Roth suggests the efficiency gains associated with a competitive environment in urban transportation are probably great enough to temporarily compensate government workers as the transition towards a free market is made. Naturally, the driver and operator unions of existing monopoly franchise systems are unalterably opposed to such open competition. And third, the inertia for no change stems in part from the power held by local politicians with respect to the granting of a franchise. The status and power of those issuing licenses and charged with running the local transit monopoly are naturally resistant to proposals suggesting they are unnecessary.

Unfortunately, the situation in many cities seems to be getting worse. Rather than decentralizing and moving toward an open and competitive urban transportation network of jitneys, vans, and shared taxis, a number of large American cities are buying, via higher tax burdens, extremely expensive fixed rail systems. Believing federal monies to be free, like manna from heaven, Los Angeles, Washington, D.C., and other cities are choosing to emulate (attracted largely by the prospect of federal tax monies) the massively inefficient BART system (Bay Area Rapid Transit) in San Francisco. The Los Angeles system is especially revealing. Given the sprawling nature of the city, the proposed 18.6 mile heavy rail system in Los Angeles will be horrendously expensive and, in the end, transport an insignificant fraction of metorpolitan commuters. The heavy rail system in the nation's capital is equally expensive.

However, there is hope. The people of Harris County, Texas,

(Houston) in June, 1983, rejected by a two to one margin a $2.35 billion bond issue proposed by the area's Metropolitan Transit Authority. Perhaps its defeat was in part a protest against the local transit board purchasing $139 million worth of Japanese rail cars three months before the bond issue vote. Most of the money was to be used for an 18.2 mile heavy rail system of mass transit in the Houston area. Like Los Angeles, Houston has a relatively low population density in comparison with the cities of New York or even Washington, D.C., While the project had estimated costs of $200 million per mile of track, calculations of ridership have been highly inflated. In spite of the low population density, the planners optimistically estimated that by the turn of the century the Houston rail system would be carrying more passengers than any heavy rail system in the United States except New York. But transit experts generally agree that heavy-rail systems are viable only in metropolitan areas with high population densities. In Houston even a traditional bus system with special bus lanes would cost only one-tenth the per mile cost of the proposed rail system. The record is clear. The BART system in San Francisco has simply not made a dent in the transportation congestion in the San Francisco bay area. There is little reason to believe that any of the new systems will be any different. We do know, however, that the burden on the taxpayer will be great.

## EMERGENCY SERVICES

Although fire protection and emergency medical services are deemed "public safety" issues, the benefits nevertheless accrue to specific individuals. The notion that fire protection is a "public good" and, therefore, must be provided by a municipal monopoly dies hard. Nevertheless, change is coming, and the special interests which currently benefit from the absence of competition will have to face reality. Police chief Charles Monzillo of Willimantic, Connecticut, participant in a controversial attempt to privatize the city's fire department, recognizes that private fire fighting companies "...are reputable concerns who claim they can give the same or better level of services than communities now have, at less cost." Unless municipal fire departments cut costs and increase efficiency, the emergence of private fire departments will be common.

In Januray, 1982, a number of firms got together in Las Vegas to form the Private Sector Fire Association. The purpose was to coordinate their efforts in order to convince local governments that privatization, either through contracting or subscription service, of fire and emergency services costs less, is more efficient, is conducive to the rapid introduction of new technologies, and is equally capable of minimizing fire damge. One study by the Institute for Local Self

310

Government in 1976 compared the private fire protection in Scottsdale, Arizona, with the municipal fire companies in the comparable cities of Glendale, Mesa, and Tempe, Arizona. In terms of engine response time, fire insurance rates, and average annual fire loss, the private department in Scottsdale performed as well as the government fire departments. At the same time, per capita costs in Scottsdale averaged only $6.48 over the period 1971-75, roughly half as much as in Glendale ($12.62), Mesa ($11.43), and Tempe ($10.68)!

At the Valley Fire Service, a privately owned company, in the suburban and rural areas around the city of Grants Pass, Oregon, the ratio of property value lost to the total insured value of property was 3.3 percent, compared with a statewide average of 8.5 percent. At the same time Valley Fire Service's cost per household is only about one-fifth as much as nearby government operated fire departments. In 1982, Wackenhut Services, Inc., a Florida based company, made a bid on the provision of fire protection in Willimantic, Connecticut, which promised to save the town $1.4 million over a five year contract. Private fire companies are saving the taxpayer money in a number of other states including Tennessee, Georgia, Illinois, and Montana. In California some of the benefits of privatization are realized through contracting for fire and emergency services with other governmental units (the so-called "Lakewood Plan").

Lower costs are also achieved by the private companies through the use of part-time and volunteer fire fighters in lieu of full-time people. For example, in the mid-1970's Scottsdale's private fire department employed 41 full-time firefighters in comparison with the national average of 118 full-time fire department employees for cities the size of Scottsdale. In addition, the private firms have been more innovative in the positioning of facilities and the introduction of new equipment. The "mini-pumper" was introduced by the Rural/Metro Fire Department, Inc. of Arizona. They also increased the rate at which water could be applied to a fire by replacing the standard two-and-one-half inch hose with a four-inch plastic hose. And, further, they introduced a custom designed pumper truck which, because of a portable water-pump module, is literally two pumpers in one. The essential point is that private-for-profit organizations have direct and immediate incentives to cut costs. As the CEO of Rural/Metro in Arizona has bluntly pointed out: "We have the greatest incentive in the world to innovate, to pioneer, to analyze every little step: sheer survival."

Not surprisingly, the most vociferous opposition to private fire departments comes from the organized fire fighters union. The International Association of Fire Fighters (IAFF) has demonstrated its willingness to take any measures necessary to prevent the erosion of their monopoly power in the government run fire departments. Jim Peron's study traced the confrontation between city governments and the fire fighters union in two New England towns. As a result of extremely expensive government fire departments--the price for fire protection in one of these towns was roughly $180 per household--as compared to private fire service subscriptions of $30-50 per household. Both Willimantic, Connecticut, and Dover, New Hampshire, requested private sector bids on the provision of fire protection in their communities. In both situations Wackenhut Services, Inc. made the winning bid, and the respective city councils were quite sympathetic to privatizing their fire services.

However, in both cases the International Association of Fire Fighters used intimidation, violence, and an appeal to the legislative power of state government to prevent unwanted competition. They argued it was "union busting," and the president of the IAFF local in Willimantic railed that private fire protection could "...like a cancer, spread all the way through the state of Connecticut..." if it wasn't stopped. The city of Dover, New Hampshire, through the efforts of its city manager Robert Steele, was already a leader in contracting local services to private operators. Privatization of the fire department was the next logical step after contracting with private firms for custodial services, garbage collection, data processing, heavy equipment work, and some snow hauling. The fire chief in Dover, David Bibber, found to his great surprise that "...it was a viable alternative for the city." Costs were out of control in the government department. According to the chief: "We're a monopoly...and something has to be done." Service was scheduled to begin in Dover by the Wackenhut people in late 1983, but uncertainty as to implementation remains because of the violent opposition of the fire fighters union.

If the efficiency gains are so obvious, why has privatization gone so slow? The answer, as we have already suggested, lies with the power and militancy of the monopoly labor union which represents municipal fire fighters. The Bureau of Labor Statistics in Washington, D.C., reported that during the period 1975-80 an average of twelve fire-fighter strikes per year were called by the union. In 1977, striking fire fighters in Dayton, Ohio watched twenty-two fires burn without lifting a finger, despite a state law prohibiting strikes by public employees. The *New York Times* reported in 1981 that members of the fire fighters union on strike in Yonkers, New York, actually physically harassed volunteers attempting to put out fires. Interestingly, during the strike, false alarms and reports of arson increased dramatically. Fire chief David Bibber's summary of the essential dilemma was recorded in Jim Peron's story: "I can understand the feelings of the fire fighters. The fire service is as traditional as apple pie and motherhood." On the other hand, Chief Bibber recognized that the demonstrated efficiency of private fire fighting companies is incontrovertible! The ultimate case for privatization is reflected in the example of the privately owned Falck Company in Denmark which, for close to eighty years, has provided fire protection, ambulance, and other emergency services to approximately half the Danish

312

people.

Stimulated by the excitement and glamour of emergency medical service by paramedics and motivated by the availability of "free" federal grant monies, many local governments have rushed into the rescue ambulance business. Indeed, trained paramedics have demonstrated their value in emergency situations. Nevertheless, the expense of emergency vehicle programs invites the obvious question of who should pay. More often than not the emergency ambulance units are assigned to the municipal fire department and are financed from local and/or federal taxes. As expected, the fire fighter union has welcomed this increased responsibility which requires more money and more people. Yet, there is little justification for paramedic services to be provided through tax supported government programs. The private sector has demonstrated an ability to provide emergency medical services at a significantly lower cost. Robert Poole in *Cutting Back City Hall* reports on a study by the Illinois Department of Transportation which indicated that the costs associated with private paramedic services are, on average, about *half* that of government operated services. The Ambulance Medical Service Association of America found the cost of private service to be only one-third as high as the government service.

There are at least four alternatives to government-run and tax-supported emergency medical sevices. They are: subscription services, volunteer services, fee services, and contract services. An example of subscription medical emergency service is that of the Falck Company in Denmark. Most Danish cities contract with Falck for ambulance service, but by subscription can also purchase more extensive emergency services. In Louisiana, residents in nine parishes (counties) subscribe to the Acadian Ambulance Service. Another example of subscription emergency medical service is found in Oklahoma where the Central Oklahoma Ambulance Trust and the Emergency Medical Services of Central Oklahoma combine to provide emergency paramedical service to Oklahoma City and a surrounding four-county region. Services are provided to non-subscribers for a fee. While partially supported by government monies, the Oklahoma operation remains mostly user-financed.

The Bethesda/Chevy Chase Rescue Squad, Inc. represents an important example of a volunteer ambulance service. Serving the northern end of the District of Columbia and Bethesda and Chevy Chase, Maryland, the volunteer system provides reliable and efficient emergency services. In spite of the rigorous training, there is always a waiting list for those who wish to volunteer their time and service. Services are provided free, and they are financed by the volunteer workers plus an annual fund raising drive. Many local governments contract with private firms for emergency services, and the resulting competition is an improvement on government run systems.

In summary, fire and medical emergency services can be provided

313

in urban and rural areas across the United States far cheaper than they have traditionally been provided by government owned and operated units. In fact, the problem is particularly relevant in large urban areas because in rural and small town America the overwhelming majority of fire fighting units and other services remain voluntary and, therefore, are not supported by government taxes. These voluntary organizations are consistent with the underlying case for privatization: the immorality of forcing individuals, through taxation, to support services they either don't want or that could be provided at less cost by the private sector. The general case for privatization rests on the proposition that freedom of choice is important.

## SOLID WASTE DISPOSAL

There are many other goods and services traditionally provided by municipal governments which can be, indeed are being, provided at lower cost by private firms that are under the pressures of the market place. Solid waste disposal by local government was, according to economist E. S. Savas, found to be at least 68 percent more expensive than private contracting. Sava's research, to illustrate the potential savings of private contracting, found absenteeism less, labor requirements lower, households served per shift greater, and time spent servicing each customer lower than for the government operated system. Another study in 1971 found that private collectors in New York City could pickup garbage for $17.50 per ton compared with the city's cost at that time of $49 per ton. William Burt, in his *Local Problems: Libertarian Solutions,* reported that collection costs for the City Sanitation Department in New York were $207 for twice-a-week service, while a few miles away in a similar neighborhood a private firm was picking up the garbage three times a week for just $72. Comparable service in San Francisco by private contracting firms was $40 per household in 1975. In San Francisco, one of the private waste disposal companies, Golden Gate Disposal Company, reported that their employees ''...actually run at the job...They have a route to cover, and the faster they can cover it, the earlier they can quit.''

Garbage collection is potentially a highly competitive business. While many American municipalities are contracting the collection function to private companies, the ultimate objective should be complete privatization. Government franchise and the municipal contract have generally lowered costs, but they have precluded the competitive process from working even more efficiently. Savas' study suggested that open competition would produce optimum size service areas of about 50,000 people. Municipal governments have, through territorial franchises, prevented these scale economies from being achieved and have prevented competition in larger metropolitan areas. He found, for example, that private collection firms restricted to suboptimal size were 34 percent more expensive than the optimal size.

Fortunately, progress is being made in the privatization of waste disposal. The garbage business is big business. The largest waste disposal firm in the nation is Browning-Ferris Industries in Houston, Texas. It operates collection firms in more than 100 towns and cities in the United States. Other large disposal companies include Waste Management, Inc., in Oak Brook, Illinois, and Boston's SCA Services, Inc. These private firms have pioneered in the utilization of modern trucks whith save on labor requirements, have introduced important productivity incentives for workers, and have introduced efficient management techniques. All this in the name of profit. The private firm faces a structure of incentives which demands efficient operation and lower costs. The end result for citizens, of course, is lighter tax burdens.

Private waste disposal firms offer the additional advantage of being alert to new technologies in the disposal process. These include such innovative ideas as burning refuse for the generation of electricity and heat. However, the tax-subsidized municipal "dump" threatens to discourage or even prevent the profitable application of new ways of dealing with the garbage problem. The local dumping subsidy in effect taxes alternative private sector solutions to the disposal problem. Savas found that 58 percent of the counties in his sample used general funds as the main source of capital funds for local landfills. Further, operating expenditures at municipal landfills were subsidized by general tax revenues in 56 percent of the counties. Given these tax supported subsidies of the local dump, recycling of solid waste remains needlessly expensive. According to William Burt, "...as long as most solid waste goes to a site where it is randomly mixed with incompatible elements, it will remain next to useless--instead of the valuable resource it could be." Local governments should get out of the municipal waste business.

## OTHER MUNICIPAL SERVICES

Partly a result of historical accident and partly at the urging of special interests who stand to profit personally, city and county governments continue to provide numerous leisure and recreational services, including tennis courts, libraries, museums, golf courses, auditoriums, parks, and many others. Invariably these facilities are offered to the public under an equal access provision without a direct payment. Yet, given the existence of specific and readily identifiable beneficiaries of these services, providing them "free" of charge is both inefficient and inequitable. As many researchers have pointed out, none of these goods and services are public goods in the sense

315

that would require equal access for everyone. The restoration of economic freedom requires that services currently being provided to special interests at taxpayers expense be made self-supporting whenever possible. The private provision of leisure and recreation activities by the free market, or at the very least utilizing full payment through charges when government is the provider, can be counted on to lower costs and eliminate the inequities associated with taxpayer financing.

Municipal tennis courts should be privatized or at the very least be provided to beneficiaries who pay the appropriate user charge. Santa Barbara, California, and a number of other local governments have either contracted the operation of tennis courts to the private sector or imposed user fees for those who actually play. In 1978, California's Proposition 13, which mandated lower property taxes, contributed importantly to an increased recognition of the fiscal value of fees for services rendered.

The "public library" in most communities is tax financed in the name of equal access and the importance attached to "free" public libraries. The fact of the matter is that the public library represents a significant subsidy to a very select group. Since libraries provide services to readily identifiable users, there is no reason why, on both efficiency and equity grounds, those who use the library should not pay for that service. In a study by economist Lawrence J. White for the Twentieth Century Fund, it was determined that only 30 percent of the adult population in the U. S. makes use of public libraries, and one-fourth of that select group accounts for three-fourths of adult use. Not surprisingly, the frequant users of the public library are more than proportionately represented by higher income, white collar individuals. The most elementary concept of justice would suggest that these beneficiary groups should pay for the services rendered to them. Where is the fairness in a system that provides higher income families a service "free" but is paid for out of sales and property taxes collected in large part from the poor and middle class?

Similarly, municipal and state museums have specific beneficiaries, and those individuals should also be charged for that use. An interesting example of a pay-as-you-go success is the Oregon Museum of Science and Industry in Portland which is entirely self-supporting. An increasing number of museums all over the country are operating in-house retail outlets whose profits are used to support the museum's exhibits. An additional advantage of pricing these services is the role that prices play in providing information to the local government regarding the demand for the service in question. When local services are provided "free" to the public, there is no way to ascertain the appropriate amount to be produced. Congestion costs are frequently generated, efficiency lags, and local governments are forever overestimating the value the community places on additional amounts of particular services.

Even city parks need not be provided at taxpayer's expense. Urban parks across the United States are being privitized in response to the high and rising cost of government. Because of the budget stringency brought about by the tax revolt in California in 1978, Oakland, California, introduced an "adopt-a-park" program. Kaiser Aluminum and Chemical Corportion, Atlantic-Richfield Company, and other firms took up the challenge. Municipal golf courses are also being contracted to the private sector, and recreation user fees are being utilized to a much greater extent. Given the growth of tax burdens in recent years, local governments are making use of entrance fees to parks, zoos, beaches, and campgrounds; rental fees for sporting equipment; user fees for picnic areas; and permit fees for access to hunting and fishing areas. Enormous potential also exists for spot checking services which have an admission fee. Like many bus and trolley systems in the cities of Europe, spot checking can be used to deter the use of a facility without the appropriate permit. The potential for privatization and user fees is large indeed.

An important argument made by those wanting "free" services is that equal access facilitates provision for the poor. However, the notion that a good or service should be made available without charge to everyone so that the poor would have access is economically inefficient and morally absurd. If the poor cannot afford the museum, the zoo, the tennis courts, the library, or whatever, clearly it would be preferrable to attack the problem directly. Means are available to reduce the impact on low income groups for those services the community somehow decides ought to be available to all citizens. Fees, for example, could be waived on particular services on an individual basis. Differential fee structures might be utilized or admission could be tied to a work activity in exchange for admission. Private charity by individual citizens, businesses, service clubs, or churches could also subsidize programs designed to gain admission for lower income groups. These and other kinds of programs would deal with the poverty question directly and avoid the inefficiencies and inequities created by the "free" provision of valuable services. Wherever possible access should be selective and rationed by the imposition of the cost of admission. There is little moral justification for having all taxpayers subsidize special interest group activities.

There are also many other areas where the competitive market process would bring important benefits. Government contracts with the private sector for services like data processing and the cleaning and maintenance of city and county buildings are examples which promise lower costs. Consideration should also be given to the private provision of water and sewers. Economies from market alternatives in the prevention of crime and the apprehension of criminals promise to improve efficiency and lower costs. Police departments, like municipal fire departments, are in need of "mood of experimentation." Needless to say, local governments should not be adding to their responsibilities. Government building codes have increased the costs of new buildings, as new construction technologies have been suppressed. Land use legislation and zoning laws should, following the recommendations of law professor Bernard Siegen, be significantly relaxed if not repealed. Houston, Texas, with a minimum of planning and zoning is just as habitable as Dallas, Texas, with its comprehensive *and* expensive planning and zoning bureaucracy.

Space precludes dealing with the many other experiments in privatizing local government activities. The studies of Robert Poole, E. S. Savas, and William Burt, among others, detail many of the private alternatives. The evidence is universally the same. When government acts as a producer of "free" goods, costs are high, incentives for efficient operation are generally missing, and innovation and new technologies are suppressed. Furthermore, under existing arrangements, the distribution of tax burdens to pay for these goods and services falls heavily on the poor and those who do not benefit; not exactly an equitable outcome.

## LOCAL SUBSIDY OF INDUSTRY

In recent years local governments have entered another area: the issuance of tax-exempt bonds to mainly subsidize industry and housing. Here again the distributional problems are significant. Specific groups benefit while the general taxpayer loses. In the last decade or so the volume of tax-exempt bonds has more than tripled. John E. Chapoton, an assistant Treasury Secretary, during 1983 told a congressional committee that "...since 1979, over one-half of all long-term tax-exempt bonds issued have been for the direct benefit of private businesses, organizations, or individuals, rather than for use..." by local governments. He continued, that these bonds are simply "...a backdoor means of obtaining federal subsidies." And to the extent the federal government loses tax revenues (the municipal bonds are not subject to federal taxes), individual tax burdens are higher than they otherwise would be. It is interesting that some of the more enthusiastic supporters of the rights of local governments in this matter are the bond dealers and underwriters who have profited from the expanded sales of these bonds. Like the proponents of free public libraries, free tennis courts, and highly subsidized urban transportation, special interests actively lobby for the tax-exempt bonds which subsidize their particular project. The agenda for restoring economic freedom must include eliminating tax-supported subsidies for those who politic the loudest.

## USER FEES VERSUS PRIVATIZATION

User fees imposed by local governments are economically pre-

318

ferrable to the provision of "free" services. There are a number of advantages. As already noted, user fees insure that those who receive benefits are those who pay for them. By charging consumers a price which at least covers operating and maintenance costs, the benefits accrue to those willing to pay. Furthermore, congestion in the use of the good or service can be eliminated. User fees of course provide important information to local governments on the real "needs" of individuals based on their willingness to pay, a reliable indicator of effective demand. When offered "free," the incentive to exaggerate one's "needs" is surely strengthened.

There are other, more subtle advantages of user fees over equal access. The incentive for individuals to expend resources in order to earn entitlements to under priced goods and services is reduced. When governments charge prices covering costs, the potential for competition from private firms is increased and efficiency gains are inevitable. Finally, in light of our concern with the incentives facing private decision makers, user fees will reduce the need for tax funds and very likely lower marginal tax rates. In this way, user fees can indirectly encourage work effort, saving, and capital investment; the ultimate sources of rising productivity and, therefore, rising standards of living.

While user fees are beneficial, competition through privatization is clearly the best solution. As repeatedly observed, the market provision of goods and services when compared to the provision by government under similar circumstances is usually about half as expensive. Private business must gain its revenues voluntarily and, therefore, monitor costs very closely. The potential always exists that customers will leave in favor of the competition. Rarely is there an equivalent discipline for a government agency. Based on many examples, efficiency gains can be derived from the competitive market process. Though user fees are acceptable when complete privatization is not possible, we must not be fooled by the "user fee mirage." Rather the goal should be to eliminate those obstacles which prevent competition. Privatization must be the ultimate goal.

## GOVERNMENT AND EDUCATION

The appropriate model for American education, assuming there is a single model, swings like a pendulum between a back-to-the-basics approach and the "progressive" view of being all things to all children. However, whatever the school of thought in vogue, America's government schools seem to be spending more to produce students who can do less. Compounding the problem is a school atmosphere, especially in the large central cities, characterized by violence to teacher and student alike. While parents are encouraged to "get involved" and teachers are urged to "care," the systemic problem of government-run schools is monopoly. Many parents are forced by cumpulsory attendance laws to use, in spite of the known enefficiencies and injustices, a system thay would not voluntarily choose. Paradoxically, while opposing the monopoly power possessed by the OPEC oil cartel, ridiculing the inefficiency of the U. S. Postal Service monopoly, and concerned with the asserted monopoly power of the big oil companies or IBM, educators continue to defend the existence of a monopolistic educational system which by law in most states determines what and how much our children are to learn.

The National Education Association and the American Federation of Teachers (the educator's labor unions) continue to insist that the answer is more money and higher teacher salaries. The evidence, however, indicates the problem is more than a matter of money. During the period of 1950 through 1976, for example, per pupil expenditures in America's public schools increased in *real* terms, after adjusting for inflation, from $553 to $1,523 or almost by a factor of three. Further, a marked increase in the number of teachers during this period produced smaller class sizes. And, in the name of "consolidation" of school districts, supposedly to increase efficiency, the number of non-teaching personnel in government schools exploded. In many large city school systems, more than *fifty* percent of the public school system's employees are not in the classroom. Furthermore, per pupil costs have in most cases *increased* with district size. Surely administrators are aware of the positive relationship between district size and their *own* salaries. In short, government operated schools in America have not been starved of money. But, what about performance?

Unfortunately, if the purpose of the public school system is to educate students, the performance has not been encouraging. Standardized test scores have, in fact, shown a steady decline since the early 1960's and have occurred in all ethnic groups and economic classes. For example, the Scholastic Aptitude Test (SAT) average score in mathematics in 1963 was about 505 but had fallen to 467 in 1982. The verbal score was 478 in 1963 and was down to 426 in 1982. The American College Testing Program (ACT) composite score fell from 455 in 1963 to 413 in 1982. It is important to note that the scores have fallen among all test groups. In the decade ending in 1977, the fraction of students scoring more than 700 on the SAT verbal test declined by 48 percent. At the same time the proportion of those completing school in the late 1970's who were functionally illiterate was higher than in the decade of the 1950's. Interestingly, close to half of the black and Spanish surnamed people tested functionally illiterate, a rather perverse result in light of the argument that public schools are necessary to protect the educational opportunities of the poor and minorities. The universal experience in America's colleges and universities in recent years has been the inferior preparation of high school graduates to do college level work.

Some would argue that the declining scores on standardized tests have been the result of lower performing students reducing the overall average. But as already noted, the highest scoring students have shown the largest deterioration in scores. Others have argued that scores have fallen because of more students taking the tests. However, the absence of any increase in the "spread" of scores would hardly substantiate this assertion. Performance, we repeat, has fallen among all regions of the country, all socio-economic groups, ethnic and racial groups, and the deterioration seems to be especially pronounced in the basic skills of verbal and mathematical competence. In addition there are studies that indicate the standardized tests are actually easier than they were twenty years ago. Though the average number of years of schooling has increased in recent decades, functional illiteracy has not been reduced, if anything it is higher than in the 1950's. The conclusion is inescapable: explosive increases in expenditures on primary and secondary education in the United States have been accompanied by significant declines in student performance.

Not only are public schools accomplishing less with more money, many schools, especially in the metropolitan areas of the country, are no longer safe for teacher or student. Violence has become a way of life in many schools. In the 1978 report of the National Institute of Education (NIE), *Violent Schools--Safe Schools,* the following facts were discovered: twenty-five percent of American public schools experience significant problems with vandalism, theft, and personal attack; in an average month, one out of nine secondary school pupils and one out of eight teachers will have something stolen from them; and, during an average month, more than 5,000 teachers will be physically attacked. Vandalism and violence, however, are not restricted to just the urban core areas. The problem has also affected suburban and rural schools according to the NIE report. "Thus," from a biting summary of this problem in Robert Poole's *Cutting Back City Hall,* "we have a public school system that doesn't work: horrendously costly, decreasingly effective, and physically dangerous to pupil and teacher alike."

As we move into the 1980's, cosmetic changes proliferate: "merit pay," "peer group competency review," more teachers, a return to this or that educational theory, and of course the need for more taxpayer's money. But little attention is paid to the fundamental and underlying problem: monopoly. The "fatal flaw" is the suppression of competition. Only a competitive market process can offer alternatives and freedom of choice to the consumer. Monopoly power is maintained by restricting potential competitors. And the monopoly power of the government school system is supported by law. Competition is made rather difficult, to say the least, when the existing producer is giving the product away "free." In addition, whether parents use the free government schools or not, they are compelled to pay for them. As the Canadian scholar E. G. West has pointed out, government schools "...do not have to wait for customers to come into their 'store', the customers have their income 'garnished' well in advance and in substantial proportions." Those who would send their children to private schools must pay twice for the opportunity of choosing an alternative to the government monopoly. Parochial and other private schools must endure this tremendous disadvantage when soliciting students and trying to balance their budgets. Finally, the monopoly power of the public school system is reinforced by compulsory education laws which force many if not most parents to send their children to a government school.

Needless to say, the compulsory attendance laws and provision of "free" educational services by tax supported government schools have served the interests of teachers and administrators alike. Not surprisingly, important sources of support for continuing present policy include the National Eduation Association (NEA) and the American Federation of Teachers (AFT). For these special interests the problem continues to be a matter of money. The issue of monopoly and the potential for competitive alternatives are ignored. Both the NEA and the AFT are militantly opposed to the fundamental changes required if increased educational efficiency and quality are to be achieved. Despite the massive increase in tax revenues to public education and the decline in student performance over the past twenty-five years, the teachers' unions, unblushingly and with discouraging repetition, ask for more certified people and more money. The answer, however, is not more money. But rather it must include a fundamental change in educational arrangements, a change that encourages alternatvies to government's monopoly grip on education. Similar to our analysis of the post office, solid waste disposal, and urban transportation, competition in education must be part of the solution.

In the late 1970's there were roughly five million children attending private schools in the United States and about 42 million in public schools. A large majority of the private schools are affiliated with a particular religion, and most of their students are from lower and middle income families. On average, the private schools were about half as expensive as the public school system, and the standardized test scores for comparable school populations were as high or higher according to the Coleman study. The private schools, in spite of the disadvantage of competing with "free" public schools, do at least as well with less money for a number of reasons. Competition requires they obtain tuitions voluntarily. Furthermore, they have a strong incentive to keep administrative overhead to an absolute minimum. Parents and other community volunteers are naturally encouraged to help in the educational process. And contrary to the widely held perception, private shcools are not just teaching the rich. Close to twenty percent of the students in Catholic grade schools are non-white, and a number of parochial shools in the core urban areas now find half or more of their enrollments represent inner city blacks or hispanics.

The claim is also made that a monopoly government school system is necessary to guarantee the poor an adequate educational opportunity. Yet, despite its documented failure to provide an adequate education to the poor and disadvantaged, especially in large cities, public school teachers and administrators still argue that competition would be disastrous for the poor. Their claim is doubtful. During the mid-1770's in Philadelphia, more than 100 schoolmasters advertised in newspapers for students to their private academies. The Quakers were very keen on finding poor children and seeing to their literacy. Learning took place in the home, in church, through library companies and circulating libraries, and in hundreds of private schools which more often than not admittted the poor without charge. Samuel L. Blumenfeld, for example, has documented the successful introduction of literacy to the overwhelming majority of Americans, rich and poor, early in the last century. With private schools still dominant, and public schools relatively unimportant, literacy was nevertheless widespread. For example, an attempt was made in Boston in 1818 to increase the role of the public schools at the expense of private education. Because of excessive delinquency and inadequate education for the poor, as perceived by some, a committee was appointed to study the situation. The school committee found there were about 2,360 pupils attending eight public schools, more than 4,000 attending a large number of private schools, and about 500 students not attending school. In other words, more than 90 percent of Boston's children were attending school in the absence of compulsory attendance laws, and the great majority of the poor were receiving a basic education.

By the time the first state compulsory attendance law appeared in 1852, the overwhelming majority of Americans were already literate. Without "big brother" requiring schooling, the parents of both rich and poor children demonstrated an interest in the education of their offspring. The economist Thomas Sowell points out that although blacks were not permitted to attend public schools in the North or the South, and in some parts of the South were *forbidden* to attend any school at all (the penalty for teaching blacks was frequently harsh physical punishment), nevertheless, three out of five free blacks were found to be literate in the 1850 federal census. In the cities the proportion was even higher. There were "underground" private schools for free blacks throughout the south, and literacy rates continued to rise although it was 1918 before the number of black children in public high schools exceeded the number in private high schools. In 1860, on the eve of the industrial transformation of the American economy, a remarkably well educated population existed. But in that year there were still only about 300 public schools in the U. S. and more than 6,000 private schools.

The argument favoring government schools because poor parents supposedly don't know or care enough to obtain an education for their children is the most vulgar paternalism one can imagine! The evidence from history is clear. If given a choice, parents, rich or poor, white or black, will choose literacy over illiteracy for their youngsters and will go to great lengths to obtain it.

Early in the nineteenth century private education flourished. Private schools were the primary means to educate young Americans, and literacy was widespread. Yet, the stampede to government schools occurred anyway. If the problem, as proponents of public schools argue, was universal access to education, why then didn't they pursue a far less expensive alternative? By subsidizing only the tuition of children whose parents were too poor they could have avoided the tremendous expense of a public school system available "free" to all children, rich and poor. Why were public schools, and not private charity or vouchers to children specifically in need, the recommended solution? Samuel Blumenfeld convincingly suggests that it was a matter of indoctrinating American society to a particular view of man and the world. Proponents of government schools advocated an arrangement which they believed would form the right "character" in man. Why public schools? Blumenfeld provides us with an answer: "Because private schools were run and controlled by individuals who might have entirely different views concerning the nature of man." Besides, private owners were forced by economic reality to concentrate on teaching skills rather than forming "the public man."

Robert Owen, the "father of socialism" according to some, introduced his experiment with the Institution for the Formation of Character at New Lanark. He wanted to produce human beings who would cooperate and be devoid of the selfishness which might be favorable to a capitalist order. For Robert Owen, communism could only be achieved if the young were indoctrinated through government schools. Blumenfeld analyzes the views of the Owenite feminist Frances Wright on the value of a national system of education through government operated public schools in a *Reason* magazine article. In 1829 in the *Free Enquirer* she described how the government schools would honor the state: "It is national, rational, republic education; free for all at the expense of all; conducted under the guardianship of the state, at the expense of the state, for the honor, the happiness, the virtue, the salvation of the state." Though a popular view at the time, it conflicts with the mythical notion that it was all done in the name of the poor and universal literacy! From the very beginning, the public education movement was designed to glorify the state and produce a uniformity of belief clearly contradictory to the principles of the founding fathers. Particular ideological groups then promoted a compulsory, monopoly school system to indoctrinate the young to their personal view of the good society. A growing danger is the risk that a particular ideological movement will, as E. G. West has noted, see the monopoly public school system as the cheapest and most effective avenue of achieving a uniformity of public opinion.

Unfortunately, the consolidation into larger school districts, and to a significant extent in state and federal hands rather than at the local level, threatens to further corrupt our constitutional democracy by reducing the incentive for parents to take an active interest in the education of their children. As school districts have merged and consolidated since the end of World War II, parental influence regarding educational issues has diminished. As funding and other educational decisions are first made at the state level and then (through the new federal Department of Education and dozens of other federal programs) at the national level, the purpose of educating young people is lost in the shuffle. Confronted with mandatory tax payments and compulsory attendance laws, freedom of choice is sacrificed to the ambitions of the *private* interests of public school teachers, administrators, and various other advocates. Thomas Sowell, in his stimulating book *Pink and Brown People and Other Controversial Essays,* captures the essential nature of this point: "In a country founded on freedom of choice, it is amazing how many battles still have to be fought over that issue...Everybody is for freedom in the abstract. It is only when you get to freedom in the concrete that you run into opposition. To many of the Olympians in our universities, government, and courts, concrete free choice by ordinary grubby mortals is a scary, if not repulsive, idea. It is especially likely to be repulsive as regards to children, for whom the Olympians have their own grand designs."

Yet, there is nothing mysterious about educating children. The human race, after all, has been doing it for thousands of years and without the attention of trained experts and educationists. But the teachers of old stressed the training necessary to participate in a society and economic system. Verbal and quantitative skills were important, as were good manners, disicipline, and solid citizenship. Today the hundreds of thousands of experts impose their truths about the building of a utopian society, a world no doubt superior but unfortunately non-existent. "Warm fuzzies," "creative curriculums," and a more "relaxed" school ethos have in part produced the present crisis.

It is absolutely essential that the American people begin to rethink the question of the monopolistic nature of the public schools, of compulsory attendance laws and the implications for economic efficiency, and of the fairness of an educational system which provides its product "free" of charge. What are the inequities which necessarily follow when an educational system is supported by the general taxpayer? Education, like the consumption of apples, television sets, and medical care, is a service for which specific beneficiaries can be identified and, therefore, costs can be allocated. Though monopoly is almost universally distrusted, we, nevertheless, continue to fall victim to the myth that government needs to be in the education business. The NEA and AFT spend vast amounts of money and lobbying time trying to justify government's role, while holding our children hostage to its demonstrated inefficiency. The National Commission on Educational Excellence in 1983 aptly described the "wreckage": "If an unfriendly foreign power had attempted to impose on America the mediocre educational performance that exists today, we might well have viewed it as an act of war." In this report sponsored by the prestigious Twentieth Century Fund, the blame rests in good part with the unions. While the NEA and AFT use their power to protect poor teachers from public scrutiny, good teachers expectedly leave the system.

Or again, as Thomas Sowell reminds us: "In many ways school children are not beneficiaries but pawns--creating jobs for teachers and empires for layers of administrators ranging all the way up to the Department of Education. Children are merely the raw material that keeps this vast machinery turning for the benefit of others." Though the taxpayer has given government schools almost everything they have wanted for over 30 years, performance nevertheless declines. That one-in-five adult Americans are incapable of dealing with the everyday requirements of living in a modern economy must be changed. The restoration of economic freedom includes an agenda for educational reform. The answer includes realistic alternatives so that parents, as sovereign consumers, can enroll their children in schools which perform. Legion are the stories of parents who remove their children from public schools to send them to the Catholic school to "straighten him out." In his 1981 study, James S. Coleman compared public and private schools, and when account was taken of income levels, ethnic groups, and other demographic factors, the typical private school out performed the typical public school. Sociologist Andrew Greeley found that minority students benefited *most* from parochial schools. Economic freedom invariably produces more efficient outcomes. While performance results are comparable, Catholic schools spend between $500 and $1,500 per pupil; far less than the average of $2,000 to $4,000 per pupil in the government schools.

The issue, therefore, is how to introduce competition into the existing monopoly system. There are essentially three interrelated questions that need to be answered. First, should parents be required to send their children to government approved schools? Second, should schooling be financed by government taxation or financed privately? And third, how should the education industry be organized: privately or publicly?

Nobel prize winning economist Milton Friedman, for example,

accepts the idea of compulsory attendance and government finance. Therefore, to introduce competition and reduce the costs associated with monopoly power, he advocates a voucher system. Taxpayer dollars would be given to parents who would spend these vouchers at the school of their choice. Schools would compete for customers by offering particular educational packages in the market place. Those with incompetent teachers and inferior performance would lose students, and those with innovative curriculum, good teachers, and verified performance would attract them. The teaching profession would, in turn, have to respond to merit and productivity rather than longevity and tenure. If competition is important in most everything we buy, then why not education? The voucher system would surely represent a significant improvement on the existing system where schools are *both* financed by taxes and run by government. It is exciting to imagine the prospect of parents with a voucher worth $1,000 or $1,500 shopping for a school which they thought would best educate their children. The increased efficiency, freedom of choice, and undoubtedly higher scores, which would follow the implementation of competition through vouchers, represent potentially far reaching improvements on the existing monopoly system. Denis P. Doyle, the head of the education-policy studies group at the American Enterprise Institute, argues that an immediate and promising federal program in educational vouchers proposed by the Reagan administration involves the distribution of the very popular federal Title I funds for low-achieving, disadvantaged youngsters. Instead of distributing $2.7 billion to schools and school districts, the money would be made available in the form of vouchers to the parents of eligible children. The parents and/or students would then select the school at which they would spend the voucher.

The teacher unions are correct when they say that vouchers would result in a proliferation of new private schools. The poor performance of the past two decades in public schools suggest a booming business in private school alternatives. However, it is clearly unwarranted to assume, as many public school teachers do, that drastically fewer teaching opportunities will exist or that teacher's salaries will necessarily be lower. Nevertheless, strenuous opposition to a voucher system of any kind is guaranteed from the education establishment. *Any* concession to the notion that parents ought to have some choice in where and how their children recieve an education would certainly mean the eventual demise of the existing monopoly public school system in America. The idea that the educational bureaucracy can choose better than parents will die hard.

There are those, however, who believe the voucher system has serious limitations. Samuel Blumenfeld believes that vouchers or tax credits would reduce the degree of autonomy private schools currently possess. For some like Jule R. Herbert of the National Taxpayers Legal Fund in Washington, D.C., who favor an absolute separation of education and the state, the voucher plan contains a fatal flaw: government finance means government control. Robert Poole, Milton Friedman, and others, however, believe this fear to be insignificant compared to the daily costs imposed on American youngsters in the existing monopoly system.

Educational tax credits offer an alternative to the voucher. The separation of church and state issues is neutralized because *not* taxing an individual can hardly be considered a government expenditure. Unfortunately, a successful tax credit bill in Congress would likely prescribe standards and other control devices on eligible public or private schools. A recent case in Minnesota suggests that the U. S. Supreme Court is prepared to permit tax credits for education if they are available to the parents of children in both public and private schools. Encouragingly, the Court also indicated its unwillingness to tie the financing of education with additional significant government "entanglements."

Tax credits, of course, are only a step removed from the truly fundamental question: whether government should even be involved in education. The traditional argument suggests that "external benefits" acrue to society from universal education. But that is also true of nearly everything: bathing, breathing, or even belching. Ultimately, almost all of our actions have an effect on others. But, do external benefits justify coercion? Pursuing E. G. West's example, if we wash our bodies daily benefits accrue to all those within close proximity. But, does this mean that society, through compulsory taxation, should provide us with free soap and hot water? "Where is the evidence," West asks, "that people will not purchase education and become literate in the pursuit of their own private benefits, and in sufficient quantities to make the marginal benefits to society not worth the marginal cost of further encouragement?"

Given the weaknesses of both the voucher system and tax credit systems (that is to say the coercive power of the state to compel individuals to finance the education of others), serious consideration should be given to gradually privatizing all education. Following the example of Samuel Blumenfeld, a program needs to be implemented in which the *incremental* cost of schooling should be provided by parents of the children in shool. Instead of increasing the sales or property tax, the annual increase in the education budget would be billed to the parents. The "marginal user tax" would be paid at the door of the school. School administrators and teachers would recognize that parents are buying a product and could always take their money to another school. Over a period of years the marginal user fee collected at the school from parents would gradually rise. Parents would then have the option of spending this increasing fraction of the cost of the child's education at the school of their choice. Competition would commence, alternatives would appear, and the illusion that public education is "free" would be eliminated. The problems associated with monopoly would also be reduced through competition and consumer sovereignty, and innovation in learning technologies, lower costs, increased productivity, and most important of all freedom of choice, would be restored.

Finally, compulsory attendance laws should be repealed. The evidence already cited indicates that parents of the rich *and* the poor are far more likely to possess a genuine interest in the education of their children than does the state. As Thomas Jefferson said: "It is better to tolerate the rare instance of a parent refusing to let his child be educated than to shock the common feelings and ideas by forcible aspiration and education of the infant against the will of the father."

The education establishment will surely counter with the frequently heard complaint that the poor would be the losers. There are, however, problems with this argument. First, the poor appear to be the big loosers from the *existing* government run system. Second, the notion that education is in fact "free" to the poor is nonsense. Unfortunately, the existing state and local tax system, frequently regressive in terms of its burden as a fraction of people's income, clearly documents that the poor are already paying dearly for the mediocre education they currently receive in the public schools. Finally, we must remember that tax rates will fall as parents pay a larger and larger fraction of the cost of education at the schoolhouse door. Lower tax rates will mean two things. First, work effort, savings, and investment will be encouraged by the lower marginal tax rates thereby contributing to faster productivity gains and, therefore, increasing standards of living. In turn, as people keep a larger fraction of their incomes, individuals and businesses will be more inclined *and* able to voluntarily assist the poor and disadvantaged. Second, the private, intermediate institutions such as churches, clubs, fraternal groups, and charity organizations of all kinds will reclaim their important role of dealing with human problems.

In the interim, a voucher or tax credit plan should remain a high priority. To summarize our case, let Thomas Sowell in his book *Pink and Brown People and Other Controversial Essays* speak to the vital role of competition, privatization, and freedom of choice:

> The public school establishment is by no means indispensible as they would have us believe. Where they have something good to offer, let them offer it. But don't let them continue to cram their product down people's throats. It doesn't make sense to deny parents a choice. And, it is inexcusable when the real victims are children.

# CHAPTER 22

## THE 'NEW' NATIONAL INDUSTRIAL POLICY

The trouble with this new talk about industrial policy is that it is not new. It is at least as old as the 18th century's mercantilism and as familiar as this century's disastrous experiments with central planning, the corporate state, and five-year plans. From what industrial policy proponents have been saying so far, there is no reason to believe that their repackaged schemes will be any less catastrophic than the earlier models.

--Richard B. McKenzie

The term 'fascist' is an emotionally charged, vituperative label more often mindlessly affixed to one's opposition than dispassionately analyzed. Yet the political/philosophic/economic system called fascism has distinct, paradigmatic economic characteristics. The description of those characterisics....raises a provocation and rather frightening question: Does this model also describe the economic system emerging in the United States?

--Charlotte Twight

The evidence seems clear: government, as a delivery system to provide people with what they want, is very inefficient and seemingly incapable of serving this mysterious thing called the "public interest." Government regulation invariably benefits those it regulates and suppresses competition. On average, goods and services provided through the public sector are twice as expensive as the performance in the private sector. The anatomy of government failure is characterized by its tendency to provide benefits to those with political power, while spreading the costs of such entrepreneurship among those with little political influence. In spite of government's poor record as a "social organizer," both in democratic and totalitarian states, the newest game in town urges an even greater politicization of American society. Arguing that the United States is experiencing a "de-industrialization" of its economy, influential academicians like economist Lester Thurow of M.I.T., political scientist Robert Reich of Harvard, investment banker Felix Rohatyn, Gar Alperowitz of the Center for Economic Alternatives, and the so-called "Atari Democrats" like 1984 presidential candidate Senator Gary Hart all maintain that our economic salvation depends on adopting a "national industrial policy." Industrial policy, which is simply another name for central economic planning, would assign to the federal government a powerful role in directing resources to particular industries in the economy, away from "losers" and toward "winners." Unfortunately, the proposal for a "reindustrialization" of the American economy through "coherent planning" is neither a new idea nor is it likely to improve upon the demonstrated efficiency and wealth creating powers of private enterprise and the competitive market process.

## THE CALL FOR A NATIONAL INDUSTRIAL POLICY

The central proposition of policy recommendations entitled "national industrial policy" is the assertion that the United States is "deindustrializing" and that simultaneously, through wise centrally planned government initiatives, our major competitors in world markets have been improving their competitive positions relative to our own. Or, according to the intellectual guru of the "industrial policy" movement, Robert B. Reich, the U. S. has experienced a significant deterioration in our "competitive productivity" relative to Japan, Germany, France, and other industrial countries. According to Ira Magaziner and Reich in their *Minding America's Business,* the business community and government have failed to make the most productive use of the resources in their care. Citing statistics on the declining shares of world export markets in manufacturing industries, Reich in his newest book, *The Next American Frontier,* tells us that the "...central problem of America's economic future is that the nation is not moving quickly enough out of high-volume, standardized production" into what he calls "flexible systems of production."

While Reich does not use the terms "winner" and "loser," the idea of encouraging selected strategic industries and anticipating declining industries are central to the proposal. According to Reich, "America's manufacturing base was eroding *precipitously...*" (emphasis added) during the decade of the 1970's, and he recommends, as the solution, a central planning agency which would anticipate, forecast, and coordinate investment decisions in the economy. What is needed is a "consciously constructed policy" in which government would plan a central role in subsidizing growth industries and assist in reducing the size and/or "rationalizing" the declining industries. Or, as economist Lester Thurow maintains in his book *The Zero-Sum Society:* "Major investment decisions have become too important to be left to the private market alone." Thurow proposes that government create "...the national equivalent of a corporate investment committee" to redirect investment funds from "sunset" to "sunrise" industries. Put another way, Reich, Thurow, and Rohatyn propose, using Amitai Etzioni's phrase in his *Public Interest* article, "The MITIzation of America."

In November 1983, a Democratic Party caucus unanimously recommended the formation of a "council on economic competitiveness and cooperation" in the federal government to implement an "industrial policy." Former Vice President and 1984 presidential hopeful Walter Mondale has endorsed it. Senator

Edward Kennedy calls it "a clear alternative to Reaganomics." And Senators Gary Hart of Colorado and Alan Cranston of California, with some differences in approach, believe it to be our industrial salvation.

MITI, Japan's Ministry of International Trade and Industy, has, in some circles, been given superhuman powers of foresight and economic understanding. Magaziner and Reich are deeply concerned that there is no centralized agency in the U. S. government with "overall responsibility" for directing the economy in the right direction. Many proponents of an industrial policy call for a Department of Trade and Development, patterned after the MITI, under which each industry in the economy would have a "trilateral committee" composed of "government, business, and labor" to ascertain an industry's future. Unfortunately, the discovery of Reich's "declining" and "growing" industries would be difficult if not impossible on a timely basis. It is not, as Etzioni points out, "...as if there were labels pinned to their smokestacks or written on their laboratory flat-roofs."

Reich explicitly rejects the notion that there is already too much government intervention in economic life. "Whenever possible, it is crucial to act in anticipation of events," according to Magaziner and Reich, because "an interdependent world economy...is prone to sharp and often sudden changes in supply, demand, technololgy, and politics." Therefore, "active government policies are necessary to enable the economy to respond quickly and efficiently to worldwide structural changes." There is, however, a problem with this scenario: where is the evidence that representative governments can "respond quickly and efficiently" to anything?

Nevertheless, according to Magaziner and Reich: "The U. S. needs to institutionalize four prerequisites for sound industrial policymaking: coherence, foresight, accountability, and competence." Under coherence, government is asked to "...reconcile the diverse and sometimes inconsistent industrial policies that emanate from different parts of the government." Foresight requires that government take "responsibility for sophisticated analytic or predictive work on a business or industry level." By accountability they mean to evaluate the international competitive consequences of government programs and policies." And finally, under the heading of competence, "the major prerequisites of effective industrial policy is a sufficient level of competence and business experience among the officials participating in the effort." In this grandiose scheme the knowledge problem, about which Friedrich Hayek has written so eloquently, is simply ignored. Note the implied wisdom of the planners from the following sentence of *Minding America's Business:* "Government officials *must have a vision* of the *overall structural development* of the international economy, and a *thorough knowledge* of the products, markets and competitive dynamics of individual businesses." (emphasis added) Is that all these mortal bureaucrats will need to know?

It almost takes your breath away; an all knowing, all fact finding, omniscient, imnipotent tripartite committee. The impossibility and arrogance of such a sentence defies description. What we have, according to George Gilder, is "...rather an ambitious new supply-side microeconomics of the left." But the competitive process of the market involves millions of decision-makers and continuously changing plans. It is the process of change which mobilizes socially useful information for consumers and producers.

## THE EVIDENCE OF AMERICA'S ECONOMIC DECLINE

A major proposition of the new industrial policy is the asserted "precipitous" de-industrialization of the American economy during the 1970's, Especially when compared with our important international competitors. In The Next American Frontier, Robert Reich provides a profusion of statistics to document the severe erosion of America's industrial base. The rate of increase in productivity in the economy declined quite significantly during the 1970's. But Reich asserts that this was not the result of government regulation, larger federal budget deficits, an inadequate rate of new capital formation, or even the decline in our research and development efforts during the decade. Instead the problem with productivity and international competitiveness stems from "the way the nation organizes itself for production."

During the first half of the twentieth century the principles of "scientific management" were, according to Reich, employed in the American economy to standardize output, simplify work-place tasks, monitor performance, and take advantage of the economies of large scale output. Unfortunately, these standardized production processes are easily duplicated by the other industrial countries, and during the past decade or so have been progressively adopted by the so-called newly industrializing countries. Although "standardized production had brought America unparalleled wealth," these are the very industries which are under competitive presure from abroad, such as automobiles, textiles, steel, and consumer electronics. Given the standardized production processes and the availability of modern machinery and equipment from industrial countries, lower-wage countries often have a distinct cost advantage. As a reault of such dynamic shifts in international competitiveness, the major industrial countries have recognized the need for a "worldwide reorganization of production" to Reich's "flexible production processes." The fundamental problem has been "America's failure to adapt to it."

The "sunrise" industries which emphasize advanced technology, precision engineering, complex testing, and sophisticated maintenance--Reich calls them the "custom-tailored" and "technology-driven" industries--require that flexible production systems be employed to adjust to rapidly changing circumstances and specialized orders. Essential to these growth industries is highly skilled labor. Reich argues, and many of his critics would agree on this point, that "American firms failed to respond by adopting the new products and processes." American business leaders, hiding behind tariffs and quotas and made complacent by the economic dominance of the U. S. economy in the early years following World War II, have, according to Reich, "...forfeited world industrial leadership to Japan." The managers of America's old industrial base remain locked into standardized, rigid production processes and management techniques. They have, in some instances, failed to adopt a flexible-system approach which is critical to high-technology industries where discovering and solving new problems is absolutely essential.

Robert Reich's criticism of American management in the steel, automobile, and other industries, represents an important contribution. His identification of the interdependence of the world economy as a fundamental source of change is also important. Unfortunately, he fails to realize or appreciate the beneficial nature of rivalry and competiton. The "restructuring" of American industry, as a result of competitive pressures from Japan and to a lesser extent Germany, France, and other industrial countries, is already well underway. As Reich recognizes in *The Next American Frontier:* "The distinct principles of flexible-system production are understood--perhaps intuitively--by many small, upstart companies in America producing new micro-electronic products and computer software or creating advertisements and films. They are also understood by a few highly successful larger companies--IBM and Hewlett-Packard, for instance."

Encouragingly, the competitive market process suggests that successful adaptation to changing circumstances will be imitated and, therefore, continue. The great success of Peter and Waterman's best selling book *In Search of Excellence* surely substantiates this point. Reich's lagging perceptions are perhaps comparable to John Kenneth Galbraith's preoccupation with the smokestack industries in *The New Industrial State* in 1967, while simultaneously the new electronic revolution, apparently without his knowledge, was emerging and hence blindsiding his argument. American industry *is* responding to the pressures of international competition. If anything, government should gracefully acknowledge this fact and just get out of the way.

There is a great deal of evidence indicating that Reich, Magaziner, Thurow, Rohatyn, and the rest have significantly overstated the "deindustrialization" of America. Charles L. Schultze in *The Brookings Review* convincingly maintains that the asserted decline in America's industrial base is "a nonexistent trend." The entire industrial world experienced a noticeable decrease in productivity gains during the 1970's. But Charles Schultze, Richard McKenzie, Amitai Etzioni, and others have shown that the U. S. economy's performance in the decade of the 1970's, when compared to other countries, was quite good. Manufacturing employment actually increased slightly, and the share of private Gross National Product (GNP) accounted for by manufacturing industries did not decline significantly. In fact, the relative decline in shares of manufacturing employment and output in the economy is accounted for by the higher rates of growth in productivity in that sector relative to most sectors of the economy. Manufacturing employment in Japan, for example, actually declined by more than 10 million persons during the decade. But of course that cannot be described as "de-industrialization" either. It is mostly a reflection of rapid productivity gains (i.e., increases in output-per-worker in manufacturing) and therefore suggests economic strength not weakness.

The decade also witnessed an incredible number of new jobs in the American economy. While the American economy was generating about 19 million new jobs during the 1970's, the net gain in employment in the European Economic Community (the Common Market) was roughly zero. The Germans were sending tens of thousands of temporary foreign workers back to their resident countries as a means of fighting unemployment. The claim of greater structural unemployment in the United States is also unsupportable. Although U. S. unemployment rates have tended to be higher than the corresponding figures for the industrial countries of Europe and Japan, "dislocated workers" (unemployed people whose last jobs were in so-called declining industries) who had been unemployed for more than eight weeks were a tiny fraction of the total labor force. At the end of the decade, long-term unemployment, meaning roughly 15 weeks or more was lower in the United States than most of the large European countries. The *increases* in unemployment rates in Europe during the 1970's were in all cases much *greater* than the United States. International trade performed quite well also. Charles Schultze cites a study by the Brookings Institute indicating the U. S. trade surplus in the high-tech industries increased from $12 billion in 1972 to $40 billion in 1979. George Gilder in a *Public Interest* article indicates that in the five year period ending in 1982, employment in computer-related manufacturing rose from 50 percent of employment in auto manufacturing to 140 percent.

Admittedly, the United States does have examples of Reich's standardized industries suffering from difficult structural problems (for example, labor costs completely out of line with productivity) in their attempt to remain competitive. These, however, are *not* typical of American industry in general. Since the economic recovery that began in the final quarter of 1982, industrial production and manufacturing output have grown very rapidly, and productivity gains have been encouraging. Many are already speaking of a new, leaner industrial America capable of demonstrating a more rapid increase in productivity and an improvement in our international competitiveness. These changes, however, appear to be contingent on reducing the uncertainty associated with large federal budget deficits, monetary policy, and interest rates.

Simultaneously, many of the European economies are sputtering and in deep trouble. Many years of government planning and the welfare state are apparently coming home to roost. Mitterrand's industrial policy of nationalization and "indicative" central planning appear to have devastated the French economy. The Federal Republic of Germany, with increasing government intervention, continues to lag and experience an historically high unemployment rate. Sweden, Italy, and the United Kingdom were mired in problems stemming from the collectivist, welfare-state mentality practiced by most Western governments. Even the Japanese miracle of 10 percent annual rates of growth is now averaging just 4 percent.

The foreign exchange value of the dollar has increased markedly in the early 1980's, and this stronger dollar is partly the result of higher "real" interest rates in the U. S. than abroad. In the context of the asserted "precipitous" decline in America's industrial strength, would foreign individuals, businesses, and governments be investing in the dollar, even with higher yields, if the U. S. economy were truly on its last leg as Reich would have us believe? As Robert J. Samuelson has clearly stated in a review of Robert Reich's work: "Anyone presenting Europe as a model of successful economic readjustment ought to have his head examined." In fact, the relatively strong recovery of industrial production and manufacturing output during 1983 and into 1984, in spite of the appreciation in the foreign exchange value of the dollar, demonstrates not weakness but an underlying strength. The U. S. is still the world's unchallenged economic leader. Problems with the U. S. economy, and they exist as already illustrated, are solvable by reducing the scope of government interference in the competitive market process.

Magaziner and Reich in *Minding America's Business* assert that in the late 1970's many developed countries had achieved higher per capita incomes than in the United States. But such claims are just plain hogwash. Studies of relative purchasing powers across countries show living standards in the United States to be substantially higher than all European countries and Japan. One study by the Organization for Economic Cooperation and Development demonstrated that statistics, supposedly showing per capita incomes to be 17 percent higher in West Germany, when adjusted for purchasing power for selected consumption categories indicated in fact that the standard of living is roughly 17 percent *higher* in the United States. Statistics on infant mortality rates, length of paid vacations, number of homicides, and pollution levels notwithstanding, very few people seriously believe that living standards are generally higher outside of the United States.

Finally, it *is* important to recognize the very serious decline in the growth rate of productivity in the U. S. during the 1970's. Indeed, there are undoubtedly public policies, such as lower tax rates, deregulation, and privatization, which can contribute to a reversal of the relatively poor performance of the U. S. economy when compared to that of the 1950's and 1960's. But in spite of the mysterious bending of the data by Reich and others, and quoting Charles L. Schultze, the chief economic advisor to President Carter in the late 1970's: "There is no evidence that this decline stems from a tendency for the private market system to allocate investment to the 'wrong' places--away from the manufacturing sector or, within manufacturing, to the wrong firms or industries. The decrease in productivity growth in no way bolsters the case for an industrial policy."

As economist George Daly has observed, "industrial policy" was applied to the energy sector of the American economy during the 1970's and the results were very disappointing. Energy studies in the Nixon and Carter administrations uniformly failed to anticipate events. In the "Project Independence Report" of 1974, energy czar John Sawhill said the purpose of the study was "...to evaluate the nation's energy problems and provide a massive framework for developing a national energy policy." The report anticipated that world oil prices would *fall* slightly from $11 per barrel, and that by 1985 nuclear power would account for *thirty* percent of total electric power generation in the U. S. President Carter's "National Energy Plan" of April 1977, proved to be equally unreliable. George Daly summarized the results of national planning in energy markets:

> Taken together, the studies prove rather damaging to the information-gap hypothesis: Two analyses undertaken by experts within a 2½ year period arrived at radically different visions of the future, both of which proved to be inaccurate. In retrospect, the widespread conviction among policy makers of that era--that they had a clearer, further vision of the future, one so superior that sensibility demanded that it be imposed on those who could not or would not see--seems at least faintly ironic.

Advocates of a national industrial policy ought to have the "Project Independence Report" and the "National Energy Plan" as required reading.

## INDUSTRIAL POLICY IN JAPAN

The proponents of a national industrial policy want government's police power be used to create a pattern of industrial investment and output which is somehow different from what the market and/or the existing mismash of government policies would have otherwise produced. According to Magaziner and Reich: "We suggest that U. S. companies and the government develop a coherent and coordinated industrial policy whose aim is to raise real income of our citizens

337

by improving the pattern of our investments rather than by focusing only on aggregate investment levels." In large part, these proposals stem from a near mesmerization of certain American intellectuals and politicians with respect to the heralded successes of Japan's industrial policy. With Japanese television sets, cameras, RAM chips, video recorders, automobiles, and steel flooding the American market (in the process bringing *higher* real incomes to the American people), "Japan, Incorporated" is viewed as a formidable adversary to be copied. Ignoring for the moment that historical, cultural, and other factors make Japan the industrial country from which we probably can borrow the least, what are the facts about Japan's phenomenal growth?

We are told that industrial policy, reflected primarily in the activities of the Ministry of International Trade and Industry (MITI), the Fiscal Investment and Loan Program (FILP), and the Japan Development Bank (JDB), has been an economic panacea--moving resources to high-productivity industries, stimulating rapid economic growth, and increasing shares of world export markets. The obvious solution to America's "de-industrialization" for many American politicians is to copy the Japanese miracle.

Unfortunately for the myth makers, actual experience with industrial policy in Japan indicates the truth lies elsewhere. Arthur T. Denzau at the Center for the Study of American Business in St. Louis, economists Paul Krugman at MIT and Hugh Patrick at Yale, and many others question the role central planning in Japan has played in their industrial success since World War II. Attempts by MITI to direct Japanese investment to leading sectors and away from declining industries have frequently been counter productive and outright failures. One early example was the attempt in 1955 of MITI to have Japanese auto makers concentrate on a single car model, the "People's Car." Later the planners tried unsuccessfully to keep Honda out of the automobile industry and attempted to "rationalize" the industry by allowing just two or three companies. MITI also discouraged the Japanese automobile industry from developing export markets. Fortunately, for both Japanese and American consumers, the planners at MITI failed in these policies of industrial reorganization.

Similar setbacks in textiles and clothing, shipbuilding, agriculture, and coal have been documented in the recent study by Arthur T. Denzau. Government planners, for example, once tried to discourage a small, struggling Japanese electronics firm from investing money and personnel in American transistor technology because of an inadequate yield. The company prevailed over government pressures. Its name: the Sony Corporation. The success of the Japanese steel industry in foreign markets is frequently credited to MITI and its encouragement of high rates of investment and a domestic cartel. But unfortunately, as Paul Krugman at MIT points out, a significant fraction of that investment lies idle, as thirty percent or more of the Japanese steel industry represents excess capacity. At the same time, other industries in Japan, influenced very little if at all by MITI policy, for example the cement, paper, glass, bicycle, and motorcycle industries, have been very successful.

MITI planners have repeatedly encouraged cartels in industries where competition was deemed to be "excessive." Frequently, these actions have sustained industries, for example textiles, which are subject to foreign competition. But an efficient national industrial policy would presumably be planning its "sunset" rather than its subsidization. While Chalmers Johnson's account of MITI is generally favorable, his discussion provides, at best, mixed evidence on the value of MITI's work. The robotics policy of MITI was not in place until 137 Japanese robotics firms were already in existence. MITI's policy of favoring consumer electronics began after the advent of transistor radios and their shipment abroad. And more recently, the Japanese government's decision to subsidize Very Large Scale Integration (VLSI) efforts in the semiconductor industry was finalized just as the Japanese companies were about to capture a sizeable fraction of the U. S. market for these random access memory (RAM) devices. Indeed, certain Japanese electronic companies not importantly influenced by MITI, for example Sharp and Matsushita, have been technologically and economically successful in state-of-the-art semiconductor products.

What about the allocation of public funds by government to Japanese industry? Have government investment funds in fact gone to the leading, "sunrise" industries like electronics, machine tools, and computers and away from the declining industries? The answers, given the mythical quality of government planning in Japan, might be surprising to many. The allocation of investment funds through the public sector in representative democracies is quite predictable and always the same. The criteria of economic efficiency, which Robert Reich suggest can be employed, is invariably sacrificed to allocation schemes dominated by political considerations. Philip Trezise in his summary of the data in the *The Brookings Review* verifies the predicted pattern: only a very small fraction of government funds have been directed to the leading sectors. In fact, government subsidy is frequently in exactly the opposite direction.

If resources are to be intentionally directed by government to growth industries, public budgetary expenditures are usually the method most used. Trezise points out that Japan's fiscal system has four budget types: the general account which includes the normal governmental activities; certain special accounts for government-affiliated agencies, such as the nationalized railways; budgets for prefectures and municipalities; and the Fiscal Investment and Loan Program (FILP), a government capital budget. A significant fraction of government expenditures, especially through the FILP and related agencies, is devoted to the production of capital goods for the domestic economy. The government's share of gross domestic capital formation since World War II has been between 20 and 30 percent each year. This means, of course, that the Japanese government could indeed, through public spending, loan programs, etc., allocate investment funds to "strategic" industries at the expense of those not targeted. Especially important in this regard, the Japan Development Bank (JDB) within the FILP has the potential to direct investment funds in the direction of industries targeted as "winners." In 1980, for example, the FILP was responsible for the allocation of $80 billion, something more than $10 billion of that being channeled through the JDB.

All the pieces are clearly in place. The Japanese government and the bureaucratic officials announce an industrial policy apparatus which they assert encourages growth industries. Since many of Japan's industries have done very well, government strategies are given the credit. There is, however, a major problem with this interpretation: government capital expenditures through FILP and JDB have *not*, to any appreciable extent, been directed to the high-technology, strategic sectors! Trezise's study shows quite clearly that the bulk of public investment in the regular budgets goes into public works. Sixty percent of the FILP budget in 1979 went to the Housing Loan Corporation, the People's Finance Corporation, the Small Business Finance Corporation, and the Japan National Railways, none having a very close connection with the "sunrise" industries. An additional 27 percent of the FILP funds went to the Japan Highway Corporation, the Agriculture, Forestry, and Fisheries Finance Corporation, and the JDB. Most of the remaining 12 percent of the 1979 FILP budget went to a number of smaller government corporations and special accounts.

The Japan Development Bank (JDB), supposedly an ideal instrument to direct loan funds to growth industries, allocated 53 percent of its budget during its first twenty years to merchant shipping and electric utilities. If one includes urban development commitments (e.g., shopping centers, warehouses, truck terminals) with merchant shipping and electric utilities, then these industries absorbed more than seventy-five percent of all JDB loans. The amounts available for other Japanese industries were relatively insignificant. For example, the Japanese steel industry over a twenty year period received less than one percent of total JDB lending, totaling $110 million. The JDB's net lending over the twenty year period amounted to just one percent of total capital formation by the private sector, excluding housing. Just 11 percent of all JDB lending during the two decades was devoted to technology development, or about $313 million per year. "All this can be summed up in the conclusion," according to the study by Philip Trezise, "that in Japan public funds have not been directed in any sizable amounts, relative to total investment requirements, to the private industries or economic sectors with high growth potential." Or, more specifically and following the implications of our earlier discussion of the anatomy of government failure, economist Charles Schultze summarizes the fiscal implications of representative democracy:

> Thus, in Japan as in any other democratic country, the public investment budget has been divied up in response to diverse political pressures. It has not been a major instrument for concentrating investment resources in carefully selected growth industries. Indeed, if one changed the institutional labels, the Japanese government's investment budget looks remarkably like what might have emerged from a House and Senate conference committee on public works in the United States Congress.

Trezise points out that Japanese tax and international trade policies have similarly been relatively unimportant factors in the success of Japan's leading industrial sectors. Trade policy has in fact protected and subsidized certain declining sectors, including textiles and agriculture. Though Japan's export subsidies have recently become relatively less important, they are practically mirror images of the policies utilized to stimulate exports by the United States and Europe: export-import banks which finance exports on subsidized terms, tax deferrals for exporting firms, overseas commercial offices, and insurance programs.

In fact, a strong case can be made that the rapid economic growth in Japan since World War II is a reflection of *less* government involvement in industry rather than more. Japanese tax burdens have consistently been a smaller fraction of economic activity than in the U. S. or the European industrial countries. Not surprisingly, the Japanese have had higher annual personal saving rates and have, as a consequence, devoted 30 to 35 percent of their Gross National Product to investment in domestic capital formation. To suggest, as Robert Reich implicitly does, that this massive capital investment program, to quote Charles Schultze, "...would have gone mainly into such [declining] industries as textiles, shoes, plastic souvenirs, and fisheries" in the absence of the MITI "is sheer nonsense."

The driving force of Japan's success in raising living standards rests with the intense competition which characterizes most of their economy. There are more automobile firms, camera, stereo equipment and television manufacturers, and more robotics companies in Japan than in the U. S. Most, if not all, of their success stories in exporting to the United States were preceded by intense competition and innovation in the Japanese home market. And in spite of the efforts by MITI to form industrial cartels, a robust pattern of rivalry and competition has been the essential characteristic of the Japanese economy. There is little evidence that MITI has improved the allocation of resources and therefore helped the Japanese economy in any major way.

In summary, as we review the conclusions of a number of studies on industrial policy in Japan, a convincing argument can be made that the success of Japanese industry has frequently been in spite of government planning. It is difficult to accept the idea that industrial policy in Japan has been an important, let alone essential, reason for their industrial success. Perhaps MITI has done more good than harm, "but to attribute to industrial policy a crucial role," according to Philip Trezie, "is an expression of faith, not an argument supported by discernible facts." That it takes ten to twenty percent fewer man-hours of labor to assemble an automobile in Japan--irrespective of the question of lower wage rates--and fifteen or twenty percent fewer man-hours to produce a ton of steel, suggests another answer. High rates of saving and capital investment, entrepreneurial initiative, a skilled and hard-working labor force, innovative labor/management relationships, a catching-up period following the devastation of World War II, and outright fear arising from their dependence on foreign raw materials have played the crucial roles in the phenomenal economic successes of Japan's past thirty years.

### PROBLEMS IN IDENTIFYING WINNERS

Robert J. Samuelson notes that the proposals by Reich, Thurow, Rohatyn, and Senator Hart to adopt public policies that favor growth industries and simultaneously care for the losers are clearly of noble intent: "This is like saying we should have policies to promote happiness. Who could be against them? But what's happiness? What policies would promote it? The formulation is almost childish." Experiences with industrial planning abroad, in France, Germany, the United Kingdom, and Japan are mixed at best, and at worst seem counterproductive. It is fascinating that in Part III of *Minding America's Business,* the survey of foreign experience with national industrial policy by Magaziner and Reich clearly suggests that things have not gone well for past national planning efforts. Since its publication, more recent evidence for France, Germany, and even Japan casts further doubt over the value of an industrial policy.

But this should not surprise us. As already emphasized, there are costs associated with the mobilization of socially useful knowledge, a characteristic of all social systems. Economists such as Ludwig von Mises, Friedrich Hayek, Israel Kirzner, and Thomas Sowell have identified the limitations to directing economic life which follow from the "knowledge problem." Before the fact, we know precious little about a "winning industrial structure." Just five years ago only a very few correctly guessed the current strength and size of the personal computer market. The future, after all, is unknowable and therefore uncertain. Forecasters of every description are notoriously wrong: estimates of the GNP two or three quarters into the future turn out

342

to be way off the mark; engineers and geologists predict oil shortages in 1907; that consumers will never accept electronic banking; that population will outstrip the food supply; and the errors roll on. The economist Richard B. McKenzie, in a review of Robert Reich's *The Next American Frontier*, captured the implications of mobilizing socially useful information in an uncertain and complex world:

> NIP [National Industrial Policy] advocates say little about how industrial policy engineers will secure the information they need to achieve goals of what must be construed as 'plans.' To assume that government officials can, with reasonable clarity, assess the wants and needs and calculate acceptable tradeoffs of those living across this enormous nation is to assume cognitive skills so far undemonstrated by any group of men or cluster of computers...How are they to pick and favor those industries designed to emerge in the intermediate future, much less the distant future? How are they to identify the industries that will 'win' in the competitive struggle for resources and the pocketbooks of the consumers? What will happen is that the managers of NIP will only be able to subsidize 'winners' after they have been picked by the market or, even worse, impose their own vision of what should 'win.'

The founder of Atari, Inc., Nolan Bushnell, has noted that the "Atari Democrats," people like Senator Gary Hart, Senator Hollins, and their intellectual advisors Robert Reich, Lester Thurow, and Felix Rohatyn, "would never have targeted Atari." "Or, to put it another way," Louis Rukeyser said, "I personally have never met any bureaucrat who would have had the foresight to give seed capital to the prickly mavericks who started Apple Computer." Charles Schultze cites a study by the Swedish economist Assar Lindbeck who has analyzed industrial specialization among advanced countries. Lindbeck demonstrates quite convincingly that a country's industrial specialization rests to a significant degree on "historical coincidence and momentum." "In short," according to Charles Schultze, "the winners emerge from a very individualistic search process, only loosely governed by broad national advantages in relative labor, capital, or natural resource costs. The competence, knowledge, and specific attributes that go with successful entrepreneurship and export capability are so narrowly defined and so fine-grained that they cannot be assigned to any particular nation. The 'winners' come from a highly decentralized search process." Louis Rukeyser is rightly concerned that the "doctors" employed by the "new" industrial policy advocates "May kill [the] patient"--that an appropriate national industrial policy in Washington, D. C. would be "government butt out."

Recognizing the difficulty of anticipating the future accurately, and witnessing the depressing results of the actual experiments with central planning, what are we to make of the following bit of grandiose nonsense from Magaziner and Reich in *Minding America's Business*?

> And yet, these [European] countries continue to develop industrial policies that are *becoming more sophisticated in design and application.*

343

Since the *most effective* of these industrial policies are often the *most subtle*, it is very *difficult to evaluate precisely their extent and effects.* With some *notable exceptions,* however, these policies are playing a positive role in the countries' economic development. (emhpasis added)


## POLITICS AND INDUSTRIAL POLICY

There is little reason to believe that government bureaucrats will be more successful than private business management in making efficient production and marketing decisions. Furthermore, the essential nature of politics compounds the problems confronting the politician and civil servant. Representative democracy guarantees that numerous political constituencies will have to be served by political entrepreneurship. Political solutions--the application of the "political means"--to social problems will rarely, if ever, be devoted to economic efficiency. Magaziner, Reich, and Thurow all document the inadequacy of government policy initiatives in the past. The federal government's model cities program, for example, which was to be an experiment in a very few cities, eventually provided federal subsidies to more than 150 American communities. The Economic Development Administration of the U. S. Department of Commerce likewise was created to provide economic assistance to distressed areas. But the political process produced eligibility standards so loose that 80 percent of the communities in the United States are now eligible. With respect to the Urban Development Action Grant program, over half of America's cities and towns qualify for aid.

The political process of interest group pressures has produced a tariff schedule in the United States which protects declining industries at the expense of the more productive high growth industries. Federal subsidies and tax breaks accrue to politically powerful interest groups and *not* to strategic industries. Aid to the high-technology industries in the United States is mostly an accidental by-product of our national defense budget. Government budgetary outlays, loans, guarantees, tariffs, subsidies are usually distributed on political grounds that have little to do with economic efficiency. Yet, Robert Reich would have us believe that errors of the past can be eliminated by rationalizing government and more "coherent" planning. He suggests that "the process of economic policy formation remains decentralized and chaotic," and that "if an industrial policy is to enhance the economy's international competitiveness, it must do so with a scalpel rather than with a sledgehammer," The new industrial policy will require, according to Magaziner and Reich, a centralized planning bureaucracy with responsibilities in four areas: "coherence, foresight, accountability, and competence." Mystical dreams and political systems notwithstanding, the evidence of history runs exactly counter to such wishspeak.

Considerable scholarship indicates that the very essence of political institutions prevents government from making hard choices. "The formal and informal institutions of the political system," Schultze reminds us, "are designed to hinder government from making hard choices among specific individuals, rewarding some and penalizing others." When government is "taking" from one group to provide subsidies to another, politicians will attempt to disguise the essential nature of these transfers. It is the market means on the other hand-- the competitive market process--which makes the hard choices and therefore improves efficiency and stimulates economic growth. The politics of public investment, as we have shown to be true in Japan, requires that gifts be distributed among all politically influential constituencies. Neither the American political system nor any other will make critical choices on the basis of economic efficiency. Government policies toward particular industries are seldom decided on economic merit.

Indeed, the founding fathers distrusted the power of king or parliament to distribute government favors and were apprehensive about politically motivated decisions to affect the circumstances of particular individuals. Such government policy, they argued, would often be capricious, arbitrary, and hence should be avoided at all costs. "The question again facing Mr. Mondale and other liberals...is," according to *New Republic* columnist Morton M. Kondracke: "How much do we want government to do?...[The] persistent disparagement of government impels liberals to look for new ways to answer: More." In November of 1983, as already noted, a Democratic Party caucus voted unanimously to create a Council on Economic Competitiveness and Cooperation which would sponsor greater governmental involvement in industrial decision making in the United States. Senator Edward Kennedy pronounced this move "a clear alternative to Reaganomics." Unfortunately, any attempt by government to achieve a degree of "coherence" and "coordination" supposedly unattainable by the market process is doomed to failure. What kind of madness is it to cite innumerable examples of how the political process has created distortions and inefficiencies in the American industrial structure as an argument for giving the government *even greater* powers? The idea that a triumvirate of "government, labor, and business" be placed in charge of "industrial policy" in the United States is, as Mancur Olson in his book *The Rise and Decline of Nations* observes, the equivalent of "asking people with a vested interest in the firms and jobs that now exist to make decisions about those that should exist. It is anti-entrant, pro-establishment, and status-quoist."

The case for a national industrial policy, in summary, is simply without merit. To quote the chairman of President Carter's Council of Economic Advisors once again:

> America is *not* de-industrializing. Japan does *not* owe its industrial success to its industrial policy. Government is *not* able to devise a 'winning' industrial structure. Finally, it is *not* possible in the American political system to pick and choose among individual firms and regions in the substantive, efficiency-driven way envisaged by advocates of industrial policy.

Government's role should be restricted, not enlarged. And Federal budget deficits need to be progressively reduced, through *spending* cuts, not tax increases. Monetary policy, in turn, must reduce the inflationary increases in the money supply which have occurred in the past. Market alternatives coupled with sound fiscal and monetary policies are, after all, the prescription for economic progress.

## THE FASCIST ANALOGY

The fervent advocacy of a new national industrial policy in the United States raises, as suggested in the lead quotation, another important question. Following the arguments made forty years ago by John Flynn, in his book *As We Go Marching,* and the more recent work of authors like Charlotte Twight in her *America's Emerging Fascist Economy,* we question the attachment of many public officials to the ideas of capitalism and private ownership. It seems that many proponents of a new industrial policy reflect an underlying ideological commitment to a societal order which only permits private property when it facilitates production, military prowess, and other collectivist goals.

Fascist regimes, like those of Italy, Germany, Japan, and Spain during the 1930's, are representative of a totalitarian order in which the nebulous idea of group "rights" are placed above individual rights. As Charlotte Twight has noted, "although fascism gives lip service to capitalism, a fascist economy is essentially orchestrated from the top by its political authorities." For example, Italy's "Program Manifesto of the Fascist Republican Party" asserted the following claim: "In the national economy, everything that, in scope or function, goes beyond private interests and affects those of the community comes within the State's sphere of action,." By definition, the "national interest" requires that a fascist government determine what goods are produced and which industries are given preferential treatment. The outcome of this allocation process, orchestrated from above, must obviously differ from what a truly free competitive market would have produced. The Italian and German experiments with fascist regimes began by imposing central government control over a few key industries, but eventually and predictably the sphere of government control over the nominally capitalist economy was widened to include almost every sector of the economy.

346

Fascism has always been associated with the creation of industrial cartels. Germany and Italy in the 1930's, like the Ministry of International Trade and Industry in Japan today, encouraged the "rationalization" of industry. Mandatory trade associations and laws which forced business firms to join existing cartels to suppress competition were present in the 1930's in Italy, Germany, and Japan. As John Flynn pointed out in *As We Go Marching*, in 1933 Franklin Roosevelt's National Recovery Administration (NRA) authorized and encouraged American businesses to band together and "rationalize" their industries. In effect the NRA was an agency designed to cartelize American industry, suppress competition, and protect existing producers from potential competitors. These kinds of associations, cartels, and government enforcing agencies favor existing, large firms against new, entrepreneurial businesses. Many of the richest and most influential owners of the large German industries in the early 1930's, for example, assisted in Hitler's rise to power. According to Charlotte Twight, "...a symbiotic relationship between large corporations and the fascist state emerges, as big business envisions fascism's political decision-making to be a means of excluding competitors without facing the rigors of the marketplace."

When Robert Reich and the Democratic Party caucus refer to a triumvirate of "government, business, and labor," we should be aware of what they mean. "Business" does not refer to the thousands of small entrepreneurial firms emerging all around the country in electronics, software, bio-engineering, communications, engineering, etc. The word refers to the National Association of Manufacturers and the large American steel and automobile firms which are finding it difficult to compete with the more efficient and dynamic Japanese companies. "Labor" means the AFL/CIO---"big labor;" not the individual technician or engineer working in Silicon Valley, the IBM service representative, the accountant in the U. S. headquarters building of Toyota, Inc. in Torrance, California, or the successful auto salesperson working in the Buick dealership.

As political allocation of resources invariably leads to economic inefficiency and higher costs, and as imports in turn become more competitive, fascist governments inevitably turn to trade protectionism to escape the reality of their economic failure. Government intervention synergistically leads to more government influence and power until the very life blood of a private property and individualistic society is extinguished. "As a fascist government increasingly usurps the functions of private enterprise in providing the daily necessities of its citizens such as health care, food, housing, energy, and insurance," according to Charlotte Twight, "the individual becomes acutely aware that his survival is dependent upon government decisions that he, as an individual, cannot significantly influence."

Ayn Rand, in her essay "The New Fascism: Rule by Consensus," points out that a central tenet of fascism, or socialism in any of its forms, is "rule by consensus." Individual rights are sacrificed to the needs of the state, and "compromise" is required "in every realm...so that no group would step over the line by demanding too much and topple the whole rotted structure." Do the Robert Reich's, Felix Rohatyn's, Lester Thurow's, Gal Alperowitz's of the world, unknowingly and we presume without malice, push us toward a collectivist system of fascism?

The claim of something "new" in the collection of proposals known as national industrial policy is without foundation. Walter Mondale, Senator Gary Hart, Senator Alan Cranston, and Senator Edward Kennedy no doubt believe that they have discovered a refreshing and beneficial way to increase the scope of government in our individual lives. Nevertheless, they make a grievous error. The fundamental problem with their scenario has been clearly identified by Robert Nozick in his famous book *Anarchy, State, and Utopia:* "To strengthen the state and extend the range of its functions as a way of preventing it from being used by some portion of the populace makes it a more valuable prize and a more alluring target for corrupting by anyone able to offer an officeholder something desirable; it is, to put it gently, a poor strategy."

## SUPPLY-SIDE ECONOMICS

While we question the degree to which industrial policy in Japan has been an important source of economic growth, there are other facts of the Japanese experience since the end of World War II which are not debatable. First, the tax burden on the people of Japan has been lower than in any of the other industrial countries thorugh the whole period. Second, the fraction of the Gross National Produce saved and therefore devoted to domestic capital formation--the additions to plant, equipment, and capital infrastructure--has been greater than 30 percent over the past three decades. A striking statistic on the comparative performance of productivity gains in Japan, Europe, and North America is the strong, positive correlation between the rate of capital formation and the rate of increase in labor force productivity and therefore standards of living. Countries with high rates of investment, for instance Japan, and to a lesser degree Germany and France, are the countries which have shown the highest rates of growth in productivity. Countries with slower rates of capital formation, like the United States and the United Kingdom, have had slower rates of gain in labor productivity.

Supply-side economics is a phrase which reminds us of certain characteristics of human behavior. If you pay people to work, they will work; if you pay people not to work, they won't. Work effort is sensitive to the reward associated with an *extra* hour of work. High marginal tax rates--the tax rate imposed on *additional* income--influence our behavior with respect to work versus leisure (or possibley decisions on joining the "underground" economy). Similarly, if the reward to saving rises relative to the reward to current consumption, individuals are very likely to increase saving and therefore contribute to a higher rate of capital formation. Again, high marginal tax rates on income from captial and entrepreneurial activity tend to discourage saving and therefore investment. While average tax burdens in most European countries are higher than our own, the structure of their tax systems tends to favor saving and capital investment and discourage current consumption. The European Economic Community's value added tax (VAT) increases the cost of present consumption and lowers the cost of future consumption, that is, saving. In most European countries and Japan, capital gains are either not taxed or if they are, at considerable lower rates than in the United States. Our practice of taxing both corporate profits and dividends as personal income is almost unheard of in Europe.

The goal remains, however, to reduce tax burdens, not just redistribute them. While perhaps overstated by George Gilder in his *Wealth and Poverty,* the fact remains that incentives do matter. Governments do not create jobs by taxing others who would otherwise have hired people. Jobs and wealth are created by entrepreneurs who mobilize capital in an attempt to satisfy consumer wants. What is needed in the United States is not a new industrial policy, but a reinvigoration of the entrepreneurial spirit which has contributed so importantly to our position of economic preeminence in the world. High tax burdens not only discourage work effort and saving, but shift large parts of our highly skilled and educated population to employments which assist people in reducing their tax burdens. Late in the 1970's Italy's Institute Centrale de Statistica revised the domestic production statistics upward by 10 percent to account for what is now called the "underground economy." Upward revisions have been made in other countries for the same reason. A number of studies in the United States suggest Americans are avoiding taxes (and also avoiding prosecution for activity which is illegal under the existing law) to such a degree that the underground economy--economic activity taking place outside the purview of the Internal Revenue Service--might be as much as 10 percent of the Gross National Product or in excess of $300 billion. The veterinarian neuters the lawyer's cat in exchange for some legal advice. A house is painted at an extremely attractive price, but the entrepreneurial painter insists that payment be in cash. Unfortunately, a substantial underground economy distorts economic signals, hides socially useful information regarding relative scarcities, and is generally inefficient. Unemployment figures are probably overstated, and inflation is quite likely less than the published indices, thereby giving misleading signals to policy makers.

If tax rates are to be lowered, government expenditures must be reduced. Significant personal income tax rate cuts initiated by the Reagan administration in 1981, without equivalent reductions in federal spending, have produced massive federal deficits. The deficits have in turn produced a great deal of uncertainty regarding the federal government's budgetary decisions and the course of action the Federal Reserve System will take regarding the money supply and, as a consequence, inflation. Ultimately the supply-side agenda will have its true test when federal spending is reduced. Whatever we might say about the incentive effects of lower marginal tax burdens, the fact remains that it is government *spending* which transfers resources out of the private sector and into the public sector. It is the outlay side of the budget which exhausts resources and makes those resources unavailable for capital formation or personal consumption.

# CHAPTER 23

## CONTROLLING THE SIZE OF GOVERNMENT

In the year of the American Declaration of Independence, Adam Smith observed that 'what is prudence in the conduct of every private family, can scarcely be folly in that of a great kingdom.' Until the advent of the 'Keynesian Revolution' in the middle of this century, the fiscal conduct of the American Republic was informed by this Smithian principle of fiscal responsiblity...the message of Keynesianism might be summarized as follows: What is folly in the conduct of a private family may be prudence in the conduct of the affairs of a great nation.
--James M. Buchanan and Richard E. Wagner

There is no surer means of overturning the existing basis of society than to debauch the currency. The process engages all the hidden forces of economic law on the side of destruction, and does it in a manner which not one man in a million is able to diagnose.
--John Maynard Keynes

Through the processes of deregulation and privatization, ways have been shown where specific categories of federal, state, and local government expenditures and intervention in the economy can be significantly reduced. The restoration of economic freedom, individual responsibility, and a commitment to a society devoted to human liberty mandates that government's role be constrained. The anatomy of government failure suggests that using government as a social delivery system violates individual rights and suppresses purposeful and peaceful human action. In addition, existing arrangements indicate a fundamental defect in democracy in the sense that special interest groups seem capable of pushing government spending higher and higher. Solutions must be found to the dilemma of controlling this leviathan that is government.

### GROWTH IN THE FEDERAL GOVERNMENT

Federal budget outlays in fiscal year 1983 reached $795.9 billion, almost *double* the $400.5 billion six years earlier and more than *four* times larger than $195.7 billion in 1970. President Reagan's fiscal 1985 budget proposes outlays of $925 billion, an increase of $130 billion in just two years. It was barely two decades ago that annual federal spending passed the $100 billion mark. While total budget outlays were 9.7 percent of the gross national product (GNP) on the eve of World War II, they had climbed to 14.7 percent of GNP by 1950, 18.2 percent in 1960, 21.5 percent in 1977, and in 1981 22.3

percent. By the end of the third year of the Reagan administration total federal outlays had risen to 25 percent of the GNP.

Even after adjusting for inflation, "real" federal budget outlays were 62 percent higher in fiscal 1983 than in 1970 and 27 percent higher than they had been as recently as 1977. The explosive growth in federal spending has occurred primarily in three areas: the so-called "entitlements" programs, interest payments on the national debt, and in the last few years defense spending. Payments to individuals under social security, medicare, and other welfare programs in 1970 were $63.3 billion, in 1977 $192.4 billion, and in 1983 reached almost $400 billion, a doubling in six years. By 1986 these payments to individuals are expected to be more than $450 billion. Health care services under medicare and medicaid almost tripled in the six years ending in 1983, and social security benefit payments doubled, ballooning to $176.2 billion in 1983 from $88.6 billion in 1977. Defense spending was $97.5 billion in 1977; by 1983 it had reached $215 billion. The Reagan administration's request for fiscal 1985 amounted to $315 billion in new spending authority, with actual outlays reaching about $265 billion. After adjusting for inflation, defense outlays were up 31 percent during the six year period ending in fiscal 1983. If the Reagan administration plans for defense spending reach $325 billion in 1986, it would represent a 71 percent increase in real terms since 1977. With federal outlays growing much faster than federal tax revenues, massive federal deficits and higher interest rates have produced large increases in interest payments on the outstanding national debt. Net interest payments in the federal budget were $7.7 billion in 1963, $14.4 billion in 1970, $29.9 billion in 1977, and by fiscal 1984 exceeded $100 billion.

Of course, with federal spending growing at 10 percent per annum, federal taxes have also risen. Individual income taxes approached $300 billion in 1982, an increase from $157.6 billion in 1977, while Social Security and related taxes went from $92.2 billion in 1977 to $180.7 billion in 1982, a doubling in just five years. In fiscal 1984, social security taxes are expected to be more than $215 billion. Fortunately, the Reagan administration's reductions in tax *rates* on personal incomes have kept individual income tax revenues roughly unchanged since 1981. However, unless something substantial is cut from the 1985 budget, personal income taxes will renew their seemingly relentless upward climb.

Actually the startling increase in the size of the federal budget over the past twenty years significantly understates the magnitude of government's size and impact on the American ecnomy. Quoting bank economist Irwin Kellner: the budget is just "the tip of the iceberg...If Washington cannot control the visible portion, how can it be expected to reduce the portion that lies beneath the surface, away from public scrutiny." For example, the Federal Financing Bank (FFB), supposedly as an efficiency move, was created in 1974 to facilitate federal borrowing for "off-budget" spending programs. In 1983 the FFB assisted federal agencies to raise more than $26 billion "off the books." The Export-Import Bank, Farmers Home Administration, Postal Service, Rural Electrification Administration, and other federal agencies have all used the FFB for funds not appearing as federal budget outlays. Prior to 1974 these off-budget outlays had been negligible.

In addition, there are numerous federally sponsored enterprises which, as a result of Washington's backing, borrow in the capital markets at lower than market rates. These quasi-private enterprises include, among others, the Federal National Mortgage Association, Banks for Cooperatives, Federal Home Loan Banks, and the Student Loan Marketing Association. These federally sponsored programs borrow tens of billions of dollars each year to subsidize particular interest groups in the economy. Finally, there has been an explosive increase in guaranteed loan programs by both on-budget and off-budget agencies. In 1982 these commitments were $53 billion. Shockingly, in fiscal 1983 they almost doubled to $102.7 billion. While the federal government does not borrow this money, the guarantee in effect allows special interests preferential and easy access to the economy's money markets. Such subsidies misallocate scarce capital funds and distort efficiency signals regarding capital market priorities. In the 1960's these guaranteed loans averaged about $5 billion per year, $15 billion in the 1970's, and lately have ranged from $32.4 billion in 1980 to the $102 billion already cited for 1983. Borrowing by federally sponsored enterprises averaged about $1.5 billion a year in the 1960's, but has exceeded $20 billion per year since 1978. If these off-budget and guaranteed loan borrowing programs are added to the massive budget deficits, in fiscal 1983 total federal borrowing absorbed roughly 130 percent of our nation's total net saving. Stated differently, the federal demand for credit in recent years represents more than half of the total flow-of-funds in the economy's credit markets.

Unfortunately, budget outlays, off-budget spending, and loan guarantees also fail to measure the full burden of the government on the economy, not to mention human freedom. Though difficult to measure and frequently hidden from view, indirect and qualitative changes in the federal government have enlarged its sphere of influence. For example, standard measures of government employment understate its true magnitude. The U. S. Census Bureau reported that in 1982 total civilian government employment in the U. S. was 15,932,693, representing roughly 15 percent of the civilian labor force, or about one out of every seven working people are employed by government. Federal employment was reported at 2,862,000, which was actually down three thousand from the previous year. But in fact, these statistics fail to measure the very large number of "invisible workers" in the federal government. How is it possible that federal employment has remained stable, when four new cabinet-level departments have been created over the past twenty-five years: Urban Development, Transportation, Energy, and Education?

Economist James Bennett has documented changes in the "qualitative aspects" of federal employment which significantly enlarge the real presence of government workers. First, there has been an explosive increase in workers, supposedly in the private sector, who are paid by government. Hundreds of thousands of consultants, contractors, and state and local government workers draw their paycheck from the U. S. Treasury. In 1979, Joseph Califano, Secretary of Health, Education and Welfare (HEW), reported that HEW was paying the salaries of almost one million people in think tanks, universities, and other units of government. The Department of Defense alone hires contractors and subcontractors numbering over 2 million. Barbara Blumenthal in her article "Uncle Sam's Army of Invisible Employees" estimates this "indirest" federal employment to be about *eight* million workers! In other words, total federal employment, both official and indirect, is closer to 10 million rather than the official statistics of less than 3 million. Even the official figures are biased downward as a result of the time-honored practice of hiding federal employees among the "25-and-ones," a term describing the practice of federal employees being full-time for 25 of the 26 annual pay periods, but in the pay period in which total employment is to be counted they are shifted to part-time status.

The federal work force has also experienced dramatic shifts in its composition and grade levels. The white collar, General Schedule (GS) federal employees have multiplied much faster than the blue-collar workers. Between 1959 and 1978 James Bennett reports that GS employees increased by 44 percent while the number of blue-collar workers decreased by 33 percent. Although total direct federal employment has grown slowly since 1959, the *type* of work done has changed a great deal. Instead of cleaning a building or typing a letter, federal employees today are more involved in regulaton, examination, auditing, investigating, and generally interfering with the market economy. In other words policymakers and regulators have gained stature and power while lower grade blue-collar workers have dwindled in number. Within the GS civil service schedule, the senior grades have also increased relative to the lower grades. During the period 1959 through 1978, for example, the executive grades GS-13 to GS-18 *tripled* to 134,049, while those in the lower GS grades decreased by almost 90,000. The statistics on total, direct federal employment unfortunately do not reveal this massive shift. In terms of economic efficiency, the blue-collar worker's cost to the economy is basically salary and fringe benefits. The impact on the economy of a senior GS rating, however, far exceeds salary: the regulator, examiner, and OSHA inspector impose additonal costs of compliance

354

on the private sector.

The size and impact of the federal government is also understated by a failure to explicityly recognize the costs of future commitments to spend. The federal government rarely reminds us of the unfunded and uncounted liabilities arising from many federal programs. The U. S. Department of the Treasury reported at the end of 1977 that government liabilities and commitments from all sources exceeded $7 *trillion*. Funding deficiencies for social security, federal retirement programs, international commitments, and government guarantees, to name the larger ones, were almost $5.4 trillion. The $200 billion federal budget deficits now discussed by Congress and the President seldom mention the degree to which the future holds the American people hostage. If modifications are not made in the military retirement program, the federal civilian retirement programs, and the social security system, federal tax burdens could very shortly crush the economy. The adverse incentive effects of required tax increases will also discourage production and therefore make it even more difficult to pay these unfunded liabilities. The word entitlement" will take on its real meaning--an empty phrase.

Finally, it is important to understand the magnitude of the problem associated with the regulators and inspectors employed by the federal bureaucracy. Murray Weidenbaum, economist and former Chairman of the President's Council of Economic Advisors, estimated that in 1979 the total cost of federal regulations-- administrative *and* compliance costs--was in excess of $100 billion per year, or more than a 50 percent increase in three years. The federal budget, however, reports only the administrative costs which are only about five percent of the total. In 1977 the Commission on Federal Paperwork estimated that the total cost of processing paperwork, including that associated with regulation, was approximately $100 billion each year. The federal government's share was $42 billion, and the rest was born by the private sector and state and local government. The Internal Revenue Service, in 1977, used 13,200 different kinds of forms and letters. Early in the 1970's, the Office of Management and Budget reported that federal agencies and offices other than the IRS used 5,567 forms which generated more than 418 million responses from the private sector of the economy. Of course, the paperwork has grown since then.

In summary, the leviathan known as the federal government seemingly grows out of control. James Dale Davidson of the National Taxpayers Union makes the useful analogy of issuing 535 American Express credit cards to House and Senate members, but where no one is responsible for paying the monthly bill. Is it any wonder that federal spending, whether tabulated on the official or hidden budgets, continues its relentless upward march? The share of federal budget spending to the GNP has risen during the first Reagan administration almost three percentage points from 22.3 percent in fiscal 1980 to about 25 percent in 1983. Federal spending during peacetime has never been higher as a fraction of economic activity. The hidden part, and obviously the part less subject to public scrutiny, has grown even faster in the past decade. Whether measured in terms of "off-budget" spending, loan guarantees, or indirect federal employment, the size and impact of the federal government continues to expand and threatens the very survival of the market system.

## THE ADVERSE IMPLICATIONS OF FEDERAL DEFICITS

The explosive increase in federal expenditures has not been matched by an equivalent increase in tax revenues. The politician, of course, is rewarded by appropriating more money, but very seldom admired for raising taxes. Federal budget deficits have necessarily risen with the rapid growth in spending. During the 1950's, the largest federal deficit was almost $13 billion, during the 1960's $25 billion, the 1970's $66 billion, and since 1980 and through fiscal year 1985 the *smallest* federal deficit has been $58 billion. The red ink for fiscal 1983 reached $195.4 billion, and both 1984 and 1985 are expected to also push $200 billion. The cumulative deficit during the first four years of the conservative Reagan presidency will approach $600 billion. There are many who believe federal deficits will rise to the $300 billion level and even higher in the late 1980's, if spending programs, especially "entitlement" programs, are not cut back. In recent years "entitlements" have accounted for about 50 percent of federal outlays, military and international spending more than 30 percent, and interest on the national debt roughly 12 percent. If *all* other federal outlays were eliminated, amounting to about $70 billion in 1983, the federal deficit would only be *reduced* by less than 40 percent.

Given the staggering deficits, the national debt naturally continues to grow. In 1970 the national debt, representing the interest bearing bonded indebtedness of the U. S. Treasury was $383 billion, by 1975 $544 billion, and in 1980 $914 billion, or about 35 percent of the GNP. At the end of fiscal 1983 it had risen to a staggering $1.4 trillion, almost *triple* what it had been just eight years earlier and amounting to almost half of GNP. The President's Office of Management and Budget (OMB), given current forecasts of federal spending and taxes, believes it likely that the national debt will reach $2 trillion by the end of 1987. Without spending control, the Reagan administration's Economic Recovery and Tax Act (ERTA) of 1981--which the OMB calculates as more than $600 billion in "lost" tax revenues between 1982 and 1986--produced the widening gap between federal outlays and receipts.

The pattern of recurrent budget deficits, growing progressively larger over the past three decades, represents a fundamental break from our past. From the first U. S. Treasury budget of 1789 through 1930, the U. S. ran 45 deficits and 95 surpluses. Most of the deficits, however, were incurred during war or economic distress. But following these emergency periods, surpluses were invariably maintained and the national debt was reduced. Since 1931, on the other hand, the federal budget has been in deficit close to 90 percent of the time. There have been only five surpluses since 1950, the *last* being in 1969. And, as noted, the national debt continues to explode with what appears to be a whole series of $200 billion deficits in the 1980's. The OMB now predicts that by the late 1980's the annual *interest* burden of the national debt might easily exceed $150 billion per year or almost 14 percent of federal expenditures.

Federal deficits, in turn, have become public enemy number one. Politicians of all ideologies are stressing the need to lower the deficits. The results of a Wall Street Journal/Gallup survey released early in January 1984 showed, for example, that business executives of large, medium and small firms believe the size of the federal budget deficit to be the most bothersome economic problem. Or as one executive commented, ''all of the other problems depend on it.'' Though economists quarrel over the exact nature of the problems presented by the deficits, they universally recommend a significant reduction in the imbalance between federal outlays and tax revenues. In the survey of business executives the most popular solutions to the deficits were to trim the so-called entitlement programs and defense spending. Increasing taxes finished a distant third.

The concern over federal red ink arises from perceptions regarding the impact of large deficits on inflation, interest rates, capital spending, and therefore the health of the economy in general. Unfortunately, economists differ a great deal with respect to the impact of deficits on the economy. Nevertheless, the most believeable scenario is that large budget deficits absorb domestic saving, push up real interest rates, and ''crowd-out'' private sector spending, especially capital outlays on plant and equipment so necessary to sustain economic growth and modernize the U. S. economy. Large federal deficits require that the Treasury enter the capital markets in competition with private sector borrowers for a limited amount of savings. Although higher interest rates probably tend to increase saving, the competition between federal borrowing and private credit demands pushes up real interest rates and therefore reduces the number of new, profitable business investments in the private sector. This interpretation maintains that the principle cost to the economy of large deficits is the reduction in the rate of capital formation. And significantly, these costs show up only years later in the form of lower standards of living than otherwise would have occurred.

However, supply-siders, supported in part by another group of economists who subscribe to "rational expectations," remind us, importantly we believe, that it is government *spending* which absorbs resources and reduces the size of the private sector, not deficits. "The villian," supply-side economist Norman Ture tells us, "is government spending. This is what crowds out, not the deficit." Government outlays, after all, on typewriters, battle tanks, subsidized housing, and agriculturel surpluses, for example, withdraw resources from the private sector. And this is true regardless of how the expenditures are financed--taxes, printing new money, or the issuance of more government bonds. Admittedly, the means of financing federal outlays do determine the distribution of burdens among individuals in the economy; *but*, it is imperative to recognize that it is the level of government spending on the nation's output of goods and services which determines what remains for the private sector. In this view, the deficit is not the main concern; rather, it is the outlay side of the federal budget. Both "entitlement" programs--including social security, medicare, and other welfare programs--and defense spending continue what seem to be an irresistable upward climb. For this reason, the health of the American economy depends far less on deficit reducing increases in taxes than it does on our ability to first slow the rate of growth in spending and eventually to cut the size of government.

Richard Wagner and Robert Tollison, in their monograph *Balanced Budgets, Fiscal Responsibility, and the Constitution,* emphasize the important categorical destinction between tax financed government outlays and the issuance of bonded indebtedness and/or new money creation. It does not matter, in fact, how expenditures are financed; government outlays transfer resources in the economy from individuals to government. "The fundamental distinction is really not so much one of balance or imbalance in the budget," according to Wagner and Tollison, "but rather is one of whether the balance was achieved explicity and openly or was achieved implicitly and secretively." When we balance the federal budget with tax revenues the costs are above-board and explicit and therefore thought to be proper. On the other hand, the act of financing government expenditures through interest bearing bonds and printing more paper money is deemed improper, expedient, and therefore wrong. There is an openness in tax finance which is clearly absent when government borrows or uses the printing press. There is a feeling of deceit and underhandedness. The fundamental argument for a balanced budget, where outlays are financed by taxes and fees, is simply a call for "truth in packaging." When the federal government makes expenditure commitments, the requirement that the transfer of resources to government be through higher taxes reflects the view that the costs be made explicit and clearly understood by the citizenry.

# CONTROLLING FEDERAL SPENDING

The startling increase in federal spending over the past half century, and the extraordinary increase in budget deficits which have accompanied this growth, stems from a veritable collapse in fiscal discipline in the United States. Following the Keynesian Revolution's arrival in the U. S. during the 1930's, "functional" federal finance, or what others call the "compensatory budget philosophy," captured the attention of most economists, and the "unwritten" constitutional prohibition on budget deficits rapidly dissolved. Following the lead of American economists like Alvin Hansen and Abba Lerner, a fiscal revolution transpired which eventually destroyed the American politician's allegiance to balanced budgets and fiscal responsibility. Or, as economist Paul McCracken has pointed out, "compensatory fiscal policy introduced the view that there are times when the budget should not be balanced. And it has been easy for government to conclude that 'now' is one of those times."

With the erosion of the unwritten constitutional prohibition on budget deficits, an underlying bias--what some call a fundamental defect in democracy--came to be recognized in the budget process. Similar to the present behavior of most of the 50 states, prior to the Great Depression federal expenditures were also largely determined by revenue estimates. Especially since the mid-1960's, all this has changed. Spending bills are passed, appropriations made, and *then* means are found to raise the necessary money. The bias in favor of ever larger government spending follows the reality of interest group politics in which the benefits of outlays are concentrated among a relatively small group, and the costs are dispersed among a much large and less well organized group of citizen/taxpayers. Politicians naturally respond to special interest pleading for immediate benefits, and try to shift the cost to the general taxpayer, preferably with payments at a later date. The "committee system" in Congress guarantees that members serve on those committees representing their own geographic constituencies. They are rewarded of course by re-election for serving their district's particular interests. A profound dilemma, therefore, is how to control the growth in federal spending, given the implications for the behavior of politicians by the "economic theory of democracy."

There have been numerous proposals, short of amending the Constitution, which proponents hoped would slow the rate of increase in federal spending and/or tax revenues. On the revenue side, President Reagan has proposed a far-reaching revision in the U. S. tax code labeled by some as "tax simplification." The proposale include closing loopholes, repeal of tax exemptions and deductions, a consumption tax, and a "flat rate" personal income tax. Democrats have proposed similar changes. However, the great unknown is the degree to which the proposed changes are tax reductions or, as some would describe them, "revenue enhancers." Tax simplification has been a topic for a long time. Presidents Nixon, Ford, and Carter all studied the issue. Unfortunately, the ultimate outcome of all this "simplification" usually means higher, not lower, taxes. When politicians talk about "broadening the tax base," they are referring to raising *more* money, not less.

Full "indexing" of the federal personal income tax, scheduled to go into effect in 1985 under the Economic Recovery and Tax Act of 1981, must be retained. In the past, politicians have driven American's into higher tax brackets through inflationary financing of government expenditures. Given the progressive nature of the income tax schedule, and the fact that tax liabilities are currently based on money incomes before adjustment for inflation, a rising price level pushes taxpayers into higher marginal tax brackets. This "bracket creep" has raised personal tax liabilities significantly over the past ten or fifteen years. Many in Congress are lobbying for the repeal of tax indexing before its scheduled implementation in 1985. It is imperative that full indexing be retained so that tax burdens cannot be increased simply through the devious method of higher rates of inflation. To a degree, indexing will instill some discipline on the outlay side of the federal budget. Unlike President Carter's last budget, the promise of a balanced federal budget should not be based on higher taxes from the bracket creep associated with inflationary finance.

The revenue side of the budget is not the fundamental problem. The point bears repeating: it is government expenditures which transfer resources from the private to the government sector. Crowding-out arises not from deficits, but from the spending which generates the red ink. An editorial in the *Wall Street Journal* made the relevant point:

> The choice is as clear as it can be. If we want America to have primarily a public economy, we should quit whining about the deficit and let congressional policies proceed toward that goal. If instead we want primarily a private economy, we simply have to cut spending

A number of economists and budget watchers believe that the president should be given a "line-item-veto" over the federal budget. Most, if not all, governors have the power to veto individual items in the budgets of state legislatures. For example, the governor of California, George Deukmejian, has used the line-item-veto to slow the growth in state spending in California since being elected in 1982. All presidents have requested this authority, including Franklin Roosevelt. The national constituency which elects a president would permit a greater degree of discipline on appropriations, and therefore offer significant gains in fiscal prudence. Of course, Congress has traditionally opposed the line-item-veto as an invasion of its responsibilities. A variant on the line veto proposes an "omnibus of item vetos" which would be voted up or down as a total package. The president would not have veto authority on a particular item, but would submit to Congress a whole group of line vetos on which the House and Senate would vote as a unit.

Longtime congressional budget expert Allen Schick has proposed an amendment to the 1974 Budget Act which he believes would mean a greater fiscal discipline to the budget process. Total outlays woud be established and fixed at the start of the budget process in light of the state of the economy and spending requirements. In turn, the allocation within the total budget by budget function and therefore Congressional committee would be binding on the entire Congress. The relevant committees would allocate funds within the functional categories. Committee members would be forced to allocate revenues among competing uses and therefore recognize priorities.

There have been other reform proposals short of a constitutional amendment, but unfortunately experience with the Budget Impoundment and Control Act of 1974, given existing attitudes and political pressures, provides little evidence that Congress can discipline its actions. As Joe Cobb of the Choice in Currency Commission in Washington, D.C., has said, "the more Congress tries to deal with the problem by statute, the worse the problem gets." The 1974 legislation was to enforce a "discipline of the total" on Congress by requiring an outlay total be established during the budget process. Since this would have represented a true constraint, Congress has been incapable of agreeing on the budget total and has dodged the issue by authorizing federal agencies to spend at "current levels." Deadlines pass, and budgets are not finalized. The Budget Impoundment and Control Act of 1974, instigated by President Nixon's refusal to spend certain appropriated monies, was heralded and sold as the means by which fiscal discipline would be restored. Unfortunately, it is a demonstrable failure. Since 1974, federal expenditures have risen much faster than ever before, and government deficits are of course much higher than could have been imagined just a few years ago.

## CONSTITUTIONAL REFORM

The abject failure of the Budget Control Act of 1974 to slow the growth in federal spending, and reinforced by the Reagan administration's inability to control spending and therefore deal with the staggering deficits, suggests to many that the only solution is an amendment to the U. S. Constitution. The National Tax Limitation Committee and the National Taxpayers Union, historically not particularly friendly, have joined forces to establish a ceiling on federal outlays and implement a plan requiring that Congress plan for balanced budgets.

Constitutional restraints on the federal budget process come in three basic varieties. First, there are those who propose a balanced budget amendment. The executive branch and the Congress would be required to determine the revenues which would be available before spending commitments are made. Or as Wagner and Tollison have observed, "the balanced budget requirement is simply a requirement that government should make explicit the resource extractions promised by and implied in its expenditure promises." Although a balanced budget amendment would not establish explicit limits to the growth in government spending, at the very least Congress would have to openly vote to raise taxes to pay for larger outlays. Public opinion polls in recent years have repeatedly shown a strong interest in an amendment to the Constitution requiring a balanced budget. Gallup, Harris, Roper, the New York Times/CBS polls have found the proportion in favor of an amendment ranging from 63 to 75 percent of those questioned. Opponents see difficulties in accurately forecasting tax revenues, defining government outlays, and the amendment's inflexibility. On the other hand, there are those who oppose this approach because it fails to provide for a control on the *level* of government expenditures. Given the progressive nature of the personal income tax, inflation-fueled increases in federal revenues would support higher spending. Most of the 50 states have constitutional prohibitions on deficits, but spending and taxes have continued to rise.

The second proposal is a spending limitation amendment. Given the present congressional practice of considering federal programs separately in the budgetary process, nobody, in spite of the Budget Control Act of 1974, focuses on the size of the total budget. The purpose of a spending limitation is to place a cap on federal outlays, usually expressed as a fraction of the level of economic activity, such as the national income. In contrast to the balanced budget amendment proposal, the spending cap would be based on actual outlays and therefore be easier to implement. Tax revenues, responding to the state of the economy, would add a stabilizing role to the budget over the business cycle. And for those who wish to restrict the growth in government and increase the flow of resources to the private sector, the spending limitation is clearly superior to the balanced budget proposal. On the other hand, for those who want an absolute reduction in the size of the federal government the problem remains.

Unfortunately, if somehow the unwritten consitutional restraint on the scope of government in our society cannot once again become a part of the belief system of the American people, and therefore among the politicians, even a constitutional amendment would remain unenforceable. For example, the constitutional limit on spending adopted in California in 1979 has been evaded by innovative maneuvers by local governments and the state legislature. In 1980 the Missouri voters approved a constitutional spending cap, but, with its first serious test in 1982, state courts have in effect negated its intent. Or as Alvin Rabushka has noted, "one can question whether any well-designed amendment can permanently withstand the creativity of persistent political challenge and clever judges."

The third proposal involves a constitutional limit on federal taxes. Sadly, the tax control amendment has most of the disadvantages of the balanced budget and spending limitation proposals, with few if any advantages. Tax revenues are largely a function of the level of economic activity, and legislatures, federal and state, are notoriously poor revenue forecasters. A tax ceiling amendment would neither control the growth in government outlays or provide for a balanced budget. In fact, federal borrowing and money creation would be encouraged as politicians attempted to respond to constituents' demands in an environment in which tax revenues were constrained. The problems associated with "crowding-out" the private sector would remain. A final possibility is the adoption of a combination of the three described proposals.

## THE BALANCED BUDGET/TAX LIMITATION AMENDMENT

In August 1982, the United States Senate, by a vote of 69 to 31, passed and sent to the House the Balanced Budget/tax Limitation Amendment to the U. S. Constitution. Later in the House of Representatives, while failing to receive the required two-thirds majority, the bill received a 236-187 majority vote in favor. Currently, 32 of the 34 states required to call the Congress to convene a constitutional convention have acted. The National Tax Limitation Committee and the National Taxpayers Union, as noted, have suppressed past differences and jointly support the proposed amendment. In the House of Representatives, spearheaded by Congressman Larry Craig of Idaho, a number of House members, and a few Senators, have formed a group called the Congressional Leadership United for the Balanced Budget (CLUBB) to push for the enactment of the Balanced Budget/Tax Limitation Amendment to the Constitution.

The proposed amendment reads as follows. Note that the combination of tax limitation and balanced budget provisions have the implication of also establishing a spending limitation.

### JOINT RESOLUTION

Joint resolution proposing an amendment to the Constitution altering federal budget procedures--

Resolved by the Senate and House of Representatives of the United States of America in Congress assembled (two thirds of each House concurring therein),

That the following article is proposed as an amendment to the Constitution of the United States, which shall be valid to all intents and purposes

363

as part of the Constitution if ratified by the legislatures of three-fourths of the several States within seven years after its submission to the States for ratification.

Secion 1. Prior to each fiscal year, the Congress shall adopt a statement of receipts and outlays for that year in which total outlays are not greater than total receipts. The Congress may amend such statement provided revised outlays are no greater than revised receipts. Whenever three-fifths of the whole number of both Houses shall deem it necessary, Congress in such statement may provide for a specific excess of outlays over receipts by a vote directed solely to that subject. The Congress and the President shall, pursuant to legislation or through exercise of their powers under the first and second articles ensure that actual outlays do not exceed the outlays set forth in such statement.

Section 2. Total receipts for any fiscal year set forth in the statement adopted pursuant to this article shall not increase by a rate greater than the rate of increase in national income in the year or years ending not less than six months nor more than twelve months before such fiscal year, unless a majority of the whole number of both Houses of Congress shall have passed a bill directed solely to approving specific additional receipts and such bill has become law.

Section 3. The Congress may waive the provisions of this article for any fiscal year in which a declaration of war is in effect.

Section 4. Total receipts shall include all receipts of the Unites States except those derived from borrowing and total outlays shall include all outlays of the United States except those for repayment of debt principal.

Section 5. This article shall take effect for the second fiscal year beginning after its ratification.

Section 6. The Congress shall enforce and implement this article by appropriate legislation.

Section 1 establishes a "norm" of a balanced budget. The Congress would be required to submit a "statement" or budget in which planned outlays equal revenues. It would require a three-fifths vote of the "whole number" of both houses to adopt a planned deficit. The amendment would not require a balanced budget, but would establish a presumption in favor of that norm. Politicians would have to stand up and be counted if they want to raise taxes or the national debt. Section 1 also provides that actual outlays cannot exceed the planned level of outlays recorded in the "statement." In other words, while deficits are possible under this proposed amendment, they must not be the result of an increase in spending. The planned budget may be amended upward, but if that meant a budget deficit, it would require a three-fifths vote. The term "outlay" refers to both unified budget expenditures and "off-budget" federal spending, but does not include the retirement of outstanding bonds.

Section 2 provides for the ultimate control over the rate of growth in spending. Given the statement of balanced outlays and receipts, Section 2 mandates that tax revenues cannot grow faster than the national income except by the explicit vote of a majority of the "whole number" of the membership of both the House and Senate. If tax receipts appear to be growing faster than permitted under the proposed amendment, Congress must change the tax laws and/or vote to allow taxes to rise faster than the national income. Section 3 of the amendment permits the Congress to waive the provisions of the article during a declaration of war. Sections 1 and 2 in tandem provide for a fiscal norm of a balanced budget in which federal outlays shall not rise faster than the growth in the economy. The revenue provisions of Section 2 represent a *de facto* spending cap for total on-budget plus off-budget outlays. Alvin Rabushka in his analysis of the Balanced Budget/Tax Limitation Amendment has captured the essential character of the discipline to be established:

> By shifting the focus from hundreds of individual spending measures to two or three critical votes each year relating to aggregate levels of taxation and deficits, the amendment is designed to enable the electorate to better identify those members of Congress most responsible for higher levels of spending, taxing, and deficits.

Although blue ribbon support for the Balance Budget/Tax Limitation Amendment continues, including for example the Nobel Laureate Milton Friedman, there are those who do not support the idea of a constitutional amendment. Louis Rukeyser, for example, believes that "we are asking the thieves to write the criminal code." He makes the valid point that "if you could get a balanced budget amendment, you would not need one. Congressmen do not vote for runaway spending because they are inherently evil; they do it because it is popular." For Rukeyser the answer is to make it popular to be fiscally responsible. Only then will government spending decline and budget deficits wither away. Or, according to Joe Cobb, "only an intellectual revolution can force the consistency in the direction of *lower spending,* rather than 'adequate revenues' for a balanced budget."

However, Lewis Uhler, president and founder of the National Tax Limitation Committee, reminds us "to claim perfection would be foolish and arrogant." He believes the proposed amendment moves us in the right direction: "What can be claimed is that the Tax Limitation/Balance Budget Amendment is thoughtfully and soundly crafted to achieve a specific objective: reversal of the current Washington bias toward higher taxes and spending and unbalanced budgets." It is truly problematical whether the "unwritten constitution" against cumulative deficits and a rising national debt can ever be restored. Without some movement in that direction, California and Missouri, among other states, have unfortunately shown the ease with which well motivated politicians can ignore their constitutional mandates about government spending. The basic dilemma was noted by the University of Chicago economist Henry Simon: "Constitutional provisions are no stronger than the moral consensus that they articulate."

## CUTTING THE LEAN OUT OF GOVERNMENT

Staggering increases in federal spending threaten the vitality of the American economy and therefore standards of living and our preeminence among industrial countries. Public sector outlays transfer resources from the private sector and in the process crowd-out modernizing capital expenditures. Future prosperity is held hostage to the relentless growth in government spending. However financed--taxes, bonds or new money, a progessively larger fraction of society's resources continue to be absorbed by government. The appropriate agenda for the American people in the last years of the twentieth century must include a significant *reduction* in federal spending. Our prosperity and freedom depend on it.

As opposed to suggestions for limiting the *growth* in federal outlays, the following proposed budget *cuts* represent a "laundry list," illustrating some measure of the work that needs to be done and difficulties to be encountered when confronting the strongly entrenched special interests. The following proposals are only suggestive of the magnitude of wasteful unproductive federal programs which should be reduced or eliminated. A complete menu of the opportunities for cutting government down to size can be obtained from three detailed studies undertaken in recent years. First, in 1980 the Libertarian Party candidate for President, Ed Clark, commissioned a *White Paper on Taxing and Spending Reduction*. The Clark for President Committee produced a detailed and annotated proposal based on President Carter's fiscal 1981 budget which identified approximately $200 billion in spending cuts. Second, David Boaz in an article in *Inquiry* also produced a long list of recommended budget cuts of almost $280 billion based on the Reagan administration's 1983 budget. Finally, the President's Private Sector Survey on Cost Control chaired by J. Peter Grace, submitted to President Reagan in January 1984, identified potential expenditure reductions of $424 billion over a three year period. Each of these proposals recognized the social benefits of large cuts in federal tax burdens which would accompany the recommended spending reductions.

Unavoidably, this discussion of spending reductions and smaller government will be brief. The possibilities for extended discussion are suggested by the scope of the so-called Grace Commission effort. The President's Private Sector Survey on Cost Control included 18 months of research, $75 million of personally donated time, and $3.3 million in business contributions. It represented the work of 36 task forces, 161 executives, and 2,000 volunteers. The process produced 47 separate reports on waste in government and 23,000 pages of examples of "needless spending." The final report identified 2,500 separate recommendations which would save $424 billion. The Clark and Boaz proposals were much shorter but nevertheless identified

dozens of places to cut. For example, David Boaz specifically identified more than 60 federal agencies, offices, and programs which
were providing subsidies directly to the business sector alone.
In the fiscal 1983 budget of the Reagan administration Boaz found
$48 billion in subsidies to business. In the U. S. Department of
Agriculture, subsidies included agricultrue sales resulting from the
U. S. Foreign Assistance Program, price support payments and loans
through the Commodity Credit Corporation, direct subsidies derived
from the Soil Conservation Service, and more than $3 billion in aid to
agriculture from the activities of the Farmers Home Administration.
The U. S. Department of Commerce, under a number of programs,
spent almost $3 billion in various subsidies to business. Subsidizing
export efforts, weather gathering, the Economic Development Administration, the Minority Business Development Agency, are a few
of the examples. Many federal programs, ostensibly for the benefit of
the poor, in fact provide very lucrative subsidies to business interests.
Programs in the Department of Housing and Urban Development
spent at least $12 billion in 1983 which directly benefit the construc-
tion, real estate, and mortage lending industries. The Urban Mass
Transportation Administration spent more than $3 billion in ineffi-
cient ways in America's cities. The Export-Import Bank provides
massive subsidies to a handful of corporations. The Federal Maritime
Commission offers incredibly generous subsidies to the merchant
marine interests. Synfuels development, college housing loans, the
Federal Railroad Administration, the Kennedy Center, and the
U. S. Travel and Tourism Administration, just begin to scratch the surface.
   The issue of bureaucracy, regulation, and red tape has already
been addressed. Direct budgetary savings among the regulatory
agencies in 1983, for example the CAB, NHTSA, CPSC, FTC, NTSB,
FERC, ad infinitum, could have totaled $3.2 billion. Many federal pro-
grams involve outlays which deprive individuals of their civil rights.
And of course there are tens of billions spent on programs which the
private sector could accomplish at half the cost. Privatization of the
Tennessee Valley Authority has already been advocated. Many other
programs, like the Foundation for Education Assistance, Human
Development Services, Small Business Administration, National
Capital Planning Commission, Community Services Administration,
the Legal Services Corporation, and dozens of other programs should
be seriously reviewed in terms of elimination or sizeable reduction.
   "Entitlements" programs and defense expenditures represent
more than eighty percent of the federal budget. Significant cuts in
total federal spending must address these two areas. An immediate
benefit freeze on social security payments should be adopted until
more substantive reform measures, including privatization, can be
implemented. In terms of all other so-called entitlement programs,
Boaz points out that if we lowered the so-called entitlements to the

fraction of the gross national production in 1970, which is *after* the growth in the Great Society programs, fiscal 1983 entitlement outlays of $168 billion could have been cut by $76 billion. More generally, Martin Feldstein, President Reagan's chief economic advisor, points out that federal civilian spending was 13 percent of the GNP in 1970. Returning current levels of civilian spending to that earlier figure, "hardly back to the Dark Ages in terms of economic and social spending," according to Feldstein, would represent a reduction in federal outlays of more than $160 billion.

The issue of defense spending is more difficult. There are the obvious savings, as noted by the Grace Report, associated with closing surplus military bases, obtaining competitive bidding on replacement parts for military equipment (why should a ten cent bolt cost $91?), reducing the incidence of duplicate weapons systems among branches of the service, and many others. However, a realistic and pragmatic approach also strongly suggests that the Japanese and Europeans be required to increasingly provide for their own defense. Having accomplished economic reconstruction since Worle War II, they are once again included in the ranks of the highest income countries of the world. More than $130 billion of the U. S. defense budget is devoted to defending Europe and East Asia. Given the realities of the world economic scene, it becomes more difficult to justify U. S. ground forces, air units, and equipment in these theaters. What economic, or even strategic, rationale is there that allows Japan to spend something more than one percent of their GNP on defense and West Germany three percent, while the United States spends six or seven percent?

Is it truly in the long-run interests of the United States to support an International Security Assistance program which aids totalitarian dictatorships? Should we continue to support the International Development Assistance program which more often than not funnels U. S. aid to government bureaucrats and politicians instead of the people in the less developed countries? Respected diplomats, politicians, and academicians increasingly question whether America is in fact safer as a result of adding to our stock of more than 9,000 strategic nuclear warheads. George Kennan, the architect of the cold-war policy toward the Soviet Union in the forties and fifties now questions our direction and has advocated a 50 percent reduction in our nuclear arsenal. George Ball, former Under-Secretary of State, has doubts whether the U. S. is safer through a policy of confrontation in El Salvador, Honduras, Lebanon, and Grenada. In the 1980's there is something wrong with a defense budget which spends more than $100 billion for the defense of *Western Europe,* the largest item in the entire federal budget except for social security benefit payments and interest on the national debt. Significant budget reductions are only possible if entitlement and defense expenditures are seriously re-examined.

Serious attention to the idea of cutting the size of federal government, however, awaits an intellectual revolution; a reversal of the love affair the American people have had in the past with larger outlays in response to special interest group pleading. The problem is characterized as the "anatomy of government failure." The federal budget will ultimately be cut only if individuals recognize the nature of the "road to serfdom" over which we have been traveling. Ideas do have consequences, and it is our goal to make the idea of human freedom once again an exciting and worthwhile objective. A "moral consensus" for limited government must be re-established.

## BUDGET DEFICITS, MONEY, AND INFLATION

Though the relationships are more complicated than most realize, the explosive increase in federal budget deficits over the past twenty years has been associated with an acceleration in the rate of money growth which has, in turn, produced greater rates of inflation. Increases in federal spending, combined with the political difficulty of raising taxes, means that budget deficits must be financed either by the U. S. Treasury selling bonds or the Federal Reserve System increasing the money supply. The inflationary effect of printing new money represents another means by which government imposes implicit taxes by debasing the country's currency. The massive increase in the national debt has already been described. The process by which the Federal Reserve System (the "Fed") "prints money," however, remains to be explored. For as John Maynard Keynes warned the industrial democracies decades ago, "there is no surer means of overturning the existing basis of society than to debauch the currency."

Since World War II, the U. S. has experienced the longest sustained period of rising prices in its history. Almost forgotten are those earlier periods, under the discipline of gold, when the price level could be expected to both rise and fall, but maintain its purchasing power over long periods. For example, Great Britain was on the gold standard for the two-hundred year period before the beginning of World War I, and at the end of that time the price level in England was roughly what it had been in 1815. Prices in the United States during its gold standard days between 1879 and 1933 were at about the same level on the eve of the Great Depression as they were in 1879 when the U. S. officially adopted the gold standard. Following the Civil War and into the 1890's, prices actually trended *downward*. However, things have changed since World War II. Beginning with the increased U. S. involvement in Vietnam in the mid-1960's, this country entered a period during which the *rate* of inflation has persistently risen.

It is no accident that accelerating inflation was preceded by an increase in the trend rate of growth in the money supply. Inflation is a monetary phenomenon. Following the evidence of history, inflation has always been fueled by governments coining or printing too much money. Milton Friedman, a leading authority on the subject, has summarized the basic point:

> There is perhaps no empirical regularity among economic phenomena that is based on so much evidence for so wide a range of circumstances as the connection between substantial changes in the stock of money and the level of prices. To the best of my knowledge, there is no instance in which a substantial change in the stock of money per unit of output has occurred without a substantial change in the level of prices in the same direction. Conversely, I know of no instance in which there has been substantial change in the level of prices without a substantial change in the stock of money per unit of output in the same direction. And instances in which prices and the stock of money have moved together are recorded for many centuries of history, for countries in every part of the globe, and for a wide diversity of monetary arrangements.

If money is the reason for inflation, then what can be made of the popular view that inflation is caused by large federal budget deficits? Though complicated, the relationship between deficits, money, and inflation can be explained by analyzing the behavior of the U. S. central bank--the Federal Reserve System. Large federal deficits increase the U. S. Treasury's demand for credit. Government borrowing in the nation's money markets, competing with private sector credit needs, tends to push interest rates upward as competition for the ecomomy's savings pool intensifies.

However, higher interest rates "crowd-out" private sector borrowing and in the process put political pressure on the Fed to do something about higher borrowing costs. The Federal Reserve System responds by lending money to the Treasury by buying U. S. Government bonds from the public. Hopefully, this eases money market conditions and pushes interest rates down. When the fed buys bonds, it automatically creates additional cash reserves for the banking system. Commerical banks and other financial institutions can in turn increase their lending and in the process create more checking and saving deposits, or in other words more money. This process by which interest bearing Treasury bills and bonds are converted, almost if by slight of hand, into more deposit money is called "monetization" of the national debt.

Political pressure on the Fed to lower interest rates is not the only important reason for the acceleration of money growth in the past two decades. Monetization has also followed political demands to lower the unemployment rate. The proposition was especially popular in the 1960's and early 1970's that the country could "buy" lower rates of unemployment by allowing more inflation. The idea of a policy trade-off between inflation and unemployment contributed importantly to an inflationary bias in the implementation of monetary policy by the Fed. Faster money growth could make an important

370

contribution to economic stability, it was argued, by reducing the economic and social costs of unemployment. "Creeping inflation," after all, was a small price to pay for more jobs and prosperity. Unfortunately, an extended trade-off was a cruel mirage. During the 1970's faster money growth was indeed accompanied by more rapid inflation, but the unemployment rate, rather than falling, also continued to edge upward in the 1970's and early 1980's.

The extent of monetization by the Fed is illustrated by the following figures. In 1965 the Federal Reserve System owned about $40 billion in U. S. government securities. By the end of 1983 Fed holdings exceeded $155 billion. In general, this increase in the Federal Reserve System's "assets" was matched by an increase in its "liabilities" --namely Federal Reserve Notes and the cash reserves of commercial banks at the Fed. In other words, the money induced acceleration of inflation in the U.S. has been a direct result of actions by the Federal Reserve System.

And it is interesting that there is an increased awareness among the American people that actions by the Fed are responsible for not only our problems with inflation but also the cyclical instability of the American economy. But quite frankly, the Federal Reserve System is simply an agency of the government. Though supposedly an independent agency, economist and long-time Fed watcher Edward Kane has poignantly dispelled that myth:

> The Fed is a political institution designed *by* politicians to *serve* politicians. Its chief officials (i.e., the Board of Governors) are nominated by the President and their appointments are cleared with the Senate. They are forced to defend their performance before Congressional committees several times a month and must be prepared to respond expeditiously to letters and telephone calls from Congressmen and Senators at a moment's notice.

The increase in money which drives the inflationary spiral is a political phenomenon determined by government's *monopoly* on the money supply process. Everybody wants more money. Unfortunately, greater stocks of money, if not matched by an icrease in productivity, will result in higher prices. Printing more money does not create wealth. Politicians recognize, of course, that more money means more votes. Inflation is, in fact, the process by which politicians increase the money supply, while imposing a tax on the money already held by the public. The U. S. government has ruled that only fiat currency or paper money issued by the Fed is "legal tender." And the Federal Reserve System, by law, has a monopoly in producing additional money. The kings of old use to melt silver or gold coins and mint new ones with less weight. Today, the techniques differ, but the printing of paper money has the same effect. It represents a form of counterfeiting in which government imposes "the cruelest tax of all"--the purchasing power of existing money is debased by augmenting its supply.

The broad sweep of human history suggests a profound constant in political life: governments have always sought a monopoly on the production of money, and once achieved, use the power to tax the citizenry through inflation. Importantly, government usually spends the newly created money first, before prices have risen. The political temptation is irresistible. Print more money before the election to stimulate economic activity and lower the unemployment rate with the full realization that more inflation and higher interest rates will be born much later after the election. The structure of incentives confronting the politician, and their operatives at the Federal Reserve System, permit the interested observer to question the government's self-proclaimed commitment to a non-inflationary economy. As economist Dwight Lee has noted: "There are compelling reasons for believing that political decision makers are less than completely sincere in their professed desire to bring inflation under control." Inflation, as a monetary phenomenon, *can* be controlled if government, through the Fed, is prepared to control the growth in the money supply. Inflation and interest rates will come down permanently only if the rate of growth in the money supply is reduced to correspond to the economy's ability to produce goods and services. In fact, the federal government invariably fails to perform the very task which supporters of a politically controlled monetary system insist is essential: a stable monetary framework which encourages the specialization in production requisite to economic and social harmony.

The existing inflationary bias demands a fundamental change in the rules of the game. Politics must be removed from the money production business. As Milton Friedman commented: "Money is too serious a matter to be left to the central bankers--or, for that matter, to economists." "Our only hope for a stable money," according to Friedrich Hayek, "is indeed now to find a way to protect money from politics." The claim is repeatedly trumpeted that government, through the Federal Reserve System, needs the authority to "fine-tune" the economy, to lean against the wind and moderate the business cycle. Unfortunately, economists simply do not have the necessary knowledge to predict the economy's direction. Policy lags--the time interval between the policy recognition and actual impact--are notoriously long and variable. Finally, as economist Dwight Lee in his excellent monograph points out, politicians have their own interests which must be served:

> The assumption behind discretionary monetary policy is that a collection of individuals, whose interests are served by increasing the wealth of government can be given control over the supply of money with confidence that they will ignore their personal interest and be guided only by the public interest. Political decision makers benefit from inflationary increases in the money supply in much the same way an individual counterfeiter does, and it should surprise no one that political control over the money supply is a sure prescription for inflation.

Or, as Richard Wagner has realistically observed, "it is contrary to reason and to history to expect that a monopoly position will fail to be exploited for the benefit of those in a position to practice such exploitation."

## ALTERNATIVE VIEWS ON MONETARY REFORM

Though government continues to "fight" inflation by declaring "war" on it and then claiming to have "turned the corner," in actual practice, anemic and cosmetic efforts have only dealt with symptoms. John McClaughry, former senior policy adviser in the Reagan White House, has provided a useful catalog of public policy options for restoring "sound money." Three of the policy alternatives retain the fundamental defect of placing politics in charge of the money business. The first "school" McClaughry labels the "Trust the Fed" approach. Given an imperfect world and the reality of politics, it is argued that the "financial priesthood" at the Fed will control money growth in the public interest. Popularity notwithstanding, this point of view must be rejected in light of the Fed's record. Second, there are those who would "Seize the Fed," where existing powers of the Federal Reserve System would be assumed by the U. S. Treasury, or at the very least, Fed governors would be subject to immediate dismissal by the President and/or Congress if they failed to toe the line. Third, while the Fed would retain its separate existence, the Congress would "Instruct the Fed." Marching orders would be given by Congress, and the Fed would obey. Each of these proposals, however, accepts the existence of a national central bank and its monopoly power over the issuance of paper money. Politics remains integral to these schools of thought.

### A Monetary Rule

There are many, as a fourth option, who propose that we "Automate the Fed." Skillfully articulated by the Nobel Laureate economist Milton Friedman, this school advocates the adoption of a "monetary rule." Though the existence of the Federal Reserve System and its monopoly is accepted by these "monetarists" (although not all so-called monetarists advocate a rule approach), the money supply process is taken out of politics by eliminating discretionary, fine-tuning policy by the Fed. Stop-start-stop monetary policy, as experienced over the past 20 years--frequent and abrupt changes in the rate of growth in the money supply induced by the Fed--would violate the monetary rule. The Federal Reserve System, or the computer that replaces the Board of Governors, would be charged with establishing a known and therefore predictable rate of growth of money or, for some proponents, the target would be an index of the price level. Rather than week-to-week, or even month-to-month, a more realistic quarter-to-quarter basis would be used. The Fed's only responsibility would be to "hit" the target rate of growth in money. Instability in the economy *caused* by periods of accelerating or decelerating money growth would be eliminated. Problems associated with correctly anticipating turning points in order to fine-tune the economy are avoided. Frankly, those who advocate fine-tuning a modern industrial economy suffer from "Potomac fever," an illness driven by "illusions of grandeur."

The problem with this approach, and the others to be discussed below, is in obtaining the agreement and then compliance of the politicians who benefit directly from the process of "debauching the currency." Proponents of the monetary rule generally recognize this special interest problem, and therefore advocate a "constitutional" change in the monetary rules. But analogous to the unwritten constitution against deficit financing in budgetary matters, a monetary rule would be unnecessary if the underlying distrust of government written into the U. S. Constitution could be restored. Unfortunately, as Henry Simons warned, "constitutional provisions are no stronger than the moral consensus that they articulate." Even so, we believe a "constitutionally constrained" government monopoly would be an improvement over existing arrangements. Other reform schools, however, question the need for retaining the government monopoly on legal tender money. Friedrich Hayek is representative of this point of view: "What is so dangerous and ought to be done away with is not government's right to issue money but the *exclusive* right to do so and their power to force people to use it and to accept it at a particular price."

### The Gold Standard

The fifth school of thought identified by John McClaughry advocates a return to a national gold standard. The price of gold would be pegged and the federal government, presumably through the Federal Reserve System, would be required to buy and sell gold at the official price. Paper money, token coins, and deposit money would then be convertible into gold. A two hundred percent increase in the price level since 1967 has caused many Americans to advocate a return to the gold standard. The attractiveness of the gold standard has been described by one of its leading proponents, economist Hans Sennholz:

> It is undoubtedly true that the fiat [paper] standard is more workable for economic planners and money managers. But this is the very reason why we prefer the gold standard. Its excellence is its *unmanageability* by government.

The price level would respond to new gold discoveries and changing demands for nonmonetary purposes, sometimes rising and sometimes falling. The great attraction in the long-run, however, is that economic pressures associated with the changing purchasing power of gold would tend to stabilize the price level over long periods of time. For example, between 1869 and 1896 the price level in the U. S. fell almost 40 percent, but in the period following the gold discoveries of the 1890's prices increased until the Great Depression. Nevertheless, over the entire period the price level was roughly the same in 1929 as it had been a few years after the Civil War. Compare that long-run stability to the post-World War II period during which the longest sustained and accelerating inflation in U. S. history threatens to sever the social fabric. Under the gold standard, politicians are disciplined by the requirement that they defend the price of gold. The existing paper standard offers no such discipline to inflationary finance.

The poor performance of government and the Fed spurred the Congress in 1980 to create a U. S. Gold Commission. The commission's membership, including two members from the Board of Governors of the Federal Reserve System, the Secretary of the Treasury, and members of Congress, guaranteed the rejection of a gold standard for the United States. Nevertheless, the commission represented the first official government investigation into the feasibility of a gold standard in more than 100 years. Texas Congressman Ron Paul and New Yorker Lewis Lehrman issued a minority report of the Commission, *The Case for Gold*. It makes an excellent case for "hard money" reform. Again, however, to successfully institute a gold standard in the political market place would in fact mean the real battle had already been won. A prerequisite to adopting a national gold standard is building the appropriate social consensus on the immorality of taxing people by printing more money.

Proponents of the monetary rule, like Milton Friedman, argue that the gold standard has significant economic costs. While the long-term benefits of price stability and a depoliticized monetary framework are potentially large, the immediate costs include a greater short-run potential for economic instability and the resource costs of maintaining gold convertibility at a fixed price. Economist Michael David Bordo, for example, has shown that *short-run* instability in employment and prices was greater during the gold standard period than during the post-World War II period.

## Money Competition

A sixth policy recommendation that approximates the stability benefits of a monetary rule, removes government's monopoly on money, and at the same time avoids the potential pitfalls of a gold standard, is the idea of competing monies. Inspired by Friedrich Hayek's 1975 article "Choice in Currency: A Way to Stop Inflation," economists and others are considering the competitive market process as a way to discipline the politician. In an excellent survey article concerning alternative monetary arrangements, Pamela Brown has summarized the position of the "competition in currency" advocates: "Proponents of free trade in currency predict that a program for monetary reform which places *competitive* rather than 'constitutional' constraints on the individual money producer will prove to be far more effective" in countering government's irresistable temptation to print more money and debase the money supply. In Hayek's words, "the past instability of the market economy is the consequence of the exclusion of the most important regulator of the market mechanism, money, from itself being regulated by the market process."

Pessimism regarding the likelihood of a gold standard proposal from the U. S. Gold Commission and following the intellectual lead of Hayek, an "alternative voice" was created: the United States Choice-in-Currency Commission. Recognizing the political and practical difficulties in restoring, at least in the near term, a gold standard, the private Choice-in-Currency Commission advocates market competition in money. Rather than the "discipline of gold" in the traditional sense, competition in currencies would impose the discipline of consumer choice. While Hayek's original inspiration emphasized multiple national currencies being used as money within a country, the Choice-in-Currency Commission favors the minting of gold coins in the United States to compete with the Federal Reserve System's monopoly money. Gold coins would circulate as money in competition with Federal Reserve Notes. If the American government, through its operative the Fed, inflated the paper money supply, its value in terms of gold coins would fall. Depreciating Federal Reserve Notes would signal authorities that too many were being issued. Consumers in turn would reject the depreciating money and insist that prices be set in terms of gold coins. Under existing legal tender laws, the U. S. government has monopoly power to protect its paper money from competition. With market competition, as Hayek has noted, "the reputation of financial righteousness would become a jealously guarded asset of all issuers of money," government included. Individuals would simly be unwilling to loan money in a currency expected to depreciate because of inflation. Debtors would likewise avoid borrowing money that was expected to appreciate. The issuance of money by the Federal Reserve System would be constrained by the competitive pressures of the market place.

In response to the growing public pressures to eliminate inflation and therefore government's monopoly on the money supply process, Senator Steve Symms of Idaho and Congressman Dan Crane of Illinois have introduced similar bills in the Senate and the House of

Representatives which are designed to introduce "freedom of choice in the marketplace." On October 5, 1981, the Free Market Gold Coinage Act was introduced in the U. S. Senate with the following introduction by Senator Symms:

> Today, I am introducing the Free Market Gold Coinage Act with [cosponsors]..., which calls for the establishment of gold coins as an alternative lawful or legal tender without abandoning the dollar and without fixing the price of gold. My bill is designed to put the two systems of currency into direct competition, and let the market choose, at the margin and over a long-run period of time, which kind of currency shall predominate.

The proposal calls for the Secretary of the Treasury to offer the gold reserves of the United States for sale in the form of four gold coins that would be minted by the government. The Treasury would mint gold coins of one troy ounce (31.103 grams), one ounce (28.349 grams), 10 grams, and 5 grams. The coins would bear the likeness, respectively, of John F. Kennedy, Abraham Lincoln, Thomas Jefferson, and Adam Smith. Furthermore, "It shall be the policy of the United States to recognize the right of free coinage of gold at a free market price." The Act provides for the private minting of the coins except they would not bear the inscription "United States of America." The "Official Conversion Rate," or the market price of gold, would be determined by the Secretary of the Treasury from gold prices determined in the world's organized gold exchanges. The Treasury would be required to exchange these gold coin or gold bullion "from any source" at the Official Conversion Rate.

The government would be required to avoid regulations or legislation which would place the new gold coins at a competitive disadvantage in their function as money. Accordingly, the United States and individual states would not be permitted to impose excise, transaction, or capital gains taxes on "the use of gold or upon banking services that involve the promise to pay with gold." Restrictions on the "convenient transfer" of interests in gold would be illegal. Finally, and most important, "neither gold nor dollars shall be an exclusive lawful tender in payment of debts." The Free Market Gold Coinage Act forcefully proposes the end of government's monopoly in the money business. It represents a giant step towards restoring a truly free society. Let Friedrich Hayek summarize the point:

> I believe [government's] claim to a *monopoly*, or their power to *limit* the kinds of money in which contracts may be concluded within their territory, or to determine the *rates* at which monies can be exchanged, to be wholly harmful...I hope it will not be too long before complete freedom to deal in any money one likes will be regarded as the essential mark of a free country.

Progress has been made in the past decade or so. In 1974, largely as a result of the lobbying effort of Representative Ron Paul and Senator Jesse Helms, Congress legalized gold ownership by voiding the

Franklin Roosevelt administration's law which had forbidden Americans to own gold. In 1977 gold-clause contracts were once again made legal and enforceable. Even the U. S. Gold Commission recommended that Congress enact legislation to resume minting gold coins, and that "the coins shall be exempt from capital gains taxes and that the coins shall be exempt from sales taxes." Early in 1983, Representative Ron Paul introduced the American Gold Eagle coin Act which, following the earlier proposals of the Free Market Gold Coinage Act, provides for minting a one ounce and one-half ounce gold coin. There would be no tax imposed on the exchange of the coins.

Under Article I, section 8 of the U. S. Constitution, the Congress is given power "to coin money." The founding fathers, however, did *not* mean the power to print paper money. At the Constitutional Convention in the summer of 1887 opposition to paper money was overwhelming. When the delegates voted on the issue of printing paper money, nine states opposed giving the government authority to issue paper money, while only two states favored such power. James Madison, in defending the Constitution in one of the Federalist Papers, explained the preference for the "coinage" of commodity money when he referred to the "pestilent effects of paper money on the necessary confidence between man and man, on the necessary confidence in the public councils, on the industry and morals of the people, and on the character of republic government." The restoration of sound money and therefore a sound environment for social coordination and harmony in a free society waits only for that "moral consensus" necessary to the unwritten constitution of fiscal and monetary prudence.

Then of course, following John McClaughry's final "school fo thought," why not think the unthinkable? Why have a central bank at all? Why not abolish the Federal Reserve System?

# CHAPTER 24

## FREEING UP THE SYSTEM

History shows that freedom is a fragile and fleeting possession. It also shows that governments expand. It is not likely that the two are unrelated.

--David Osterfeld

But nothing guarantees that this system [of capitalism] will endure forever. It is an experiment. Our failure to defend it well, with spirit and with intelligence, would be an unforgivable failure, a tragedy for the world.

--Machael Novak

For you and me, the picture is pretty clear: we either restore the American Dream, right here and now, or we most certainly will never live to experience it again.

--Robert Ringer

On August 13, 1961, the socialist government of East Germany closed its borders to Berlin and began to build the Berlin Wall. East Germans had previously been free to choose between two radically different systems of political economy, and they fled by the tens-of-thousands to the West. People voted with their feet for democracy and the market system and against a socialist dictatorship. The startling contrast between the drab of East Germany and the "economic miracle" of West Germany just across the border demonstrates the benefits of the market system and freedom. Rejecting price controls and centralized intervention in the private sector, capitalism in large measure was permitted to function in West Germany. The one system proposed a limited role for government and a wider liberty for individuals to associate voluntarily and live their own lives. The alternative system advocated socialism and the idea that political solutions would advance the prospects of mankind. This book has sought to expose the mirage and to demonstrate the comparative efficiency and justice of these systems. Both theory and history show quite convincingly, we believe, that the system of private property and voluntary exchange is more conducive to the good society.

The relevant insights stem principally from the pronouncements of the founding fathers. Thomas Jefferson in his First Inaugural Address advocated a government "which shall restrain men from injuring one another, which shall leave them otherwise free to regulate their own pursuits of industry and improvement, and shall not take from the mouth of labor the bread it has earned." The Declaration of Independence, following the call for "unalienable rights," complained that King George III "...has erected a multitude of new offices, and sent hither swarms of officers to harass our people and eat out their substance." While admitting that men were not angels, James Madison warned of the problem of controlling the size and scope of government.

Today, we are about to celebrate the bicentennial of the U. S. Constitution, yet political economist William H. Meckling justifiably writes of "American Capitalism at Sunset." If America continues to be the world's economic leader and a singular example of the presence of a degree of human liberty, it is largely because of the social and economic "capital" accumulated during the previous two centuries when individuals--at least up until the past fifty years or so-- lived their entire lives with few encounters with the insitutions of government. From a country of individuals who simply wished to be left alone to pursue their goals, government now threatens to fulfill the wishes of those who advocate an all-powerful, leviathan state demanding absolute obedience.

America is at a crossroads. Like it or not, fundamental choices are being made between the "market means" and the "political means." The Great American Experiment of our ancestors--that government by and for the people is to be strictly limited--is faltering. The totalitarian-collectivist arrangements of earlier times have resurfaced with a vengence and now threaten to deny this magnificent experiment in liberty. Robert Ringer is right in his book *Restoring the American Dream* when he argues that "we either restore the American Dream, right here and now, or we most certainly will never live to experience it again."

Unfortunately, the restoration of freedom and the market economy is going to be difficult. Since the acceleration in the growth of government power, during the Roosevelt adminstrations of the 1930's especially, a third generation of Americans have grown to adulthood, conditioned to the reality of government as the dominant social institution. They do not remember, or more realistically the schools fail to teach, that the birth of this nation rested on the proposition that governments were inevitably tyrannical and were to be distrusted because they extinquished liberty. "The proponents of the 'welfare state,' or collectivist society," according to Ringer, "have succeeded in making millions of people believe that the American Dream is 'outdated'." Although our freedoms are now restricted far below that which is consistent with a free society, there is still time. "Fortunately," Milton and Rose Friedman remind us in their powerful book *Free to Choose*, "...we are as a people still free to choose which way we should go--whether to continue along the road we have been following to ever bigger government, or to call a halt and change direction."

But there is indeed a sense of urgency if the path toward human liberty and a market order is to be resumed. The intellectual "reality makers" continue to propose increments to government power via taxation, spending, regulations, restrictions, and interventions of all kinds to answer the purported failures of the market. However, political solutions to social problems have invariably generated collectivist arrangements which deny peaceful and voluntary relationships between individuals and therefore sacrifice liberty at the alter of the almighty state. The economist Arthur Shenfield has captured the essential character of this misguided view:

> All socialists are utopians in some measure or other. They propose a powerful state, but their powerful state will be caring, compassionate, benevolent. It will be incorruptible, efficient, far-seeing, progressive, and adaptable. Its politicians will think only of the public welfare, and its bureaucrats will think only of service to the people. The rule of law will prevail, and yet the government will have a wide discretion, so that it may do the utmost good. The government will control all essential sources of livelihood; yet criticism will be free and, mirabile dictu, also effective.

There is a serious problem with this scenario. History reveals no leviathan which remained benevolent. Even democracy, as Alexis de Tocqueville warned early in the last century in his *Democracy in America,* has tended to dissipate into special interest excesses and the tyrannical rule of the majority. "Majority rule," Robert Ringer notes, "has evolved into a free-for-all stampede of citizens appealing to politicians to give them more of the plunder. On the horizon is chaos, and just beyond is totalitarian rule." If the American people are to stop this slide into a police state without individual liberties, it is important that the restoration recommended by the agenda in *Part III* of this book begin at once.

The constitutional lawyer Henry Mark Holzer in his book *Sweet Land of Liberty* identifies the essential nature of the issue:

> Freedom will only come to America when our intellectual leaders reject altruism-collectivism-statism and replace it with an unyielding commitment to *individual rights.* We must return to the basic principle of our Declaration of Independence: We *are* created equal; as individuals, we *do* possess unalienable rights; we *have* a right to our life and our liberty and the pursuit of our own happiness. It is *we* who created government and it is government which derives its just powers from *our* consent.

To regain this revolutionary spirit, the American people must renew both a moral and intellectual consensus that liberty is a paramount attribute of the good society. Liberty, private property, individual autonomy, and responsibility must once again become exciting issues worth defending. Rather than a blind allegiance to beneficent dictatorships or tyrannical majorities, government must be recognized for what it really is--a necessary evil. The founding fathers had no doubt regarding the essential truth of this proposition. Their defense of the Constitution repeatedly tried to convince the people of the thirteen colonies that the leviathan state needed to be *and* could be controlled through the separation of powers among branches of government and between the different levels of government.

In large part, the original experiment has failed. The moral consensus for limited government has dissipated, especially in the twentieth century, and therefore, as views changed, the Lockean-Jeffersonian conception of liberty was increasingly left undefended. Milton and Rose Friedman in *Free to Choose* have shown the key relationship between belief systems and government actions:

> In order for a written--or for that matter, unwritten--constitution to be effective it must be supported by the general climate of opinion, among both the public at large and its leaders. It must incorporate principles that they have come to believe in deeply, so that it is taken for granted that the executive, the legislative, and the courts will behave in conformity to these principles. As we have seen, when the climate of opinion changes, so will policy.

The restoration of freedom and the market economy will require a fundamental change in the "climate of opinion"--a renewed commitment to a free society in which human cooperation and the coordination of economic and social action will be based on voluntary relationships.

If we wish to halt and reverse the trend towards larger government, and therefore a shrinking sphere of individual autonomy, the proposals of politicians and special interests to expand the police power of the state must be rejected. Existing ordinances, regulations, and laws which intervene in economic matters should be repealed wherever the competitive market process is adaquate to the task. *Part III* of this book documents the vast potential for market solutions to economic problems. On both grounds of efficiency and individual justice the market system has been shown to be a superior delivery mechanism.

Most of the tasks currently performed by federal, state, or local governments should be shifted to the private sector where costs are demonstrably lower. From municipal garbage collection to airport control towers to the task of educating America's young people, the market produces more and better for less. The deregulation movement in recent years has shown the benefits that competitive markets bring to consumers. Trucking, the airlines, broadcasting, and telecommunications all promise long-term benefits even larger than the intitial advantages of lower prices and more alternatives. Government ownership and regulation do not improve on market outcomes, but invariably thwart and suppress competition. It is important that the American people renew their support of the socially beneficial implications of privatization and deregulation.

Those who favor the restoration of liberty should lend their support to politicians who vote to restrict the size of government. Unfortunately, there are many, including most of those economists who write of the anatomy of government failure, who do not believe traditional political channels--the legislative and executive branches of government--will be effective in turning the tide. The Friedmans in *Free to Choose* favor the use of "package deals" in which "self-denying ordinances" are employed to amend the constitutional order. Analogous to First Amendment rights in the Constitution to freedom of speech, what is needed is "an economic Bill of Rights." Their chapter "The Tide Is Turning" offers a list of possible amendments to the U. S. Constitution. The Friedmans believe there are two important advantages to this type of revision of the constitutional order. First, in the process of formulating the amendments on particular economic issues, the climate of opinion would itself be shaped. The discussion of the issues would itself contribute to a reaffirmation of the positive value which attaches to human freedom. Second, through the process of referendum or constitutional convention the limitations of the legislative process and its defects are avoided. The proposals for a constitutional convention on the issue of an amendment requiring the federal government to balance its budget is one example of this approach.

A variation on this general theme has been proposed by economist William Meckling. Following the implications of political entrepreneurship, "the answer," according to Meckling, "...lies in the representative nature of lawmaking. Our representatives are simply capitalizing on the opportunity they have to market the use of the police powers." He continues:

> The revolution in mass media that has taken place, particularly since the advent of the radio in the 1920's, has converted Congress into an association of hucksters who employ a simple marketing strategy. First, they interpret the current state of affairs for their clientele. The interpretation always points to the existence of evil or of imminent disaster or both. In any case, congressional action is required. A prescription is offered which will remedy the problem. All of the prescriptions tend to have one thing in common. The role of government, and Congress particularly, is expanded. In their marketing endeavors, congressmen are given support and comfort by the journalism community. The latter has long understood that evil and disaster attract viewers and sell newspapers.

As already noted, "the opportunity to sell the use of the police powers is a problem inherent in the structure of our political democracy." Meckling therefore proposes a device by which he believes "self-denying ordinances" might be adopted by the people: "My first preference for repairing this structural defect is to get rid of representatives in the legislative process by abolishing Congress and the state legislatures...There is no reason why all statutes, including budgets, couldn't be submitted to a popular vote; that is to a referendum." The market for political favors for special interest groups would dissolve before the onslaught of direct democracy. The illness is severe, possibly terminal, and therefore the solutions will necessarily require strong medicine.

Although radical proposals, the answers to combat larger and larger government proposed by the Friedmans, Meckling, and others confront directly the inherent problems associated with representative democracy. They also call attention to the importance of changing people's ideological frame of reference. It is worth repeating the eloquent description by Nobel Laureate Friedrich A. Hayek of the nature of the crossroads which this book has attempted to depict:

> Unless we can make the philosophic foundations of a free society once more a living intellectual issue, and its implementation a task which challenges the ingenuity and imagination of our liveliest minds, the prospects of freedom are indeed dark. But if we can regain that belief in the power of ideas which was the mark of liberalism at its best, the battle is not lost. The intellectual revival of [classical] liberalism is already under way in many parts of the world.

# EPILOGUE

My name is the United States of America. I was born in 1776 in freedom and that lure has caused millions of people to cast their fortunes with me. For over 200 years I have offered hope and opportunity to people taking refuge on my shores, My soil is stained with the blood of Paul Revere and Nathan Hale, and the world still reverberates with the shot heard "round the world," Thomas Jefferson and Patrick Henry are just a few who have understood that the wealth of a nation is its people and that left alone, and guided by enlightened self-interest, individuals could create riches and opportunities like the world has never seen before.

But freedom has not been cheap, My sons have spilled their blood on the battlefields of Europe and Asia, in defense of freedom, free enterprise, and the principle that all individuals have inalienable rights to life, liberty, and the pursuit of happiness. Literally millions of families have cried in anguish as they learned their sons, husbands, and fathers were killed in battle. But thank God those lives counted for something.

I am big. From the Atlantic Ocean to the Pacific — as far flung North as Alaska, as far west as beautiful Hawaii. My three million square miles pulsate with activity and opportunity. I have forests in Oregon, wheatfields in Kansas, oil in Texas, and coal in Virginia. I am the Empire State Building in New York, the Sears Tower in Chicago, and Disneyland in California. I have over two million farms whose productivity is unequaled in the world. I have given birth to thousands, nay millions of producers. Men and women like Cyrus McCormick, Thomas Edison, George Washington Carver, Sandra Kurtzig, and Barbara Proctor. I am Babe Ruth and the World Series. I am Chris Everrett Lloyd and professional tennis. And no one slams it better than Dr. J.

But more than that, I am a nation where we not only work and play, but we pray. I have over 400,000 churches where people praise and worship the God who is there, and He is not silent.

Really, what I am is individuals. People, individually who matter. America after all has been the world's showcase for private achievement. In freedom I was conceived, and in freedom I want to live the rest of my days. But liberty requires vigilance. A constant effort by the people to insure that government protects private property, rather than seeking to own it or control it; that it encourages rather than discourages work and production; that it recognizes the sanctity of each and every individual.

Abraham Lincoln, in the dark hours of the Civil War was asked the question: "Can a nation of, by, and for the people survive?" He answered by saying, "I don't know how history will speak of America. But I do know that Americans were born to be free."

# APPENDIX

## SELECTED SOURCES AND RECOMMENDED READINGS

### Chapter 1
The quotation at the head of the chapter is from Milton and Rose Friedman, *Free to Choose.* (Harcourt Brace Jovanovich: New York), 1979.

The extended quotation by Clarence B. Carson is from his series of articles with the generic title of "World in the Grip of an Idea" which appeared in *The Freeman,* Foundation for Economic Education, Irvington-on-Hudson, New York during 1978 and 1979. The words of Fox Butterfield are from his book *China: Alone in the Bitter Sea,* (Times Books: New York), 1982, and the citation for Malcolm Muggeridge is John Bright-Holmes, ed. *Like It Was: The Diaries of Malcolm Muggeridge,* (William Morrow & Co.: New York), 1982.

### Chapter 2
The quotation at the head of the chapter is from Adam Smith, *The Theory of Moral Sentiments,* (1759), (Liberty Classics/Liberty Fund, Inc.: Indianapolis), 1976.

The interesting contrast between the increasing role of government and simultaneously a loss in our confidence in government appeared in Walter Lippman, *The Good Society,* (Little, Brown and Company: Boston), 1937. An important discussion of the purposefulness of human action is found in the treatise by Ludwig von Mises, *Human Action: A Treatise on Economics,* (Henry Regnery Co.: Chicago), Third revised edition, 1966. Another approach to the relationship between human action and the idea of human rights can be found in the writings of Ayn Rand, especially the small paperbacks *For the New Intellectual,* (Random House, Inc.: New York), 1961 and *The Virtue of Selfishness,* (The New American Library, Inc.: New York), 1964, Chapter 12 — "Man's Rights."

The distinction between the political means and the market means was emphasized in Franz Oppenheimer, *The State,* (Free Life Editions, Inc.: New York), (1914) 1975 and employed by Albert Jay Nock in his profound little book, *Our Enemy, The State,* (Free Life Editions, Inc.: New York), (1935) 1973.

Our understanding of the meaning of individual human rights stems from the work of Tibor Machan, *Human Rights and Human Liberties,* (Nelson-Hall: Chicago), 1975; Robert Nozick, *Anarchy, State, and Utopia,* (Basic Books, Inc.: New York), 1974; Murray N. Rothbard, *The Ethics of Liberty,* (Humanities Press: Atlantic Highlands, New Jersey), 1982; and David Osterfeld, *Freedom, Society and the State,* (University Press of America: Boston), 1983. Short quotations are from Robert Paul Wolf, *In Defense of Anarchism,* (Harper & Row Publishers: New York), 1970 and Auberon Herbert, *The Right and Wrong of Compulsion by the State,* (Liberty Press, Inc.: Indianapolis), 1978.

For an excellent survey of the history of the idea of natural rights see Richard S. Tuck, *Natural Rights Theories: Their Origin and Development,* (Cambridge University Press: London), 1979. Of course John Locke, *Two Treatises of Government,* (Cambridge University Press: London), (1691) 1960 is crucial and is discussed in Chapter 3. For the development of the notion of natural rights and human liberties in the American experience see Bernard Bailyn, *The Ideological Origins of the American Revolution.* (Harvard University Press: Cambridge), 1967.

### Chapter 3
The references to John Locke are from *Two Treatises of Government,* especially the second treatise, "An Essay Concerning the True Origin, Extent, and End of Civil Government." The evolution of the ideological foundations of a free society after Locke and through the American Revolution is found in Bernard Bailyn, *The Ideological*

*Origins of the American Revolution* and Murray N. Rothbard, *Conceived in Liberty: 'Salutary Neglect': The American Colonies in the First Half of the 18th Century*, Vol. II, 1975 and *Conceived in Liberty: Advance to Revolution, 1760-1775*, Vol. III, 1976 both (Arlington House: New York). The early chapters in Arthur A. Ekirch, Jr., *The Decline of American Liberalism*, (Atheneum: New York), 1967 deal with the revolutionary and constitutional periods. Jacob E. Cooke, ed., *The Federalist*, (Wesleyan University Press: Middletown, Connecticut), 1961 provides the classic defense of the Constitution by James Madison, Alexander Hamilton and John Jay. Herbert J. Storing, *What the Anti-Federalists Were For: The Political Opponents of the Constitution*, (University of Chicago Press), 1981 and Jackson Turner Main, *The Anti-Federalists*, (University of North Carolina Press: Chapel Hill), 1961 present the arguments of those who opposed the ratification of the U. S. Constitution. The quotation by Frank Chodorov is from his *Fugitive Essays*, (Liberty Press, Inc.: Indianapolis), 1980. William D. Grampp, *Economic Liberalism: Volume I, The Beginnings*, (Random House: New York), 1965 also covers this same ground.

## Chapter 4

The quotation at the head of the chapter is from Robert G. Perrin, "The Dynamics and Dialectics of Capitalism," *The Journal of Libertarian Studies*, Vol. 5, Number 2, Spring 1981.

The pre-capitalist periods of fuedalism and mercantalism are analyzed in Douglas C. North and Robert Paul Thomas, *The Rise of the Western World: A New Economic History*, (Cambridge University Press: London), 1973; in the classic Eli Heckscher, *Mercantalism*, Revised edition, 2 vols., (The Macmillan Company: New York), 1955; and Dudley Dillard, *Economic Development of the North Atlantic Community*, (Prentice-Hall: Englewood Cliffs, New Jersey), 1967 among other sources.

A good brief summary of the role of protestantism can be found in the article by Christopher Hill, "Protestantism and the Rise of Capitalism," in D. S. Landes, ed., *The Rise of Capitalism*, (Cambridge University Press: London), 1966. The classic volumes are of course Max Weber, *The Protestant Ethic and the Spirit of Capitalism* and Richard Tawney, *Religion and the Rise of Capitalism*.

We have relied heavily on the classic treatise on the history of economic ideas by Charles Gide and Charles Rist, *A History of Economic Doctrines*, (George G. Harrap & Co.: London), 1948 and Robert E. Keleher, "Supply-Side Economics and the Founding Fathers: The Linkage," Working Paper Series, Federal Reserve Bank of Atlanta, July 1982 for the material describing the evolution of the 'classical liberal' tradition. A recent volume by Karen I. Vaughn, *John Locke: Economist and Social Scientist*, (University of Chicago Press), 1980 analyzes Locke as an economist. Of course Adam Smith's, *Wealth of Nations* remains worthwhile reading more than two hundred years after its publication. An important bibliographical work on Smith by E. G. West, *Adam Smith: The Man and His Works*, (Liberty Classics/Liberty Fund, Incl: Indianapolis), 1976 puts the man in perspective and documents the importance of his contribution. Another important work on Smith is Gerald P. O'Driscoll, ed., *Adam Smith and Modern Political Economy*, (Iowa State University Press: Ames, Iowa) 1978.

The classical liberal tradition in France continued after J. B. Say in the writings of Frederic Bastiat. See for example his short but powerful book *The Law*, (Foundation for Economic Education: Irvington-on-Hudson), 1950.

An excellent summary of the modern work of English speaking economists following the tradition established by Adam Smith can be found in Henri Lepage, *Tomorrow, Capitalism: The Economics of Economic Freedom*, (Open Court Publishing Company: London), 1982.

## Chapter 5

A brief but excellent summary of the nature and character of the Industrial Revolution in England and the source of the quotation at the head of the chapter is T. S. Ashton, *The Industrial Revolution, 1760-1830*, (Oxford University Press: New York), 1962. Phyllis Deane and W. A. Cole, *British Economic Growth, 1688-1959: Trends and Structure*, (Cambridge University Press: London), 1962 is a detailed and factual account of the industrial revolution as well as the periods before and after. Another excellent account is Sir John H. Clapham, *An Economic History of Modern Britain*, (Cambridge University Press: London), 1926. For a description of the living conditions of the peasant prior to the Industrial Revolution see P. Boissonnade, *Life and Work in Medieval Europe*, trans. Eileen Power, (A. A. Knopf: New York), 1927.

The importance of the assignment and enforcement of private property rights for incentives and therefore economic growth can be found in Douglas C. North and Robert Paul Thomas, *The Rise of the Western World: A New Economic History*.

The conventional view of this period as one of falling incomes and misery is forcefully challenged in the collection of articles in Friedrich A. Hayek, ed., *Capitalism and the Historians*, (University of Chicago Press), 1954, especially the articles by T. S. Ashton, "The Treatment of Capitalism by Historians and L. M. Hacker, "The Anticapitalist Bias of American Historians;" and in the collection R. M. Hartwell, ed., *The Long Debate on Poverty*, (Institute of Economic Affairs: London), 1972. The positive case for the beneficial effects of the industrial revolution can also be found in an excellent three part film program "The Industrial Revolution: A Program in Three Parts," produced by Liberty Fund, Inc., Indianapolis, Indiana. A recent book by sociologist Robert Nisbet, *History of the Idea of Progress*, (Basic Books: New York), 1980 traces mankind's close attachment to the idea of progress and the ways in which attitudes influenced the period of the industrial revolution.

A demonstration of the welfare gains associated with population growth and increased longevity can be found in P. T. Bauer, *Dissent on Development*, (Harvard University Press: Cambridge), 1976 and Julian A. Simon, *The Ultimate Resource*, (Princeton University Press), 1981.

## Chapter 6

An excellent source of material on the economic history of the United States, representing the collective effort of twelve eminent economic historians is Lance E. Davis, Douglas C. North, Nathan Rosenberg, Richard A. Easterlin, et. al., *American Economic Growth: An Economist's History of the United States*, (Harper & Row Publishers: New York), 1972. The book by Dudley Dillard, *Economic Development of the North Atlantic Community* places the American growth experience into the context of the European situation. The provocative book by Douglass C. North, *Growth and Welfare in the American Past: A New Economic History*, (Prentice-Hall: Englewood Cliffs, New Jersey), 1966 is also a valuable source of information and interpretation.

The gradual erosion in the political and institutional commitment to an economy driven by capitalism during the 19th century is documented in Arthur A. Ekirch, Jr., *The Decline of American Liberalism*. The revisionist view of the importance of monopoly in the post-Civil War Period can be found in Gabriel Kolko, *The Triumph of Conservatism: A Reinterpretation of America's History, 1900-1916*, (Free Press: New York), 1977 and in Dominick T. Armentano, *Antitrust and Monopoly: Anatomy of a Policy Failure*, (John Wiley & Sons: New York), 1982. The classic illustration of the robber barons interpretation of this period is de-bunked in Lawrence W. Reed, "Witch Hunting for Robber Barons: The Standard Oil Story," *The Freeman*, (Foundation for Economic Education: Irvington-on-Hudson, New York), March 1980.

The negative view of the so-called gilded age by social historians is effectively refuted by L. M. Hacker, "The Anticapitalist Bias of American Historians," in F. A. Hayek, ed., *Capitalism and the Historians*. The comparative experience of different minority groups migrating to the United States is analyzed by Thomas Sowell in *Race and Economics*, (David McKay Company, Inc.: New York), 1975 and more recently in *Ethnic America*, (Basic Books, Inc.: New York), 1981.

## Chapter 7

The treatise by Henry Hazlitt, *The Foundations of Morality*, (Nash Publishing Company: Los Angeles), 1964 is the source of the quotation at the head of the chapter. The article by Benjamin A. Rogge, "The Case for Economic Freedom," reproduced in *The Freeman*, February 1981 is an inspiring defense of capitalism on moral grounds. The articles by Arthur Shenfield, "Capitalism Under the Test of Ethics," *IMPRIMIS*,

(Hillsdale College, Hillsdale, Michigan), December 1981 and Paul Johnson, "Is There a Moral Basis for Capitalism?", *PAIDEIA*, Spring 1980 were very useful and are strongly recommended to the reader's attention. Also see Friedrich A. Hayek, "The Moral Element in Free Enterprise," *Studies in Philosophy, Politics and Economics*, (University of Chicago Press), 1967 and Leslie Snyder, "Justice and Freedom," *The Freemen*, March 1980.

Other recommended readings in this area include Friedrich A. Hayek, *The Road to Serfdom*, (University of Chicago Press), 1944; Ludwig von Mises, *Liberalism: A Socio-Economic Exposition*, (Sheed Andrews and McMeel, Inc.: Kansas City), 1976; Murray Rothbard, *The Ethics of Liberty*.; and for a somewhat different twist the writings of Ayn Rand. In addition there are other important works by Hayek including *The Constitution of Liberty*, (University of Chicago Press), 1960 and the three volume series *Law, Legislation and Liberty*, (University of Chicago Press), 1973, 1976 and 1979.

## Chapter 8

Fundamental to the development of the arguments in this chapter is the book by Arthur A. Ekirch, *The Decline of American Liberalism* and the volumes in Vernon L. Parrington, *Main Currents in American Thought*, (Harcourt, Brace, Jovanovich: New York), 1927-1930.

The legal and judicial changes are captured in the powerful books by Morton J. Horwitz, *The Transformation of American Law, 1780-1860* (Harvard University Press: Cambridge), 1977; Henry Mark Holzer, *Sweet Land of Liberty: The Supreme Court and Individual Rights*, (Common Sense Press, Inc.: Costa Mesa, California), 1982; Bernard H. Siegen, *Economic Liberties and the Constitution*, (University of Chicago Press), 1980; and Raoul Berger, *Government by Judiciary*, (Harvard University Press: Cambridge), 1977. An excellent short summary of the "economic due process" issue can be found in Bernard H. Siegen, *The Rise and Fall of Economic Due Process--When the Supreme Court Championed and Then Curtailed Economic Freedom*, (International Insitute for Economic Research: Los Angeles), February 1983.

The story of the conflicting preferences and attitudes of the American people for freedom and/or equality, limited government versus a more powerful state is provided by Michael Kammen, *People of Paradox: An Inquiry Concerning the Origins of American Civilization*, (Alfred A. Knopf: New York), 1973. See Herbert J. Storing, *What the Anti-Federalists Were For: The Political Thought of the Opponents of the Constitution*, (University of Chicago Press), 1981 for the anti-federalist point of view.

Murray N. Rothbard in *Power and Market: Government and the Economy*, (Sheed Andrews and McMeel, Inc.: Kansas City), 1970 has identified the long list of existing interventions by government in our economic and personal affairs.

## Chapter 9

The quotation at the head of the chapter is from Herbert Spencer, *Social Statics*, (Robert Schalkenbach Foundation: New York), (1850) 1970.

The material of this chapter has relied mostly on the work of Friedrich A. Hayek. He has written extensively on the contrasts between the spontaneous order and rational constructivism and the differences between the negative law which is "grown" and the results of legal positivism which is "made." See for example his "The Errors of Constructivism," and "The New Confusion About 'Planning'," in *New Studies in Philosophy, Politics, Economics and the History of Ideas*, (University of Chicago Press), 1978; "The Results of Human Action But Not of Human Design," and "The Legal and Political Philosophy of David Hume," in *Studies in Philosophy, Politics and Economics*, (University of Chicago Press), 1967; *Law, Legislation and Liberty: Rules and Order*, (University of Chicago Press), Vol. I, 1973; and "The Use of Knowledge in Society," in *Individualism and Economic Order*, (University of Chicago Press), 1948.

A short summary of the issues raised in this chapter can be found in George C. Roche III, "The American Collectivist Myth: Its Roots, Its Results, Its Downfall," *IMPRIMIS*, Vol. II, no. 2, February 1982. An important contemporary analysis of the possibilities of centralized economic planning in the United States is Herbert Stein, *Economic Planning and the Improvement of Economic Policy*, (American Enterprise Institute:

Washington, D.C.), 1975. The whole question of "reindustrialization" and the proposals for a "National Industrial Policy" receives critical attention from Richard B. McKenzie, "Blueprint for Economic Decay," in *Competition*, (Council for a Competitive Economy: Washington, D.C.), Vol. 4, number 5, September/December 1983.

## Chapter 10

The power and relevance of Friedrich A. Hayek's views on "social justice" are found in *The Constitution of Liberty; Law, Legislation and Liberty: The Mirage of Social Justice*, University of Chicago Press), Vol. II, 1976; and "The Atavism of Social Justice," in *Social Justice, Socialism and Democracy*, (Center for Independent Studies: Sydney, Australia), Occasional Papers 2, 1979. While difficult going, Robert Nozick's *Anarchy, State, Utopia*, (Basic Books, Inc.: New York), 1974 is an important contribution. The chapter "Created Equal" in Milton and Rose Friedman, *Free to Choose*, (Harcourt, Brace Jovanovich, Inc.: New York), 1979 is must reading for everyone.

The discussion of the "welfare state" in Murray Rothbard, *For a New Liberty*, (Macmillan Publishing Company: New York), revised edition, 1978 provided facts and figures on the dimensions of the welfare problem. Evidence on the high degree of income mobility in the American economy is from Bradley R. Schiller, "Equality, Opportunity, and the 'Good Job'," *Public Interest*, Spring 1976 and Greg J. Duncan, "An Overview of Family Economic Mobility," *Economic Outlook*, 8, Number 2 (Spring, 1981).

We also made use of Robert Nisbet, "The Pursuit of Equality," *Public Interest*, Spring 1974; Robert G. Perrin, "The Dynamics and Dialectics of Capitalism," *The Journal of Libertarian Studies*, Vol. V, no. 2, Spring 1981; Jarret B. Wollstein, "The Idea of Equality," *The Freeman*, April 1980; Eric Mack, "Individualism, Rights, and the Open Society," in Tibor Machan, ed. *The Libertarian Alternative*, (Nelson-Hall Publishers: Chicago), 1974; Irving Kristol, "What is 'Social Justice'?," in *The Wall Street Journal*, August 12, 1976; and especially David Osterfeld, "The Government, the Market and the Poor," *The Freeman*, November 1980. Adam Smith's earlier work was *The Theory of Moral Sentiments*, 1759. The role of envy in human behavior is analyzed in great detail in Helmut Schoeck, *Envy, A Theory of Social Behavior*, (Harcourt, Brace and World Inc.: New York), 1969.

Roland Huntford, *The New Totalitarians*, (Stein and Day Publishers: New York), 1972 in his study of the Swedish welfare state draws attention to the collectivist mentality which "breaks the spirit and will of the people." One pathbreaking study on the net impact of government spending and taxation on the poor and income distribution is Henry Aaron and Martin McGuire, "Public Goods and Income Distribution," *Econometrica*, Vol. 38, no. 6, November 1970.

## Chapter 11

The quotation at the head of the chapter is from Frank Chodorov, "The Dogma of Our Times," in his *Fugitive Essays*.

Our brief survey of the various socialist movements relied on the treatise by Charles Gide and Charles Rist, *A History of Economic Doctrines*, Second English edition, 1948. Joseph Schumpeter's *Capitalism, Socialism and Democracy*, (Harper and Brothers: New York), third edition, 1950 is another important source on this topic. The article by Peter L. Berger, "The Socialist Myth," *Public Interest*, No. 44, Summer 1976, contributed importantly to our discussion.

The question of the possibility of economic calculation under socialism is analyzed in Ludwig von Mises, *Socialism*, (Liberty Fund, Inc.: Indianapolis), (1936) 1981. A good short summary of the writings of Karl Marx can be found in *Capital and Other Writings by Karl Marx*, (The Modern Library: New York) 1959 which contains "The Communist Manifesto," important sections from *Das Capital* and an essay on Marx by Lennin. For an excellent summary of the relationship between the state and the individual under socialism see the essay by Murray Rothbard, "The Anatomy of the State," in Tibor Machan, ed., *The Libertarian Alternative*, (Nelson-Hall: Chicago), 1974.

Recently Michael Novak has offered a refreshing look at the alternative available to us between capitalism and socialism in its many variations. See Michael Novak,

*The Spirit of Democratic Capitalism,* (Simon & Schuster: New York), 1982 and *The American Vision: An Essay on the Future of Democratic Capitalism,* (American Enterprise Institute: Washington, D. C.), 1978. The quotation from Vladimar Bukovsky is from "The Soul of Man Under Socialism," *Commentary,* January 1979.

### Chapter 12

With respect to the appeal of socialism to the intellectual see Friedrich A. Hayek, "The Intellectual and Socialism," in *Studies in Philosophy, Politics and Economics,* (University of Chicago Press), 1967 and George Roche, "The American Collectivist Myth," *IMPRIMIS,* (Hillsdale College: Michigan), February 1982. Joseph Schumpeter's views are in *Capitalism, Socialism and Democracy.*

The volume of essays in Kenneth S. Templeton, Jr., ed., *The Politicization of Society,* (Liberty Fund, Inc.: Indianapolis), 1979 is well worth the reader's attention, especially the introductory essay by R. M. Hartwell. An excellent survey of the implications of the "mixed economy" can be found in S. C. Littlechild, *The Fallacy of the Mixed Economy,* (Institute of Economic Affairs: London), 1978. The quotation by Murray Rothbard is from his *For a New Liberty,* (Macmillan Publishing Company: New York), Revised edition, 1978, and the brief quotation by Frank Chodorov is from his collection of essays *Fugitive Essays.* The words of George Barnard Shaw and Upton Sinclair are cited in Paul Hollander, *Political Pilgrims,* (Oxford University Press: Oxford), 1982

Roland Huntford, *The New Totalitarians,* (Stein and Day Publishers: New York), 1972 documents the adverse consequences of the Swedish welfare state. John Flynn, *As We Go Marching,* (Doubleday: New York), 1944 compares the fascist experiments in Italy and Germany with the efforts by the intellectuals in the United States to politicize the American economy. In order to get a feel for what the advocates of "economic democracy" have in mind see Martin Carnoy and Derek Shearer, *Economic Democracy: The Challenge of the 1980's,* (M. E. Sharpe: New York), 1980; Bill Anderson, "Economic Democracy," *The Freeman,* November 1982; and Justin Raimondo, "Inside the CED," *Reason,* February 1982 for its application to California politics by Tom Haden and Jane Fonda.

William L. O'Neill's *A Better World: The Great Schism: Stalinism and the American Intellectuals,* (Simon & Schuster: New York), 1982 tries to explain the American intellectual's interest, especially during the 1940's, in the Stalin dictatorship. A short article "Marxism In U. S. Classrooms," *U. S. News and World Report,* January 25, 1982 provides an interesting insight into the influence of left/Marxist scholarship on the campuses of America's colleges and Universities.

### Chapter 13

The quotation at the head of the chapter and the key source for the contradictory nature of the collectivist's solutions to the question of economic growth are from Murray N. Rothbard, *For a New Liberty.*

The material of this chapter is treated at greater length in especially William Breit and Roger L. Ransom, *The Academic Scribblers: American Economics in Collision,* (Holt, Rinehart and Winston: New York), 1971 and Herbert Stein, *The Fiscal Revolution in America,* (University of Chicago Press), 1969. Also see Robert Lekachman, *The Age of Keynes,* (Random House: New York), 1966 and Murray N. Rothbard, *America's Great Depression,* (Sheed and Ward, Inc.: Kansas City), third edition, 1975. On Alvin Hansen see his *Fiscal Policy and Business Cycles,* (W. W. Norton & Co.: New York), 1941; *Full Recovery or Stagnation?,* (W. W. Norton & Co.: New York), 1938; and later his *The Economic Issues of the 1960's,* (McGraw-Hill Publishers: New York), 1960. An excellent brief description of the changing view of budget deficits and the politics of fiscal policy can be found in Richard E. Wagner and Robert D. Tollison, *Balanced Budgets, Fiscal Responsibility, and the Constitution,* (CATO Institute: Washington, D. C.), 1980.

Both sides of the "limits to growth" question are presented in the important little volume H. S. D. Cole, ed., *Models of Doom: The Limits to Growth,* (Universe Books: New York), 1973. For a truly upbeat view on the prospects of growth and rising standards of living in the U. S. see George Gilder, *Wealth and Poverty,* (Basic Books, Inc.: New York), 1981.

On the government's role in generating the Great Depression of the 1930's see Milton Friedman and Anna Jacobson Schwartz, *A Monetary History of the United States, 1867-1960,* National Bureau of Economic Research, (Princeton University Press), 1963, Peter Temin, *Did Monetary Forces Cause the Great Depression,* (W. W. Norton & Company: New York), 1976, as well as Rothbard's *America's Great Depression.*

## Chapter 14
The quotation at the head of the chapter is from Robert Nisbet, *History of the Idea of Progress,* (Basic Books, Inc.: New York), 1980. This scholarly effort was crucial to our discussion in this chapter. A good short summary of the issues in Nisbet's book can be found in his survey article "The Idea of Progress, *Literature of Liberty,* (Institute of Humane Studies: Menlo Park, Califonia), Vol. II, no. 1, January/March 1979. Quotations by Robert L. Sinsheimer, Gifford Pinchot and Bayard Rustin are cited in Nisbet's *History of the Idea of Progress.*
Other important works on the issue of progress include Herbert E. Meyer, *The War Against Progress,* (Storm Publishers, Inc.: New York), 1980; J. B. Bury, *The Idea of Progress,* (Allen & Unwin: London), 1920; William Tucker, *Progress and Privilege: America in the Age of Environmentalism,* (Anchor Press-Doubleday: New York), 1982; and Mary Douglas and Aaron Wildavsky, *Risk and Culture,* (University of California Press), 1982. The chapter "The Common Sense of Progress," in Friedrich Hayek's *Constitution of Liberty,* and the article by Robert Nisbet, "Modern Man and The Obsession," in *The American Spectator,* Vol. 16, no. 5, May 1983 have been important sources. Also see the article by Robert G. Perrin, "The Dynamics and Dialectics of Capitalism."
We have cited a number of books which make the case for economic growth. Among the more important, although for reasons that differ quite significantly and in terms of arguments which we do not necessarily share, there are Alvin Toffler, *The Third Wave,* (William Morrow and Company: New York), 1980; H. S. D. Cole, ed., *Models of Doom: A Critique of the Limits to Growth;* Herman Kahn, *World Economic Development: 1979 and Beyond,* (Westview Press, Inc.: Boulder, Colorado), 1979; Julian L. Simon, *The Ultimate Resource;* Herman Kahn, *The Coming Boom,* (Simon & Schuster: New York), 1982; Michael Novak, *The Spirit of Democratic Capitalism* and John Naisbitt, *Megatrends.*

## Chapter 15
The quotation at the head of the chapter and the best survey of the issues and personalities involved in the transformation of the economics profession in the United States are in Henri Lepage, *Tomorrow Capitalism: The Economics of Economic Freedom,* (Open Court Publishing: La Salle, Illinois), 1982.
The two important books which truly marked the counter revolution in economics are Friedrich A. Hayek, *The Road to Serfdom,* (University of Chicago Press), 1944 and Milton Friedman, *Capitalism and Freedom* (University of Chicago Press), 1962.
Important insights into the role of Frank Knight and Henry Simons in keeping the private property, voluntary exchange paradigm alive are found in William Breit and Roger Ransom, *The Academic Scribblers: American Economists in Collision.* Quotations are from Henry Simons, *Economic Policy for a Free Society,* (University of Chicago Press: Chicago), 1948. A brief but excellent introduction to the Austrian School can be found in S. C. Littlechild, *The Fallacy of the Mixed Economy: An 'Austrian' Critique of Economic Thinking and Policy.*

## Chapter 16
The quotations at the head of the chapter are from Peter F. Drucker, "The Sickness of Government," *Public Interest,* Winter 1969 and Milton Friedman and Rose Friedman, *Free to Choose.*
A brief but excellent summary of the issues surrounding the question of government's limitations as a delivery system is William C. Mitchell, *The Anatomy of Public Failure: A Public Choice Perspective,* (International Institute for Economic Research: Los Angeles), June 1978. Another important summary of the theory of public choice is in Henry

Lepage, *Tomorrow, Capitalism*. A few of the more accessible sources would include the relevant chapters in Milton and Rose Friedman, *Free to Choose*, (Harcourt, Brace Jovanovich: New York), 1980; William E. Simon, *A Time for Truth*, (McGraw-Hill Publishers: New York), 1978; Bernard H. Siegen, *Economic Liberties and the Constitution*, (University of Chicago Press), 1980; and Richard B. McKenzie and Gordon Tullock, *Modern Political Economy: An Introduction to Economics*, (McGraw-Hill Publishers: New York), 1978.

The following are generally more demanding reading but classics. The pioneering study of the ideas contained in the public choice model was Anthony Downs, *An Economic Theory of Democracy*, (Harper & Row Publishers: New York), 1957. Other key contributions to our understanding of the anatomy of government failure include James M. Buchanan and Gordon Tullock, *The Calculus of Consent: Logical Foundations of Constitutional Democracy*, (University of Michigan Press: Ann Arbor), 1962; William Niskanan, *Bureaucracy and Representative Government*, (Aldine-Atherton: Chicago), 1971; Mancur Olson, *The Logic of Collective Action*, (Harvard University Press: Cambridge), 1971; George Stigler, *The Citizen and the State*, (University of Chicago Press), 1975; and Albert Breton, *The Economic Theory of Representative Government*, (Aldine Publishing Company: Chicago), 1974. A rigorous survey of the public choice field can be found in Dennis C. Mueller, *Public Choice*, Cambridge Surveys of Economic Literature, (Cambridge University Press: New York), 1979.

The quotation on the emptiness of the phrase the "public interest" is from M. Bruce Johnson, "Planning Without Prices: A Discussion of Land Use Regulation Without Compensation," in Bernard H. Siegen, ed., *Planning Without Prices*, D. C. Heath: Lexington, Mass.), 1977.

Two fairly short and very readable discussions of the defects in our democratic institutions can be found in Robert A. Nisbet, *The New Despotism*, (Institute for Humane Studies: Menlo Park, Calif.), 1976 and Richard E. Wagner and Robert D. Tollison, *Balanced Budgets, Fiscal Responsibility, and the Constitution*. Henri Lepage in *Tomorrow, Captialism*, Chapter 7 — "Reinventing the Market" also offers a good summary of the means by which government might be made more responsive to individual wants.

From a somewhat different approach than the public choice people, the "Austrian School" has also made important contributions to our understanding of the limitations of government as a delivery system. See for example the classic Ludwig von Mises, *Bureaucracy*, (Yale University Press: New Haven), 1946 and *Socialism*, (Liberty Fund, Inc.: Indianapolis), (1936) 1981; and in the work of Friedrich A. Hayek, *The Road to Serfdom* and Part III of *The Consitution of Liberty*. A powerful account of the implications of government intervention in the free market is the important book by Murray N. Rothbard, *Power and Market: Government and the Economy*. An excellent short summary of the factors contributing to the growth in government is Allen H. Meltzer, *Why Government Grows*, (International Institute for Economic Research: Los Angeles), August 1976.

**Chapter 17**

The quotations at the head of the chapter are from Frederic Bastiat, *The Law* and S. C. Littlechild, *The Fallacy of the Mixed Economy*.

The two classic works on the dynamic and ever changing nature of the system of competitive capitalism are Ludwig von Mises, *Human Action; A Treatise on Economics*, (Henry Regnery Company: Chicago), third revised edition, 1966 and Joseph Schumpeter, *Capitalism, Socialism and Democracy*. Following the lead of these two intellectual giants, Friedrich A. Hayek's volume *Individualism and Economic Order*, (University of Chicago Press), 1948 contains two classic articles: "The Use of Knowledge in Society" and "The Meaning of Competition." The Austrian perspective on the nature of the competitive process is developed at length in the important book by Israel Kirzner, *Competition and Entrepreneurship*, (University of Chicago Press), 1973. S. C. Littlechild, *The Fallacy of the Mixed Economy* has analyzed the post-World War II British economy in terms of the market process view. The important work by Murray N. Rothbard, *Man, Economy and State: A Treatise on Economic Principles*, (Nash Publishing: Los Angeles), 1962 also emphasizes the competitive process. A very important book by Thomas Sowell, *Knowledge and Decisions* (Basic Books, Inc.: New York), 1980, drawing on the earlier work of Hayek and Kirzner, continues the important task of discovering the implications of a world in which knowledge is itself scarce and must be mobilized for decision making. There are additonal articles by Ludwig Lachmann, another Austrian economist and Kirzner on the nature of the competitive process in Edwin G. Dolan, ed., *The Foundations of Modern Austrian Economics*, (Sheed and Ward, Inc.: Kansas City), 1976. Walter Wriston has captured the implications of the factor risk in all this in a little monograph *Risk and Other Four Letter Words*, (International Institute for Economic Research: Los Angeles), August1980.

Two recent survey articles in *Literature of Liberty*, (Institute for Humane Studies: Menlo Park, California), Summer 1982 and Winter 1982 by Norman Barry, "The Tradition of Spontaneous Order," and John N. Gray, "F. A. Hayek and the Rebirth of Classical Liberalism" which, along with Friedrich Hayek, "Competition As a Discovery Procedure," in Hayek, ed., *New Studies in Philosophy, Politics, Economics and the History of Ideas*, (University of Chicago Press), 1978, are well worth reading.

With respect to the question of monopoly and the antitrust laws the basic contribution is Dominick T. Armentano, *Antitrust and Monopoly: Anatomy of a Policy Failure*, (John Wiley & Sons: New York), 1982. An important collection of papers on this issue is H. J. Goldschmid, H. M. Mann, and J. F. Weston, eds., *Industrial Concentration: The New Learning*, (Little, Brown and Company: Boston), 1974. Among other important and readable sources on the question of monopoly power and industrial concentration the following are recommended: Yale Brozen, *Is Government the Source of Monopoly? and Other Essays*, (CATO Institute: Washington, D. C.), 1980; Harold Demsetz, *The Market Concentration Doctrine*, (American Enterprise Institute: Washington, D. C.), August 1973; and Harold Demsetz, *The Trust Behind Antitrust*, (International Institute for Economic Research: Los Angeles), March 1978.

For a revisionist interpretation of the nature of the competitive process and government intervention in the economy at the turn of the century see Gabriel Kolko, *The Triumph of Conservatism: A Reinterpretation of American History, 1900-1916*, (The Free Press: New York), 1963. On the pricing practices of the Standard Oil Company see John S. McGee, "Predatory Price Cutting: The Standard Oil (N.J.) Case," *Journal of Law and Economics*, Vol. 1, October 1958.

**Chapter 18**

The quotation at the head of the chapter is Ronald H. Coase, "Economists and Public Policy," in J. Fred Weston, ed., *Large Corporations in a Changing Society*, (New York University Press: New York), 1975.

The different types of government intervention have been distinguished by Murray N. Rothbard, *Power and Market: Government and the Economy*. The ways in which economic regulation through price controls suppresses socially useful knowledge is identified in Thomas Sowell, *Knowledge and Decisions*. Sowell also has an excellent discussion of the adverse implications of occupational licensing.

Sowell, *Knowledge and Decisions*, Rothbard, *Power and Market*, and Bernard Siegen, *Economic Liberties and the Constitution* speak to the issue of price ceilings and price floors. Rent controls are analyzed in Charles W. Baird, *Rent Control: The Perennial Folly*, (CATO Institute: Washington, D. C.), 1980 and Eric K. Hemel, "What Does Rent Control Control?," in Institute for Contemporary Studies, *Taxes and Spending*, Fall 1979. The terribly adverse implications of the energy price controls in the 1970's are described in J. Clayborn La Force, *The Energy Crisis: The Moral Equivalent of Bamboozle*, (International Institute for Economic Research: Los Angeles), April 1978 and Jai-Hoon Yang, "The Nature and Origins of the U. S. Energy Crisis," Federal Reserve Bank of St. Louis, *Review*, July 1977.

The problems in agriculture are characterized in a good summary in Clifton B. Luttrell, *Down on the Farm With Uncle Sam*, (International Institute for Economic Research: Los Angeles), June 1983.

The disasterous consequences of minimum wage legislation are described in Walter Williams, *The State Against the Blacks*, (McGraw-Hill Publishers: New York), 1982.

Government intervention in the area of medical care, regulation, licensing, etc.

and the economic consequences are described in John C. Goodman, *The Regulation of Medical Care: Is The Price Too High?*, (CATO Institute: Washington, D. C.), 1980 and Elton Rayack, "The Physicians Service Industry," in Walter Adams, ed., *The Structure of American Industry*, Sixth edition, (Macmillan Publishing Co.: New York), 1982.

The so-called traditional, old-style economic regulation of air travel, surface transportation, communications, broadcasting, banking, etc. is analyzed in a number of studies in Robert W. Poole, Jr., ed., *Instead of Regulation: Alternative to Federal Regulatory Agencies*, (D. C. Heath and Company: Lexington, Mass.), 1982 and in Almarin Phillips, ed., *Promoting Competition in Regulated Markets*, (The Brookings Institution: Washington, D. C.), 1975.

See the interesting article by Tom Hazlett, "The Viewer is the Loser," *Reason*, July 1982 on the new attempt to declare cable television a "natural monopoly" and to deny competition in this arena.

Sources for the so-called new social regulation were the studies in Robert W. Poole, *Instead of Regulation* and Murray L. Weidenbaum, *Business, Government, and the Public*, Second edition, (Prentice-Hall: Englewood Cliffs, New Jersey), 1981. With regard to consumer protection, also see Richard B. McKenzie, *Caution: Consumer Protection May Be Hazardous to Your Health*, (International Institute for Economic Research: Los Angeles), December 1978.

The interesting question regarding the private interest which some firms and industries have in maintaining the old regulated ways is analyzed in Robert W. Crandall, "Twilight of Deregulation," *The Brookings Bulletin*, (The Brookings Institution: Washington, D. C.), Vol. 18, no. 3 & 4, Winter-Spring 1982. The difficulties we can expect in completing the deregulation movement are identified in Donald J. Mullineaux, "Regulation: Whence It Came and Whether It's Here to Stay," Federal Reserve Bank of Philadelphia, *Business Review*, September/October 1978 and Tom Alexander, "Why Bureaucracy Keeps Growing," *Fortune*, May 7, 1979.

**Chapter 19**

The quotation at the head of the chapter is from Ludwig von Mises, *Bureaucracy*. This little volume also makes the general case for privatization.

Our discussion of the federal government involvement in transportation relied on Paul Feldman, "Free the D. C. 2!," *Reason*, September 1983; John Doherty "Towering Entrepreneurs," *Reason*, May 1983; Patrick Cox, "Fair Weather," *Reason*, June 1983; Jack Williams, "Private Weather Firms Boom," *USA Today*, January 10, 1984; and George W. Hilton, "Ending the Ground-Transportation Cartel," in Robert Poole, ed., *Instead of Regulation*.

The brief look at energy utilized the following sources: Yvonne Levy, "Synfuels Subsidy," Federal Reserve Bank of San Francisco, *Weekly Letter*, March 28, 1980 and Elena Folkerts-Landau, "The Sinful Cost of Synfuels," *The Wall Street Journal*, May 13, 1983 speak to the synthetic fuels issue. An excellent short summary of the "energy crisis" is J. Clayborn La Force, *The Energy Crisis: The Moral Equivalent of Bamboozle*. With respect to nuclear power we relied on Arlen J. Large, "U. S. Subsidized Growth in Nuclear Power By $37 Billion Over 30 Years, Study Says," *The Wall Street Journal*, December 15, 1980, Caroline J. C. Hellman and Richard Hellman, "The Lousy Economics of Nuclear Power," *The Wall Street Journal*. August 2, 1981 and *The Competitive Economics of Nuclear Power and Coal Power*, (Lexington Books: Lexington, Mass.), 1983; and Barry P. Brownstein, "The Market's Case Against Nuclear Power Plants," *Dow Jones, Inc., The Collegiate Forum*, Spring 1980. The announcement of the termination of the breeder reactor project was Arlen J. Large and Leonard M. Apcar, "Clinch River Nuclear Project Dies in Congress," *The Wall Street Journal*, October 27, 1983.

On TVA see Douglas C. Lyons, "After 50 Years, TVA Is Still In Hot Water," *U. S. News & World Report*, May 23, 1983 and North Callahan, *TVA: Bridge Over Troubled Waters*, (Cornwall Books: New York), 1980. A sampling of comments on the Washington Public Power Supply System (WPPSS) can be found in James T. Bennett and Thomas J. DiLorenzo, "Beefy Bailouts: First Big Mac and Now a Whooper?," *The Wall Street Journal*, August 8, 1983 and *Underground Government: The Off-Budget*

Public Sector, (CATO Institute, Washington, D. C.), 1983; Carrie Dolan, "Debt-Ridden WPPSS Gets NRC License to Operate Long-Delayed Nuclear Plant," The Wall Street Journal, December 21, 1983; Yvonne Levy, "Power to the Northwest," Federal Reserve Bank of San Francisco, Weekly Letter, April 7, 1978; "The Fallout From 'Whoops'," Business Week, July 11, 1983; "WPPSS to Sell Acres of Hardware," The Idaho Statesman, February 21, 1984; and "Questions on WPPSS Revealed," The Idaho Statesman, January 2, 1984.

The implications of the monopoly U. S. Postal Service are analyzed in Jeff Sampson, "Denationalizing the Mails," Reason, September 1979 and Kathleen Conkey, The Postal Precipice: Can the U. S. Postal Service Survive?, (Center for the Study of Responsive Law: Washington, D. C.), 1983. The issue of "cream skimming," which appears as a problem in a number of cross-subsidization schemes of government intervention is identified in its true colors by Alan Reynolds, "A Kind Word for 'Cream Skimming'," Harvard Business Review, November/December 1974.

Our sources for the social security mess included Peter J. Ferrara, Social Security: Averting the Crisis, (CATO Institute: Washington, D. C.), 1982; Colin D. Campbell, Social Security's Financial Crisis, (International Institute for Economic Research: Los Angeles), October 1983, Martin Feldstein, "Social Security Induced Retirement and Aggregate Capital Accumulation," Journal of Political Economy, September/October 1974; and Ed Clark, A New Beginning, (Caroline House: New York), 1980. The entire issue of The CATO Journal, Vol. 3, No. 2, Fall 1983 is devoted to the social security problem.

The potential for the independent sector or the third sector of the economy can be found in Richard Cornuelle, Healing America: What Can Be Done About the Continuing Economic Crisis, (G. P. Putnam's Sons: New York), 1983.

The issue of federal government money going to subsidize housing is discussed in Sydney Smith Hicks, "Federal Housing Agencies: How Effective Are They?," Federal Reserve Bank of Dallas, Voice, October 1978; William R. Sayre, "Subsidized Housing--Costs and Benefits," Federal Reserve Bank of Chicago, Economics Perspectives, May/June 1979; and Randall Pozdena and William Burke, "Housing: Sacred Cow?," Federal Reserve Bank of San Francisco, Weekly Letter, November 28, 1980. The interesting question of whether the federal subsidies to housing are coming at the expense of investment in new plant and equipment in American industry is raised by Anthony Downs, "Too Much Capital for Housing," The Brookings Bulletin, Vol. 17, no. 1, Summer 1980.

The date on the relative efficiency of private and public enterprises in Europe is from R. Joseph Monsen and Kenneth D. Walters, Nationalized Companies, (McGraw-Hill Publishers: New York), 1983.

**Chapter 20**
The quotation by Robert J. Smith at the head of the chapter is from his Earth's Resources: Private Ownership vs. Public Waste, (Libertarian Party National Committee: Washington, D. C.), 1980.

The citations and quotations by Richard Stroup and John Baden are from their Natural Resources: Bureaucratic Myths and Environmental Management, 1982 published by the Pacific Institute for Public Policy Research, 177 Post Street, San Francisco, California, 94108.

Garrett Hardin's classic article, "The Tragedy of the Commons," which first appeared in Science in 1968 has been reproduced in many anthologies. It can be found, for example, in Alain C. Enthoven and A. Myrick Freeman III, eds., Pollution, Resources, and the Environment, (W. W. Norton & Company, Inc.: New York), 1973.

Important sources on the long-run scarcity of resources and sources of quotations on the issue are Anthony Scott, Natural Resources: The Economics of Conservation, (University of Toronto Press: Toronto), 1955; Harold J. Barnett and Chandler Morse, Scarcity and Growth: The Economics of Natural Resource Availability, (John Hopkins University Press: Baltimore), 1963; and Julian L. Simon, The Ultimate Resource, (Princeton University Press: Princeton, New Jersey), 1981.

The argument on the aristocratic and elitist nature of the environmental movement is developed at length in William Tucker, *Progress and Privilege: America in the Age of Environmentalism*, (Anchor Press/Doubleday: Garden City, New York), 1982. The quotation by Vernon Jordan is from a speech reprinted as "Forging New Alliances," in the *New York Times*, May 27, 1979.

An excellent introduction to environmental economics and the source of the quotation on excess taking is Edwin Dolan, *TANSTAAFL: The Economic Stragedy for Environmental Crisis*, (Holt, Rinehart and Winston: New York), 1971. The quotation which equates pollution emisions to physical aggression and therefore a fundamental violation of human rights is by Robert Poole, Jr., "Reason and Ecology," in D. James, ed., *Outside Looking In*, (Harper & Row Publishers: New York), 1972. The best summary of the change in the common law tradition by the courts in ruling on environmental matters is Morton J. Horwitz, *The Transformation of American Law, 1780-1860*, (Harvard University Press: Cambridge), 1977.

Other worthwhile sources, among many, on the issues of conservation include John Baden and Richard Stroup, "A Radical Proposal: Saving the Wilderness," *Reason*, July 1981; Robert J. Smith, "Resolving the Tragedy of the Commons by Creating Private Property Rights in Wildlife," *The CATO Journal*, Vol. 1, no. 2, Fall 1981; William C. Dennis, "The Public and Private Interest in Wilderness Protection," James P. Beckwith, Jr., "Parks, Property Rights, and the Possibilities of the Private Law," and Charles R. Batten, "Toward a Free Market in Forest Resources," all from the same Fall 1981 issue of *The CATO Journal*; Bruce Ramsey, "Forest Socialism," *Reason*, December 1983; William Tucker, "Conservation in Deed: Saving the Environment Through Ownership," *Reason*, May 1983; and Dwight R. Lee, *Environmental Versus Political Pollution*, (International Institute for Economic Research: Los Angeles), September 1982.

An excellent collection of articles is John Baden and Richard L. Stroup, eds., *Bureaucracy vs Environment*, (University of Michigan Press: Ann Arbor), 1981. An excellent brief intoduction to the water conservation issue can be found in Terry L. Anderson *Water Crisis: Ending the Policy Drought*, (CATO Institution: Washington, D. C.), 1983.

Milton Friedman in Chapter 2 — "The Role of Government in a Free Society," *Capitalism and Freedom*, (University of Chicago Press), 1962 explicitly identifies national parks as a function government currently performs which cannot be justified in a free society of limited government.

The original contribution on the idea of a market in pollution rights was J. H. Dales, *Pollution, Property, and Prices)*, (University of Toronto Press: Toronto), 1968. An excellent short summary of the air pollution issue is in Theodore Crone and Robert H. DeFina, "Cleaning the Air with the Invisible Hand," Federal Reserve Bank of Philadelphia, *Business Review*, November/December 1983.

Soviet environmental problems are documented in Marshall I. Goldman, *The Spoils of Progress: Environmental Pollution in the Soviet Union*, (M.I.T. Press: Cambridge), 1972 and Fred Singleton, ed., *Environmental Misuse in the Soviet Union*. (Praeger Publishers: New York), 1976.

**Chapter 21**

An important source of material on the question of privatization at the local level and the source of the quotation at the head of this chapter is William D. Burt, *Local Problems: Libertarian Solutions*, (Libertarian National Committee: Washington, D. C.), 1979.

Especially valuable is the important book by Robert W. Poole, Jr., *Cutting Back City Hall*, (Universe Books: New York), 1980. Also see E. S. Savas, *How to Shrink Government: Privatizing the Public Sector*, (Chatham House Publishers: Chatham, New Jersey), 1982. Background on the public versus private issue can be found in Ludwig von Mises *Bureaucracy* and Murray Rothbard, *Power and Market*.

On the question of urban tranportation valuable sources included Gabriel Roth, "Free-Lance Transit," *Reason*, October 1982; Gabriel Roth and George G. Wynne, *Free Enterprise Urban Transportation*, (Council for International Urban Liason: Washington, D. C.), 1981; Thomas Sowell, *Knowledge and Decisions;* and "Houston Voters Derail Boondoggle," *Reason*, September 1983; in addition to Poole and Burt.

The interview with Richard Page, former federal mass-transit chief was in Albert R. Karr, "Despite Improvements, Local Transit Line Must Raise Standards Further, Expert Says," *The Wall Street Journal*, July 19, 1983.

Additional material on privatization of emergency services came from Jim Peron, "Blazing Battles," *Reason*, November 1983; Robert W. Poole, "Private Fire Departments Come of Age," Center for Education and Research in Free Enterprise, Texas A & M, *Pathfinder*, October 1983; and Theodore Gage, "Cops, Inc.," *Reason*, November 1982.

The expert on solid waste disposal is E. S. Savas, "Public vs. Private Refuse Collection: A Critical Review of the Evidence," *Journal of Urban Analysis*, Vol. 6, 1979.

For a discussion of the other local services which are capable of being taken to the private sector see Poole, *Cutting Back City Hall*, Burt, *Local Problems: Libertarian Solutions*, and Savas, *How to Shrink Government*. We utilized Dick Bjornseth, "No-Code Comfort," *Reason*, July 1983 on the issue of building codes; "A Clean Sweep for Contracting Out," *Reason*, June 1983 on contracting for custodial services in public buildings; Lynn Asinof, "Growth of Tax-Exempt Financing Stirs Battle on Revenues and Rights," *The Wall Street Journal*, November 7, 1983 with respect to the issuance by local government of tax exempt financing of housing and industry; and Bernard Siegen, *Land Use Without Zoning* on the merits of zoning ordinances.

A comparative look at the employment of user fees by government operated businesses versus complete privatization is undertaken by Steven H. Hanke in the short piece "The User Fee Illusion," *Reason*, August 1983.

On the important question of public versus private education the following studies were especially useful. On the history and success of private education in the United States before the Civil War see Samuel L. Blumenfeld, "Why Schools Went Public," *Reason*, March 1979 and his book *Is Public Education Necessary*, (Devin-Adair Co., Inc.: Old Greenwich, Connecticut), 1981. A very important work on the evolution of the relationship between government and education and an evaluation of proposals for privatization is Robert B. Everhart, ed., *The Public School Monopoly: A Critical Analysis of Education and the State in American Society*, (Pacific Institute for Public Policy Research: San Francisco), 1982. The important work on this issue by E. G. West is illustrated in his article "The Perils of Public Education," *The Freeman*, November 1977. Another important collection of articles can be found in James S. Coleman, et. al., *Parents, Teachers, and Children: Prospects for Choice in American Education*. (Institute for Contemporary Studies: San Francisco), 1977. Two short pieces by Thomas Sowell provide some interesting facts on the viability of private schools: "Educators' Treat Parents Like Children," and "Educational Draftees," in his *Pink and Brown People and Other Controversial Essays*, (Hoover Institute Press: Palo Alto, Calif.), 1981. A brief but insightful comparison of vouchers and tax credits can be found in the letter to the editor by Jule R. Herbert, Jr., "Credit Risks," in *Reason*, November 1983.

Denis P. Doyle recommends that funds appropriated under existing Title I programs be made available as vouchers to students rather than schools as a device to encourage competition in education in "Let Title I Fund Pupils Rather Than Schools," *The Wall Street Journal*, October 4, 1983.

Finally the entire issue of *Conservative Digest*, Vol. 9, no. 8, August 1983 was devoted to the question of private versus public education and "Education's New Dark Age." Chapters in Poole and Burt also deal at some length with the education issue.

## Chapter 22

The quotations at the head of the chapter are from Richard B. McKenzie, "Blueprint for Economic Decay," *Competition*, (Council for a Competitive Economy: Washington, D. C.), September/December 1983 and Charlotte Twight, "The Economics of Fascism: 'National Interest' Above All," *Perspectives on Public Policy*, (Council for a Competitive Economy: Washington, D. C.), 1980.

Our interpretation of "national industrial policy" is based on the works by Robert B. Reich, *The Next American Frontier*, (Random House: New York), 1983; Ira C. Magaziner and Robert B. Reich, *Minding America's Business: The Decline and Rise of the American Economy*, (Harcourt Brace and Jovanovich: New York), 1982, and

Lester Thurow, *The Zero-Sum Society*, (Basic Books, Inc.: New York), 1981.

Key sources for our critique of the industrial policy proposals are Charles L. Schultze, "Industrial Policy: A Dissent," *The Brookings Review*, (The Brookings Institution: Washington, D. C.), Fall 1983; Richard B. McKenzie, "Blueprint for Economic Decay,"; Amitai Etzioni, "The MITIzation of America?," *The Public Interest*, No. 72, Summer 1983; Robert J. Samuelson, "Harvard's Industrial-Policy Peddlers," *Harpers Magazine*, June 1983; George Gilder, "A Supply-Side Economic of the Left," *The Public Interest*, No. 72, Summer 1983; Paul R. Krugman, "Targeted Industrial Policies: Theory and Evidence," Federal Reserve Bank of Kansas City, *Industrial Change and Public Policy: A Symposium*, August 24-26, 1983; and Mancur Olson, *The Rise and Decline of Nations*, (Yale University Press: New Haven), 1982.

Explanations of the decline in the rate of growth in productivity in the American economy during the 1970's can be found in Timothy Hannan, "The Productivity Perplex: A Concern for the Supply Side," Federal Reserve Bank of Philadelphia, *Business Review*, March/April 1980; John Tatom, "The Productivity Problem," Federal Reserve Bank of St. Louis, *Review* September 1979; and Edward F. Denison, "Explanations of Declining Productivity Growth," *Survey of Current Business*, August 1979.

The important summary of Japan's experience with allocating public investment funds is in Philip H. Trezise, "Industrial Policy Is Not the Major Reason for Japan's Success," *The Brookings Review*, Spring 1983.

We quoted from the following newspaper articles: Art Pine, "Industrial Policies? It's no Panacea in Japan," *The Wall Street Journal*, September 19, 1983; Louis Rukeyser, "Industrial-Policy Backers--'Doctors' May Kill Patient," *The Idaho Statesman*, September 25, 1983; and Morton M. Kondracke, "A Liberal-Activist Alternative to Industrial Policy," *The Wall Street Journal*, December 15, 1983.

There have been a number of critical reviews of the books by Robert Reich, including Alan Reynolds, "A Confederacy of Drones," *Inquiry*, August 1983; Richard W. Wilcke, "Economic Elixir," *Reason*, December 1983; and Tom Bethell, "Sunset for Industrial Policy?," *National Review*, December 9, 1983.

Material on the scope of the underground economy in the United States is summarized in Vito Tanzi, "Underground Economy Built on Illicit Pursuits Is Growing Concern of Economic Policymakers," International Monetary Fund, *Survey*, February 4, 1980 and Richard D. Porter and Amanda S. Bayer, "A Monetary Perspective on Underground Economic Activity in the United States," Board of Governors of the Federal Reserve System, *Federal Reserve Bulletin*, (Washington, D. C.), March 1984.

Our interpretation of fascism is based on the works of John Flynn, *As We Go Marching* and Charlotte Twight, *America's Emerging Fascist Economy*, (Arlington House: Westport, Connecticut), 1975.

An excellent survey of the supply-side issues is Robert E. Keleher, "Supply-Side Economics and the Founding Fathers: The Linkage," Working Paper Series, Federal Reserve Bank of Atlanta, July 1982. Also see the collection of papers in Richard H. Fink, ed., *Supply-Side Economics: A Critical Appraisal*, University Publications of America: Frederick, Maryland), 1982.

### Chapter 23

The quotations at the chapter heading are from James M. Buchanan and Richard E. Wagner, *Democracy in Deficit*. (Academic Press: New York), 1977 and John Maynard Keynes, *The Economic Consequences of the Peace*, 1919.

On the size and growth of the federal government, see Executive Office of the President, Office of Management and Budget, *The United States Budget in Brief: Fiscal Year 1984* and *Fiscal Year 1985*, (U. S. Government Printing Office: Washington D. C.), February 1983 and February 1984; James T. Bennett, "How Big Is the Federal Government," Federal Reserve Bank of Atlanta, *Economic Review*, December 1981; Irwin L. Kellner, "The Tip of the Iceberg," The Manufacturers Hanover Bank, *Economic Report*, November 1981; Stephen H. Pollock, "Off-Budget Federal Outlays," Federal Reserve Bank of Kansas City, *Economic Review*, March 1981; Keith M. Carlson, "Trends in Federal Spending: 1955-1986," Federal Reserve Bank of St. Louis, *Review*, November 1981; and Barbara Blumenthal, "Uncle Sam's Army of Invisible Employees," *National*

*Journal*, May 5, 1979.

Off-budget financing by state and local government has been summarized by James T. Bennett and Thomas J. DiLorenzo, "the Limitations of Spending Limitation," Federal Reserve Bank of Atlanta, *Economic Review*, December 1982.

With respect to fiscal discipline in the U. S. past see Richard E. Wagner and Robert D. Tollison, *Balanced Budgets, Fiscal Responsibility, and the Constitution* and James M. Buchanan and Richard E. Wagner, *Democracy in Deficit*, (Academic Press, Inc.: New York), 1977. The results of the Wall Street Journal/Gallup poll are in Mike Connelly, "Executives Say Size of U. S. Deficit is Most Serious Economic Problem," *The Wall Street Journal*, January 12, 1984.

The issue of "crowding-out" is analyzed in standard macroeconomic textbooks. The quotation from Norman B. Ture is from "What Really Does the Crowding Out," *The Wall Street Journal*, September 14, 1983. The competition for domestic savings between the private sector and the federal government is highlighted in Irwin L. Kellner. "The Deficit," The Manufacturers Hanover Bank, *Economic Report*, January 1984.

The quotation from Henry C. Simon on the requirements of a "moral consensus" is from his *Economic Policy for a Free Society*, (University of Chicago Press), 1948.

Proposals for "tax simplification are discussed in a lengthy article by Robert Reno, "Major Change in Tax Code--Lots of Talk, Few Specifics," *The Idaho Statesman*, February 12, 1984. The question of indexing has been discussed in Paul Craig Roberts, "Senator Domenci Takes On Indexing," *The Wall Street Journal*, April 13, 1981; Lindley H. Clark, Jr., "Indexing: An Idea Only Politicians Could Hate," *The Wall Street Journal*, March 8, 1983; and Martin Feldstein, "Why Indexing Must Not Be Repealed," *The Wall Street Journal*, March 1, 1983; and Beryl W. Sprinkel, "More Taxes Feed More Spending," *The Wall Street Journal*, November 10, 1983.

Quotations on the budget balancing issue are from Paul W. McCracken, "A Consensus to Live Within Our Means?," *The Wall Street Journal*, June 28, 1983 and the editorial "Budget Solution," *The Wall Street Journal*, September 14, 1983.

Our analysis of constitutional proposals to control the growth in federal government utilized Alvin Rabushka, "Fiscal Responsibility: Will Anything Less Than a Constitutional Amendment Do?," in Michael Boskin & Aaron Wildavsky, eds., *The Federal Budget: Economics and Politics*, (Institute of Contemporary Studies: San Francisco), 1982; Wagner and Tollison, *Balanced Budgets, Fiscal Responsibility, and the Constitution;* Joe Cobb, "Balancing Act," *Reason*, June 1983; Russell Shannon, "Curbing Congressional Inebriation," Dow Jones & Company, Inc., *The Collegiate Forum*, Spring 1983; Lewis Uhler, "The Case for an Amendment to Limit Spending," *The Wall Street Journal*, April 28, 1982; Louis Rukeyser, "5 Reasons to Oppose Budget-Balancing Amendment," *The Idaho Statesman*, and William N. Cox, "Constitutional Limitation of the Federal Budget," Federal Reserve Bank of Atlanta, *Economic Review*, May/June 1979.

Illustrative examples of prospects and problems in budgetary control from California and Missouri are from Michael Francheti, "California Learns to Live Within Taxpayer's Means," *The Wall Street Journal*, November 4, 1983 and Alvin Rabushka, "Missouri Ruling Makes You Wonder if Taxpayers Have Their Limits," *"The Wall Street Journal*, June 23, 1983.

The proposals for drastic cuts in federal spending are from David Boaz, "How to Really Cut the Budget," *Inquiry*, April 12, 1982; Taxing and Spending Task Force of the Clark for President Committee, *White Paper on Taxing and Spending Reduction*, Clark for President, Washington, D. C., 1980; and *War on Waste: President's Private Sector Survey on Cost Control*, J. Peter Grace, Chairman, (Macmillan Publishing Company: New York), January 12, 1984. The Grace Commission report was analyzed in the print media in J. Peter Grace, "Little Things Mean a Lot, Grace Panel Found," *The Wall Street Journal*, January 12, 1984; Ann Hughey, "Congress in Dis-Grace," *Newsweek*, January 16, 1984; "Business Panel Targets $424 billion in U. S. Waste," *The Idaho Statesman*, January 13, 1984; and John Cunniff, "Tough Talk From Grace Panel About Cutting Runaway Taxes," *The Idaho Statesman*, January 15, 1984. The Heritage Foundation has also announced a study which proposes $119 billion in budget cuts in the 1985 fiscal year.

The mechanics of Federal Reserve System "open market operations"--the means by which "monetization" takes place--can be found in any good money and banking textbook. The quotation from Milton Friedman on the association between money growth and inflation is from "The Supply of Money and Changes in Prices and Output," in Milton Friedman, ed., *The Optimum Quantity of Money*, (Aldine Publishers: Chicago), 1969. The quotation from Edward J. Kane is from his "Politics and Fed Policymaking: The More Things Change the More They Stay the Same," *Journal of Monetary Economics*, April 1980. An excellent and fairly short summary of monetary policy under the influence of politics can be found in Dwight R. Lee, *Inflation and Unemployment: The Case for Limiting Political Discretion*, (International Institute for Economic Research: Los Angeles, Calif.), September 1983.

John McClaughry's seven schools of thought on alternative reforms to monetary arrangements in the United States is in "A Battle Over Monetary Policy," U. S. Choice in Currenty Commission, *Currenty Competition*, January 1983. In analyzing the various alternatives we have utilized the following sources: Pamela J. Brown, "Constitution or Competition?: Alternative Views on Monetary Reform," Institute of Humane Studies, *Literature of Liberty*, Autumn 1982; Friedrich A. Hayek, "Choice in Currency: A Way to Stop Inflation," in his *New Studies in Philosophy, Politics, Economics and the History of Ideas*, 1978, "Toward a Free Market Monetary System," *The Journal of Libertarian Studies*, Vol. III, No. 1, 1979, and *Denationalization of Money--The Argument Refined*, (Institute for Economic Affairs: London), 2nd edition, 1978; Michael David Bordo, The Classical Gold Standard: Some Lessons for Today," Federal Reserve Bank of St. Louis, *Review*, May 1981; Joe Cobb, "Going for Solid Gold," *Reason*, September 1981; Martin Bronfenbrenner, "The Currency-Choice Defense," *Challenge*, January/February 1980; and Representative Ron Paul and Lewis Lehrman, *The Case for Gold*, (CATO Institute: Washington, D. C.), 1982.

Reference to the American Gold Eagle Coin Act of 1983 is from Hon. Ron Paul, "The New American Gold Coins," *Currency in Competition*, April 1983, and the citation on the Free Market Gold Coinage Act is drawn from the *Congressional Record*, Washington, D. C., October 5, 1981. The quotation by Hans F. Sennholz was taken from Pamela Brown, "Constitution or Competition?: Alternative Views on Monetary Reform," who quotes from Sennholz's book *Inflation or Gold Standard*.

## Chapter 24

The quotations at the head of the chapter are from David Osterfeld, *Freedom, Society and the State*, (University Press of American: Lanham, Maryland), 1983; Michael Novak, "Capitalist And Proud Of It," *IMPRIMIS*, Vol. 12, No. 10, October 1983; and Robert Ringer, *Restoring the American Dream*, (Harper and Row Publishers: New York), 1979.

References and quotations for William H. Meckling are from his article "American Capitalism at Sunset," *Reason*, April, 1984. The quotation from Arthur Shenfield is in "A Durable Free Society: Utopian Dream or Realistic Goal?," *IMPRIMIS*, Vol. 12, No. 3, March 1983 and the quotation by Henry Mark Holzer in his *Sweet Land of Liberty*. The Quotation by Ringer, and an important resource with regard to the restoration of liberty, is Chapter 9 — "Taking Back America," in his *Restoring the American Dream*. The words of Milton and Rose Friedman are from their book *Free to Choose*, Chapter 10 — "The Tide is Turning."

Benjamin A. Rogge, "Will Capitalism Survive?," *IMPRIMIS*, Vol. 3, No. 5, May 1974 summarizes Joseph Schumpeter's famous interpretation of the internal collapse of the market order as a result, primarily, of the defection of the intellectual class. Schumpeter's argument was originally made in *Capitalism, Socialism and Democracy*.

# INDEX

Pinchot, Gifford, 168, 170
Plato, 121
Political Action Committee, 192
Political means, 13, 143, 188, 191, 198, 200, 207, 218, 249, 304, 344, 380
Pollution, 297, 300
Pollution fees, 298, 300
Poole, Robert J., 185, 233, 297, 303, 304, 313, 321
Poor, 6, 33, 45, 193, 223, 227, 245, 329
Pound, Rosco, 100
Poverty, 70, 113
Power, 136
Prices, 152, 305, 369
Price-Anderson Act, 264, 290
Price ceilings, 221
Price floors, 223
Price system, 202
Private express laws, 267, 268
Private schools, 324
Private ownership, 13, 31
Privatization, 249, 253, 291, 303, 304, 367
Productivity, 51, 115
Profits, 58, 144, 146, 206, 282
Progress, 40, 160, 162, 165, 168, 170, 172
Property rights, 40, 89, 281, 291
Proposition 13
Proudhon, Pierre Joseph, 198
Public choice, 188, 193
Public good, 93, 95, 194
Public interest, 79, 194, 195, 275

Quesnay, 30

Rabushka, Alvin, 365
Railroading, 52, 55
Rainey Wildlife Sanctuary, 289
Ramsey, Bruce, 294
Rand, Ayn, 186
Ranson, Roger, 180
Rapid transit, 306, 307, 308, 309
Rational constructivism, 93
Rayack, Elton, 229
Read, Leonard, 145, 185
Reagan, President Ronald, 190, 218, 294, 350, 352
Regulation, 218, 231
Reich, Robert, 330, 331, 332, 333, 334, 341, 342, 343
Reindustrialization, 152
Reisman, George, 166, 171
Religion, 67, 174
Rent controls, 221, 222
Reynolds, Alan, 269
Ricardo, David, 122

Ringer, Robert, 145, 379, 380, 381
Risk, 207, 264
Rist, Charles, 122
Robbins, Lionel, 183
Robinson-Patman Act, 210
Rockefeller, John D., 56, 212
Rogge, Benjamin, 182
Rohatyn, Felix, 334, 342
Rome, City of, 4, 36
Roosevelt, President F. D., 74, 82, 96, 106, 360, 378
Roosevelt, President Theodore, 290
Rosenberg, Nathan, 53
Roth, Gabriel, 308
Rothbard, Murray, 35, 66, 137, 145, 146, 150, 154, 183, 185, 219, 220
Rousseau, 94, 165
Rukeyser, Louis, 343, 365
Rule of law, 94, 99, 100
Rural/Metro Fire Department, 311

Sage Brush Rebellion, 295
Saint-Simon, 122, 123
Samuelson, Paul, 147
Samuelson, Robert J., 342
Savas, E. S., 304, 314
Say, Jean Babtiste, 34
Schick, Allen, 361
Schiller, Bradley, 115
Schultze, Charles L., 334, 335, 337, 341, 343, 345
Schumpeter, Joseph, 120, 135, 136, 205
Schwartz, Anna, 155
Scott, Anthony, 283
Sedition Act, 77
Seldon, Arthur, 185
Self-interest, 63, 204
Senior, Nassau, 34
Sennholz, Hans, 374
Shapiro, David, 86
Shaw, George Bernard, 135
Shearer, Derek, 142, 144
Shenfield, Arthur, 64, 68, 185, 381
Sherman Anti-Trust Act, 81, 212, 214, 215
Sidney, Algernon, 20
Siegen, Bernard, 89, 318
Sierra Club, 168, 286, 294
Simon, William, 145
Simons, Henry, 34, 148, 180, 365, 374
Simon, Julian, 41, 173, 284, 286
Sinclair, Upton, 143
Sinsheimer, Robert L., 169
Sixteenth Amendment, 81
Smith, Adam, 8, 10, 13, 15, 16, 17, 24, 30, 31, 33, 40, 48, 60, 74, 85, 118, 160

91159